THE NEW MIDDLE AGES

BONNIE WHEELER, *Series Editor*

The New Middle Ages is a series dedicated to transdisciplinary studies of medieval cultures, with particular emphasis on recuperating women's history and on feminist and gender analyses. This peer-reviewed series includes both scholarly monographs and essay collections.

PUBLISHED BY PALGRAVE:

Women in the Medieval Islamic World: Power, Patronage, and Piety
    edited by Gavin R. G. Hambly

The Ethics of Nature in the Middle Ages: On Boccaccio's Poetaphysics
    by Gregory B. Stone

Presence and Presentation: Women in the Chinese Literati Tradition
    by Sherry J. Mou

The Lost Love Letters of Heloise and Abelard: Perceptions of Dialogue in Twelfth-Century France
    by Constant J. Mews

Understanding Scholastic Thought with Foucault
    by Philipp W. Rosemann

For Her Good Estate: The Life of Elizabeth de Burgh
    by Frances A. Underhill

Constructions of Widowhood and Virginity in the Middle Ages
    edited by Cindy L. Carlson and Angela Jane Weisl

Motherhood and Mothering in Anglo-Saxon England
    by Mary Dockray-Miller

Listening to Heloise: The Voice of a Twelfth-Century Woman
    edited by Bonnie Wheeler

The Postcolonial Middle Ages
    edited by Jeffrey Jerome Cohen

Chaucer's Pardoner and Gender Theory: Bodies of Discourse
    by Robert S. Sturges

Crossing the Bridge: Comparative Essays on Medieval European and Heian Japanese Women Writers
    edited by Barbara Stevenson and Cynthia Ho

Engaging Words: The Culture of Reading in the Later Middle Ages
    by Laurel Amtower

Robes and Honor: The Medieval World of Investiture
    edited by Stewart Gordon

Representing Rape in Medieval and Early Modern Literature
    edited by Elizabeth Robertson and Christine M. Rose

Same Sex Love and Desire among Women in the Middle Ages
    edited by Francesca Canadé Sautman and Pamela Sheingorn

Sight and Embodiment in the Middle Ages: Ocular Desires
    by Suzannah Biernoff

Listen, Daughter: The Speculum Virginum and the Formation of Religious Women in the Middle Ages
    edited by Constant J. Mews

Science, the Singular, and the Question of Theology
    by Richard A. Lee, Jr.

Gender in Debate from the Early Middle Ages to the Renaissance
  edited by Thelma S. Fenster and Clare A. Lees

Malory's Morte D'Arthur: *Remaking Arthurian Tradition*
  by Catherine Batt

The Vernacular Spirit: Essays on Medieval Religious Literature
  edited by Renate Blumenfeld-Kosinski, Duncan Robertson, and Nancy Warren

Popular Piety and Art in the Late Middle Ages: Image Worship and Idolatry in England 1350–1500
  by Kathleen Kamerick

Absent Narratives, Manuscript Textuality, and Literary Structure in Late Medieval England
  by Elizabeth Scala

Creating Community with Food and Drink in Merovingian Gaul
  by Bonnie Effros

Representations of Early Byzantine Empresses: Image and Empire
  by Anne McClanan

Encountering Medieval Textiles and Dress: Objects, Texts, Images
  edited by Désirée G. Koslin and Janet Snyder

Eleanor of Aquitaine: Lord and Lady
  edited by Bonnie Wheeler and John Carmi Parsons

Isabel La Católica, Queen of Castile: Critical Essays
  edited by David A. Boruchoff

Homoeroticism and Chivalry: Discourses of Male Same-Sex Desire in the Fourteenth Century
  by Richard E. Zeikowitz

Portraits of Medieval Women: Family, Marriage, and Politics in England 1225–1350
  by Linda E. Mitchell

Eloquent Virgins: From Thecla to Joan of Arc
  by Maud Burnett McInerney

The Persistence of Medievalism: Narrative Adventures in Contemporary Culture
  by Angela Jane Weisl

Capetian Women
  edited by Kathleen D. Nolan

Joan of Arc and Spirituality
  edited by Ann W. Astell and Bonnie Wheeler

The Texture of Society: Medieval Women in the Southern Low Countries
  edited by Ellen E. Kittell and Mary A. Suydam

Charlemagne's Mustache: And Other Cultural Clusters of a Dark Age
  by Paul Edward Dutton

Troubled Vision: Gender, Sexuality, and Sight in Medieval Text and Image
  edited by Emma Campbell and Robert Mills

Queering Medieval Genres
  by Tison Pugh

Sacred Place in Early Medieval Neoplatonism
  by L. Michael Harrington

The Middle Ages at Work
  edited by Kellie Robertson and Michael Uebel

Chaucer's Jobs
  by David R. Carlson

Medievalism and Orientalism: Three Essays on Literature, Architecture and Cultural Identity
  by John M. Ganim

Queer Love in the Middle Ages
  by Anna Klosowska

Performing Women in the Middle Ages: Sex, Gender, and the Iberian Lyric
  by Denise K. Filios

Necessary Conjunctions: The Social Self in Medieval England
  by David Gary Shaw

Visual Culture and the German Middle Ages
  edited by Kathryn Starkey and Horst Wenzel

Medieval Paradigms: Essays in Honor of Jeremy duQuesnay Adams, Volumes 1 and 2
edited by Stephanie Hayes-Healy

False Fables and Exemplary Truth in Later Middle English Literature
by Elizabeth Allen

Ecstatic Transformation: On the Uses of Alterity in the Middle Ages
by Michael Uebel

Sacred and Secular in Medieval and Early Modern Cultures: New Essays
edited by Lawrence Besserman

Tolkien's Modern Middle Ages
edited by Jane Chance and Alfred K. Siewers

Representing Righteous Heathens in Late Medieval England
by Frank Grady

Byzantine Dress: Representations of Secular Dress in Eighth-to-Twelfth Century Painting
by Jennifer L. Ball

The Laborer's Two Bodies: Labor and the "Work" of the Text in Medieval Britain, 1350–1500
by Kellie Robertson

The Dogaressa of Venice, 1250–1500: Wife and Icon
by Holly S. Hurlburt

Logic, Theology, and Poetry in Boethius, Abelard, and Alan of Lille: Words in the Absence of Things
by Eileen C. Sweeney

The Theology of Work: Peter Damian and the Medieval Religious Renewal Movement
by Patricia Ranft

On the Purification of Women: Churching in Northern France, 1100–1500
by Paula M. Rieder

Writers of the Reign of Henry II: Twelve Essays
edited by Ruth Kennedy and Simon Meecham-Jones

Lonesome Words: The Vocal Poetics of the Old English Lament and the African-American Blues Song
by M.G. McGeachy

Performing Piety: Musical Culture in Medieval English Nunneries
by Anne Bagnell Yardley

The Flight from Desire: Augustine and Ovid to Chaucer
by Robert R. Edwards

Mindful Spirit in Late Medieval Literature: Essays in Honor of Elizabeth D. Kirk
edited by Bonnie Wheeler

Medieval Fabrications: Dress, Textiles, Clothwork, and Other Cultural Imaginings
edited by E. Jane Burns

Was the Bayeux Tapestry Made in France?: The Case for St. Florent of Saumur
by George Beech

Women, Power, and Religious Patronage in the Middle Ages
by Erin L. Jordan

Hybridity, Identity, and Monstrosity in Medieval Britain: On Difficult Middles
by Jeremy Jerome Cohen

Medieval Go-betweens and Chaucer's Pandarus
by Gretchen Mieszkowski

The Surgeon in Medieval English Literature
by Jeremy J. Citrome

Temporal Circumstances: Form and History in the Canterbury Tales
by Lee Patterson

Erotic Discourse and Early English Religious Writing
by Lara Farina

Odd Bodies and Visible Ends in Medieval Literature
by Sachi Shimomura

On Farting: Language and Laughter in the Middle Ages
by Valerie Allen

Women and Medieval Epic: Gender, Genre, and the Limits of Epic Masculinity
edited by Sara S. Poor and Jana K. Schulman

Race, Class, and Gender in "Medieval" Cinema
edited by Lynn T. Ramey and Tison Pugh

Allegory and Sexual Ethics in the High Middle Ages
  by Noah D. Guynn

England and Iberia in the Middle Ages, 12th-15th Century: Cultural, Literary, and Political Exchanges
  edited by María Bullón-Fernández

The Medieval Chastity Belt: A Myth-Making Process
  by Albrecht Classen

Claustrophilia: The Erotics of Enclosure in Medieval Literature
  by Cary Howie

Cannibalism in High Medieval English Literature
  by Heather Blurton

The Drama of Masculinity and Medieval English Guild Culture
  by Christina M. Fitzgerald

Chaucer's Visions of Manhood
  by Holly A. Crocker

The Literary Subversions of Medieval Women
  by Jane Chance

Manmade Marvels in Medieval Culture and Literature
  by Scott Lightsey

American Chaucers
  by Candace Barrington

Representing Others in Medieval Iberian Literature
  by Michelle M. Hamilton

Paradigms and Methods in Early Medieval Studies
  Edited by Celia Chazelle and Felice Lifshitz

The King and the Whore: King Roderick and La Cava
  by Elizabeth Drayson

THE KING AND THE WHORE

KING RODERICK AND LA CAVA

Elizabeth Drayson

palgrave
macmillan

THE KING AND THE WHORE
Copyright © Elizabeth Drayson, 2007.

All rights reserved. No part of this book may be used or reproduced in any manner whatsoever without written permission except in the case of brief quotations embodied in critical articles or reviews.

First published in 2007 by
PALGRAVE MACMILLAN™
175 Fifth Avenue, New York, N.Y. 10010 and
Houndmills, Basingstoke, Hampshire, England RG21 6XS
Companies and representatives throughout the world.

PALGRAVE MACMILLAN is the global academic imprint of the Palgrave Macmillan division of St. Martin's Press, LLC and of Palgrave Macmillan Ltd. Macmillan® is a registered trademark in the United States, United Kingdom and other countries. Palgrave is a registered trademark in the European Union and other countries.

ISBN-13: 978–1–4039–7436–5
ISBN-10: 1–4039–7436–5

Library of Congress Cataloging-in-Publication Data

Drayson, Elizabeth.
  The king and the whore : King Roderick and La Cava / Elizabeth Drayson.
    p. cm.—(The new Middle Ages)
  Includes bibliographical references.
  ISBN 1–4039–7436–5
  1. Roderick, King of the Visigoths, d. 711?—In literature. 2. Florinda (Legendary character)—In literature. I. Title.

PN57.R58D73 2007
809'.93351—dc22   2007012363

A catalogue record for this book is available from the British Library.

Design by Newgen Imaging Systems (P) Ltd., Chennai, India.

First edition: December 2007

10 9 8 7 6 5 4 3 2 1

Printed in the United States of America.

To
Kiernan Ryan

CONTENTS

Acknowledgments	xi
Introduction	1
1 The Birth of a Legend	9
2 Cultural Filters: Roderick and La Cava through the Eyes of Medieval Historians	17
3 True and False Histories: The Case of the Master Forger Miguel de Luna	47
4 Metamorphosis into Song	59
5 New Life in Drama and Music: From Poetry to Theatre	75
6 Censored!—The Eighteenth Century	107
7 Romanticism and Renewal	129
8 Multiple Perspectives in Hispanic Romanticism	167
9 The Once and Future King	199
Conclusion	213
Appendix 1 Genealogy of the Crónica de 1344 Manuscripts (according to Cintra)	225
Appendix 2 Visual Images of King Roderick and La Cava	227
Notes	229
Bibliography	245
Index	257

ACKNOWLEDGMENTS

Chapter 1 is a condensed and revised version of "Ways of Seeing: The First Medieval Islamic and Christian Depictions of Roderick, Last Visigothic King of Spain," in *Al-Masāq*, Vol. 18, Number 2, September 2006, pp. 115–128. Chapter 2 contains material drawn from "Penance or Pornography? The Exile of King Roderick in Pedro de Corral's *Crónica sarracina*," in *Al-Masāq*, Vol. 17, Number 2, September 2005, pp. 193–204, and Chapter 3 includes revised extracts from "Medieval Legend and False History: King Roderick and La Cava Reinvented by Miguel de Luna," in *Proceedings of the Thirteenth Colloquium*, Papers of the Medieval Hispanic Research Seminar, 51, ed. Jane Whetnall and Alan Deyermond (London: Department of Hispanic Studies, Queen Mary, University of London, 2006), pp. 75–82. Chapter 6 contains revised material from "The King and the Whore: The Musical Life of a Spanish Legend," in *Antes y después del Quijote*, Asociación de Hispanistas de Gran Bretaña e Irlanda (Valencia: Generalitat Valenciana, 2005), pp. 181–90. The author is grateful to the publishers for permission to reprint this material.

My thanks are also due to the many students and colleagues at Cambridge and elsewhere who have shown such interest in my project and lent great encouragement to me. Bonnie Wheeler, Julia Cohen, Kristy Lilas, and Maran Elancheran have provided invaluable assistance, expertise, and patience, for which I shall remain extremely grateful. I would also like to thank Jan Gilbert for first drawing my attention to the musical *La Cava*, without which the book would not have been conceived. Words are inadequate to express my gratitude to Kiernan Ryan, who inspired and supported me throughout.

INTRODUCTION

In 2001 the Piccadilly Theatre in London was the scene of a tale of passion and revenge whose theme may be perpetual, but whose circumstances were unique. At the finale of the musical *La Cava* staged by the Florinda Company, King Roderick of Spain lies dying on the battlefield after his army has been defeated by the Moors. Florinda, alias La Cava, has staggered through the smoke and devastation to find him and tell him she is bearing his child, but the confession of her love has come too late to stop the carnage. Roderick breathes his last, and Spain is lost. This tragic and sentimental storyline, based on a novel by Dana Broccoli, offered twenty-first-century audiences an unlikely encounter with early medieval Iberia in its reenactment of the story of the eighth-century Visigothic king whose army was defeated by a Moorish raiding party on 19 July 711. The ensuing conquest of the peninsula by mixed Arab and Berber tribes gave rise to the foundational legend of the Spanish people, in which Roderick's love affair with the beautiful woman known as La Cava, the whore, was seen as the original cause of war. The lovers' uncontrollable passion led to the cataclysm of invasion and a powerful Arab presence in Spain for over seven hundred years.

A secret confraternity of writers and composers as diverse as the Spanish dramatist and poet Lope de Vega, the Jacobean playwright William Rowley, George Friedrich Handel, Sir Walter Scott, Robert Southey, Walter Savage Landor, and the contemporary Spanish novelist Juan Goytisolo were all drawn irresistibly to the tragedy of King Roderick and La Cava, one of the most extraordinary legends ever produced by Western European culture. The astonishing and enduring afterlife it has enjoyed in the thirteen centuries since its conception, in inexhaustible re-creations in diverse artistic forms, bear witness to the medieval scholar Alan Deyermond's observation that "it appeals so deeply and insistently to common imaginative patterns that it could be used as political fiction in the last years of Franco's Spain, in Juan Goytisolo's *La revindicación del conde don Julián*."[1] The success of the London musical further attests to the perpetuity of this narrative of invasion and conquest, which has since acquired added significance in the light of existing tensions between Middle East and West, and between Islam and Christianity.

The purpose of this book is to chart the history of the reception of the legend in historical, literary, and musical forms from the Middle Ages to the present, within both Spain and Latin America, and in other European countries. The study seeks to uncover a process of continuous appropriation of the story, used as a means to confront issues such as political crises, national identities, religious conflicts, gender, and the nature of history and fiction.

The crucial importance of Spain in the Middle Ages and since as the meeting point of Europe and the Orient, of Christianity and Islam (and Judaism, though this is not directly relevant to the subject of this book) is amply illustrated by the discussion of both medieval and subsequent perceptions of Islam by Christians, and of Christianity by Muslims, in the rich vein of recently published books in this area. The historian Richard Fletcher identified the two essential ingredients of the Christian image of Islam in the Middle Ages, namely that Mohammed was a pseudo-prophet, impostor and heretic whose followers were men of blood and violence, arising from the view of the Muslims as conquerors, and of Islam as an aberrant form of Christianity. This was countered by the Muslim attitude of lofty disdain toward the Christians because of their perceived barbarism.[2] The natural dichotomies inherent in this debate, such as those between Hispanic and Arabic ethnicities, between Christian and Muslim, history and myth, are fundamental to the development of the story of the king and the whore, and as such emphasize its perennial relevance and value inside and outside Spain.

Islam had been established as a faith for less than a hundred years at the time of the Moorish invasion of Spain in 711. Possibly the earliest known Christian writer to concern himself with Islam was John of Damascus, who composed a *Dialogue between a Saracen and a Christian* of uncertain date, although he was known to be writing about 745.[3] The Venerable Bede, also writing in the eighth century, describes the Christian idea of the legendary origin of the Muslims, who were allegedly descended from Hagar, Abraham's concubine, while Christians came from his lawful son Isaac. Although there is a parallel between Hagar and La Cava who are both concubines of the patriarchal figure, the point of Bede's story of origins lies in the fact that it rendered all Muslims illegitimate, as bastards, while Christians belonged to the legitimate blood line. Muslims were also believed to be lineal descendants of Cain, the murderer. As the historian Andrew Wheatcroft observes, the earliest Muslim invasions, such as that in the Levant in 634 were consequently described in Christian sources as apocalyptic, as the wreaking of a symbolic vengeance of God upon his sinful people: "This instrument of devastation was the bastard line of Abraham: protected by God and yet at an infinite distance from the love of Christ."[4] It was in this broad context of religious prejudice and anxiety that Roderick came to the throne of Spain in 710.

It is important at this stage to set out the established facts pertaining to the conquest of the Visigothic kingdom of Spain by the North African invaders. In spite of the extensive treatment of this subject by medieval historians, both Christian and Arabic, these facts remain frustratingly sparse and obscure. While the Visigoths had entered Spain in the fourth century and established a thriving kingdom under the aegis of Catholicism, the expansion of the Arab states was more recent, corresponding to the rise of Islam, which was waxing strong by the eighth century. Spain's geographical proximity to Africa rendered it vulnerable to attack, though it seems likely that expeditions to Spain from Africa had been undertaken for trading purposes for some years. At the same time, the newly crowned king, Roderick, was also vulnerable from the outset of his reign. His legitimacy as ruler was questioned, for he was not a royal heir, and was presented as a candidate by certain members of the nobility who were at odds with the sons of the previous king, Witiza. There will be more to say on this score later, but the salient point at this stage is that Roderick was perceived by some powerful factions to be a usurper. As the eminent historian of medieval Spain, Roger Collins, comments, the king's standing may have been weak due to the controversy over succession, and his authority was open to challenges that he needed to counter with a convincing display of military capability.[5]

His first recorded campaign was against the Basques in the North of the Peninsula, and it was while he was occupied in this way that disaster struck in the south. Having subjugated most of North Africa, the Arab governor of Ifrikiya (the new northern Africa) Mūsa ibn Nuṣayr sent an expedition to Spain in 711, believed to be a probing raid, under the command of his former slave Tarīk. Roderick hurried south to meet the invaders, but was defeated in the valley of the river Guadalete, probably near Medina Sidonia, his demise no doubt hastened by the collusion of the usurped sons of Witiza with the Arabs, who deserted their king in his final battle. Although it may have been on a comparatively small scale, the ease of the Arab victory is thought to have been greatly due to the unfamiliarity of Tarīk's tactics. Instead of moving inland to attack Roderick as he hastened south, a move that would have deprived the Arab forces of the opportunity of rapid withdrawal if circumstances dictated it, Tarīk chose to wait at Algeciras for reinforcements. Their arrival increased his army to 12,000 men and battle was finally joined on 19 July 711. It was a battle that ended Roderick's reign and the Visigothic kingdom with it. His death, like his life, is shrouded in mystery and uncertainty. It was not recorded in reliable accounts, though according to Collins,[6] it is reasonable to assume that he died in battle. After this, Tarīk quickly captured Toledo, and his success encouraged Mūsa to follow his lead and capture Seville.

Collins comments upon the remarkable parallels between the Arab invasion of Spain and the Norman conquest of England, where in both cases a single battle effectively decided the issue and in both instances the defending ruler was forced to make a rapid, lengthy march to meet the invader. The deaths of both monarchs, the scattering of their immediate and highly influential military following and the fall of the capitals convert both battles into conquests. Collins concludes with an important point relating to the interpretation of historical facts in both circumstances: "That these events have more to do with the social and political organizations of the defeated state than with the supposed morals or morale of their citizenry has now fortunately been recognized in respect of Anglo-Saxon England, though not yet of Visigothic Spain."[7] The Western view of the invasion of Spain as a disastrous defeat for the Christian Spaniards is one that has endured, and its association with sexual morality was important in both the creation and future development of the Roderick legend.

The essential elements of the legend are sexual passion, vengeance, and treachery, the centerpiece of which is King Roderick's desire for a beautiful girl who is the daughter of his general, Count Julian. Finding herself in an impossible and compromised situation, the girl informs her father of the illicit sexual relationship and in his overwhelming need for vengeance, Julian colludes traitorously with the Arabs to facilitate the invasion of Spain. This triangular relationship of transgressive passion and treason has flourished in numerous variations that will be explored during the course of this book. From a historical perspective, only Roderick is known unquestionably to have existed, although the earliest accounts of the invasion also give credence to the existence of Julian as the king's governor of Ceuta in north Africa. There is no historical evidence whatsoever for the existence of La Cava. It is therefore of fundamental importance to consider the possible reasons both for the creation of such a story and for its perpetuity in so many forms. Once again, Collins' comments in this respect are significant. He notes that the invasion itself and the easy victory of the Arabs were imbued with an apocalyptic quality for both the conquered and the conquerors. This is illustrated by the earliest Muslim accounts that describe premonitory signs heralding the invasion and the fabulous treasure that the victors acquired afterward (usually including the original 'Table of Solomon' that formed part of the treasures of Jerusalem).[8] The principal story of supernatural warning relates to a house, palace, or tower, allegedly built by Hercules, which no Visigothic king had previously entered. Instead, each time a king came to the throne, he added another lock to the door. Roderick is the only monarch to ignore this, against the advice of his counselors, breaking into the palace to find auguries of his downfall and of the invasion in the depiction of Arab horsemen on the walls inside. An inscription in Arabic states that whoever breaks the locks will lose his kingdom to the men depicted there. Collins remarks that this story has interesting parallels with certain Jewish stories and others that describe a chamber in which successive Visigothic kings hung up their crowns. This prefigurative story forms part of many later versions of the Roderick and La Cava legend, and its variants and development are interesting in their own right. It represents the king as a man who cannot escape his destiny, which is fulfilled through the consequences of his violation of La Cava. The legend might never have been intended to be historically accurate; however, some historians have been persuaded of the authenticity of the story of the two lovers,[9] though the majority has remained skeptical. Since the figures of Roderick and Julian are historically verified, the latter may plausibly have had a daughter, making such a situation perfectly within the bounds of possibility. To date, no evidence exists to prove it, but equally none exists to disprove it.

This vexed problem of the distinction between history and legend is fundamental to the exploration of the afterlife of the story of the king and the whore. The historical circumstances become overlaid with the resonances of legend and myth in a way that revitalizes and manipulates the story according to the dictates of literary or artistic medium and contemporary response. The Muslim invasion of Spain was an event of such magnitude that a mythical story was needed to explain or reconcile, to act as a spur to action or even to legitimate the event. In Christian terms, there appeared to be a need to re-create the narrative in order to make sense of and understand the momentous upheavals the conquest brought about.

Roderick was not the first monarch to abuse his power through sexual violation, as later writers and historians showed. There were biblical and classical precedents in King David's rape of Bathsheba, and in Tarquin's abuse of Lucretia, while early narrative versions reveal the imprint of motifs from Germanic legends and Nordic sagas, which will be referred to in more detail later. The philosopher Paul Ricoeur notes that the word 'mythos' in Greek means both a 'fable' or imaginary story and also 'plot' in the sense of well-constructed history. The term itself encapsulates the tension between fact and fiction that empowers the historical events through creative interpretation, transcending them to produce new possibilities. Ricoeur speaks of the symbolic function of myth in releasing precisely this power of discovery and revelation, which may exceed its origin. His discussion of the simultaneously foundational and liberating nature of legendary and mythical stories is directly applicable to that of King Roderick and La Cava. Myth is "a disclosure of unprecedented worlds, an opening onto other possible worlds which transcend the established limits of our actual world." It carries with it the promise of another existence entirely, as well as being paradigmatic and implying a social or cosmic order or perfection.[10]

The overlap between historical events and mythical motifs invested the legend with a creative energy that flowed into a variety of artistic vessels, whose scope remained uncharted until the early twentieth century. The renowned Spanish scholar Don Ramón Menéndez Pidal was a pioneer in writing his three-volume survey of the Roderick legend that was published between 1924 and 1927. No one before had considered the story as a living entity or marked its progression from the eighth century onwards; his compendium of the large corpus of writing that tells the story of the last Goth is indispensable, and this book is greatly indebted to it. Pidal notes that it is Spain's oldest legend, surviving, in his opinion, due to the historical magnitude of the catastrophe it entails and the violent passions involved, to become one of the most ubiquitous literary themes. He states: "...para los creyentes musulmanes representaba uno de los milagrosos triunfos del Islam, y para los cristianos inducía a meditar cómo el pecado de los pueblos acarrea su ruina"[11] [...for Muslim believers it represented one of the miraculous triumphs of Islam, and for Christians it led to a meditation upon how the sin of a people brings about its ruin].

Pidal's introductory comments are characteristically perceptive, and underline certain unusual qualities, notably a reputed origin in either Arabic or a remote Germanic tradition (Ermanarich) rare among Spain's heroic legends, which tend to be Castilian, and the fact that in spite of being by far the oldest legend of the Peninsula, it is one of the most widespread poetic themes, whose unity and continuity of value, even in works of average quality, is important in constituting what he describes as "un conjunto orgánico"[12] [an organic whole]. This in turn leads to "...un interés superior al de la leyenda en sí misma, cual es el de la leyenda afectada y sacudida por las corrientes literarias o culturales de las varias épocas que atraviesa"[13] [...a point of interest greater than that of the legend itself, namely, the way it is affected and shaken by the literary or cultural currents of the various times it traverses]. Menéndez Pidal identifies another intriguing aspect of the study of the legend of King Roderick and La Cava when he describes it as a kind of episodic history of literature, whose generic and stylistic evolution can be charted through the progression of the narrative, which in his opinion tends to demonstrate ". . .la complicada mecánica de lo colectivo y lo personal en el desenvolvimiento de una literatura"[14] [. . .the complicated mechanisms of the collective and the personal in the evolution of a literature].

This story from the past that looks into the future has special relevance to the present moment. As John Tolan notes, the Middle Ages are of more than academic interest for those concerned with relations between Europe and the Muslim world.[15] That the question of Islam in Spain and Europe is still firmly anchored to the history of the Spanish Middle Ages from the Arab invasion in 711 until their expulsion from the peninsula by Ferdinand and Isabella in 1492 is abundantly illustrated by articles published recently. The Granada Journal in the *New York Times* of October 21, 2003 relates how "Muslims are back in this ancient Moorish stronghold, the last bastion of Islam in Spain before the fifteenth-century emir Boabdil kissed King Ferdinand's hand and relinquished the city with a legendary sigh." The article states that a generation of post-Franco intellectuals is reassessing the country's Moorish past and recasting Spanish identity to include Islamic influences rejected as heretical centuries ago. While the converted Scot Abdalqadir al-Murabit's aim to found an Islamic caliphate with an economy of gold dinars may meet with some opposition, Islamic converts living in Granada have taken significant steps, for example, lobbying to prevent the annual celebrations of the fall of Granada into Christian hands, and opening a mosque in the city in July 2003.

This longing to reinstate Islam and the Muslim community in Andalusia has a darker side directly linked to terrorism. In *La Vanguardia* of May 4, 2002, an essay by Amatzia Baram on the Israeli-Palestinian conflict states: "De hecho, algunas organizaciones radicales del mundo árabe albergan una visión aún más ambiciosa—y más ilusoria-: reconquistar España como forma de volver a la época dorada del islam" [In fact, some radical organizations in the Arab world cherish an even more ambitious—and illusory—vision: the reconquest of Spain as a way of returning to the golden age of Islam]. On November 7, 2001, the terrorist al-Zawahiri spoke on an al-Quaeda tape recording about offenses against Islam including the appropriation by the Christians of the Arab lands of Spain, expressing a wish "que no pase con Palestina lo mismo que con al-Andalus" [not to let the same thing happen to Palestine that happened in al-Andalus], and these words were echoed in a newspaper report on the atrocities of March 11, 2004 in Madrid that stated "bin Laden, in a broadcast shortly after 11 September, referred to the former Islamic kingdom of al-Andalus, in what is now Spain, whose artistic scholarship was crushed by the crusading Catholic Christian monarchs Ferdinand and Isabella, who expelled all Muslims from Spain after 1492. There are therefore 'old accounts' for Islamic fundamentalists to settle with Spain."[16] These newspaper articles confirm the persistence and living importance of the religious, racial, and political conflict arising out of the Arab invasion of Christian Spain in the eighth century, at the heart of which is the catalyzing story of King Roderick and La Cava.

CHAPTER 1

THE BIRTH OF A LEGEND

> "History is our way of giving what we are and what we believe in the present a significance that will endure into the future, by relating it to what has happened in the past."
>
> Fred Donner

The Desert Kings

The first cultural reference to King Roderick does not appear in Spain, but in the Middle East, within the ruined medieval palace of Qusayr 'Amra (meaning the 'little palace of 'Amra'), which lies in the remote Jordanian desert, amid a limitless expanse of sand traversed only by Bedouins. Built in the early eighth century with hard reddish limestone quarried from the surrounding hills, the palace dome and rounded arches have resisted the passage of time to blend unassumingly with the tones of the landscape. Yet inside a marvel is hidden, for virtually every wall is covered with fresco paintings vibrant with color and movement, which constitute one of the most important and unique art treasures of the medieval Islamic era. On the west wall, an image survives of six world rulers, one of whom is Roderick, last Visigothic king of Spain, whose startling presence in this painting predates the earliest known written accounts of the Muslim conquest of his country. The significance of this depiction of King Roderick is particularly important in terms of its implications for the earliest written Christian and Arab records of the Visigothic king's demise, which are the sources of the legend of the king and the whore.

The world heritage site of Qusayr 'Amra was discovered in 1898 by Alois Musil, who had heard from the Bedouin of the existence of a palace decorated with paintings in a dangerous part of the desert. He had scarcely set foot in it when an alarm was raised and he and his guides had to leave in haste. He managed to return in 1900 under cover of a tribal raid, and stayed three days measuring and photographing. In 1901 he visited it a third time with the painter Mielich, who made some valuable copies of the frescoes. The palace stands in what used to be the Syrian desert to the east of the northern end of the Dead Sea, fifty miles east of Amman, and consists of two main elements, a rectangular audience hall with an alcove and two rooms, and a bath, consisting of three small rooms, the third of which is domed. Experts[1] consider that the size of the building and its remoteness point to a function as a private pleasure domain, a kind of desert retreat from the city.

The historical and cultural context is crucial in understanding the inspiration for such a building. As David Talbot Rice explains,[2] within twenty years of Mohammed's migration to Medina in 622, both Syria and Egypt had been wrested from the Byzantine Empire by the Muslims, and Iraq and Persia from the Sassanian Empire. The powerful Byzantine state, heir of Roman glory, was brought to its knees by the loss of two of its most important provinces, and Persia was entirely subjugated. The dual heritage of these two great empires, both culturally and artistically, would affect the world of Islam for centuries.

As Islam waxed and a new capital was established at Damascus, the earliest development of a truly Islamic art began, and initially took its name from the first dynasty of Islam, the Ummayad, which was its patron. This continued until 750 when the capital was transferred from Syria to Mesopotamia, and the new Abbasid dynasty came to power. Religious and secular buildings survive from the earliest period, notably the Dome of the Rock and the al-Aqsa mosque in Jerusalem, the Great Mosque of Damascus, and a series of palaces in the desert built by the caliphs and their sons as places to retire from the cares of state and the ties of urban life. As Creswell notes,[3] the armies of the Muslim conquest were composed of Bedouin from Arabia who found it hard to abandon their former way of life. He comments: "The instincts of the Ummayad caliphs were nomad. They preferred spring pasture, where the desert is covered with green after the winter rains. Each Ummayad caliph possessed their own camping grounds, at first tents, but gradually increasing in luxury to develop into a standing camp, and later with permanent buildings."[4] Qusayr 'Amra was just such a place, free from the plague and fever of the city.

However, while the nature of the palace itself is unproblematical, significant controversy still bedevils its remarkable frescoes in relation to their date, subject matter, purpose, and even the artists who painted them. This controversy centers upon the great painting of the figures known as the six kings, among whom Roderick appears. The intense scholarly disputes surrounding this painting are due in part to the irretrievable loss of vital information through damage to the frescoes, and in part to the deeply ambiguous nature of the subject. It is precisely this ambiguity that will become an important positive element in the development of the King Roderick legend in later times.

In order to appreciate the diverse interpretations of this painting, it must first be described. The six figures depicted on the west wall of the main hall are richly dressed, three in the foreground with what appear to be their right hands open, and three placed between and behind them, their costumes partly concealed by those in front. Above the first four remain fragments of superscriptions in Arabic and Greek that are crucial to the recognition of the figures and to the accurate dating of the painting. The four persons have been identified as the Byzantine emperor or Kaisar, wearing imperial robes and a tiara on his head, Roderick, Visigothic king of Spain, of whose image little remains, though in Musil's time it was possible to see the top of a Visigothic helmet, third, the Sassanian emperor, beardless and youthful, with thick curly hair and dressed in a purple cloak and shoes with the Sassanian crown on his head, and fourth, the Negus of Abyssinia, wearing a light-colored garment with a dark stole. The identity of the other two figures is a mystery, though it has been proposed that these were the emperor of China and an Indian or Turkish monarch.

In the alcove at the back of the hall a figure with a nimbus is depicted seated on a throne, toward whom the six rulers are gesturing. He is flanked by two other figures, possibly servants, below whom is a stretch of sea with four figures in a boat, sea monsters, and a bird. There is a Kufic inscription in white invoking a blessing on a person whose name is now, frustratingly, eroded. Alongside the fresco of the rulers, on the south wall is a depiction of a very tall woman, above whom is the word VICTORY.

The unresolved controversy among art historians regarding the significance of the images has a bearing upon the role and importance of King Roderick in this ancient painting. Oleg Grabar, who has written extensively on the frescoes of Qusayr 'Amra, notes that for the art historian, each image is liable to elicit different interpretations of its value and importance. Scholars have consistently linked the purpose of the six kings painting to the time of its creation, thereby firmly anchoring its meaning to its historical context. Grabar himself believes the picture to have a specifically Muslim meaning, but does not support the idea of a representation of kings conquered by Islam favored by previous scholars like van Berchem and Creswell in his early work; he interprets the hand gesture of the figures as one of deference rather than submission. He states that in both Sassanian and Byzantine art, the iconography of defeated enemies shows specific traits absent in Qusayr 'Amra. His solution, expounded in his 1954 article, is to give a comparatively late date to the work, whose earliest possible date of 710 is based on King Roderick's presence in the picture and upon his accession to the throne in that year. The latest possible date must be 750, which marked the end of the Ummayad dynasty.

Grabar suggests that the painting draws on the idea, both ancient and medieval, of a family of kings. He notes that in many Persian written sources, such as those by Mas'ūdī, Qazwīnī, and Ferdowsī, all the kings of the earth are brothers.⁵ Such texts were known to the Ummayads and Grabar posits that emphasis on the actual human relationship rather than on a spiritual one was more likely to appeal to the uncouth Ummayad princes and points out that the Ummayad caliph Yazid III (who reigned for six months in 127/744 AD) created a lineage written by himself in verse, which linked him to his Sassanid origins.⁶ This asserted Yazid's right to the throne via an imagined ancestry as the descendent and heir of kings who had been defeated by the Arabs. Grabar's theory is that the palace frescoes, created, in his view, in Yazid's reign, are a visual version of a literary myth, rendering them unique in Islamic art. Each of the six kings illustrates a specific phase of Ummayad history, and is hence a representation of a Sassanian idea converted into an Ummayad concept and adapted to the specific historical situation in order to imply that the Ummayad dynasty was the descendant and heir of the dynasties it had defeated. The picture is thus meant to convey the idea of a new culture being fully aware of its membership of the ancient and traditional family of world rulers.⁷

Creswell's later study⁸ of Qusayr 'Amra in 1969 is superlative and persuasive in its thoroughness. He notes that the frescoes exemplify the Hellenistic art of Syria with the exception of the painting of six kings, which he declares to be Persian in inspiration, reiterating the idea that a Persian prototype of the kings of the earth paying homage to their emperor is known to have existed. The arrangement in rank is characteristically Persian, as is the position of the right hand of the three figures in the foreground, which is the symbol of paying homage in Sassanian sculpture. However, he discounts Grabar's theory of an allegorical significance to the fresco, instead emphasizing its historical meaning. He is able to state categorically that the painting of the enthroned figure in the alcove was a representation of the person for whom the palace was built, precisely because the alcove was intended for the throne recess. It is this function that defines the person depicted. Presenting some very convincing historical detail,⁹ he hypothesizes that this painting symbolizes the victories of caliph al-Walīd I. Known as a great builder, Creswell feels no doubt that al-Walīd authorized the building of the palace, thus dating it between 711–12 and 715, the year of his death. This is further reinforced by the historical significance of the presence of Roderick, defeated during al-Walīd's reign and thereafter known only to the learned, and seemingly confirmed by what Creswell identifies as the personification of Victory in the female figure on the left.¹⁰

A radical interpretation of the six kings fresco appears in Garth Fowden's 1993 study of Qusayr 'Amra in his book on monotheism in late antiquity. His chapter on Islam aims to study "Islam's appropriation and fulfilment of the Old World through the unique buildings constructed in this early period."[11] In his view Qusayr 'Amra emphasizes the strength and prestige to be gained from Islam's appropriation of earlier traditions, an important factor in the success of the Islamic Empire, which was willing to coexist with internal dissenters. I would add that this spirit of 'convivencia' or coexistence was similarly a crucial element of life for hundreds of years in the Spanish medieval era, when Christians, Muslims, and Jews lived and worked side by side.

Fowden remarks on the striking impact of the representation of Roderick. He says: "The whole panel is unique, but King Roderick in particular betrays an artist not afraid of unconventional allusion."[12] At the time of writing, Fowden believed that the explanation of the painting lay not in the enthroned figure, but in the female figure adjacent to it. He interpreted the visible title originally thought to mean "Victory" to "Victory of or to Sarah," an allusion suggesting that the female figure is not the wife of the man depicted in the throne recess, nor a classical personification. However, the identification of Sarah with the Arabs that Fowden felt was crucial would have been underlined if the wife of Qusayr 'Amra's patron had sat in front of the fresco on formal occasions. The Sarah fresco would therefore legitimate the Arabs by making them descendants of Abraham's lawful wife, emphasizing Arab kinship with Isaac's descendants, and thus proclaiming Sarah's victory over the six kings before her. Although there is undoubted artistic pride and prestige in the unusually precise and up-to-the-minute reference to Roderick, the victory depicted is not just a military one, but was the key, according to Fowden, to political legitimation and cultural appropriation. The six kings fresco carries the message that while Islam triumphed, it had to accept and transform what had gone before.

In his monograph on Qusayr 'Amra published in 2004, Fowden entirely retracts the Sarah hypothesis because of insufficient evidence to support it, and somewhat modifies his ideas on the political and cultural dimensions of the fresco. He concedes that there may not be one 'correct' interpretation of the panel, though he reaffirms that the six kings symbolize the entire political and cultural heritage of the world the Arabs had recently inherited. He makes the interesting point that the depiction of the kings as beardless identifies them as representatives of an older, more sophisticated but less dynamic civilization than that of the Arabs.[13] The kings' significance is as much cultural as political, hence their portrayal in court, rather than military, attire, and Fowden concludes that the painting implies a greater interest in the cultural legacy of the six kings than in their (or their people's) spiritual subjection to Islam. The Ummayad patron thus annexes their political and cultural prestige rather than imposing his religious revelation upon them.[14]

The prevalent view is therefore that the enthroned figure is an eminent Muslim to whom the six rulers, probably three kings and three emperors, are paying their respects, and that this can be evaluated in historical, iconographical, imperialistic, or Islamic terms. But no scholar to date has considered the presence of the Spanish king in the fresco in any detail. The recent inclusion of a Western Christian king among Oriental and Eastern rulers raises a number of important issues. First, in purely practical terms, how did the artists know of Roderick's appearance and clothing? The first visual images of Roderick appear on the coins minted during his brief reign and form a fascinating contrast with the Qusayr 'Amra image. On one side of the coin is a bust of the king wearing a helmet, with laurels, presaging the intended triumphs over the Basque region he never achieved in reality. The legend reads: "In the name of God, King Roderick." On the reverse appears a Greek Cross, with vases of flowers, and the inscription "TOLETO PIUS" [pious in Toledo], referring to his coronation in that city. The coins depict a triumphant, not defeated, monarch and warrior, firmly aligned with the Greek and therefore Byzantine heritage, with all its links with the Roman Empire and Christianity. They communicate authority, military power, and prosperity.

But the image on the coins would not have provided sufficient clues for the Qusayr 'Amra artists, even if they had had access to them. One must assume that they relied upon some written account of Visigothic apparel and of the king's own appearance. It is established that many Ummayad caliphs enjoyed reading and listening to history, but no historical account of the invasion of Spain is known to have existed before the end of the Ummayad reign in 750. However, later historians do record details of epistolary contact between caliph al-Walīd and Musa ben Nosair, of Syrian descent himself, and governor of Ifrikiya and adjacent countries, who led the victory over Roderick in 711. The anonymous eleventh-century chronicle *Ajbar Machmuâ* relates the story of the love affair between King Roderick and La Cava, and adds that Musa wrote to al-Walīd with the news of early successes in Spain and of the plan suggested by Julian, Roderick's governor in Ceuta, to collude with the Moors and defeat the king. Similarly, a twelfth-century Arabic codex, *Fatho-l-Andaluçi*, reports that al-Walīd wrote to Musa ordering him to send troops to Spain.[15] The implication is that al-Walīd was kept up to date with progress by letters, so it is equally possible that the fresco artists, presumably based in the capital Damascus, heard of or were given access to the information they needed, perhaps from a brief description in a letter, or even an anecdotal conversation with someone who had been in Spain.

In the palace fresco, Roderick is aligned, not with the authority and power of Byzantium or Christianity as on the Visigothic coins but with that of the empire of Islam. He is without question a king conquered by Islam, who is, if not subjugated by, then certainly deferential to its military power. As a representative of Christianity in the fresco, he is also suggesting the deference of his religion to Islam. Yet in his role as monarch, Roderick himself is an ambiguous and dualistic figure of cultural appropriation. Linked to Greek and Roman heritage in his own country, he is also linked to Islam in the fresco through the caliph, who heads an ancient and venerable religious and imperial lineage embodied in the six rulers. Roderick, Janus-like, looks back toward Christian imperialism and forward to the new empire of Islam.

The special fascination of his image at Qusayr 'Amra lies in the fact that it predates any written record of his reign and defeat at the hands of the Muslims, yet still survives. What is also fascinating and of the greatest importance in charting the evolution of the Roderick legend is that the essential ambiguity of his status discussed above shapes the first historical narratives of the invasion. The two earliest accounts are Christian texts written in Spain, which will be discussed in more detail in chapter 2. The first account, known as the *Crónica bizantino-arábiga* [Byzantine-Arabic Chronicle], was probably written by a Christian recently converted to Islam. Perhaps for this reason his chronicle shows minimal interest in Hispanic matters, and focuses upon the life of Mohammed and of Muslims, referring to Roderick in the briefest of terms. Of far greater significance is the *Crónica mozarábe de 754* [Mozarabic Chronicle of 754], written anonymously, probably in Toledo or al-Andalus by a Mozarab, or Spanish Christian living in Muslim Spain. Given its early date, this chronicle carries great weight, though it is written with a brevity that makes its meaning ambiguous, if not cryptic. It contains a discussion of political and military events, such as Roderick's accession to the throne, and his human, intellectual, and military qualities as reflected in his government and military action. Its author clearly saw the Muslim invasion as a disaster of the first magnitude, likening it to the destruction of Troy, Jerusalem, and Babylon and the sack of Rome by Alaric, viewing it as divine retribution for the sins of the Visigothic people. Divine Providence was the agent of history, and all events formed part of God's plan. This powerful idea of the defeat of Roderick and of Spain as the punishment of God lent it the quality of a catastrophic disaster that had lasting resonance in the future.

In the ninth century, Asturian chronicles use the figure of Roderick to link the Asturian royal line to a Gothic and Roman heritage, while the early-tenth-century *Crónica de Alfonso III* [Chronicle of Alfonso III] reasserts the link between Visigothic and Asturian monarchies by claiming that their first king, Pelayo, was related to Roderick and therefore definitely of royal blood. This allowed the Asturians to illustrate their own myth of Pelayo and thus reinforce the contemporary royal authority of Alfonso III. These first accounts are characterized by their explanation of the Muslim invasion within the Christian Catholic framework of God's punishment of a wayward people and in the Asturian chronicles by the exploitation of a historical event for ideological and political purposes.[16]

No early Islamic accounts of the invasion of Spain survive, largely due to the attempts by the Abbasids to erase all memory of the Ummayad reign resulting in the destruction of many documents. Existing records only begin in the tenth century AD, but show that for Islamic historians as well as for Christian writers, the conquest of Spain constituted an event of overwhelming, though not catastrophic, significance and took on an apocalyptic quality, while the former both viewed and wrote about it in a quite different way. As part of a narrative of conquest and victory, it lacked the negative cadence of Christian historiography. Arab chroniclers reported the events of 711 as the result of the actions of Muslim troops and generals acting as part of the broader expansion policy of the government of Damascus. The occupation of Hispania was therefore part of a much wider Islamic conquest taking place outside the peninsula and late-Roman Empire.

So for early Islamic and Christian historians, Roderick was a man of destiny, albeit an equivocal destiny, fundamental to the fortunes and futures of both sides. For Christian writers he was the vessel through which God wreaked punishment upon the corrupt through defeat and invasion, and for Islamic historians, he was the instrument of conquest, fulfilling the prophecy embodied in the Muslim legend of the enchanted tower of Toledo. In a sense the Qusayr 'Amra fresco could be seen as the response to these visionary images in the tower legend, showing that the prophecy has been fulfilled.

For both sides, Roderick was also an instrument of genealogical reinforcement, on the one hand cementing the Gothic alliance with the Roman past and Christian Catholic future, and on the other, as manifest in the fresco, legitimizing the new religious and military regime of Islam by linking it with those of both the distant and recent past. The tension between the visual image of a triumphant Roderick on Visigothic coinage and the defeated monarch in the Ummayad fresco therefore develops into the tension between the conquered and the victors in written form.

It is precisely this ambivalence as a figurehead that lends Roderick extraordinary regenerative power, not only in terms of his own legendary story, but also in his ability to stimulate the new visions and recreations of artistic, literary, racial, and religious conventions and traditions that made him such a rich source of inspiration in Western and Eastern cultures for thirteen hundred years.

CHAPTER 2

CULTURAL FILTERS: RODERICK AND LA CAVA THROUGH THE EYES OF MEDIEVAL HISTORIANS

> History is philosophy from examples.
>
> Dionysius of Halicarnassus, 30–37 BC
>
> History is the propaganda of the victors.
>
> Avi Shlaim, 2000

The Earliest Christian Accounts

The divergent views of history expressed in the two quotations above reflect one of the fundamental oppositions between medieval Christian and Arabic historians as they strove to record the events that took place in Spain in the year 711. Conflicting historiographical traditions and the interplay between historical fact and fiction created disharmony among the ancient voices of the past, rendering their accounts of King Roderick's demise opaque and confusing. No two exact contemporaneous accounts exist, since the first written records, produced in Spain, date from 741 and 754. The earliest reference to the Muslim invasion appears in the *Crónica bizantino-arábiga*[1] that Chalmeta suggests may have been written by a Christian from the Levante, possibly a convert to Islam.[2] However, the *Crónica mozarábe de 754*[3] is of exceptional importance and was written anonymously, again according to Chalmeta by a Mozarabic clergyman from either Cordoba or Levante.[4] This chronicle carries great weight since it is the best-informed source on this era and reflects Christian peninsular views.

It is thought that there was a coup d'état in Toledo upon the death of the previous Visigothic king Witiza's son Akhila in 710. Roderick seized power, defeating the army of Akhila and his brothers, though he was apparently not a member of the ruling family. Roderick may well have been a legitimate king by election, in compliance with the Visigothic system,[5] but there were a number of influential people at court who felt wronged, viewing him as a usurper. José Antonio Maravall makes an interesting point in relation to the designation as usurper and tyrant in Visigothic times, noting that the concept of tyranny falls upon a king who is not legitimate, but a rebel or usurper. He uses the example of Roderick's predecessor Witiza as a Visigothic king who governed unjustly but was never described as a tyrant, while Hermenegild, who was deemed a good Christian king, was considered a tyrant because he rebelled against a legitimate monarch. King Roderick's portrayal as a tyrant in many versions of the legend as late as the nineteenth century may well have its roots in this point of Visigothic political thought.[6] The *Crónica de 754* reports that "Rudericus tumultuose regnum ortante senatu inuadit"[7] [Roderick seized the throne with force and at the instance of the Senate]. According to Georges Martin, the Senate consisted of an assembly of representatives of the lay nobility who were traditionally involved, alongside the church, with the nomination and legal election of the monarch. Martin suggests that the coronation took place without ecclesiastical consent, thereby intensifying the conflict between the great noble families and the church evident in the reigns of the last three Visigothic kings.[8]

While the chronicler blames Roderick's ambitions, and the treachery and cowardice of those around him for the success of the Muslims, possibly revealing the author to be a supporter of Witiza, he shows a preoccupation with ecclesiastical affairs, even in his language, which is heavily influenced by the liturgy and canonical documents. As Collins notes,[9] he drew on both the learning of the Visigothic church and on a historiographical tradition in chronicle writing that stretched back to Isidore and Eusebius before him: "Sed ut in brebi cuncta legenti renotem pagella, relictis seculi inumerabilibus ab Adam usque nunc cladibus, quas per infinitis regionibus et ciuitatibus crudelis intulit mundus iste inmundus, quidquid historialiter capta Troia pertulit, quidquit Iherosolima predicta per prophetarum eloquia baiulabit, quidquid Babilonia per scripturarum eloquia substulit, quidquid postremo Roma apostolorum movilitate decorata martirialiter confecit, omnia et toth ut Spania condam deliciosa et nunc misera effecta tam in honore quam etiam in dedecore experibit"[10] [in order that I might offer to the reader a complete account within the space of a single short page, leaving aside all the other countless disasters of human history from Adam until now, which this cruel, foul world had brought about throughout an infinite number of regions and nations, he will have everything unfolding in front of him: anything that captured Troy has borne, according to history, anything which Jerusalem, which had been forewarned through the words of the prophets, suffered, that undergone by Babylon, according to the Scriptures, and finally, anything that Rome, which has been made glorious by the heroism of the apostles, accomplished through the example of the martyrs, and what Spain, which was once full of delights and is now in a miserable state, did both to her credit and to her disgrace]. Divine Providence was the agent of history, and all events formed part of God's plan. However, at this stage there is no mention of La Cava, although the *Crónica de 754* corroborates an important element of later Arab accounts, which is the existence and role of Count Julian, identified with the man named once in the text as Urbanus. For some historians, this ancient document has authenticity and presents the facts in a way not skewed by ideological preoccupations.

Over one hundred years elapsed between this and the next known written accounts of the story, which originate in Asturias in northern Spain. Last bastion of native resistance to the Muslims, the mountainous northern kingdoms remained the stronghold from which the Asturians won a significant battle against the Muslims at Covadonga, led by their first king Pelayo (or Pelagius) in 722. The *Crónica albeldense* [Chronicle of Albelda], written c. 881–83 during the reign of Alfonso III, describes Pelayo as a grandnephew of Roderick, who fled to Asturias after being expelled from Toledo by King Witiza. The focus of the account is the establishment of continuity between the Asturian monarchy and the earlier Visigothic one, proclaiming an exclusive ethnic connection between both lineages. The kinship between Roderick and Pelayo remains important and is an element used to good effect in certain future versions of the legend.

A key work in the rich vein of Asturian historiography was the marginally later *Crónica profética* [Prophetic Chronicle], dated about 883. It consists of a brief compilation of pieces on the history of Islamic Spain, probably written by a learned Mozarab because of the influence upon it of Muslim historiography, its focus upon Andalusia, and its originality in comparison with other northern histories. The section on Roderick's defeat is brief yet while the theme is by then traditional—the punishment of the Visigothic people for its sins—it is written in a new, interpretative way deriving from books of prophecy whose visions describe a moment of restoration arising at a time of destruction or captivity. There are two points of interest. First, the rejection of the myth of Pelayo, suggesting that Mozarabic historians never considered him as a Goth. Martin comments that this introduces the idea that the Gothic people still remained in Spain, waiting to have their sovereignty and territory restored. This first version of the myth of the Christian reconquest was not based on the idea of a new Asturian king and kingdom, but on the permanence of the Gothic people in the peninsula, thus effacing the history of Asturian royalty. The second point of interest is that the chronicle describes the mystery surrounding the fate of Roderick. There is no official record of his death, which, as Martin observes astutely, seems to leave the issue in a state of suspension, of implicit continuity and permanence.[11] The unresolved question of Roderick's final outcome elicits manifold creative responses in future centuries and lends the legend some of its mystery and dynamism. The early-tenth-century *Crónica de Alfonso III* sought to redress the suppression of Asturian connections, using a wide range of sources including the *Crónica profética* to reassert the link between Visigothic and Asturian monarchies by claiming that Pelayo was definitely of royal blood and elected king of Asturias by members of the royal family. This allowed the Asturians to illustrate their own myth of Pelayo and thus reinforce the contemporary royal authority of Alfonso III.

These first accounts are characterized by their explanation of the Muslim invasion within the Christian Catholic framework of God's punishment of a wayward people and in the Asturian chronicles by the exploitation of a historical event for ideological and political purposes. King Roderick is a real if mysterious figure at the core of the story, while Count Julian appears only once, and his daughter as yet has no existence at all.

The First Arabic Versions

For Islamic historians as well as for Christian writers, the conquest of Spain constituted an event of enormous significance. Fred Donner notes that the earliest Believers developed a rich historiographical tradition because they discovered, in historical narration, a way of legitimizing the religious and political community in relation to the claims of other communities, similar to that used by the Christian historians of the Asturian chronicles.[12] Arab chroniclers reported the events of 711 as the result of the actions of Muslim troops and generals acting as part of the general expansion policy of the government of Damascus. The occupation of Hispania was therefore part of a much wider Islamic conquest taking place outside the peninsula and late-Roman Empire. Arab historiography was, nevertheless, fundamentally divergent from its Christian counterpart for various reasons. Roger Collins is again eloquent on this subject, drawing attention to two apparently contradictory aspects, which subsequently had a profound influence upon the development of the narrative relating to Roderick and La Cava. First, the importance of citing sources was paramount in Islamic tradition because it gave stature to a book and allowed readers to assess the credibility of any anecdote. This derived from the idea of collecting the sayings and teachings of the prophet Mohammed in order to supplement the Koran itself. As a result, Islamic historiography developed in a unique way, which tended to be anecdotal while emphasizing the need for careful reference to the sources of the information. Although this lends it detail and immediacy, the linking of the names of recognized authorities to fabricated stories was a danger. This was further compounded by the fact that unlike their Christian counterparts at the time, Muslim historians were secular men, and usually not legal or religious authorities. Islam never produced a religious caste like the one existing in medieval Christianity, and therefore most historians focused upon edification through the expression of Muslim ideals.[13]

Consequently, Arab records of the conquest became infused with elements of fiction and fantasy. Their first accounts describe auguries of victory, and the fabulous treasures they won as a result; as indicated in the introduction, and the central story of King Roderick's forced entry into the locked palace or tower in Toledo originates in early Islamic history. Variations on this story, which has parallels with certain Jewish tales, were never intended to reveal reality, though this secondary event forms an important part of future versions of the story of Roderick and La Cava.[14] Any strictly historical elements in these records were affected by the need to present the invasion as proof of the validity of the message of Islam as evidenced by its military triumph. This was exacerbated by the fact that the earliest accounts date from the mid-ninth century, over one hundred years after the events themselves, without any certain oral tradition or *hadīth* to link the chronicles with the early eighth century. For Collins, all these aspects serve to diminish the value of Islamic historiography as an accurate historical record, which he describes as "just as much a repository of later legendary elaborations which curtail its value as a description of actual events."[15]

This is not the view of the Spanish Arabist Pedro Chalmeta, who comments on numerous Arabic sources of the late eighth to tenth centuries, admittedly noting that these are fewer and less detailed for al-Andalus than for the central parts of the empire, being full of legend and fable that contrast strongly with accounts of the occupation of Iraq and Syria, which contain no fantastical elements.[16] Chalmeta notes three key figures in the conquest and occupation of Hispania, namely Mūsā, Ṭāriq, and Julian, the latter being the catalyst of the action, whose offspring are praised in Arabic sources as being honored descendants of the man who introduced Islam to al-Andalus.[17] All Arabic sources state that Julian was Christian and ruled the Maghrib area of northern Africa, being based in Tangiers and later, Ceuta. Several historians describe him as Roderick's governor in Ceuta in their preamble to the dishonor of his daughter at the court of Toledo. All Arab texts are unequivocal in underlining the transcendental importance of Julian's action in facilitating the entry into Spain: "Fuente habrá que silencie los motivos, otras darán diversas razones, todas coinciden en que se realizó a propuesta del señor de Ceuta"[18] [Some sources are silent as regards motives, some give various explanations, all coincide in stating that it came to pass at the proposal of the lord of Ceuta]. For the Spanish historian this means that the existence of Julian and the historical reality of his offer are proved beyond all reasonable doubt. However, accounts seem to date Julian's intervention in the last years of Witiza's reign, around 709, and therefore prior to Roderick's accession to the throne. This would necessarily call into question the legendary rape of Julian's daughter by Roderick as a motive for the governor's action. Chalmeta concurs with Howell's view that since there is no known source for the story of La Cava's violation, it may well have originated with Julian himself, who could have presented it exclusively to the Arabs as a secret in order to cast himself in the role of dishonored father rather than traitorous betrayer of his country. This might well account for the first appearance of the story in Arab, not in Christian writings, and would vindicate the last Visigothic king of Spain of his catastrophic and legendary sin, while accusing Julian exclusively. Two notable Arab accounts of the conquest were the anonymous *Akhbār al-Majmū'a* [Collection of Anecdotes] possibly written around 940, and the tenth-century *Ta'rikh Iftitāh al-Andalus* [History of the Conquest of al-Andalus], both of which were edited and systematized by the Rāzī family in a chronicle that is now lost, only surviving in a thirteenth-century Portuguese translation known as the *Crónica del moro Rasis* [Chronicle of the Moor Rasis] discussed below.

As a result of the growth of translation activity in the peninsula after the capture of Toledo with its wealth of Arabic books by the Christians in 1085 and the strengthening tradition of Hispano-Latin historiography, it was natural that legendary elements from the Arabic sources began to be absorbed into later Christian accounts. The motif of the dishonor of Julian's daughter appears for the first time in the eleventh-century *Chronica Gothorum pseudo-Isidoriana* [Pseudo-Isidorian Chronicle of the Goths], although the girl is violated in this version by King Witiza, Roderick's predecessor. However, Pidal observes that the inclusion in this chronicle of the Arabic legend of the locked Toledan palace "tiende a presenter a Rodrigo cual hombre impío, violador de las más sagradas prohibiciones"[19] [tends to present Roderick as an impious man, a violator of the most sacred prohibitions]. The *Historia silense*, written about 1115–18 by a monk from the monastery of Santo Domingo de Silos in La Rioja, reveals special interest in the last part of the Visigothic reign that enables the history of the reign of Alfonso VI (1065–1109) to be linked with the Gothic monarchs, especially Leovigild and Reccared. This chronicle, deemed relatively reliable, also includes the story of Julian's daughter, described as a beautiful concubine who is dishonored for the first time in Christian writing by Roderick, not Witiza. The account develops the interpretation given in the earliest versions that the disastrous invasion was an act of Providence that occurred to avoid the sin and depravity of Witiza, not Roderick, from leading to greater and more widespread evil. The chronicle emphasizes the lust of Witiza, his soldiers and the clergy in particular.

In the first half of the thirteenth century, two lengthy and influential chronicles were composed in Latin, the *Chronicon mundi* [Chronicle of the World] by Lucas, bishop of Túy, finished in 1236, and *De rebus hispaniae* [On Matters Hispanic] by Rodrigo Jiménez de Rada, the famous archbishop of Toledo, completed in 1243. While Lucas of Túy's account repeats what his sources stated, the motif of the treacherous counselor is strong. The author links Julian to the two scheming sons of Witiza, describing the count as "muy amado entre sus secretarios (de Witiza)...era este Juliano varon artero y sabio, y engañosamente despertó los franceses que guerreasen a España la mas cercana; fingiose tanbien ser muy amigo al rey Rodrigo, y engañosamente le consejo que los caballos y las armas ynbiase a las Galias y Africa"[20] [highly esteemed among Witiza's secretaries...he was a crafty and learned man, who treacherously incited the French to fight in Spain because of its proximity; he also feigned great friendship with King Roderick, and treacherously advised him to send horses and arms to Gaul and to Africa]. But it is in the archbishop of Toledo's version that arguments and justifications take on a definitive form, where the catastrophe of the invasion is attributed to Witiza's exultant lechery, reiterating the old idea of the *iudicium Dei*, the judgment of God as a punishment for debauchery. The archbishop is the first to claim that Roderick violates Julian's wife, not his daughter, in contrast with the other accounts.

The Overlay of Myth

In the five hundred years from the Muslim invasion until Jiménez de Rada wrote his important chronicle of Spain, history had merged with fictional elements to establish the essential form of the story of the king and the whore. The intricate complexities of Christian and Muslim accounts of the historical circumstances created a maze of conflicting records, some of which were markedly supernatural in nature, and molded by differences in historiographical traditions, authorial intentions, religion, and ideology and not least by the difference between conqueror and conquered. Tensions between the Arab and Christian world emerged in the effort to forge a unique interpretation of momentous events. The bare bones of the narrative lay in a king's loss of his country through invasion, catalyzed by the betrayal of a trusted governor in the form of Count Julian, whose motive may have been revenge for sexual dishonor. The fusion of the individual and personal with the national and universal arose from the need to make sense of the senseless for the Christian Spaniards who found themselves suddenly under Moorish thrall, and to reinforce the rightfulness and timeliness of Muslim expansion from the Arab point of view. It is in this fusion that later historians have noted strange parallels between mythical stories and historical events, such as the disappearance of Troy, and of the Roman and later, of the Visigothic kingdoms, which appear to prefigure the albeit extended disappearance over eight centuries of the Saracens. As Chalmeta notes, the fall of the Trojan, Roman, and Visigothic Empires were all caused by a love affair. The rape of Helen of Troy by Paris enraged Menelaus and provoked the Trojan war as recounted by Homer; the rape of Lucretia by Sextus Tarquinus aroused the indignation of both father and husband, and her public denunciation and suicide brought about the elimination of the Roman monarchy and the rise of the Republic of Rome; the rape of La Cava brought about the fall of the Visigothic kingdom. Chalmeta also remarks on the fact that the invader Tarīk's companion Mummuza's passion for the sister of Pelayo roused the latter to stage a victorious uprising against the Moors at Covadonga.[21]

The motifs of rape and the treacherous counselor therefore form part of a number of narratives recounting the loss of empire or kingdom. In his study of the Roderick legend, Alexander Krappe asserts strong links with Gothic legend in the King Ermanarich cycle. The oldest version of this kind of legend existing outside Spain appears in Procopius of Caesarea's *Bellum Vandalicum*, written in the sixth century, in which the wife of a Roman senator, Maximus, is raped by Emperor Valentinian III. When Maximus finds out, he craftily conceals his anger and persuades the emperor to kill Aetius, his best general. As a result, Valentinian is helpless when Attila and the Huns invade Italy, and finally, Maximus avenges his wife's violation by killing Valentinian and marrying the empress.[22] A similar legend appears in a number of other narratives, notably in Isidore of Spain's *Historia Gothorum* of the seventh century, in which enraged nobles kill the Visigothic king Theudisclus (548–49), as well as in at least two Norse sagas. In the *Fornmanna Sögur*, the king falls in love with another man's wife and sends her husband to England to collect tribute. While he is away, the king violates his wife, only to be found out by a returning messenger who slays him with his battleaxe, prior to being slain himself. *Didreks Saga*, a Norwegian translation of a German poem, ascribes the rape to King Ermanarich, a central figure in Ostrogothic legend. There are also a number of Danish ballads with a similar plot.

Krappe suggests that since no source for Procopius' story has ever been discovered, it may have been a legend he picked up whilst in Italy during campaigns against the Goths. This implies that the rise of the story of Julian's daughter was not due to the Arab invasion, nor due to the infamy brought upon the last Visigothic kings by Christian chroniclers in the later Middle Ages, principally because the idea of rape associated with loss of empire appears in Isidore's history, which predates 711. Krappe feels certain that the Roderick legend is part of the Gothic Ermanarich cycle, part of "...the vast legendary current which contributed to swell the Spanish, the French, the Scandinavian and the German epic, supplying them with material of rare tragic power. It can be likened to a tree, its roots going deep into the unknown strata of prehistoric times and its branches overshadowing all Europe."[23] The same type of story appears in works by Byzantine historians writing in imperial Constantinople, Arabic chroniclers writing in southern Spain, a German chronicler in his monastery, a French jongleur and by Icelandic saga writers, to which Erich von Richthofen adds the influence of similar Viking legends not discussed by either Juan Menéndez Pidal or Krappe.

If the hypothesis that Julian secretly and intentionally blackened King Roderick's name by inventing the rape of his daughter or wife as a plausible reason for his betrayal to the Moors is correct, it is quite possible that Julian, as a Visigothic Christian general, had come across some legendary version that fitted perfectly with his practical intentions, and that he related this to Arab counterparts as if it were a real event. This would explain its apparent origin in Islamic accounts of the invasion. Although Julian's true motivation for his treachery may remain shrouded in the mists of time, his possible appropriation of a legendary motif as authentic fact is of extraordinary moment. In a remarkable ironic twist in which the fictitious is passed off as the factual, his fabrication could well account for the confusion that marks the chronicled history of King Roderick and the Moorish invasion of Spain from its inception until the late medieval period. Yet it was precisely this melding of the historical and fictional that lent the story such colossal narrative power and flexibility, which enabled it to be recreated according to the purposes of the narrator. The dissonant chorus of medieval voices that tell this tale beg a crucial point: to what important questions was the story of the king and the whore the answer? It was not until the fourteenth century and the rise of the Castilian vernacular that these matters became any clearer.

Hidden Agendas: The Evolution of the Legend of King Roderick and La Cava in the *Crónica de 1344* and Its Refundición (c. 1440)

When Alfonso X the Learned came to the throne of Castile and Leon in 1252, his intense Castilian patriotism asserted itself in the rise to prominence of the vernacular language, not only in official documents that had previously been in Latin, but also in his enormous cultural output that encompassed works on scientific, historical, legal, and other subjects. His insistence on the use of the Castilian vernacular arose from his strong national consciousness and his wish to encourage the only language common to the Moors, Jews, and Christians who lived in his kingdom. Alfonso X planned two historical works, the *Estoria de España* or *Primera crónica general* and the *General estoria*, which was to be a history of the world. Both tasks were gargantuan and were never completed as they had been envisaged, but their contribution to medieval historiography was great because of the historical information they made available for the first time in Castilian. It is the *Primera Crónica General* (c. 1275) that contains the first vernacular account of the legend of King Roderick and La Cava. The chronicle begins with Moses and continues with pre-Roman Spain and with Rome, whose history is presented as an important part of Spain's background. Most of the work is devoted, however, to the history of Spain, starting with the Germanic invasions and ending in the reign of Fernando III, Alfonso's father. From a historiographical point of view, the compilation of this history is exceedingly interesting because of the vast number of varied sources used, including all manner of literary material and the works of Arab historians. In terms of our legend, it is valuable as the first version of the story to exist in Castilian, and is of special importance to Alfonso X, who had a life-long, but unfulfilled aspiration to become Holy Roman Emperor. It was therefore important for him to underline his descent from the Visigothic line of kings, thus reinforcing the continuity of the Spanish royal line from the time before the Arab conquest.

The narrative in the Alfonsine history is a close translation of the thirteenth-century Latin text by Rodrigo Jiménez de Rada, el Toledano. Although nothing substantially new is added to the legend, certain details are elaborated upon which dictate the focus of this precursor of subsequent vernacular reworkings. King Witiza, denigrated predictably for his sexual corruption, is described as establishing his brother Oppa as archbishop of Seville instead of the rightful candidate. In this text, the Visigothic king strikes an allegiance with the Jews to the detriment of Catholicism: "e tornó los judíos en la tierra e dióles privilegios et franquezas, et más onrrados et más cotados eran los judíos que non las eglesias"[24] [and he returned the Jews to the land and gave them privileges and generosity, so they were more honored and illustrious than the churches]. In this history, Witiza plans to blind Roderick as he did his father Theudefredo, but Roderick is apparently greatly loved by the Roman Senate, and with their help rises up against Witiza and blinds him in turn. When Roderick is elected king, it is by the power of the Roman, not the Visigothic, Senate.

The king is depicted in shades of gray—he is strong in battle, liberal in his actions, yet has the wiliness of Witiza. Julian, however, is painted very positively as a fine, rich nobleman of impeccable Gothic lineage and a close adviser of Witiza. The account's lack of clarity regarding Roderick's crime reflects the divergences between earlier sources. The writer reports that the king did indeed rape Julian's daughter, though there was some talk of her being promised to him in marriage. The compiler also duly notes the confusion over the king's demise, quoting Lucas de Túy's belief that he may have died fighting against the Moors, while counterbalancing this with a reference to an inscription above the king's supposed grave in Viseu in Portugal.

What is quite certain, however, is the ignominy with which Julian is portrayed. He is described in the strongest possible terms, which merit quoting in full: "Maldita sea la saña del traidor Julián ca mucho fué perseverada; maldita sea la su ira, ca mucha fué dura et mala, ca sandio fué él con su ravia et corajoso con su incha, antuviado con su locura, oblidado de lealdad, desacordado de la ley, despreciador de Dios, cruel en sí mismo, matador de su señor, enemigo de su casa, destroidor de su tierra, culpado et alevoso et traidor contra todos los suyos; amargo es el su nombre en la boca de quil nombra; duelo et pesar faze la su remembrance en el coraçon daquel quel emienta, e el su nombre siempre sera maldito de quantos dél fablaren"[25] [Cursed be the anger of the traitor Julian, for it was very long-lasting; cursed be his rage, for it was hard and evil, for he was crazy with fury and irate because of his grudge, muddled with madness, his loyalty forgotten, the law disregarded, despiser of God, cruel in himself, murderer of his lord, enemy of his house, destroyer of his homeland, guilty and treacherous and betrayer of his own people; bitter is his name in the mouth of those who speak it; his memory brings grief and sorrow to the heart of any who think on him, and his name will forever be cursed by all those who use it]. Alfonso's narrative effectively exonerates Roderick, perhaps as a member of the Visigothic line the Learned King wished to be aligned with, and demonizes Count Julian as the arch-traitor, a role he played in many future incarnations.

It was not until almost a century later that the legendary story was significantly reworked to create a compelling drama of loyalty, vengeance, and betrayal in the *Crónica general de Espana de 1344*, the Castilian translation of a Portuguese chronicle. This version was widely read throughout Spain and Portugal, and was in turn amended in the fifteenth-century *Refundición toledana de la Crónica de 1344*, dated around 1440, and written by a Toledan *converso* or Jew who converted to Christianity, who develops intriguing new elements in the Roderick narrative. I would like to explore the unanswered questions to which these chronicles form a response by instigating a primary dialogue between these two texts. While acknowledging Levi-Strauss's observation that "history can be distinguished from myth by virtue of its dependency on and responsibility to those 'dates' that make up its specious objective framework," Hayden White underlines the conviction of Nietzsche, Hegel and Croce, that "history, like other formalizations of poetic insight, was as much a 'making' (an *inventio*) as it was a 'finding' of the facts that comprise the structure of its perceptions."[26] On this basis, what was the purpose of the inventions and amendments introduced by the authors of the *Crónica de 1344* and its *Refundición* in their remaking of the story of King Roderick, and do they reveal hidden agendas?

What question, therefore, was posed in the mind of the fourteenth-century chronicler by Alfonso X's account of the story in the *Primera Crónica General*, which led to the innovations and changes he made in the *Crónica de 1344* version? As the eminent Spanish scholar Diego Catalán points out, both versions represent the nationalist desires of a country watching the debacle of al-Andalus, and both harmonize the ideal of the neo-Gothic unity of Spain with Castile's aspiration to be "cabeça de reinado" (head of the kingdom).[27]

The *Crónica de 1344* is strikingly different in its development of the story of Roderick, and, as Ramón Menéndez Pidal notes,[28] its superiority over previous accounts marks an important turning point in the history of the legend. The identity of its author is crucial to this discussion because it bears directly upon the evolution of the narrative. Although no authorial name appears in the manuscripts, it has been conclusively established by Cintra, Diego Catalán and María Soledad Andrés that the author was Pedro Afonso, count of Barcelos in Portugal, bastard son of King Dinis (1279–1325). While his personal relationship with the king influenced his account of the relationship between Roderick and La Cava, as will be seen shortly, undoubtedly part of Pedro's agenda in creating the *Crónica* relates to issues of historiography. Unlike the Spanish kingdoms, prior to the reign of King Dinis, Portugal had no tradition of chronicles in Latin, and its historiography proper began only under the aegis of Dinis himself. The introduction of a Portuguese branch of the Alfonsine school of historiography was the initiative of Count Pedro, whom Cintra describes as a faithful disciple of the Castilian school of historical compilation. However, Pedro's inclusion of a history of the kings of Portugal in this general history of the peninsula indicates his desire to reinforce the idea of Portuguese autonomy and establish his native land as a kingdom with its own independent history.

The most important source for the *Crónica de 1344* was the Portuguese translation of the tenth-century *Crónica del moro Rasis*, ordered by King Dinis and carried out by a priest, Gil Perez. This willingness to import an

Arabic source at once aligned the chronicle with the Alfonsine school, and also set it apart, for the *Primera Crónica General* does not use *Rasis* for the Roderick narrative. Jiménez de Rada did use *Rasis* in *De rebus Hispaniae*, but only sparsely, yet it is fundamental to the *Crónica de 1344*. However, it is the alterations to the basic structure of *Rasis*, made either by Perez or by Pedro Afonso, that are illuminating in relation to the Rodrigo and La Cava story. I shall refer to MS M, a Castilian translation of the first redaction by Pedro Afonso. The situation regarding manuscripts of the C1344 is complex, and the Portuguese original is lost. A chart of their apparent genealogy can be consulted in the appendices.

Absent in the *Primera Crónica General* and in *Rasis*, but vital to the plot in *Crónica de 1344*, the Visigothic king Witiza is succeeded by an imaginary king, Acosta, who makes his debut here and endures in Spanish historiography until the sixteenth century. Upon Acosta's death, great discord spreads throughout the land because of antagonism between two factions, one supporting each of Acosta's two sons, and claiming the relevant son as rightful king. The conflict becomes so intense all over Spain that it is decided to avoid further dispute by electing Roderick, a relation of the king, as regent until Acosta's sons are of age. Yet Roderick assumes the role of usurper and appropriates the kingdom for himself. In spite of this, the *Crónica de 1344* portrays Roderick in a very favorable light. When he takes charge, "començó de hazer tanto de bien que maravilla era" [He started to do so much good that it seemed miraculous] (Cap. LXXVI, p. 92). He brings the two young princes to his palace "e tanto les fazia de amor e de algo, que su padre no gelo fiziera ni la mitad" [and showed them such affection and made so much of them, that even their own father would not have shown half so much] (Cap. LXXVI, p. 92). The two extensive descriptions of the enchanted house in Toledo, to which successive Visigothic kings have added a lock, and which no one dares to enter, are also new additions in their detail and invention, and again Roderick, "que era onbre de gran coraçon" [who was a man of great heart] (Cap. LXXVII, p. 96), is portrayed as powerless to escape his destiny in his desire to see what is inside the building. However, at this point he is distracted by his passion for the daughter of his governor in North Africa, Count Julian.

For the first time in the evolution of the legend, Count Julian's daughter takes on character and importance. Arabic sources had previously claimed that the raising of grandees' children in the royal palace was a Spanish custom, but in the *Crónica de 1344* this is not the case. Instead, it is a special system devised by Roderick, which enables him to request the presence of Julian's daughter in Toledo. For the first time in written accounts, she is named, as Alacaba, and the carefree incident during which Roderick is overcome by her beauty is also an innovation: "paso por ay el rrei, e acaesçio asy que lo vio vn poco del pie a vueltas con la pierna, que lo avia tan blanco e tan bien hecho que non podria ser mejor. E tanto que la ansi vio, començola de querer muy gran bien e començole de demandar muy fuertemente su amor" [the king happened to walk by and saw a little of her bare foot and leg, so white and beautifully shaped. And upon seeing this, he began to love her greatly and began to press her strongly for her love] (Cap. LXVIII p. 98).

Also new are the expressions of Alacaba's alienation, sadness, and desperation after her seduction, as well as her long conversations with her confidante, Alquifa and the text of her letter to her father, telling him of her dishonor. The chronicle underlines her blamelessness and her vulnerability as a woman placed in an impossible predicament. But Roderick cannot avoid his fate, as his second visit to the locked house in Toledo shows, for inside he finds a chest and a cloth predicting the invasion of Spain by the Arabs. Inexorably, Count Julian's revenge is plotted in another new, well-conceived episode that consists of a council meeting Julian holds in Ceuta with his supporters, among others Prince Ricaldo, Don Ximón, who is Alacaba's suitor, and Don Enrique, a resentful, impudent man who ends up betraying Julian. As Menéndez Pidal suggests, these additions to *Rasis*, plus the linking of the two episodes of the enchanted house with Roderick's affair with Alacaba, enhance the fictional, dramatic dimensions of the narrative, turning it into a compelling conflict of passion and revenge, in which Roderick is no longer the evil violator as he appears in some earlier versions, but a strong, noble man overcome by passion, while Alacaba becomes a forceful female presence in the story.

Possible origins for these innovations, in lost epic or in fictionalized chronicles, are discussed inconclusively by Menéndez Pidal.[29] However, the life of the author, Count Pedro, hints at a hidden agenda that influenced the choice of materials included or added. Pedro Afonso was either Dinis's eldest or second eldest illegitimate child, and he became steward to the wife of his half brother Afonso, who succeeded Dinis to become King Afonso IV in 1325. In 1314 Dinis granted Pedro the title of count and he enjoyed a privileged position at his father's court until 1317, when a family feud broke out between Dinis, who allied himself with two other illegitimate sons, João Afonso and Afonso Sanches, against his legitimate son Afonso, who was supported by Pedro.

Afonso feared that Dinis would name his illegitimate son, Afonso Sanches, heir to the throne, and openly rebelled against his father in 1321, seizing Coimbra. Pedro Afonso acted as mediator between Dinis and Afonso, and before long, Dinis pardoned Pedro for siding against him and reinstated him. In the 1344 chronicle, Pedro tends not to fault Afonso in the war between father and son, but places the blame on certain royal advisers, in particular one Gomes Lourenço. Nor did he bear a grudge against his father for his treatment of him, for when Dinis died in 1325, Pedro was at his bedside. It was some years later when Pedro compiled the *Crónica de 1344*, although he was already well known for his *Livro das Linaghens*, a genealogical history of Portugal written, and its author says: "por gaanhar o seu amor (de Dinis) e por meter amor e amizade antre los nobres fidallgos de Espanha"[30] [to win his love (that of Dinis) and to foster love and friendship among the noblemen of Spain]. It seems likely that his own bastardy reinforced his obsession with lineages, a preoccupation that spills over into the first redaction of the *Crónica de 1344* with its genealogy of the kings of Portugal. Similarly, his personal experiences and his father's life may have informed his reworking of the story of King Roderick, a man prey to violent passion for a woman who was not his wife, and involved in a disputed succession at the start of his reign. It does not seem implausible that those very additions Count Pedro approved of or made himself to the version of Rasis had special resonance for him. The new elements of the imaginary king Acosta and the problem of the succession of his two sons, including the portrayal of the traitorous adviser to Julian, echoed his own involvement with his father's disputed succession. The depiction of Roderick as a praiseworthy king in thrall to his sensual nature may reflect Pedro's natural admiration and sympathy for Dinis as a king, while acknowledging his human side, to which the count owed his existence.

First, it is clear, in the light of Pedro's life and education, that his exposure to Alfonsine historiography at the Castilian court where he was exiled for a short time, and his possible knowledge of the *Primera Crónica General* led him to question the impoverished status of Portuguese history writing, and to respond by compiling the *Crónica de 1344* along Alfonsine lines, while simultaneously enhancing the importance of Portugal as an autonomous kingdom. Second, his knowledge of the Arabic version of Roderick's story written by Rasis may well have raised issues of blame, guilt, and treachery that had powerful echoes in his own life, and that he sought to resolve in his portrayal of Roderick and Alacaba. The *Crónica de 1344* answers questions about the nature and status of Portuguese historiography, and also responds to the question of how the story of Roderick and La Cava might be interpreted in the context of the contemporary political situation in Portugal and Spain.

Almost one hundred years later, around 1440, a Toledan *converso* reworked his version of the legend in the *Refundición toledana de la crónica general de 1344*, a text as yet unpublished in its entirety and extant in two main manuscripts, MS 7594 in the Biblioteca Nacional, and MS 2585 in Salamanca University library. As one would expect from its title, which

Lathrop asserts to be the most accurate of several,[31] the chronicle reflects its predecessor fairly closely. Why, therefore, rewrite the same story one hundred years on? What unanswered questions in the *Crónica de 1344* is the *Refundición* itself responding to?

As in the case of the former text, one of the main issues relates to historiography, which had changed significantly over the intervening century. The trend toward the inclusion of more legendary, fictionalized material was notable, and both Lathrop and Pattison remark on the novelistic skills of the 1440 author, Pattison noting a tendency to sensationalism that is extreme in his narration of other legends in the same manuscript.[32] Once again, the nature of the author is central. First, although the author is anonymous, it is known that he came from Toledo, and several of his emendations to the Roderick story reflect the pride he felt over the city. For example, he insists that Toledo remained faithful to the sons of Acosta for a long time, accepting Roderick's authority grudgingly only. The same pride is obvious when he describes Roderick's wedding celebrations in Toledo, "por ser una delas mas singulares e reales çibdades delas Españas" [because it was one of the most unique and royal cities of Spain]. He also adds a Toledan tradition that seems to locate La Cava's tragic carelessness in revealing herself to the king, in an orchard in the city, which to that day was called "el corral de los pavones"[33] [the garden of peacocks]. Her bathing naked in the pool in that garden, unaware that she is being watched by Roderick adds an erotic touch to the *1344* account, and echoes the biblical story of the Jewish king David and Bathsheba.

King David's Jewishness leads to the second important aspect, the author's religious and racial identity as a converted Jew. Writing around 1440, at a time of aggravation of the social and religious problems of Jews and *conversos* with Christians, the origins of the Jewish presence in Spain began to be pondered. There is an early association of the Jews with Toledo, linked to the Hebrew noun 'toledot' meaning 'generations.' Their arrival in Spain and presence in Toledo dated back to pre-Christian times, and was largely usurped when Toledo began to acquire importance as the focus of the Visigothic monarchy. In 694, a newly discovered conspiracy of Jews and *conversos* altered the Visigothic ruler Egica's tolerant attitude. A plot was discovered to usurp his throne, and it was believed that the Jews had been in cahoots with the Arabs in the invasion that took place seventeen years later in 711.

Religious conversion is crucial to another telling addition to the *Refundición*, Roderick's invented marriage to Eilata, the daughter of the king of Tunis. Before she can marry him, she is obliged to convert to Christianity, and only then are they crowned monarchs of Spain. This is a surprising alteration, since it is known that Roderick's wife Egilona was of

Gothic origin, yet it is consistent with the conciliatory tone of much of the narration of the story of the Muslim invasion, and may have had personal resonance for the *converso* author. Roderick's marriage underlines the good relations between Christians and Arabs, and the text casts the king as noble, heroic, compassionate, and completely blameless in sexual terms. When he sees the beauty of Eilata, Roderick merely does what any Christian king might have done, which is to impose conversion before their union could be legalized.

The text of the *Refundición* contains another important new element in the narrative, the penance of the dethroned king. This addition evolves significantly in future recreations of the story, moving far beyond the uncertainty over the king's death expressed in the *Crónica de 1344*. Surprisingly, in the earlier chronicle, the count of Barcelos refers only briefly to the association of the penance legend with Viseu in Portugal: "e perdiose en la batalla que ovo con los moros en el campo de Medina Sidonia en tal manera que del nunca supieron parte, pero que dixeron despues algunos que moriera vrçelaño en Viseo" [and he was lost in the battle against the Moors in the battlefield of Medina Sidonia, so that nothing was ever known of him, although some said later that he died as a gardener in Viseo] (MS M, folio 11). This is an elaboration of the reference to Viseu in the *Primera Crónica General*, and relates to the famous discovery of what was alleged to be Roderick's tomb in that town, recorded in the *Crónica de Alfonso III*, when the ninth-century repopulators of Viseu came across the inscription: "Hic requiescit Rudericus ultimus rex gothorum" [Here lies Roderick, last king of the Visigoths] on a sepulchre in a basilica in the town, providing what was viewed as hard evidence of Roderick's fate after his defeat in battle.

In contrast with Count Pedro, the author of the *Refundición* develops this story in a clear, definite description of Roderick's demise: ". . .fuyó el rey don Rodrigo fasta la villa de Viseo que es en los reinos de Portugal, onde toda su vida estovo et bivió por moço de un ortelano en una huerta, fasta que murió. E cuenta la estoria que fizo en la su vida tan grand penitençia et murió tan católico que a la su fin se tañeron las campanas todas de la villa de Viseo por él, sin tocarlas alguna persona; ca dicen que crió en la huerta una muy grande culebra et, quando la vio poderosa, metióse con ella en una cueva et dexóse todo comer fasta que murió"[34] [And King Roderick fled as far as the town of Viseo in the kingdom of Portugal, where he lived the rest of his life as a helper in a garden, until he died. And the story goes that he made such great penance and died such a devout Catholic that upon his death all the bells in Viseu rang for him, without the aid of any human hand; for they say that an enormous snake was raised in the garden, and when he saw that it was potent and strong, he shut himself in a cave with it and allowed it to eat him until he died]. This gruesome death of devourment by a snake appears in a number of other versions of the legend, including Pedro de Corral's *Crónica sarracina* of 1430, where it is described particularly barbarously. While the penance legend and its origins are fascinating in their own right, Roderick's ghastly death in the *Refundición* forever exonerates the king from any blame for the Arab conquest, and establishes him as a penitent Catholic martyr.

In his study and edition of the legend of the *Siete infantes de Lara* taken from the manuscript of the *Refundición*, Lathrop describes its Toledan author as "a master story teller, who used whatever written material, epic material from the oral tradition, and his own imagination to compose his polished narrative."[35] While many of the additions and amendments to the story of Roderick and La Cava reinforce the view that the author dramatized and developed the legend in a subtle and exciting way, certain of these reworkings also point to a latent social and political agenda, both personal and universal, which relates specifically to the Jewish race and to Toledo. Combined pride in Toledo as the original Jewish settlement, together with a presentation of Roderick as blameless for his sexual passion could be seen as an attempt to discount Jewish involvement or guilt in relation to the conquest of Spain and attribute it to the usurpatory and dissolute Visigothic royal line, of which Roderick was not a direct descendant. In his absolution of Roderick, La Cava, and even Count Julian, the author equates them with the Jewish race: "Pues por un rey se pagar de una tan gentil donzella non casada nin ordenada en alguna religión, alegres devieran ser toda su generación, nin al conde don Julián comprehender deve la culpa más que oy a los judíos la muerte de Jesu Cristo, porque lo que Dios permite ninguno puede enbargar" [So for a king to take pleasure in such a lovely girl, unmarried and not ordained in any religion, all his generation should rejoice, nor should blame fall upon Count Julian any more than today the Jews should be blamed for the death of Jesus Christ, because what God permits, no one can constrain]. As these characters are blameless, so are the Jews blameless of Christ's death. The true culprit is Vitiza: "la verdadera culpa e causa catar sabés, bien allí la fallarés en el vil corronpimiento del malvado rey Vetiza"[36] [you should look more closely at the true cause and blame, and you will find that it lies in the vile corruption of the evil king Witiza]. Neither Roderick nor the Jews were to blame for the conquest of Spain, and perhaps the author of the *Refundición* felt that the Jews had done sufficient penance, akin to Roderick in the final episode. Like Eilata, Roderick's Arab bride in this version of events, the Jews were obliged to convert to Christianity, but were then also betrayed, as she was.

The author acknowledges the paradigmatic nature of the legend of King Roderick and La Cava. His rewriting responds to the implicit questions posed in the *Crónica de 1344* relating to the nature of the writing of history, by presenting a narrative in which dramatization and fictionalization enhance and underline the underlying historical truth. He also uses legend as an ethical response to the representation of Roderick, La Cava, and Julian in the earlier chronicle by suggesting an ideological subtext for the social and religious problem of Jews and *conversos* in fifteenth-century Spain. His text is magnetized for us by its implications.

Both chronicles display evidence of hidden agendas relating to contemporary social perceptions and to the personal circumstances of each author, and their reformulations of history as explanation and example wrought permanent changes in the evolution of the story. Both texts bear out Hayden White's comment that historical narratives exploit metaphorical similarities between sets of real events and the conventional structures of our fictions. Each author has a sense of what White calls 'emplotment,' the encodation of facts contained in a chronicle as components of specific kinds of plot structures, so that the historical narrative mediates between the events reported in it, and the pregeneric plot structures conventionally used in our culture to endow unfamiliar events and situations with meaning.[37] The author of the *Refundición* describes the Muslim invasion of Spain as "aquel misterio [que] despues passasse por él (Rodrigo) e por las Españas todas"[38] [that mystery which later passed through Roderick and through all Spain]. It is precisely the inexplicable, perplexing nature of this major event that both narratives under discussion attempt to frame within their own historical and social contexts in a way that highlights their contemporary dilemmas. As each author liberated the legend from historical generalization, they reformulated the old story in a way that was relevant for their time, and also provided compelling new perspectives for future writers to build upon.

Penance or Pornography? The Exile of King Roderick in Pedro de Corral's *Crónica sarracina*

The *Crónica sarracina*, written about 1430 by Pedro de Corral, and described by Ramón Menéndez Pidal as Spain's first historical novel, is of the utmost importance in the history of the reception of the legend. In a work that runs to a thousand pages, Corral reformulates the seven-hundred-year-old story, developing the significant new element of Roderick's penitential exile to create a memorable version that inspired many later European reworkings. In this version, Roderick wins respect and admiration once he is elected king. As in the *Refundición de la Crónica de* 1344, he marries an Arabic princess, Eliata, but later spies on Count Julian's daughter, here named La Cava, as she has fun with other girls in the palace gardens. Inflamed with uncontrollable desire for her, he eventually seduces her, but

La Cava is so distraught at her predicament that she writes to inform her father. As in earlier accounts, Julian seeks revenge through his alliance with Moorish invaders, and the Christians are defeated in 711 at Guadalete. However, in this rendering, Roderick flees after the battle and makes his way to Viseu in Portugal, where he is exiled, undertaking a ghastly penance to gain absolution for the sins he has committed. Tempted by a she-devil in the form of La Cava, which he resists, he entombs himself with a snake that devours his genitals in a slow, lingering death. My discussion of Corral's innovative presentation of La Cava, and of the nature of Roderick's penance, will unravel the marked ambiguities of what purports to be a Christian morality tale, destabilized by a punishment whose expression verges on pornography.

Although described in the nine extant manuscripts as the *Crónica del Rey don Rodrigo*, the popular title of *Crónica sarracina*, or *Saracen Chronicle*, immediately adds a significant Arabic flavor to a work that, though extremely popular in the fifteenth and sixteenth centuries, has been almost forgotten since. The recent edition by James Fogelquist is the first since 1587! The *Crónica* is a literary colossus, containing motifs, structures, and techniques from three different genres, historiography, chivalresque literature, and hagiography, in which the chronicle form is fundamental. Fogelquist has noted[39] that the term 'crónica' was used at this time both for authentic chronicles and for adventure stories, with no distinction, and many of Corral's contemporaries, except the historian Pérez de Guzmán, accepted the *Crónica sarracina* as genuine history, in spite of the predominance of fantasy elements in the narrative.

This illusion of authenticity was fostered by Corral's use of respected historical sources, notably the Arab historian Al-Razi's (d. 955) *Crónica del moro Rasis*, the *Crónica de 1344*, and the histories by Rodrigo Jiménez de Rada (d. 1247), López de Ayala (d. 1407), and the later *Crónica troyana*. Pedro de Corral's account of Roderick's life differs considerably from those in the *Crónica de 1344* and the *Refundición de la Crónica de 1344*, while extending and deepening the crucial issues with which they engage. His narrative does not end with the defeat of the Visigoths at the battle of Guadalete, but culminates in the king's exile, his subsequent redemption through confession and his fatal penance. Yet the description of his death is written not in the sparse style of the chronicler, but in a narrative infused with fantasy, where fictional elements override and dominate historical veracity. What, therefore, led Corral to make the extraordinary amendments to the legend of King Roderick that prompted Cacho Blecua[40] to describe Corral's work as "uno de los intentos más singulares de toda la Edad Media española" [one of the most unique and unusual undertakings of the entire Spanish Middle Ages]? What were the unanswered questions posed by earlier and contemporary chronicles, to which Corral's *Crónica sarracina* was the answer?

Certain specific questions arising from chronicled accounts and relating to the individuals at the heart of these events are answered in the text. The uncertainty over Roderick's final hours and weeks, and the exact nature of his penance are clarified in Corral's version, and the broader issue of attribution of blame for the conquest of Spain is explored in detail. Was it Roderick alone, or La Cava, or even Julian who was truly at fault? Other accounts also raise a number of more general queries relating both to the relevance of the events of 711 to the fifteenth century, and to the nature of the relationship between Christians and Muslims, as well as interrogating the purpose and method of history writing itself, all of which are responded to in different measure by Corral's text.

Undoubtedly, the contemporary political context and Corral's own involvement in it were relevant to the *Crónica sarracina*. Although very little is known of Corral's own life, and there is only one extant reference to him as the author of the *Crónica*, his brother, Rodrigo de Villandrano, count of Ribadeo (d. 1400) was clearly a prominent figure who achieved repute at the court of King Juan II of Castile (1406–54). He and Pedro de Corral later sided with Álvaro de Luna (d. 1453), the king's chief adviser, who usurped Juan's royal power and virtually ruled the kingdom himself, hoping to restore prosperity and complete the reconquest. Corral was writing in a country he saw as corrupt and detrimentally affected by long-term crises that had fragmented society, rendering it unable to regain the perceived unity of Visigothic Spain. The overall thrust of his work has been deemed to be religious and didactic, for Roderick is held up as a moral example, hence his parallel with the biblical King David. Corral may well have been making a statement about dissolute monarchy and the abuse of power in his portrayal of the Visigothic king as a man who loses his kingdom through lust and fails to uphold Christian principles. Yet the plain Christian moral that sin will be punished, and can be atoned for through contrition is challenged by Corral's insistence on elements of eroticism, violence, and even sadism in his account of the relationship between Roderick and La Cava, and of the king's exile. In fact, the entire premise of the Muslim invasion as disaster is itself compromised by such a reading, which not only undermines Catholicism, but also encourages a favorable parallel to be drawn between Álvaro de Luna, a powerful man who works against his king for the perceived greater good, and Roderick's general and ally, Count Julian, who also works against his king by leading the Muslims into Spain.

The seduction and rape of La Cava by King Roderick came to be viewed by Christian historiographers as the single specific sin that led to the fall of the Visigothic realm to the Muslim invaders, and the author's position as a Castilian writer with close ties to the monarchy would suggest his adherence to Christian Spain's interpretation of events. Yet the text intimates an equivocalness toward Spain's Arab foes that undermines that adherence, since Roderick marries a Muslim, not a Christian, princess, amid great celebration, and La Cava herself is foreign to the court, for she comes to Toledo from North Africa, where her father is governor. More crucially, Corral signals an ambivalence in both the presentation of La Cava herself and in her relations with the king that may echo the essential ambivalence of contemporary Christian-Arab relations.

The name La Cava that became familiar to future generations is used for the first time in this text. As if reinforcing this ambivalence, it immediately places her within an Islamic frame of reference, for it derives from the Arabic word meaning 'whore.'[41] The name is also judgmental and castigatory in its implication that La Cava is the wicked temptress of the gullible king, and therefore morally reprehensible. These undertones are at ironic variance with Corral's initial descriptions of her as "cortés e mesurada"[42] [polite and modest] and as a girl who "robava la fama a todas, e esto por la su bondad"[43] [stole the show over all the others, because of her goodness]. But it is her physical, not moral, beauty that attracts the gaze of the king when he first falls under her spell as he spies upon her playing a game with some friends in the garden: "E un día el Rey se fue a los palacios del mirador que avía fecho, e andovo por la sala solo sobre las huertas e vio a la Caba, fija del Conde don Julián, que estava en las huertas burlando con algunas donzellas, e ellas no sabían parte del Rey, ca bien se cuidavan que dormía; e como la Caba era la más fermosa donzella de su casa, e la más amorosa en todos sus fechos, e el Rey le avía buena voluntad, así como la vio echó ojos en ella; e como ella e las otras donzellas jugavan, alçó las faldas pensando que no la veía ninguno, e mostró ya quanto de las piernas; e teníalas tan blancas como nieve, e así lisas que no es persona al mundo que dello no atalantase"[44] [One day the king went to the chambers in the belvedere he had built, and walking alone through the room which looked out onto the gardens, he saw La Cava, daughter of Count Julian, who was in the garden joking with some other girls. They didn't know the king was watching, for they thought he was asleep; and as La Cava was the most beautiful girl in his household, and the most loving in all her deeds, the king felt good will toward her, and took immediate notice of her. And while she and the other girls were playing about, she lifted her skirts thinking no one could see her, and showed her bare legs, which were as white as snow, and so smooth that anyone in the world would have felt confusion at the sight].

While Corral hastily attributes the blame for Roderick's lustful gaze to the devil and to destiny, as Fogelquist notes,[45] this scene and its consequences reveal a variant incest theme in which the putative father/daughter relationship (since Roderick has invited the girl to his court to educate her) changes to a sexual one. Roderick cannot take his eyes off her and the description becomes more erotic: "E cresció porfia entre ellas desque una vez gran pieça ovieron jugado de quién tenía más gentil cuerpo, e oviéronse a desnudar, e quedar en pellotes apretados que tenían de fina escarlata, e parescíansele los pechos, e lo más de las tetillas"[46] [And after they had been playing for a while, a dispute arose between them over who had the best body, so that they were obliged to take their clothes off down to their close-fitting petticoats of pure scarlet, which revealed their breasts and most of their nipples]. Clearly La Cava wins this competition in the king's eyes, because his secret observation of her half-naked body (as well as those of the other girls), intensified by the sexual suggestiveness of the scarlet petticoat against her white skin, leads eventually to her violation and the resulting despair that forces her to write to her father telling him of her dishonor. Julian's rage triggers his betrayal of Roderick to the Moors and his collusion in their invasion of Spain. La Cava's paradoxical embodiment of sensuality and innocent purity is transmuted into the diabolical during Roderick's penance, where Corral converts her into a she-devil, the ultimate evil temptress, who serves to destabilize the status quo in this extraordinary finale even further.

King Roderick's exile in Viseu in Portugal following the defeat of his army by the Muslims is merely acknowledged as the barest possibility in the earlier *Crónica de 1344*, although it is alluded to in brief terms in the *Refundición*. This makes Corral's extensive development of the Viseu legend even more surprising, especially as it comes at the very end of the text, creating maximum impact. As Cacho Blecua remarks,[47] the penance should actually be narrated much earlier in the sequence in order to be chronologically accurate. Clearly then, the author should have intended this ending to convey a powerful instructional message regarding the need for contrition, penitence, and absolution. However, upon closer examination, the fantasy elements of his version contradict this reading, with interesting implications.

The episode owes much to hagiographical literature, notably in the theme of the repentant sinner, and also in the markedly supernatural quality of the events. As Roderick wanders alone and grief-stricken, he is guided to his final destination by a white cloud. He is alternately assailed by the devil, then strengthened by the voice of God and by dreams that encourage him to resist. These hagiographic motifs of temptation and dream sequences, plus the use of the ecclesiastical discursive genres of prayer, sermon, and confession emphasize a didactic message, and elevate Roderick to sainthood, earned by his final dreadful martyrdom to the snake. This metamorphosis from secular monarch into holy martyr is astonishing enough in itself, for it exonerates him unequivocally from blame, and extols him in spite of his alleged crimes.

Yet Corral's grasp of the moral message seems to slip as Roderick arrives at the place where a hermit instructs him as to the nature of his penance. As soon as the king prays and confesses his sins, the devil begins to tempt him in various guises, first, as a treacherous hermit who lures him with envy and gluttony, second, in the figure of Count Julian, who tempts him with pride by offering him the kingdom of Spain once more, with the endorsement of the nobility, and third and most notably, as La Cava herself. Again Roderick and the reader become voyeurs of a flagrantly erotic display by the La Cava-devil, who appears "muy ricamente vestida"[48] [most richly dressed], looking more beautiful than ever, and tells the king that he must give her a son and heir to the Visigothic kingdom. His secret observation of La Cava in the garden is echoed in this scene, as the she-devil assures him of the secrecy of this encounter, yet the roles are reversed, for this time the false La Cava seeks to force the king, rather than vice versa.

During his temptation, he sees her dressed in "una aljuba de escarlata apretada e corta por media pierna"[49] [a close-fitting scarlet jubbah, reaching only to the knee], echoing the sexy red petticoats of the girls in the palace gardens and again presenting La Cava in an equivocal light, since she is wearing the short-sleeved *morisco* costume of Arab origin. Next he sees her "delante una cama muy rica, e que se começava a desnudar el aljuba e que quedava en camisa e en cabellos que le llegavan fasta los pies. En aquella ora se bolvió contra el rey, mostrándole los pechos e las piernas"[50] [before a magnificent bed, where she started to take off the jubbah, leaving only her underwear and letting her hair fall to her feet. Then she turned toward the king, showing him her breasts and legs]. Roderick finally has a vision of her "asentada en almohadas muy ricas de oro en par dél en camisa, los pechos descubiertos por lo poner en tentación"[51] [lying opposite him in her underwear on cushions embroidered with gold, her breasts uncovered to tempt him]. Here Corral's alacrity in describing erotic detail conveys a pleasure inconsistent with admonishment for sin, perhaps as a means of gripping the attention of the reader. Sugaring the pill of the didactic message is a familiar feature of medieval and early modern writing, yet the insistence on sensual description in these examples by its very nature problematizes the idea of punishment for wrongdoing.

Nonetheless, Roderick resists these temptations, and can now undertake his penance. He has to seek a two-headed snake, put it in a pitcher and allow it to grow large. Then he must entomb himself with the snake and submit to his fate. Álvarez-Hesse[52] identifies penance as the main didactic theme of the *Crónica sarracina*, and notes the preponderance of this theme within the tradition of Christian asceticism. However, Corral's original interpretation, expressing erotic violence and verging on sadism, subverts ascetic precepts forcefully. The two-headed snake, which appears to have no direct source or precedent, is an ambiguous symbol, at once phallic and castigatory. In Egyptian mythology, the snake goddess Mertseger (with three heads) can punish and forgive if the sinner repents. In hagiographic legends, Saint Christina has three different kinds of snakes applied to her as a punishment, this having its source in the popular *Legenda aurea* by Jacobus de Voragine. But while snakes can be divine instruments of retribution, as demonstrated in the biblical references in Numbers 21:6, Ecclesiastes 10:11 and Jeremiah 8:17, they are also used in hagiography as symbols of sin and of the devil's power over man. Weir and Jerman identify *l'homme aux serpents*, a figure deriving from the classical figure Serpentarius, on a considerable number of medieval stone carvings, the earliest example being in the church of San Isidoro in León, where a monk is depicted coiled round by two huge serpents poised to bite his head, while his tongue protrudes as a sign of his concupiscence.[53] It may be that Pedro de Corral was inspired by a similar carving, since in the Spanish text, Roderick's nemesis is both a symbol of God's punishment and suggestive of the devil, who has just appeared to Roderick as La Cava, and whose shape ironically mirrors the phallus that has caused the king's downfall.

Once more, Corral emphasizes the erotic dimension in his account of the king's penance and suffering. Roderick seals himself into the tomb with the snake "desnudo qual nasció"[54] [as naked as the day he was born], where he remains for three days before the snake starts to eat him: "E al tercero día complido de quando allí havía entrado, la culebra se levantó de par dél e subióle desuso del vientre e de los pechos. E començó de le comer por la natura con la una cabeça e con la otra en derecho del coraçón"[55] [And when three days had passed since he entered the tomb, the snake rose up before him, moving from belly to breast. And it began to eat his genitals with one of its heads and his heart with the other]. The latent erotic violence of this episode is heightened by a shepherd who asks Roderick to describe exactly where the snake is eating him: "E él le dixo que por dos (sitios). El uno en derecho del coraçón con el qual él pensava quanto mal él avía fecho. E el otro por la natura, la qual fuera la causa de la grand destruición de España"[56] [And he told him he was being eaten in two places, one in line with his heart, with which he had conceived the evil he had done. And the other at his genitals, which may have been the cause of the great destruction of Spain]. The equivocal nature of the subject matter is reflected on a linguistic level in the choice of the tense and mood in this quotation. The verb 'pensava' [conceived] is in the Imperfect tense to express a continuous action in the past, while 'fuera' [may have been] is in the Subjunctive mood that, although commonly interchanged with the Imperfect in this era, nevertheless casts an element of doubt over whether Roderick's desire was the true cause of the invasion, thereby mitigating his guilt and revealing uncertainty and interrogation present at different textual levels.

Corral insists on drawing out the gruesome deed even further, in a manner that is positively sadistic: "E la culuebra como estava muerta de fambre e era grande en un punto ovo comido la natura, e començóle de comer por el vientre; empero ella tanto no pudo comer que no durase el Rey en esta pena desde una hora antes de la noche fasta pasado mediodía. E como le rompió las telas del coraçón allí quedó que no le comió más"[57] [And since the snake was dying of hunger, and was of great size, it ate his member in one go, and then started on his belly; but it couldn't eat sufficiently fast to prevent the king's pain from lasting from one hour before nightfall until after midday. And when the membranes of his heart broke, the snake ceased to eat him].

The prominence of pain, violence, and suffering in mystical writing is well known. In its imitation of Christ's passion, suffering is redemptive. Julie Miller draws attention, however, to the equating of intense pain and suffering with the erotic. An example is the mystical experience of Beatrice of Nazareth, which was both "awe-ful and intimate, intensely erotic and excruciatingly painful."[58] Her point is that pain, violence, and the erotic become indistinguishable, and she notes that some scholars have viewed certain kinds of medieval piety as sublimated sado-masochism. In his book on erotic writing in Renaissance England, Ian Moulton[59] also equates violence with pornography in terms of its sensual effect upon the reader. It strikes me that Pedro de Corral's narration of King Roderick's penance clearly demonstrates these aspects, but to what end? What unanswered questions in the story of Roderick and La Cava does this version respond to?

First, the doubt over the king's ultimate fate, left unexplored in earlier accounts, is clarified in great detail. He dies absolved of sin and extolled like the kings in other royal chronicles, thereby reinforcing the idea of the continuity of Spain's history from the time of Espan until Roderick's reign, which is indicated by the description of al-Andalus and the genealogy of Roderick's ancestors that Corral takes from the *Crónica del moro Rasis*. The reader gains the satisfaction of closure, in an ending that establishes the power and importance of fictional truth over and above historical truth, for Corral's finale is pure invention. However, that satisfaction is disturbed by enigma, as the standard Christian readings are subverted by violent sexual elements. This tendency for the narrative to indicate one thing and the gloss to contradict it is observed by Fogelquist in other respects, creating a smokescreen behind which the author hides in order to "lanzar una crítica corrosiva de la situación política, económica y moral de la España en que vivía"[60] [launch a corrosive attack on the political, economic, and moral situation of the Spain in which he lived]. As the editor notes, readers of the *Crónica del Rey don Rodrigo* would have naturally found parallels between Roderick and his time and the Castile of Juan II. Discontent over the expense of war, the corruption of the clergy, and the responsibility of the monarch for general social disorder expressed in the text in relation to the Visigothic king could well have applied to Juan II himself, not least because of the constant fighting between Castile and the Moorish kingdom of Granada in the early fifteenth century, a state of affairs that showed that the upheavals that had their origins in the eighth century and before still remained unresolved.

While the aim of the text purports to be the reestablishment of continuity, and restoration of Christian Catholic supremacy in the figure of Pelayo, the earlier chronicles that present Roderick as responsible for the loss of Spain are refuted by Corral's work, for the king is depicted as a man of great moral complexity. Menéndez Pidal commented that "ningún poeta posterior vio tan hondo en el carácter del rey"[61] [no later poet perceived the character of the king with such depth], a king who is presented as vulnerable to temptation, but is ultimately exonerated, particularly since the text implies that La Cava was to some extent complicit in the love affair, the scene of temptation by the she-devil in her form suggesting the corruption of innocent man by the femme fatale or Eve figure. This view of the king is presented by the historian in the text, the courtier Eleastras, who is on Roderick's side and narrates the historical account accordingly. Interestingly, Corral's narrative fails to equate the sympathy for and exoneration of Roderick with the sympathy for the Jews and their exoneration from any blame for Christ's death, which is the focus of the *converso* chronicler of the *Refundición de la crónica de 1344*. In fact, Corral shows himself to be markedly antisemitic elsewhere in the narrative.

Corral's bold, ingenious use of eroticism and violence as transgressive forces that run against the grain of Christian didacticism threatens to undermine the power structures that Catholic ideology reinforces. While apparently toeing the line by drawing strongly upon the hagiographical tradition of using explicit descriptions of sexuality to convey a didactic message, he implicitly refigures sexuality and the erotic as positive forces, and specifically foregrounds female sexuality, instead of denying it. His latent questioning of sexuality, gender, and the guilt, and abuse of power that manifest themselves in the ambiguous nature of the relationship between the king and La Cava gained response in the work of writers over the next four hundred years who presented sympathetic depictions of the king, the whore, and her father, notably in the cases of the nineteenth-century English dramatist Landor's tragedy *Count Julian*, and in María Rosa Galvez's play *Florinda*, written in 1804.

In earlier versions, the conquest of Spain and the demise of its king paves the way for Pelayo to launch the reconquest, which would draw to its conclusion in 1492, only fifty years after Corral's writing. Was he questioning the wisdom and viability of a military and political undertaking that would soon strip Spain of its highly sophisticated and civilized Moorish and Jewish inhabitants? The ballad tradition that found full expression in the two hundred years after Corral was alive certainly illustrates an ambiguous reaction to the constantly changing Christian/Moorish frontier that constituted one of the main political issues of his time. The allure of the Middle East so visible in this Arabic-tinged narrative shapes the early fictionalization of the tension between prohibition and pleasure, between official hostility of the Christians to the Moors and unofficial admiration for and fascination with Islamic culture.

Corral's fictionalization is also a response to questions regarding the nature of history that has exercised historiographers before and since. There is a sense in which the *Crónica sarracina* subverts history in its presentation of a predominantly invented account that many people read as authentic and accurate. Its author uses a number of historiographical conventions that reinforce this reading, not least in his use of 'crónica' in the title, a term that would have had certain clear expectations for the fifteenth-century reader, in line with other chronicles that present authentic accounts of the reign of a king, such as the *Crónica de Juan II*, and similarly emphasize the importance of the king as protagonist by including his name in the title, as Corral did himself. In addition, the author draws upon the figural biblical tradition that used prophesy to explain later events, applying it to a secular text in this case. Corral's work comes within the category of 'historia fingida,' described by Fogelquist as attributing "a una obra fundamentalment ficticia fuentes historiográficas imaginarias que tienen la apariencia de verdaderas para conceder al libro la autoridad moral de la historia"[62] [to a fundamentally fictional work imaginary historiographical sources that appear to be true, in order to bestow the moral authority of history upon the book]. This cleverness in imitating the chronicles, in this instance by drawing heavily upon the source of the Arabic *Crónica del moro Rasis*, which itself contained a large number of fictional elements, was consonant with the general tendency of fifteenth-century historians to write much livelier, more detailed accounts than those of their fourteenth-century predecessors, incorporating vivid narrative elements that had previously evolved in fiction.

Corral's decision to favor fiction and fantasy over historical accuracy clashes with 'historia verdadera' because of its lack of objectivity and factual reliability. It implies not only that these may be unachievable in the writing of history, but also that the fictional may have just as much, if not more, veracity than the factual in terms of exemplarity and didacticism. Yet Corral's inventiveness diverts his work away from the theme of Christian censure and toward confluence with the Oriental, as reflected in the simultaneously demonic and alluring figure of La Cava, who epitomizes the paradoxical ambivalence of male Christian reaction to both women and Muslims. It is precisely this latent acknowledgment of cultural and sexual otherness and of the possibility of their coexistence that is developed in the cycle of ballads on Roderick and La Cava inspired uniquely by the *Crónica sarracina*. The theme also manifests itself strongly in early modern Spain in such other works as Villegas' *El Abencerraje*, in which love and chivalry triumph over cultural and racial differences between Moors and Christians, and in Lope de Vega's plays *Abindarráez y Jarifa* and *El último godo*, the latter developing the story of the last Visigothic king in a drama that builds upon the ambiguities hinted at in Corral's work by addressing powerful cultural anxieties and tensions pertinent to the persistently ambivalent relationship between Christians and Muslims in the play. The *Crónica sarracina* thus brought the legend sharply into focus as a way of exploring issues of cultural and historical relevance to fifteenth-century Spain through the fictionalization of chronicled events, as well as paving the way for future generations to rewrite the story of the king and the whore.

CHAPTER 3

TRUE AND FALSE HISTORIES:
THE CASE OF THE MASTER
FORGER MIGUEL DE LUNA

> *The simulacrum is never that which conceals the truth—it is the truth which conceals that there is none. The simulacrum is true.*
>
> Jean Baudrillard, *Simulations*

The tension between fact and fiction in historiography reached a peak in the sixteenth and seventeenth centuries in Spain and its effects were plainly visible in the development of the legend. The ambiguous message inherent in a fictional narrative masquerading as authentic history, which is at the core of the *Crónica sarracina*, became significantly more pronounced in the writing of one of the most intriguing and mysterious figures of Early Modern Spain, the *morisco* Miguel de Luna, who lived in Granada toward the end of the sixteenth century. His remarkable history of King Roderick and the Muslim invasion, which is the focus of this chapter, is rendered more striking by a comparison with other contemporary versions of the story.

Menéndez Pidal identifies two other historians of the sixteenth century whose accounts had a noticeable impact upon the legend, Julián del Castillo, who wrote his *Historia de los reyes godos* [History of the Gothic Kings] in 1582, and Father Juan de Mariana, whose *Historia general de España* [General History of Spain] appeared in Castilian in 1601. These works were both historical undertakings of a universal and synthesizing nature, intended to provide a new and better history of the peninsula, and were preceded in this enterprise by a fifteenth-century history, the *Historia Hispanica*, published in 1469, one year prior to the death of its author, Rodrigo Sánchez de Arévalo, who was born in 1404 and studied law at

Salamanca university before embarking on numerous travels abroad that ended with his appointment as governor of the great Roman fortress and prison of Sant'Angelo in Italy.

His work appeared almost forty years after Corral's great novel was written, and was quite different in its intentions. Perhaps Arévalo's residence on foreign soil aroused a nostalgia for his homeland that manifested itself in a desire to praise and affirm Spain, and Castile in particular. In strong contrast with Corral, Rodrigo de Arévalo was opposed to Álvaro de Luna and his faction, and acted as ambassador for Juan II himself around 1440. Also in contrast with Corral, his intention in his history writing was to continue the work of his predecessors, notably Lucas de Túy and Rodrigo Jiménez de Rada, although in addition he draws on a number of Latin historians including Lucillus, Martinus Polonus, and Quintus Curtius. This use of Latin sources and the fact that he wrote his history in Latin indicate a nod toward the classical influence of the Renaissance as well as to the medieval past, since his model Spanish historians both wrote in Latin. Yet Arévalo's work does not embrace the trend of Renaissance humanists of developing a new historical method and applying it to assist in understanding the present. It was a method that was increasingly critical of previous historiography in the sense that it abandoned the pervasive use of legends and miracles characteristic of medieval history, bestowing more importance upon human action than upon the intervention of God. In these terms, Arévalo introduced no new method or ideas in his work, which in fact harks back to the neo-Gothic idea that the kings of Castile are direct descendants of the Gothic kings, put forward by Lucas de Túy in the thirteenth century. This implies that Juan II and Enrique IV of Castile were direct heirs of the Goths. As Juan María Laboa points out,[1] the problem with this idea was that Roderick was always deemed to be the last king of the Goths, and could therefore have no successors. Arévalo resolves this difficulty by asserting that the issue lies in Roderick's title, not in the concept itself, for until the battle of Guadalete, he was king of the Goths, and after the battle he became king of Spain or Castile, or even Leon. This is a clever reinforcement of Arévalo's argument that in this case, the unity of Spain was never destroyed, only fragmented, and that a Spanish kingdom always existed over and above the individual kingdoms of the peninsula. So this author uses the story of Roderick as a way of emphasizing the supremacy and unity of Castile, following in the tradition of Alfonso X in his aims, and in that of earlier chronicle writers in his technique. Possibly the most important aspect of Arévalo's work was that it was the first history of Spain to be printed, in Rome in 1470. Yet the advantage of reaching a wider reading public through the printing press may have been considerably lessened because the text was written in Latin, and not in the vernacular.

Over a century later in 1582, Julián del Castillo's history of the Gothic kings shows several similar characteristics. Menéndez Pidal notes the reactionary nature of the work "salida del corazón mismo de la vieja Castilla, se manifiesta tradicionalista en extremo, completamente medieval"[2] [springing from the very heart of old Castile, it reveals itself to be traditionalist in the extreme, completely medieval]. In his dedication to King Felipe II, Castillo states that his intention in writing the history is to increase the fame and glory of Felipe's ancestors, the Gothic kings, and stresses what he feels is the uniqueness of his history because it engages with matters ". . .que según entiendo, nadie las a escrito en particular, sino entremetiendo algunas breves sumas dellas en otras historias"[3] [. . .which as far as I know, no one has written upon in detail, merely inserting some brief summaries in other histories].

The interest in Castillo's case lies in his adherence to the tradition of 'historia verdadera' [true history], in opposition to the 'historia fingida' [false history] of his predecessor Pedro de Corral and in extreme contrast with the 'true history' of his contemporary Miguel de Luna. In the preface Castillo addresses the reader to reassure him or her that his intention has been to write the truth: "pues se deve creer se ha escrito la verdad con toda decencia" [you must believe that the truth has been written in all decency] and ". . .que todo lo en esta historia escripto, es tomado de muchos verdaderos autores aprobados"[4] [. . .that everything written in this history has been taken from many genuine and approved authors]. He is therefore at pains to demonstrate the veracity of his account that draws upon reliable sources, yet he goes on to justify his inclusion of fictional elements as follows: "y en todos quatro libros van tocadas muchos y diversas materias, e historias verdaderas y fabulosas, de mas dela principal: lo cual parece que excede los terminos historicos, y a lo que esta obligado quien en este genero escrive; y esto ha sido por dar mas gusto a los lectores, con la variedad de cosas tan differentes como en ellos se vera. . ."[5] [and all four books contain many varied materials, and true and fictional stories, in addition to the main one: which seems as if it exceeds the terms of history and the obligations of those who write in this genre; and this has been done in order to give more pleasure to the readers through the variety of different things they will find in it. . .].

So, even 'true history' can justifiably contain fictional elements, as one Pedro Laynez, presumably an inquisitor, agrees in his preface to the *Historia de los reyes godos*: ". . .lo que me parece es, que aunque como el mesmo confiessa en su carta a los lectores en alguna manera excede el puro termino escrevir historia verdadera, presupuesto que el advirtio antes este inconveniente, y que su fin fue deleytar co la variedad de materias differentes a los que leyeren esta historia, hasta ahora nadie escripta en nuestra lengua con tanta particularidad, pues en lo esencial ninguna cosa de las que trata contradize a la verdad que sigue, se le puede justamente conceder licencia para la impression en premio de su trabajo, y de la curiosidad que a tenido en mezclar lo dulce con lo verdadero"[6] [...and it seems to me, and he himself confesses to this in his letter to his readers, that in some way he goes beyond the simple aim of writing true history, yet taking account of the fact that he pointed out this disadvantage previously, and that his intention was to entertain his readers with a variety of different materials, which until now no one has written down in our language in such detail, and since in its essence nothing he describes contradicts the truth which follows, he can justifiably be granted a license to print as a reward for his work, and for the carefulness with which he has mixed entertainment with truth].

Castillo is therefore justified in including the story of Roderick and La Cava in his 'true' historical account, as well as the legend of the enchanted tower in Toledo which the king forces open, only to foresee his fate. But his depiction of Roderick's character lacks the subtlety and depth of Corral's creation. Castillo uses the story of La Cava's seduction as a warning against lust, which seizes the king like a madness "que priva el entendimiento y memoria de los hombres"[7] [which deprives men of understanding and memory], and forces the bedeviled king to rape her. However, Roderick's guilt is mitigated by the fact that the Muslim invasion of Spain is an inescapable part of his destiny, predicted, according to Castillo, not only by Hercules Alcides the Greek, but also by Merlin and the Venerable Bede. There is an intriguing elaboration of the legend of the king's tomb at Viseu in Portugal, in which the king's gravestone depicts not only his name but also a virulent denunciation of Count Julian: "Aqui yaze Rodrigo, ultimo Rey de los Godos, maldito sea el furor impio de Julian Conde, que ta pertinaz fue: maldita fue su indignacion tan dura: loco y cruel le torno la furia: animoso le hizo la indignacion: impetuoso el furor: olvidado de la fidelidad y de la religion cruel para si mismo: homicida contra su senor: enemigo de su casa y nacion: destruydor de su patria: culpado y mal hechor para con todos: amarga sera en la boca de todos su memoria: y para siempre se corrompera y podrecera su nombre"[8] [Here lies Roderick, last king of the Goths; cursed be the impious fury of Count Julian, who was so obstinate; cursed his hardhearted indignation; rage made him mad and cruel: indignation made him determined: impetuous his fury; forgetful of loyalty and religion for his own ends; murderer of his lord; enemy of his house and nation; destroyer of his native land; guilty and wicked in everyone's eyes; his memory will be bitter in people's mouths; and his name will suffer corruption and will rot forever].

This diatribe against the count closely follows the model in Alfonso X's *Primera Crónica General* previously discussed, although Castillo ultimately reverts to his attribution of overall guilt to the king's lust.

In 1588, the year of the destruction of the allegedly invincible Spanish Armada, Castillo's contemporary, Father Juan de Mariana, completed an altogether more ambitious project in his twenty-five-volume *Historia general de España* [General History of Spain]. The history was written in Latin originally with the title *De rebus Hispaniae*, presumably in deference to Rodrigo Ximénez de Rada's work, and twenty volumes were first published in 1592, but it seems that Mariana misjudged his public, for few could read Latin easily, causing him to produce a vernacular version (no doubt with the help of additional translators) that was ready by 1598, and appeared finally in 1601. Mariana's view of the demise of the Armada as divine judgment for the licentiousness of princes epitomizes the changing role of historical writing during this era. Although it was still a predominantly ecclesiastical product, as it had been in the Middle Ages, history began to serve religious purposes less than political ones, or else the religious meaning attached to it served the interests of princes rather than priests. Father Mariana's history of Spain was an influential and important piece of historiography and is relevant to the debate over true and false history within which the legend of Roderick and La Cava was entangled, in particular because its author was directly involved in the question of the authenticity of the lead books of Granada that later proved to be the forgeries of Miguel de Luna and his colleague Alonso de Castillo.

The influence of Renaissance historical dictums is much more evident in Mariana's work than in that of Julián del Castillo or Arévalo. He was keen to present an accurate record of the past and not be duped by it, and was doubtless aware of Cicero's statement that the historian should avoid saying anything false, and should be scrupulous about including the whole truth. What seemed to be more the issue was the nature of that truth, for the tendency, shaped by Petrarchan influences, to seek moral lessons in history led to the view (already fundamental to Alfonso X's view of history in the thirteenth century) that if fiction or legend could teach a moral truth more effectively than a fact could, then it was legitimate to include it. However, Mariana was often quoted for his own citation of the classical historian Quintus Curtius, "Plura transcribo quam credo" [I report more things than I believe], which fostered his ironic reputation as a writer of fables. Like other historiographers of his time, he incorporated large sections of battle harangues, including one from the Muslim Tariq's mouth, and portraits of individuals and letters, such as the one from La Cava to her father, which plunged him into a protracted controversy over the purpose of history writing.

In his valuable monograph on Juan de Mariana, Alan Soons[9] recounts a dispute with Pedro Mantuano, the secretary to the constable of Castile, who openly ridiculed him for using La Cava's letter to Count Julian, which was considered to be fictional, and for including tales that might be taken to be prescriptive, rather than prohibitive. In a letter to the king on this subject, Mantuano wrote: "From the story (if it were true) of La Cava ladies will learn how to take revenge for outrages committed on them in royal apartments, and the state will be in danger. Princes will imitate Rodrigo, and present-day enemies of Spain might be invited in as invaders, or they may learn to be tempted to force ladies residing in grandee's palaces."[10] Clearly the instructional message in these stories was taken very seriously. The censor of the new 1601 edition of the history, Pedro de Valencia, insisted that Mantuano's complaints should be ignored, since although these sections were legendary, they did carry important lessons for debauchees!

Mariana's account of the legend is clear and elegantly written, and is based largely upon Lucas de Túy, Jiménez de Rada, and another contemporary, Ambrosio de Morales' *Crónica general de España* [General Chronicle of Spain], which is almost scientific in approach. In spite of accusations of misogyny in his presentation of Roderick's violation of La Cava, none of the criticism leveled at him seemed to have any effect on the way he was esteemed as a historian, and in 1618, the great dramatist Lope de Vega described him as "the Christian Livy, luminary of Spanish history." Soons believes that the *Historia General de España* was influential in shaping the Spanish consciousness of the country's past right up to the time of the peninsula war in the nineteenth century, when a new historiographical awareness came into being.[11]

Among the many metamorphoses of the story of the king and the whore, the version written in late-sixteenth-century Spain by the Granadan, Miguel de Luna, constitutes a crucial reinterpretation of events, not only because de Luna's work involves a fascinating story of deception and intrigue, but also because it intensifies issues relating to the nature of history, fiction, and translation, in addition to exerting a profound influence upon the afterlife of the legend. The quotation at the head of this chapter from the Bible, which is used by Jean Baudrillard at the start of his work *Simulations* to illustrate the paradoxical power of the image or semblance to convey truth, is of direct relevance to de Luna. Highly respected as an Arabist, acting as interpreter and translator to King Felipe II and to the Spanish Inquisition, a man of standing and influence, and held in high esteem, both his cultural status as a *morisco* and his linguistic expertise were crucial to his other secret profession of master forger, not only of written documents but also of archeological artefacts. He perpetrated two exceptional hoaxes, relating in the first instance to the Lead Books of Granada, and in the second, to his faked history of the Muslim invasion of Spain in 711. The motivation that led him and his associates to construct such elaborate and daring forgeries is inseparable from the cultural context of Golden Age Spain and to the plight of its *morisco* population.

The inability to distinguish between the genuine and the faked was the Achilles heel that allowed Miguel de Luna to fascinate and delude the great and powerful of Golden Age Spain and beyond for over half a century. His forgery of the celebrated Lead Books of the Sacromonte in Granada was astounding in its audacity. These relics were discovered during the excavation of the site in 1595 and heralded as "astonishing archaeological discoveries." The unearthing of eighteen lead books containing sayings of the Virgin Mary, Saint Peter and Saint James written in Arabic rocked the whole of Spain and attracted the interest of the Vatican. The relics were extensively investigated until it was finally revealed that their celebrated translators, Miguel de Luna and his colleague Alonso de Castillo, were also the perpetrators of a remarkable hoax.[12] Juan de Mariana played his part in the debate over the authenticity of the relics, and although Father Juan was skeptical about the artefacts themselves, he was less so about a related forgery, the 'falsos cronicones' or false chronicles, a collection of documents published by the Toledan cleric Jerónimo Román de la Higuera in 1594. The latter claimed he had obtained the chronicles by Marcus Flavius Dexter, Maximus, and Eutrandus from the monastic library at Fulda in Germany. Previous minor church historians had named these chroniclers; Román went so far as to invent their works, including an account of Saint James's visit to Spain, which Mariana was unwise enough to incorporate into his own history, fuelling the criticisms of those who saw him as a 'father of lies' in the vein of Herodotus.

The fascinating forgeries of the Sacromonte and the associated chronicles were manifestations of a culture in which falsity and fakery were endemic, and within which Miguel de Luna perpetrated his other masterpiece of deception, his true history of Roderick and La Cava. In 1589 he produced a translation, from a hitherto unknown Arabic source found in the library of the Escorial, of the authentic version of the events of 711, entitled *La verdadera historia del rey don Rodrigo, compuesta por el sabio alcayde Abulcacim Tarif Abentarique* [The True History of King Roderick, Composed by the Learned Governor Abulcacim Tarif Abentarique]. It was published in 1592 and achieved great success. The violent antagonism toward it expressed by Menéndez Pidal arises from his objection to the complete departure from tradition in de Luna's text, while it still claimed to be the *true* account of the facts. He objects as follows: "Todo falsario tiene un poco de perturbado, pero Luna tiene un mucho; sus invenciones aturden y marean al lector, como las de un loco, pues desquician y contradicen sin finalidad ni fundamento todo cuanto por tradición estamos habituados a tener por cosa sabida"[13] [All forgery contains a small element of mental imbalance, but in

Luna's case it is a large one; his inventions bewilder and annoy the reader, like those of a madman, since they disturb and contradict everything we are accustomed to accept as a fact through tradition, without purpose or foundation]. Don Ramón's judgment is harsh and damning, focusing principally on the fact that in spite of the alleged authenticity of de Luna's Arabic source, substantiated by his printing as marginal notes some of the Arabic vocabulary and phrases he was apparently translating into Castilian, there is no record of the existence of the historiographer Tarif Abentarique named in the title, and it transpires that this true history was in fact a colossal fabrication, which fooled very many educated people, including the two officers of the inquisition who wrote prefaces. The second inquisitor, Doctor F. Vicente Gómez, states: "...no he hallado en el cosa que se oponga en nuestra Fe, ni contradiga a las buenas costumbres, antes me parece que ha de ser muy provechoso, haziendo memoria de los graves pecados, por los quales los Christianos antigos fueron castigados de Dios tan gravemente"[14] [I have found nothing in it which opposes our Faith, nor which contradicts good customs, but rather it seems to me to be very beneficial, bringing to mind grave sins for which the ancient Christians were so severely punished by God]. Ironically, he picks up the theme of divine punishment favored by earlier Christian historiographers and views the work as upholding Catholic didacticism.

But should Miguel de Luna be sentenced to eternal opprobrium on account of his forgery, or does the case require reinvestigation? Contemporary ballads, and the early-fifteenth-century *Crónica sarracina* by Pedro de Corral, among other versions, give what might be called fictionalized, and by that token, 'acceptable,' accounts of the affair between Roderick and La Cava. If de Luna's crime was to create a 'false' history, how far did it deviate from 'true' history, and for what reasons? The earliest forms of the legend as manifested in chronicled histories provide some answers. Differences between Christian and Arabic historiography in the medieval period are crucial both to the inception of the legend, and to Miguel de Luna's rendition of it. As we have already seen, the author of the *Crónica de 754* drew on a tradition of chronicle writing going back to Isidore and Eusebius before him, viewing the fall of the Visigothic kingdom as a disaster of enormous magnitude, akin to the fall of Adam, the fall of Troy, the capture of Jerusalem, and the sack of Rome. This was an approach in line with Christian historiography starting in the fourth and fifth centuries, in which terrible catastrophes were seen as God's retribution for evil or immorality, since history was presided over by divine Providence. The idea of catastrophe and decadence so fundamental to subsequent Christian histories of the invasion is an attitude still assumed by some contemporary Spanish historians, such as Luis García Moreno.

The different stance adopted by the Arab historians discussed in chapter 2, who presented the conquest of Spain as evidence of the power and validity of Islam, is characterized by a frequent use of legend in Arabic historiography that questions the very nature of history itself. Collins notes that, in this case, "fiction...may be said to be the root of the problem"[15] and that to charge medieval Arab historians with sheer invention is an accusation they would not necessarily have found damning. His comment that in the end "what counts is the authorial purpose"[16] is explored fully by the historian of Islamic origins, Fred Donner, who states that "People cultivate and hand on stories, poems, proverbs, genealogies, etc. because they deem them in some way significant."[17] Conquest emerges as a key historiographical theme among medieval Arab writers because, he observes, "the story of conquest provided, above all, a narrative justification of the rule by Muslims and Arabs over non-Muslims and non-Arabs."[18] There were no qualms about the historical appropriation of a good dramatic story 'confirming the idea of Islamic conquest as part of God's chosen plan.'[19]

In this context, what is the status of Miguel de Luna's 'historia verdadera'? First, he uses the device of translation to disclaim narrative responsibility and enhance the authority of his text, and has acted, he says with some irony, according to the rules of a "verdadero y fiel intérprete y traductor"[20] [true and faithful interpreter]. He capitalizes on the power of the translator and of translation itself, to render the cultural Other, here the Arab/Muslim, as acceptable and comprehensible to Christian culture. Should he be charged on this account? Only if we also charge Cervantes with using the same device in *Don Quijote*, in relation to Cide Hamete Benengeli (in that case ironically, as Professor Harvey has pointed out, aiming precisely at Miguel de Luna).[21] More recently, Umberto Eco used the same sort of device in *The Name of the Rose*.

Second, de Luna incorporates literary invention as part of his 'true history.' The indignant Menéndez Pidal, comparing the work predominantly with Pedro de Corral's historical novel, berates the *morisco* for converting Roderick from the heroic and idealized protagonist of the *Crónica sarracina* into a bloodthirsty and fearsome figure, haunted by lust: "andava descuydado, exercitando algunos vicios, mayormente los carnales"[22] [he roamed about carelessly, indulging in vice, in particular the sins of the flesh]. Unlike the gruesome demise of Roderick in Corral's story, de Luna does not describe the king's death, leaving the matter unresolved. He also changes the centuries-old name of Julian's daughter, La Cava, to Florinda, a name she has retained in the modern afterlife of the legend up to and including the recent musical version.

De Luna also makes use of letters in his narrative, which, he claims, were originals in the possession of his source historian, and which disclose highly personal information. In particular, the letter Florinda sends to her father uses the innovative symbol of an emerald ring crushed by the Royal rapier to convey her dishonor. She commits suicide, unlike in Corral's version, by flinging herself from a tower in the manner of Melibea, the female protagonist in Fernando de Rojas's famous work *La Celestina* (1499). A further instance of de Luna's inventiveness is to change the personage Egilona from Roderick's wife, as she was in earlier versions, to his daughter. The wife de Luna bestows upon the king is an Arab princess called Zahra, who, when widowed, marries not the historical figure Abdalaziz, but a new character called Mahometo Gilhair, who converts to Christianity. The list goes on.

It seems that in some cases, de Luna's fabricated translation is closer to the earliest accounts than many reworkings closer in time to 1592. For example, Roderick is certainly not idealized initially, and there is plenty of evidence to suggest that the Visigothic monarchy, at least in the time of Witiza, was a hotbed of sexual transgression. The oldest accounts do not record Roderick's death either, and his penitential demise at the fangs of the serpent is a later embellishment. In terms of history writing, Miguel de Luna seems to have adhered to certain tenets of medieval Arabic historiography, a specific example being the use of letters, a commonplace technique in which a letter was used as a device to carry the narrative forward. Although the use of letters was certainly a feature of Renaissance historiography in the vernacular, and is exemplified by Father Mariana, according to Albrecht Noth the use of letters also constituted a formal element of Islamic tradition, and their function was not that of an actual historical document.[23]

But it was not only Arab historians who mingled fact with fiction. While historicization of legendary material was standard in medieval Islamic accounts, pseudo-history also abounded in sixteenth-century Spain. L.P. Harvey cites the best known example as *Las guerras de Granada* by Pérez de Hita, a historical account also alleged to be written by an Arabic author, Aben Hamín. In the light of all this, it is hard to understand the extreme reactions of Menéndez Pidal and others, unless it is the idea of forgery itself that disturbs, for Miguel de Luna undoubtedly was a forger, as his involvement in the famous scandal of the Lead Books of the Sacromonte demonstrates.

His creation of the *Verdadera historia del rey don Rodrigo* was an act of daring intensified through his dedication of the work to King Felipe II. De Luna's manipulation of the medieval legend within the cultural context of late-sixteenth-century Spain was in my view strongly political. The situation for the *moriscos* at the time was very uncomfortable. After the Granadan rebellion of 1568–70, Spain had forced all its Muslim subjects to convert to Christianity, and when de Luna was writing, the expulsion of all *moriscos* was only a decade or so ahead. Therefore, the success of his history might seem remarkable, considering its purported Arabic authorship and the translator's status as a convert. In a climate in which the nature of history writing was being called seriously into question, and in which, as David Lowenthal remarks,[24] the appetite for relics engendered all manner of Renaissance forgeries, Miguel de Luna's faking of medieval history and his forging of the Lead Books might paradoxically be viewed as revealing hidden political and religious truths. De Luna's fakery reinforces his authorial purpose, which was precisely to legitimize the religious and political claims of the Mozarabs in relation to the Christian establishment, consonant with Islamic historians' use of narrative for similar purposes.

The text is ultimately one that upholds the legitimacy and strength of the Muslim claim to Spanish territory at a time when the Catholic church was acting fast to close out any remaining traces of religious otherness. The work was extraordinarily successful in its own time, going through seven reprintings, until the authenticity of its status was at last questioned. However, this simulacrum, in line with Baudrillard's proposition, embodies a truth, for Miguel de Luna's vision and implicit idealism sought to redress the imbalance in the perception of Spanish history and Catholicism at the time, and venture toward mutual tolerance between Arabs and Christians, capitalizing on the contemporary preoccupation with *burlas y veras*, trickery, and truth, to expose other, deep-seated falsities.

Yet it must be emphasized that the work's status as history was not a hindrance in its enormous influence on future versions of the Roderick and La Cava story. Sir Walter Raleigh drew on it for the section on the invasion of Spain in his *Life and Death of Mahomet*, and it inspired not only Lope de Vega, but later, Sir Walter Scott, Robert Southey, Washington Irving, and Deschamps among others, in their own recreations of the legend. So, the jury is still out with regard to Miguel de Luna. If his work is considered in the light of Roger Collins' and Fred Donner's remarks, then his use of invention reinforces his authorial purpose, which was precisely to legitimize the religious and political claims of the Mozarabs in relation to the Christian establishment. His 'deception' is therefore justifiable in terms of early Arab historiography, which is exactly what he was attempting to recreate. But what his intriguing work reveals about the nature of history and fiction, about the enhancement of legend in general, and the importance of this legend in particular demands further investigation, which may well lead, I suspect, to an entirely favorable verdict.

Menéndez Pidal points out that even the most serious historians of this time could not ignore the legend, and even worse, in his view, "todo el esfuerzo de Morales o de Mariana fue enteramente ineficaz para contener los desmanes del espíritu falsario"[25] [all the efforts of Morales or Mariana were wholly ineffective in containing the excesses of the falsifying spirit]. The false chronicles dominated all other accounts, and of particular interest in this respect is the history of Portuguese monarchy written by Fray Bernardo de Brito in 1609, entitled *A Monarchia Lusitana*, in which the legend of Roderick undergoes some surprising changes. Pidal[26] remarks on Brito's inclusion of a long chapter in his account of the history of Portugal devoted to the loss of Spain, in which he draws on Miguel de Luna for some of his material. Basing his version upon a false Portuguese chronicle attributed to one Laymundo, he asserts that neither Roderick nor La Cava was to blame for the ill-fated love that caused Spain's loss. Instead, the guilty party was the countess who is La Cava's mother in the story, a woman in love with the king herself who pretends that it is La Cava who is making advances toward him. The countess plans to usurp her daughter's place in the king's bed for a night and satisfy her passion, but the king forces the girl prior to this, thinking he has her consent. When her mother discovers that her plans have misfired, she incites her daughter to inform Count Julian of the king's misdemeanor. This competition between mother and daughter for the king's love has ancient origins, notably in a thirteenth-century vernacular version of Jiménez de Rada's Latin history, in which Roderick rapes the count's daughter according to some accounts, and his wife according to others. The personage of Julian's wife, an insubstantial figure from the distant past, lives on beyond Brito's history in a number of future recreations of the legend, though always in a secondary role.

Another innovation on Brito's part is the choice of his own monastery of Alcobaza as the location for Roderick's first penance, which in Corral's striking episode occurs at an unspecified place. As in the case of the *Crónica de 1344*, the legend becomes a means of privileging one part of the peninsula over another, in this instance enhancing the status of both the monastery itself and of Portugal as the final resting place of the last Gothic king.

During the course of the sixteenth and seventeenth centuries, the legend of Roderick and La Cava is again cast in fluid moulds in which the personalities of the protagonists diverge as they are appropriated by true and false historians for political and religious reasons. These reworkings of history were of enormous importance in setting the foundations for the growth of the story in different artistic forms in later centuries. The legend in its many historiographical incarnations was about to give way to new interpretations in the poetry, drama, and opera of the Early Modern age.

CHAPTER 4

METAMORPHOSIS INTO SONG

In the years of transition between the medieval and early modern eras, the legend of the king and the whore found new life in performance. As principal source, Corral's *Crónica sarracina* was fundamental to the development of the story, which evolved over two hundred years from about 1450 to 1650 in a cycle of ballads on the theme of Roderick and La Cava. The great collections of ballad songbooks known as *romanceros* are one of the treasures of the Spanish people, for the ballad tradition in the Hispanic peninsula is outstanding, if not unique, in its richness, variety, and longevity. Many ballads originating in the Middle Ages continue to be sung today, including some of those in the Roderick cycle, a good deal of their astonishing vigor being attributable to their popular appeal as poetry for everyone, as songs that were sung by all social classes from peasantry to royalty.

The earliest ballads were anonymous, though by the sixteenth century more sophisticated versions began to be written by named, erudite poets. Although their origins are uncertain and much debated, ballads have strong links with popular legend and folklore, constituting largely narrative poetry, frequently with long passages of direct speech, and being characterized by intensely powerful episodes of human drama, often, but not always, set in the context of national or regional affairs.[1] They were sung accompanied by the six- or seven-string vihuela during the sixteenth century, though by the end of the 1500s, this was replaced by the early guitar.

Certain specific aspects of balladry in Spain from the fifteenth to the seventeenth centuries are important to our contextual understanding of the cycle of poems featuring Roderick and La Cava, and also assist in its evaluation. Those ballads that had historical themes were, according to Smith, "a vast repository of fact and legend about the more picturesque parts of Spanish medieval history."[2] An instance of this is the cycle of ballads on the early life of Spain's greatest hero, Rodrigo Díaz, El Cid. The events depicted in these ballads have little or no connection with the famous epic *Poema de mio Çid*, and beg the question of whether such ballads were created by minstrels, albeit using a different tradition of stories, in parallel with the epic version, or whether they arose and developed after the epic was created. This uncertainty over the genesis of a fundamentally fluid artistic form, which Ramón Menéndez Pidal famously described as "poesía que vive en variantes" [poetry that lives through variants] continues to dog ballad scholarship. Yet the Roderick cycle is exceptional in the Hispanic ballad tradition because it is based predominantly on the then recently published written source of Pedro de Corral's *Crónica sarracina* (1430), and has no connection whatsoever with epic. This dates the first Roderick ballads after 1440, making the cycle one of the latest parts of the general *romancero*. As Pidal notes,[3] such late derivation, and from a prose work rather than poetry, as well as the late tradition that developed from it, are of special interest within the genre. What is fascinating in this regard is that while the fate of Roderick was fundamental to the unfolding of Spain's history, it is historical fiction that is the source of inspiration for ballad writers, from which they take some of the most fantastic and extreme episodes, such as the king's forced entry into the locked palace in Toledo, and his ghastly penance with the snake, as material for their songs. It emphasizes the focus of these ballads upon human drama or melodrama and compelling individual events rather than upon any kind of historical authenticity.

The *Romancero del rey Rodrigo* began to be published in the first half of the sixteenth century, in the form of *pliegos sueltos* or loose song sheets. Actual books of ballads that appeared from 1550 until almost the middle of the seventeenth century include new ballads in the cycle, but from that time until the nineteenth century, nothing new was published. Pidal notes that the Romantic revival encourage Depping to publish a collection of Spanish ballads in Germany in 1817, followed by Abel Hugo, who produced his *Romancero e historia del rey de España don Rodrigo* in 1821. Much later in 1870, Sir Walter Scott's son-in-law, J.G. Lockhart, compiled *Ancient Spanish Ballads*, which consisted of his own translations of ballads including "The Lamentation of Don Roderick" and "The Penitence of Don Roderick."

The earliest poems in the Roderick cycle reflect the mid-fifteenth century vogue for the ballad, which was embraced enthusiastically by poets and musicians at the royal court. Smith reminds us that "it was customary for court poets and musicians to 'gloss' them, that is, to revise the words (without destroying their essential brevity, directness, and lack of sophistication), to polish the form and compose new tunes."[4] During the reign of the Catholic Monarchs Ferdinand and Isabella (Isabella became queen of Castile in 1474), the genre became even more highly esteemed, the most popular being the *fronterizo* or frontier ballads, a large cycle of poems on the subject of border relations between Christians and Muslims, some of which were used as valuable propaganda in the final stages of the war against Granada waged by the Catholic Monarchs, which ended with the fall of the city of Granada in 1492. Barbara Weissberger deems it significant that the Roderick cycle began circulating at the time of the revitalization of the neo-Gothic theory already observed in the work of Rodrigo Sánchez de Arévalo. She feels that the Roderick ballad cycle is "a collective lament over a loss of a virile warrior society and a battle cry for the restoration of that society through the re-membering of the body politic, an urgent operation that requires the therapeutic expulsion of the treacherous, feminine/effeminate, Oriental Others, the fifteenth-century Muslims (and Jews) who are Cava's symbolic descendants."[5] In spite of the popularity of the frontier ballads and the ambiguous attitude toward Muslims in the Cid cycle, the perceived importance of the ballads of the king and the whore in relation to the conclusion of the Christian reconquest is certainly evident in a telling anecdote from Lope de Vega's tragicomedy *El mejor mozo de España*, published in 1624. The young princess Isabella sits sewing, while her page Rodrigo sings her the ballad "Maldiziendo va Rodrigo," in which the king curses his terrible fate. When the ballad is sung, Isabella falls asleep, saddened by the memory of the defeated Visigothic king. In her dreams, she has visions of Spain oppressed by "africanos y hebreos" [Africans and Hebrews], which reveal to her the importance of her own historical mission to reconquer Spain for the Catholic Christians.[6]

Against this background, the *Romancero del rey Rodrigo* is nevertheless strikingly unusual in several respects. In addition to its dependence on a recent, written text, the poetic elaboration of the subject matter diverges in interesting ways from previous reworkings of the story. It stands apart from other cycles both in the manner in which ballad conventions and familiar themes are used to present the legend from new angles and in its relative detachment from the contemporaneous racial and political pressures that create dramatic tension in other ballad groups. I am referring to the ambivalent portrayal of both Arabs and of relations between Christians and Arabs in the large number of *morisco* and frontier ballads so widely known, especially in the second half of the two hundred years of balladry under discussion, when the matter was of intense interest due to the imminent expulsion of *moriscos* from the country. In the Roderick cycle, there is no ambivalence in this respect because there is virtually no portrayal of Arabs, beyond a few denigratory lines relating to the invasion of the peninsula itself.

But this is not the issue in the ballads on King Roderick and La Cava, for their significance lies elsewhere. In contrast with the latent cultural agendas lurking beneath the surface of earlier reformulations of the story, these ballads are concerned with the principal actors in their drama, with the individuals involved, whose character development is essential to the performativity of the story that finds important new expression in later theatre. It is through the personal drama of this ballad cycle that the audience/reader is awakened to another crucial dimension of the legend, the issue of gender, as manifested in the diverse and ambivalent portrayals of the male and female protagonists.

There were inevitable changes in style and focus in the two hundred years during which the ballad cycle evolved. Pidal dates the earliest examples of old traditional ballads between 1450 and 1510, three of which are of particular interest. "Los vientos eran contrarios" [The Winds Blew Wildly] is probably the oldest ballad on the Roderick theme, in which the king has a prophetic vision of his fate the night before the final, decisive battle leading to his defeat by the Muslim armies. The ballad powerfully evokes the disharmony of the natural world that prefigures the impending disaster. The wind is blowing dangerously, the moon is huge, and even fish in the river are affected by the bad weather: "Los vientos eran contrarios, / la luna estaba crecida, / los peces daban gemidos / por el mal tiempo que hacía" [The winds blew wildly, / the moon was huge, / the fish wailed with fear / at the bad weather] (lines 1–4). Yet Roderick sleeps calmly beside La Cava in his tent, the harmony of their closeness heightening the contrast in external conditions, as he is sublimely unaware of Count Julian's betrayal. As the king dreams, he sees a personification of Fortune foretelling disaster, this scenario deriving from Corral's novel. The motif of omens and predictions is a compelling one, used by later writers, including Julián del Castillo in his *Historia de los reyes godos*, by the Duque de Rivas in his poem *Florinda*, and by Espronceda in his nineteenth-century poem *El Pelayo*. It is telling that Julián's vengeance for his dishonor is the root cause of the invasion of Spain in this earliest poem in the cycle, echoing Alfonso X's *Primera Crónica General*. But in characteristic ballad style, there is no overt moralizing over Roderick's relationship with La Cava. On the contrary, the scene portrayed elicits sympathy for the lovers, oblivious in their abandon to the treason and betrayal that spells their doom. The ballad was so well known and of such significance that an imitation was composed in 1512 recounting the King of Navarre's loss of his own kingdom.

A second early ballad, "Las huestes de Don Rodrigo" [The Army of King Roderick] was one of the most acclaimed in the cycle. It describes the king's desolation as he looks down on his troops defeated on the battlefield in a series of extremely moving images that contrast his present defeat and humiliation with his previous status and power. On the verge of passing out, and so drenched in blood that he appears red like a burning coal, "iba tan tinto de sangre / que una brasa parecía" (lines 17–18), his face is swollen with suffering, his jeweled sword has become like the blade of a saw with use, and his helmet is dented and ill-fitting: "la espada lleva hecha sierra / de los golpes que tenía; / el almete abollado / en la cabeza se hundía" [his sword had become a saw / from the blows it had struck; / his helmet was dented / and hung low on his head] (lines 21–25). Such images of armor and weapons were current in fifteenth-century verse, yet their cumulative force and the poetic tension deriving from the oppositions characteristic of Spanish balladry reach a climax in the king's famous words: "Ayer era rey de España, / hoy no lo soy de una villa; / ayer villas y castillos, / hoy ninguno poseía" [Yesterday I was king of Spain, / today not of a single town; / yesterday I had towns and castles, / today I possess none] (lines 43–46). The vigor of these strong, simple contrasts was sufficient to linger in the minds of later writers. Lope de Vega reworks these lines in his play *El último godo* and Cervantes' Maese Pedro quotes part of the ballad after Don Quijote has destroyed his puppet kingdom.[7] Both Smith and Menéndez Pidal relate the anecdote of the ballad being sung to King Sebastião of Portugal aboard ship on an expedition to Morocco in 1578. When the minstrel reached the line "Ayer era rey de España," a courtier ordered him to sing something more cheerful, for he sensed the words prefigured disaster. His intuition was right, for both the king and his army perished in battle a few weeks later.

A third traditional ballad of interest is "Amores trata Rodrigo" [Roderick Talks of Love] that exists in different versions of varying dates, but may well have been of early origin, as it was published in loose sheets in one of the oldest collections, the Zaragoza *Silva* of 1551. It is based directly on episodes from the *Crónica sarracina* which recount the king's seduction of La Cava. This is of special interest in its portrayal of La Cava, who is by no means passive in the poem. Weissberger feels that the blame seems to lie with the king, but notes equivocal elements, based on her interpretation of 'discreta' as 'clever' and 'descuidada' to mean 'careless' when used in relation to La Cava. She deduces that La Cava is clearly associated with the stereotypical heartless lady of courtly love.[8] However, 'discreta' can mean 'discreet' and 'descuidada' might mean 'carefree,' both of which lack a negative cadence. When Roderick reveals his feelings for her, she starts to succumb to his charms: "Ella hincada de rodillas, él estála enamorando" [she is kneeling before him, he is making her fall in love] (line 11, version 4c). When the king finally gets his way, "más por fuerça que por grado" [rather by force than by willingness] (line 14), La Cava is cast in a negative light when she reveals the truth of her seduction to her father: "La malvada de la Cava a su padre lo ha contado" [Wicked La Cava tells her father about it] (line 16), though Julián is firmly portrayed as the traitorous betrayer of his country for the sake of vengeance: "don Julián, que es traidor, con los moros se ha concertado / que destruyessen a España por le aver assí injuriado" [Julian, the traitor, has connived with the Moors / to destroy Spain because of the insult upon him] (lines 17–18). In this poem, La Cava is not entirely uncompliant with Roderick's desires. Interestingly, it is she, not the king, who is criticized for her betrayal of her lover, rather than for succumbing to his wishes.

From approximately 1480 to 1550, juglaresque ballads came to the fore. These differed in style from the traditional poems, being characterized by an abundance of conjunctions, adverbs, pronouns, and other speech or statement formulae, together with a tendency to have consonance rather than assonance, features linked to the fact that this category of ballad tended to be read aloud rather than sung. Juglaresque ballads in the Roderick cycle derive mostly from Corral. "Después que el rey don Rodrigo" [After King Roderick. . .] is the first example to present the theme of the penitent king, taken from the fantasy scene in the *Crónica sarracina*. This ballad was very popular and exists in numerous modern versions. In juglaresque style, it consists largely of dialogue, first between the king and a shepherd whom he meets as he wanders in a desperate state following his defeat in battle, and second, with a hermit who receives the divine revelation of Roderick's penance, and then gives him courage as he dies. The account is a sanitized version of Corral's story, and entirely lacks the latent eroticism of the latter. There is no ambivalence, since Roderick is absolved of his sin by receiving his punishment in the jaws of the snake, becoming "el buen rey Rodrigo" [good King Roderick] (line 54) as he complies with his penance. "Después que el rey don Rodrigo" is the other poem discussed in detail by Weissberger, who considers it to be the central ballad of the cycle. Although she does not mention Pedro de Corral as the source of the penitence episode, she makes much of the serpent's function as an instrument of punishment rather than of temptation. For her it is Roderick's castration, not La Cava's rape, that represents the "traumatic originary wound of the sexualised body politic of Hispania."[9]

What is conspicuous once more is the fertility of this episode in inspiring various later versions, notably in early modern prose (Julián del Castillo's *Historia de los reyes godos* of 1582, and Miguel de Luna's *Verdadera historia del rey Rodrigo* of 1592) and in theatre, once more in Lope de Vega's *El último godo* and in his poem *Jerusalén Conquistada*, both of which draw on the episode with the shepherd, which Calderón also relates in his play *La Virgen del Sagrario*. Later, the episode was used in Romantic poetry, where it is reworked by Émile Deschamps, and as Pidal points out, with some novelty by Jules Leclerq in his *Rimes Héroïques* [Heroic Rhymes], where he converts the hermit who decrees the king's penance into Julian, who seeks revenge and laughs at Roderick's blind faith and inevitable death.[10]

The focus is on Count Julian's treachery in "En Ceupta está Julián" [Julian is in Ceuta], a ballad with two parts, a treacherous letter from Julián, followed by a lament, and the description of Roderick's disappearance, also lamented. It is the first ballad to depart from the *Crónica sarracina* as a source, drawing instead on Alfonso X's *Primera Crónica General*, in particular in its praise of Spain (a eulogy originally deriving from Saint Isidore, c. 560–636). The poem is uncompromisingly critical of the two traitors, Julián, "un perverso traidor" [an evil traitor] (line 23) and the conniving bishop Orpas, "obispo de mala andanza" [a wicked bishop] (line 42), who together bring about the loss of Spain and its king. The count is blacker than the Muslim foe, for he forces an old Moor to write his letter of betrayal for him, making him an accessory to the deed, and then proceeds to kill him. Pidal notes that this is an element taken from another ballad cycle, that of the Infantes de Lara, where a similar letter of treachery is composed,[11] and it serves well in this case to underline the magnitude of Julian's treachery, while the poem projects some sympathy for the king, "El triste rey don Rodrigo" [sad King Roderick] (line 30), and for a somewhat diminished La Cava, "que por sola una doncella / la cual Cava se llamaba / causen estos dos traidores / que España sea domeñada" [. . .for the sake of just one girl / called La Cava / these two traitors brought about / Spain's domination] (lines 47–50).

An element of fantasy enlivens some of the later ballads in the form of the legend of the enchanted palace in Toledo mentioned in earlier chapters, which Rodcrick enters to discover images of the impending Moorish invasion of his country. Part of a tradition of fantastic tales and events named 'futuhat' or 'conquests' that related to countries conquered by Islam, the depiction of this episode of the Roderick legend is one of the few Islamic elements in the ballad cycle. The ballad "Don Rodrigo, rey de España" [Roderick, King of Spain] is essentially based on an equivalent series of chapters from the *Crónica sarracina*, and is more concise and energetic than many jongleuresque examples. At the start of a huge tournament to be held in Toledo to celebrate his coronation, Roderick is urged to add another lock to the house of Hercules, but according to this particular version, instead of doing so, he breaks all the previous locks to allow him to enter in search of treasure. Although the view shared by some critics, including Menéndez Pidal, that the violation of the house and locks symbolizes the forthcoming violation of La Cava seems unlikely to have been a contemporary interpretation of the legend, what is intriguing in terms of its development is the ambivalent depiction of Roderick in this poem. Menéndez Pidal is much nearer the mark in this respect when he observes: "El episodio del palacio cerrado es, por su espíritu, hostil a Rodrigo, ya que le presenta como violador temerario de una prohibición sagrada; pero refuerza con trágico interés el carácter del rey, que aparece como osado escrutador del misterio, hombre de espíritu indomable, de corazón fuerte y de voluntad arrolladora"[12] [The episode of the locked palace is, by its nature, hostile to Roderick, since it presents him as the reckless violator of a sacred prohibition; but it lends force and tragic interest to the character of the king, who is depicted as a daring scrutininizer of the mystery, as a man of indomitable spirit, great courage and irresistible willpower].

"En Toledo está Rodrigo" [Roderick Is in Toledo], a ballad on the same theme, forms part of the *Romancero Nuevo* or new collection of ballads, which Pidal dates from 1530 to 1640. The first of these so-called *romances artificiosos* or 'artistic ballads' appeared in the period between 1530 and 1550. They were more sophisticated poems, usually short and depicting a single scene, generally existing as independent compositions and not as part of a bigger legend. "En Toledo está Rodrigo" dates from this period and is of independent inspiration, although the eagle that descends from the sky at the end and sets fire to Hercules' house links it both to Corral and to "Don Rodrigo rey de España." The narrative centers upon the king's experience inside the locked palace, and describes the embroidered cloth depicting men in Arab costume in some detail. This version of the legend of the enchanted palace or room appears in many later works, including Lope's *El último godo* and his *La donzella Teodor*, and is also reworked in a striking way by Sir Walter Scott in his *Vision of Don Roderick* of 1811, while Victor Hugo's character Esmeralda repeats the old ballad in *Notre-Dame de Paris* (1831).

Another 'romance artificioso' from this period, "Gran llanto hazía la Cava" [La Cava Was Weeping Her Heart Out], marks a new direction in the Roderick cycle, focusing specifically upon the woman and her plight. It is the first ballad to do so, describing her desolation at the loss of Spain, which she feels has been caused by her beauty. The poem contains a monologue in which La Cava predicts her ill-repute in the eyes of future generations: "Tú eres perdición de España, / fuego que todo lo apura, / de ti quedará memoria / para siempre en escritura, unos te llamarán Diablo, / otros te llamarán diablura, / otros te llamarán dimonio, / otros que eras su hechura" [You are the cause of Spain's loss, / fire which consumes everything, / you will be remembered / forever in writing, / some will call you devil, / others will call you trouble-maker, / others will call you demon, / others that you were his creature] (lines 8–13). These words are strangely premonitory of the debate that would surround the figure of La Cava in later centuries up to the present. In this poem, it is the written word of the future that troubles her most, and the repeated 'otros' suggests that it may be the male sex who will view her most unfavorably, and by whom she will be judged. The divergent secondary meanings of 'apura,' which can also mean 'purifies' and 'diablura,' which can mean 'wonder' or 'miracle,' while possibly not present in the mind of the balladeer, are evident to later readers and hint at the ambivalent status of La Cava as the legend grows and changes. With Corral's work as its source, this ballad presents La Cava as desperate but dignified, and as Pidal notes,[13] the later 'romances artificiosos' of the period 1570–1595 and the declamatory ballads of the period 1590–1637 develop this benevolent view of Count Julian's daughter. This contrasts strongly with the old traditional ballads where she is barely referred to, and in which the focus is on the king's plight and sins.

The potential for developing the powerful drama of the relationship between the king and his lover did not escape the attention of the poets of the new ballad collection of the late sixteenth and early seventeenth centuries. The Roderick cycle was of special interest to them as they sought to renovate traditional ballad scenes and render them more poetic. As Pidal observes, the legend offered them ". . .una serie de cuadros variadísimos de interés hondamente humano, en que jugaban las más violentas pasiones: amor, venganza, desesperación. . ."[14] [. . .a series of extremely varied scenes, of deeply human interest, in which the most violent passions were played out: love, vengeance, despair. . .].

One such ballad is "De una torre de palacio" [From a Palace Tower], probably composed after 1592, since it puns on the name Florinda for La Cava, indicating that it postdates the work of Miguel de Luna, who used this name for the first time. Another nod toward de Luna's version of the legend is the tower, from which La Cava and her friends enter the garden in this poem, but from which she subsequently throws herself to her death in his rendering of the story. In the ballad, the perfection of the garden as *locus amoenus* is impaired by Roderick's voyeurism, as unbeknown to the girls, he watches them from a window as they display their legs. He is suddenly overcome with desire, and summons Florinda to his chamber. The irony of his words: "si me quieres dar remedio / a pagártelo me obligo / con mi cetro y mi corona / que a tus aras sacrifico" [if you wish to cure me / I am obliged to pay you for it / with my sceptre and my crown / which I sacrifice for your sake] (lines 17–18) is poignant, for they anticipate the king's fate. The poem ends with an assessment of who is to blame for the catastrophe that ensued, claiming with wry humor: "Si dicen quién de los dos / la mayor culpa ha tenido, / digan los hombres: la Cava, / y las mujeres: Rodrigo" [If people ask which of the two / was more to blame, / the men may say: La Cava, / the women: Rodrigo] (lines 23–24). This difference in opinion between the sexes suggests that the subject constituted a popular contemporary debate, perhaps something discussed at court after ballad performances. Michel Moner notes in his article on the emblematic figure of the violated woman that in the case of La Cava, the main point of interest lies in the extent to which a raped woman is guilty party or victim.[15] This ballad is an interesting reflection of attitudes toward sexual misdemeanor within the context of a society that regularly watched plays in which the honor code was ruthlessly enforced as women and their lovers were punished by death for infidelities.

"Cartas escribe la Cava" [La Cava Is Writing Letters] presents another entirely favorable portrayal of the king's lover. It is a poem of independent inspiration, following no specific tradition, disclosing the letters that she writes to her father telling him of her dishonor. In these letters, she describes how the king comes to her bedchamber and rapes her: "sin saberlo yo, cuitada, entró donde yo dormía, / y con fuerça muy forçosa deshonra la honra mía" [without my knowledge, wretch that I am, he entered my bedchamber, / and with great force he dishonored me] (lines 19–20). The king is likened to Tarquin and La Cava to Lucretia, as she exhorts her father to take on the role of Brutus and avenge her: "Devéis de vengar, señor, esta tan gran villanía / y ser Bruto, el gran romano, pues Tarquino él se hazía; / si no, yo seré Lucrecia, la que dió fin a su vida" [You must avenge this great villainy, my lord / and be Brutus, the great Roman, since he has become Tarquin; / if not, I shall be Lucretia, who ended her own life] (lines 21–23).

An opposing portrayal of La Cava is given in "Triste estava don Rodrigo" [Roderick Was Sad], an erudite ballad written by Lorenzo de Sepúlveda. The subject is the defeat and lament of the king, as he ascribes blame to the count's daughter. She is described as "essa maldita Cava" [that cursed Cava] (line 5) and "su malvada hija" [his evil daughter] (line 8) and is cursed in line 23: "¡Maldita sea su hija, que de tan gran mal fué causa!" [Cursed be his daughter, the cause of such great evil!].

Interest in the Roderick legend, and in the figure of La Cava in particular, reached a peak in the latest category of ballads, known as declamatory ballads, which flourished from about 1590 until 1637. These poems were variants on the *romance artificioso*, in which a rhetorical or reasoned speech forms part of the development. The narrative element is minimized, implying that the poet assumed the audience to know the story already, and many poems in this category are sophisticated in their use of the puns, conceits, and images found frequently in seventeenth-century poetry and theatre. Pidal notes that La Cava acquires greater dignity in these ballads, usually at the expense of the king's character. He also makes the significant point that it would not be until the nineteenth century that the attitude adopted by Pedro de Corral, who divided his sympathy between the victims of the disaster and the lovers themselves, gained currency once more.[16]

One of the most fascinating of these ballads is "Revuelta en sudor y llanto" [Dishevelled with Sweat and Tears], existing in three variants, the first of which was published in the 1605 edition of the *Romancero General*. The ballad is powerful and masterly in its depiction of La Cava, who is presented as pleading with the king not to force her into a sexual relationship with him. What is of special interest is the way in which the differences between the three variants convey nuances of meaning that destabilize the basic premise, namely that La Cava is an unwilling victim of the king's lust. For example, in the ballad that begins "Revuelta en sudor y llanto" (all three have different first lines) there is a suggestion that La Cava herself desires the king: "-No quieras, señor, - le dize-, / Sol del español Imperio, / escurecer con tus rayos / la nube de mi desseo" ["Do not, my lord"—she said, / "Sun of the Spanish Empire, / darken with your rays / the cloud of my desire"] (lines 7–8). This suggestion is strikingly conveyed in the unusual image of darkening rays, an antithetical conceit that surprises the listener or reader by its seeming impossibility. In the other two versions, line 8 is changed to "que escurezcan vuestros rayos / la lumbre de mis desprecios" [darken with your rays / the fire of my scorn] and "que escurezcan vuestros rayos / la nuve de mi desprecio" [darken with your rays / the cloud of my scorn] respectively, both versions reestablishing the expected meaning.

The vulnerability and physical weakness of La Cava contrasts with her spirited verbal struggle against Roderick. As she fights her battle, she evokes the name of her father, who, she points out, is fighting on the king's behalf. The variant beginning "Embuelto en sudor y llanto" [Enveloped in Sweat and Tears] is the only one of the three poems to liken Roderick, the Visigothic king, to the Moors, in La Cava's words: "El pelea con los moros, / yo con cristianos peleo, / aunque ya más parecéis / vos moro y cristianos ellos" [He is fighting against the Moors, / I with Christians battle, / although you now seem / more like a Moor, and they, like Christians] (lines 17–18). The conventional preconception that Moors were sexually indulgent is hinted at in this poem, which suggests that Roderick's lust is more typical of Arabs than Christians. The view was one that had many echoes in later texts.

The final lines of these poems dwell upon Roderick's cruelty in loving La Cava and immediately losing interest in her. This idea is developed further in "Dando suspiros al aire" [Sighing to the Winds], first published in 1629, which explores the new theme of La Cava's love for Roderick, hinted at in the previous discussion. Here named Florinda, she addresses Roderick directly, chastising him for his deception of her in a speech that mingles outrage, hurt, despair, and pride. The characteristic dualisms of balladry juxtapose her peerless beauty and her unmatched misfortune and express the emotional contrast between being loved and scorned: "Enamorada, suspira, despreciada, desespera" [In love, she sighs, scorned, she despairs] (line 5). Another, slightly earlier ballad of 1620, "Afirmada cuello y brazos" [With Arms and Neck Set Firm], also focuses on La Cava, suggesting the harrowingly ambiguous nature of her situation: "viéndose en un mismo punto amiga, reina y esclava" [finding herself all at once to be lover, queen and slave] (line 3). This poem is effective in conveying the unfortunate and inevitable lot of a woman in such a situation: "que es muger, y tal el caso, que al fin a de ser culpada" [she is a woman, and in such an event, she must in the end be blamed] (line 8).

A further consequence of the sympathetic later portrayal of La Cava was a tendency to mitigate the depiction of her father's treacherous betrayal of his country by showing the depth of his distress and dishonor at the hands of his king. In "¡O canas ignominiosas" [Oh, Ignominious Grey Hairs!] of 1604, Count Julian laments at length over what he sees as the tyranny of Roderick. His outrage is not just on the personal level of having his trust betrayed, but on a political one too, for he views the king's seduction of his daughter as an act of tyrannical power of a king over the nobility: "villana sin excepción, que a la nobleza aniquila!" [ignoble (fate) in the extreme, which annihilates the nobility] (line 10) and "No se espanten los que oyeren alguna cosa indevida, / que rey tirano y aleve vassalos traidores cría" [Those who listen should not be alarmed to hear things unheard of, / for a tyrannical, perfidious king rears treacherous vassals] (lines 15–16). Nevertheless, Julian is still cast as a traitor, although the reason for his treachery is held back until the very final lines of the poem.

Finally, a word may be said about the portrayal of Roderick in the later ballad cycles. One particularly brilliant ballad, "Cuando las pintadas aves" [When the Speckled Birds], illustrates the degree of sympathy with which he too was viewed at this stage in the evolution of the ballad form. It picks up the thread of the old traditional ballads, setting the scene once more in the aftermath of the terrible defeat on the banks of the Guadalete, from which the king flees on his horse Orelia. The poem begins by describing the silence, as no birds sing, and the earth is waiting and listening, as if shocked into quietness by the terrible events of the day: "Cuando las pintadas aves mudas están, y la tierra / atenta escucha los ríos que al mar su tributo llevan, / el escaso resplandor de cualque luziente estrella / que en medroso silencio tristemente centellea" [When the speckled birds are dumb and the earth / listens attentively to the rivers which carry their tribute to the seas, / the sparse glimmer of some shining star / which in the fearsome silence sadly twinkles] (lines 1–4). Pidal feels this beginning exceeds in beauty the famous description at the start of Virgil's *Aeneid* before Dido commits suicide,[17] and it certainly sets the tone of immense sadness before the king begins his lament, in which he describes how he was overwhelmed by La Cava's beauty and justly asks why her father could not have just killed him, rather than bringing this terrible fate upon his people and in a sense upon the Arabs, who will be henceforth viewed negatively. His touching words: "No ofendí yo africano, ¿por qué africano te venga?" [I never offended an African, why does the African avenge you?] (line 51) are eloquent in their concise summation of the act that sealed Spain's future.

The preponderance of dialogue and direct speech, narrative and scenic elements combined with the strong emotions and conflicts that are vital for performance made the ballad the ideal vehicle to convey the legend to a wide audience, effectively encompassing all social levels. The evolution of the main characters in the Roderick cycle over the two hundred years during which the *romancero* changed brought political and gender issues to the fore that had not been addressed in the same way in earlier forms of the story, allowing the individuals involved to act on a wider stage than that of their own personal circumstances.

As king of the Visigoths, Roderick's role and actions as an individual relate to the political theme of kingship, closely linked to a more pervasive theme in Spanish ballads, that of justice. Questions about the nature of monarchy are implicit in the legend itself. Should Roderick as king be more resistant than other people to the passion and temptations to which he is more subject because of his power? What does Count Julian's action say about the nature of nobility in Spain? Although Pedro Correa notes a generally favorable picture of the nobility, especially in frontier ballads, which stress their commitment to an ideal and their courage in defense of the Christian/Moorish frontier,[18] in later ballads Julian clearly believes he must not only avenge his personal dishonor but also the dishonor of the nobility, in thrall to the monarchy. This is telling, for real-life struggles between monarchy and aristocracy were threatening to disrupt the status quo virtually throughout the early modern age.

The theme of justice entails proper retribution for wrongs committed. This tends to be a retribution in general human terms, rather than one imposed by the authority of the Catholic church. Smith remarks on how surprisingly little the ballads owe to church teaching, even though they flourished at the height of the inquisition, when outward shows of Puritanism were so dominant in Spain.[19] In the Roderick cycle, the Christian dimension is nevertheless present, but low-key.[20] The horrifying penance the king undergoes is of unquestionably Christian Catholic derivation, but, as Smith astutely observes, the word 'pecado' is rarely used in ballads, shifting the emphasis onto the more secular idea of a crime committed rather than of a sin. There tends to be a predominantly straightforward attitude to sexual morality, although the specifically Castilian ballads are rather strait-laced and deal with significantly few situations of this kind. In this respect, the poems of the Roderick cycle are again exceptional.

However, Christian and political issues remain in the minor key and emotion and drama in the major, for the king is portrayed as destined to be wracked by powerful feeling, whether overwhelming sexual passion or desolation and despair, and the dominant note of his absence of emotional control is entirely consonant with the overarching theme of the tragic nature of life that is so fundamental to balladry in Spain. The destructiveness of sexual passion, a theme echoed in modern peninsula literature, particularly in the ballads and plays of the twentieth-century dramatist and poet Federico García Lorca, is explored and nuanced in the Roderick ballads in a way that presents the protagonists as neither wholly good nor wholly bad and more as victims rather than villains.

The sympathetic portrayal of the character of La Cava in later ballads is significant in the life of the legend, for it led to much more complex later reformulations of her role and relationship with the king in seventeenth- and eighteenth-century drama in particular. The influence of the courtly ethos, which placed women on a pedestal to be worshipped from afar by their chivalrous admirers, and the recent dominant role played by Queen Isabella may have reinforced this shift in emphasis to the female protagonist, though the debate over gender issues and the respective roles of men and women in society was gaining momentum, and was finding expression in other genres, especially in the plays of Golden Age dramatists such as Lope de Vega, Calderón, and Tirso de Molina, and in the work of the seventeenth-century woman novelist María de Zayas.

In terms of the overall evolution of the legend, the ballads stand strangely apart from other genres that adopted the subject, for the Roderick cycle existed in parallel with interpretations in history, theatre, and other early modern poetry, such as Fray Luis de León's *Profecía del Tajo*, yet it embraced new aspects of the story, less directly related to the racial, religious, and political dimensions of the narrative, aspects that convert the figures of early legend into flesh and blood characters with real feelings. The previous sympathy for Roderick and consequent antipathy toward Julian, with La Cava cast in a minor, largely negative, role are transmuted into complex, nuanced portrayals of the male and female protagonists as ambivalent individuals, wracked by violent emotions as they struggle with their tragic destinies. While absence of criticism of the king is a constant almost throughout the sequence, and Julian is always the evil traitor, even in the latest phase in which his conflicting feelings of betrayal and loyalty are exposed, La Cava evolves from an evil temptress into the unfortunate victim, and in later ballads, into a woman susceptible to Roderick's charms, who even finds she loves him. Her proleptic vision of the judgment of future generations is uncannily accurate. The Hispanic ballads on the legend of King Roderick and La Cava written between 1450 and 1650 were of sufficient interest and power to inspire Romantic writers and poets in England and France, such as the aforementioned Abel and Victor Hugo, Jules Leclerq, Émile Deschamps, and James Lockhart. They were also crucial in extracting the nascent dramatic potential of the legend, which found more intricate and lengthy expression in the theatre and opera of the future in Spain, England, and Latin America.

CHAPTER 5

NEW LIFE IN DRAMA AND MUSIC: FROM POETRY TO THEATRE

Even by the sixteenth and seventeenth centuries, the medieval legend of King Roderick had lost none of its vigor. While the specter of the last Visigothic king of Spain's passion for the beautiful La Cava continued to haunt early modern historians just as much as it had obsessed medieval chroniclers, the fictional possibilities of the story began to expand and develop in exciting new ways. Its vibrant poetic expression in the ballad form was not the only manifestation of the legend in verse. Renaissance humanists such as the fifteenth-century Juan de Lucena had already reiterated the similarity between the perceived catastrophe caused by La Cava and the fall of Troy caused by the rape of Helen identified in the earliest chronicle, the *Crónica de 754*. The classical analogy chimed with the Renaissance fascination with Greek and Roman culture and manifested itself in two imitations of the Horatian ode, one by a Sevillian priest, Francisco de Medrano (1570–1607), in the second half of the sixteenth century and the second by the celebrated religious poet Fray Luis de León. Medrano's poetry was mostly made up of translations or paraphrases of classical originals, and his offering, entitled *Profecía del Tajo en la pérdida de España* [Prophecy of the River Tagus on the Loss of Spain], is of this kind. In his poem the river addresses King Roderick as he lies with La Cava on its banks, and Menéndez Pidal justly comments: "Toda originalidad falta y el conjunto es duro y frío" [Any originality is lacking, and as a whole it is hard and cold]. The poem consists largely of rhetorical exclamations and questions, as well as lines that have been infelicitously translated directly from Horace and applied to the Spanish context. It is not successful either as a translation or as a poem in its own right.

In contrast, Fray Luis de León's *Profecía del Tajo*, written earlier, in 1551 or 1552, is a reworking of Horace's *Ode I, xv* on the prediction of the loss of

Troy, stirring and powerful in its vision of the imminent demise of Roderick and of Spain. As Menéndez y Pelayo remarked, this was the first time a Spanish poet had used the classical style of the sixteenth-century humanist to represent an event in national history.[1] Although the ode, like the ballad, was originally a sung form, there is little else to link the two types of verse, the former being elaborate, usually lengthy, and generally addressed to a specific person or thing. The tone is altogether different, less intimate and more formal. Like Medrano, Fray Luis uses the familiar literary device of personification of a river,[2] the Tagus, which flows through Toledo, to address Roderick as he takes his pleasure with La Cava by the river in the town where his royal court is situated. The scene of the lovers in harmony, unaware of the disharmony of the natural world and the imminent disaster, is identical to the scene described in the ballad "Los vientos eran contrarios," yet unlike this and other ballads, the subject is not the personal relationship between king and lover, nor Roderick's ill-advised passion, but the impending war with the Moors the river foresees, and of which the king is blissfully unaware. The tone is both martial and lamentatory, and tension is built upon a series of opposites, principally relating to the enjoyment of the lovers and the disaster it will bring, expressed in such phrases as "En mal punto te goces" [You take pleasure at an evil hour] (line 6), "¿Y aún te tiene / el mal dulce regazo?" [Does that sweet, evil lap still hold you?] (line 57), and "¡Ay, esa tu alegría / qué llantos acarrea!" [Oh, your joy, such weeping shall entail!] (line 12).

This conflict is further reinforced by the rhyme scheme, *ababb*, which links the concepts of beauty, weeping and loss in lines 12, 14, and 15 in 'hermosa' (beautiful girl), 'llorosa' [tearful], and 'costosa' [costly]. There are some inspired lines in Fray Luis's poem, notably in the description of the gathering army of Moors, whose innumerable squadrons leave no ground visible beneath them; the dust kicked up by their advancing horses obscures all sight: "el polvo roba el día y le escurece" [the dust robs the daytime and darkens it] (line 45).

This subject taken from national history is less familiar to readers of Fray Luis than his more frequent religious and metaphysical subjects. The *Profecía del Tajo* is infused with classical elements, not only in its imitation of a specific Horation ode that alludes to the Trojan war, but also in its references to figures of classical mythology in Mars, Neptune, Hercules and Aeolius, the wind God. The parallel between Spain and Troy, La Cava, and Helen, reinforces the idea of a continuity between the Roman state, the Visigothic king and Spain itself through the medium of a poetic culture that equates prestigious Latin verse with vernacular Spanish and thereby enhances its status. The poem is notable as a source of inspiration for later writers, including Juan Goytisolo, who uses it as a historical reference point in his novel *Reivindicación del Conde Don Julián*.

However, the legend did not flourish in learned poetic forms at this time, perhaps because those forms lacked the intensity of human interest in the individuals involved, which is so fundamental to the ballads of the Roderick cycle. It was a much more natural development for the characters so hauntingly portrayed in ballad form to evolve in the theatrical representations of the sixteenth and seventeenth centuries, and it was here that the story truly began to mature. About 1530, the Aragonese dramatist Bartolomé Palau wrote a play in six acts called the *Historia de Santa Orosia* [History of Saint Orosia], in which King Roderick is surprisingly betrothed to the saint herself, while all the time lusting after La Cava. The religious orientation of the play was characteristic of early theatre, out of which Palau created Spain's first historical drama, inspired by the Roderick legend, and on this score alone it merits discussion. The play adds a quite different dimension to the story of Roderick and La Cava by framing it within a hagiographical legend. The style typifies medieval liturgical drama, ending with an invitation to the audience to sing the final psalm, and the work was probably intended to be acted out in the cathedral, presumably on the feast day of Saint Orosia, June 25, as an act of devotion.

Orosia was a saint claimed by the Aragonese as their own. Her origins have been the subject of considerable debate, but it seems unlikely that she came from Bohemia, as Palau presents it. She may have been of noble birth, possibly from the Basque region, or France, or from Aragon itself, and legend has it that she was martyred for refusing to renounce the Christian faith and marry a Muslim caliph at the time of the Moorish invasion, an omission for which she was punished by a grisly death. Her remains were taken to Jaca in Aragon, where they lie in the cathedral. So what was Palau's purpose in linking a local saint to a Visigothic king? The answer may lie in the dramatist's strong feelings for Spain that are overlaid by notable pro-Aragonese elements. His praise of the fighting prowess of the men from Jaca in their battle against the invaders in the fifth act is individualized in the extraordinary courage of Orosia, who is aligned with Aragon in her personal defense of Christianity against the Muslim faith. In the view of the editor of the text, Olem Mazur, the tragedy of Roderick and the martyrdom of Orosia form a duality that underlines the catastrophe of the invasion of Christian territory by the Moors.[3]

In this version of the story, in the opening scene Roderick is advised by his wise and loyal counselor, Firmiano, to act according to Roman tradition and seek a wife, on the basis that a man must be able to govern his wife before he can govern a country. This links the Visigothic king firmly to his Roman heritage and also serves to contrast the treacherous behavior of Count Julian, Roderick's servant at court, with the trustworthy Firmiano. The latter's description of the king as noble and virtuous, "la gran nobleza /

de tu person y estado / según estás reputado / que no cabe en ti vileza" [the great nobility of your person and estate, according to repute, allows no room for baseness] (line 150), renders his passion for La Cava and the confusion expressed in his later soliloquy even more striking and surprising to the audience, eliciting greater sympathy, for the king is not portrayed as a villainous rapist, but as a man at the mercy of a blind and malevolent fate.

As advised, the king sends his ambassador to Orosia, the queen of Bohemia, asking for her hand in marriage. Following a scene that parallels the opening of the play in which Orosia seeks advice on ruling well from her aptly named confidante Prudencia, Roderick delivers a long monologue in which he agonizes over his dilemma, for he is now smitten with love for La Cava, and as yet has received no reply from Orosia. The king names eleven men from biblical and classical legend who were similarly overcome by transgressive sexual passion, reinforcing the mythical dimension of Roderick's story and once again linking him to the classical and biblical past. It is intriguing that the last king he mentions is Alfonso X, who is alleged to have raped his sister-in-law five hundred and forty-six years after the invasion of Spain! We have to assume that either Roderick is prophetic or that Palau let chronological verisimilitude slip.

By Act 4, La Cava has been dishonored, and her lament contrasts in its despair and anger with the arrival of Orosia and her train in war-ravaged Spain to fulfill her agreement to marry the king. La Cava's long opening monologue and her conversation with her father were probably taken from the *Crónica sarracina*, and lead to the scenes of devastation and murder perpetrated by the excessively bloodthirsty Moors Orosia and her friends encounter. A shepherd reveals the truth of Roderick's betrayal of the princess and of his country, and Orosia is cut into pieces after refusing to convert to Islam and marry a Moorish king. Her remains are recovered by the shepherd and taken back to rest in Jaca.

The plot of the *Historia de Santa Orosia* is good in principle, with a number of dramatic tensions and conflicts established, yet its implementation is ponderous and the speeches lack realism and naturalness. The exaggeration of the ghoulishness of the Moors and the pointed eulogy of Jaca are somewhat simplistic, although lightened by the shepherd's attempts at linguistic humor. Orosia herself is a poorly drawn character, overly submissive and timid in the first scenes, then subsequently showing a scorn for the Muslim faith and a Senecan stoicism for which the audience has not been prepared. Mazur notes the bellicosity of her character in contrast with the portrayal of the saint in Tirso de Molina's later play *La joya de las montañas*. Roderick's character does have nuancing, and La Cava is a much livelier figure than the eponymous heroine. Their encounter and its aftermath are certainly the most engaging parts of the drama, and although Orosia is meant to be the main protagonist, I think Mazur is right in suggesting that the major preoccupation is with Roderick's personal dilemma.

Bartolomé Palau makes a unique contribution to the legend of Roderick and La Cava in bestowing a foreign, though Christian, fiancé upon the king, while adhering otherwise to the version in Jiménez de Rada's history. His intentions in doing so were straightforward in so far as they were anchored in a religious and political conventionality that upholds the Catholic faith and the Visigothic heritage, as well as acting as propaganda for the promotion of the author's native region in political and religious terms. The importance of this play lies in particular in the innovation of the genre of historical drama. Pidal notes that the legend of the king and his lover inspired two new literary spectacles: "el nacimiento del drama histórico nacional; también un siglo antes nos dio la primera novela histórica"[4] [the birth of national historical drama and, one century earlier, it gave us the first historical novel]. Fray Luis's first poem on the theme in the classical style may be added to these. The remarkable fertility of the legend not only in inspiring innovation in terms of its plot and characterization, but also in engendering new literary forms of representation is exceptional.

Reading against the Grain: The Cultural Ambivalence, Ambiguity, and Subversion of *El postrer godo de España* by Lope de Vega

The inherent theatrical qualities of the story harnessed by Palau were enriched significantly in the hands of a genius, the early modern playwright whom Cervantes named a "monstruo de la naturaleza" [a monster of nature], Lope de Vega Carpio (1562–1635). Lope took up the gauntlet seventy years later in his little known play *El postrer godo de España* [The Last Goth of Spain], alternatively known as *El último godo* [The Last Goth], the first secular drama on the theme. Menéndez Pidal dated the play between 1604 and 1614, but more recent critics suggest a date between 1599 and 1603. It is printed twice in Lope's works, once in the *Octava Parte* of 1617, and again in *Parte 25*, produced in Zaragoza in 1647. Both versions are full of errors, due, according to Menéndez y Pelayo, to the presence of various originals, causing the playwright himself to discredit the bad emendations of his publishers. Lope also addressed the same theme in a short episode in his tragic epic *Jerusalén conquistada*, which was finished by 1605, and finally printed in 1609, although Lope had worked on it for some time, dating back to 1604 and earlier. The epic poem casts some interesting light on the interpretation of the story, which is much more fully developed in *El postrer godo de España* and was written in imitation of the Italian poet Tasso's celebrated *Gerusalemme liberata* (1580), which had the Third Crusade involving Richard the Lionheart and Saladin as its main subject. Lope's intention was to create a learned epic for Spain on a par with Camoens's *Os Lusiadas*, which he admired reverentially. He wanted to create a national poem that ennobled his native country, and considered the twenty-book work as his magnum opus in terms of poetry.

In Book VI, Lope dedicates forty-three *octavos* to King Roderick's fate. The context is Saladin's celebration of his victory over the imperial armies, during which his brother Sirasudolo reproaches him and reminds him of the fearful power of Spain and of the courage and daring of the fast-approaching King Alfonso VIII, whom Saladin has scorned. To illustrate this point, a captive relates the history of Spain from the time of the Arab invasion, including its most heroic events. King Roderick's defeat forms part of this, wherein the king is treated with great sympathy, although the poet dwells more on the character of Florinda, probing her behavior and motivation. Lope captures her beauty, especially that of her eyes, which light up the frozen mountains of Spain, and which ironically initiate the irrevocable chain of events leading to invasion. Extending the imagery of vision, Lope suggests that it would have been better if Roderick had lost his sight, instead of his father, whose eyes were gouged out by his evil predecessor, Witiza: "Esta miró Rodrigo desdichado. / ¡Ay!, si como su padre fuera ciego, / sacó sus ojos Ubitisa airado, / fuera mejor los de Rodrigo luego" [Ill-fated Roderick saw her. / Oh, if only he were blind like his father, / his eyes put out by Witiza's wrath, / it would have been better if it had been Roderick's, later] (lines 9–12 of Book 6). Yet Florinda's character does not match her beauty in this poem, for it is Roderick's cooling feelings toward her after the seduction that lead her to take vengeance by informing her father of what took place: "Dícese que no ver en el rey gusto, / sino de tanto amor tanta mudanza, / fué la ocasión; que la mujer gozada / más siente aborrecida que forzada" [They say that seeing no affection in the king, / but rather such great change after such great love / was the cause; that a woman seduced / feels abhorred more than violated] (lines 69–72).

Although a number of critics praised this episode within the epic poem, the nineteenth-century commentator Hugo Blair makes the point that it does not sit well within the crusading context, for the war between the Visigoths and the Moors had nothing to do with the crusades, and observes that instead of contributing to Sirasudolo's purpose of aggrandizing Spain, it would surely have had the opposite effect in Saladin's mind, making him proud of the Moorish victory.[5] However, it fits the poet's overall purpose in the sense that it largely absolves Roderick of blame for the invasion, and aligns him with later Spanish kings, including the advancing Alfonso VIII.

This rendering of the story is present in germinal form in *El postrer godo de España*, written earlier than the epic poem, but Lope has an entirely different agenda in his depiction of the relationship between the king and Florinda within the drama. The plot of this play is constructed as a kind of triptych, each act of which focuses on a different protagonist. In Act 1, King Roderick accedes to the Visigothic throne, having taken revenge on the evil Witiza by blinding him for his usurpation of Roderick's rightful crown. In spite of bad auguries, followed by Roderick's determined opening of the locked house in Toledo to reveal the destined Arabic invasion, the new king falls in love with Zara, a beautiful African princess, and marries her amid great celebration in Toledo. Very shortly, Roderick's general in Ceuta, Count Julian, brings his lovely daughter Florinda to court and places her under the king's protection. Suddenly and bewilderingly overwhelmed by Florinda's charms, he tries to seduce her, and she teases him with her resistance until he forces her to submit to him sexually.

In Act 2, Roderick's ardor has cooled, and Florinda writes a secret letter to her father telling him of her dishonor. Julian, whose rage and treachery are the focus of this act, discloses the situation to Muza, the African ruler, and offers to betray Spain to the Arabs to wreak vengeance upon Roderick. The cataclysm unravels inexorably from this point onward, as Florinda commits suicide by throwing herself from a tower, Julian's wife dies of cancer, and Roderick's army is defeated by Tariq's men, after which the king laments his fate, disguised as a peasant. The final act presents Pelayo as the protagonist in his efforts to rally the remaining Spaniards to defeat Julian and the Arabs, who have been aided and abetted by the wicked bishop Orpaz. Queen Zara and her Moorish admirer Abembúcar are executed for converting to Christianity, while Pelayo rescues his sister from the Moorish invaders and triumphantly gains the crown of his people.

Designated as a tragicomedy, this is a play bereft of humor, in which the constant proximity of tragedy and its resolution in Pelayo's victory typifies its category. In *Theatre in Spain 1490–1700*, Professor McKendrick notes that a tragicomedy often has a sting in its tail that compromises the satisfactory nature of its ending, and that irony and language subvert the ideas the action seems to endorse.[6] This divergence between language and action in *El postrer godo* is crucial to this discussion, for it underlines the gap between purported meaning and latent ambivalences, between what is overtly asserted and what is unconsciously disclosed.

When Lope wrote the play at the start of the seventeenth century, Spain was in a state of cultural conflict. Felipe III was poised to order the expulsion of all *moriscos*, and the themes of kingship and the Muslim invasion of Spain must have struck a profound chord with turn-of-the-century theatregoers. Contemporary echoes enhance the theatrical illusion at different levels. King Roderick's nuptial celebrations in Toledo bring to mind Felipe III's wedding in Valencia in 1599, and one of the key motifs of the legend, the intervention of a treacherous adviser or vassal, might have seemed relevant to the issue of *privanza*, or court favorites, which was high on the agenda of the time, as was the nature of kingship. Yet the key dimension of this play, the cultural interaction between Christians and Moors, implicitly addresses the growing crisis over the expulsion of *moriscos*. After 1582, when Felipe II's Council of State proposals for the expulsion were accepted, a major debate arose that indicated that the expulsion was neither inevitable nor even necessarily supported by public opinion.[7] Kamen notes that some grandees accepted that excessive religious zeal would destroy *convivencia*, and Íñigo López de Mendoza attacked Cisneros' policy toward the *moriscos*, and the harshness of the inquisition, as well as the attempt to make them change their dress. In these respects, *El postrer godo* is a work tethered to its context, whose meaning is shaped not just by our present-day interpretations, but also by the culture from which it arose.

How and why Lope chose to rewrite this story is vital in uncovering the powerful debate that underlies his development of the legend. The first important aspect is the strong influence upon the playwright of Miguel de Luna's *Historia verdadera del rey Don Rodrigo, compuesta por Abulcácim Tárif Abentarique*. The notorious *morisco*'s creative version of the Muslim invasion of Spain was extremely popular, and Lope's use of it as his prime source is strongly derided by Menéndez Pidal, who feels it renders the play inferior. In his view, *El postrer godo* was a simple attempt to remind the public of the loss and immediate restoration of Spain.[8] Lope takes all the key features of the Roderick and La Cava legend from Miguel de Luna's version, supposedly written by an Arab, and including the king's marriage to an Arab princess, the name of Florinda for Julian's daughter, and the letter she sends to her father, which Lope translates into verse. What is interesting is not only the fact that as Menéndez y Pelayo reminds us,[9] the legend of the love affair is Muslim, not Christian in origin, but also the closeness of Lope's adherence to a source written by a *morisco* largely for political and racial propaganda, aspects of the *Verdadera historia* I have already discussed in chapter 4. The synthesis of this complex material into the three thousand or so lines of the play is achieved with brilliance and innovation. Those aspects that Menéndez Pidal criticizes, such as fleeting impressions, concision, fluidity of scene changes, seem to me to be the strengths of a work that Pidal himself grudgingly avows to be "un verdadero cinedrama, superior a los modernos, claro es, por no desarrollarse en la pantalla. . ."[10] [a real cinedrama, better than the modern ones, of course, because it does not unfold upon the screen]. The prime material of the cinedrama is words, and the focus on fabrication from language in this, as in Lope's other plays, with all its subtle linguistic nuances, renders it doubly susceptible to reinterpretation, as a construct with endless potential for explication. Adherents of the classical school, such as Francisco Cascales, a Murcian theorist, were horrified by Lope's daring in abandoning classical precepts, in particular the unity of action. There is much to be said about the sophisticated economy of scene setting, the use of mise en abîme, and the painterly dimensions of this play that is outside the scope of this discussion. Such techniques serve to emphasize the portrayal of the protagonists, whose characterization subtly articulates responses to the question of why Lope chose to rework this theme as a drama.

The obvious interpretation is that he intended to write a play about royal immorality and absolutism. In fact, Melveena McKendrick argues eloquently for this theme in her recent book *Playing the King*. She finds a clue in the title—Roderick, as last Gothic king, is the end of a line of monarchs represented as unruly and decadent, unfit to govern.[11] This ties in, in her view, with the heightened interest in politics and kingship provoked by the accession of Felipe III and the rise of the Duke of Lerma, the man in effective control of Spain, who used the royal prerogative to further his own interests in a blatant and disgraceful way, in an alliance forcefully criticized by the historian Mariana, who held that rule by favorite was "el mal más terrible que se puede imaginar" [the most terrible evil imaginable], and associated it with tyranny. As McKendrick notes, many of Lope's kingship plays belong to the first decade or so of Felipe III's reign, and one of their main preoccupations is which qualities make a successful ruler. In addition, the theme of sexual unruliness also appears in two other plays by Lope, *La fe rompida* [Broken Faith], where the king seduces and abandons the heroine, and *El príncipe despeñado* [The Fallen Prince], where the king tries to rape the wife of his foremost supporter. Sexual politics therefore, reflect national politics: "The conflicts and strains inherent in kingship are mapped onto the timeless narrative of sexuality and passion rather than onto the existing political system itself, and misplaced desire in kings functions as a technique of demonization. While the body of the king relates to his private self, with all the needs and desires of the man, that body is also the incarnation of the state."[12]

Very few other scholars have given attention to *El postrer godo*, though Susan Niehoff has an article on the play written in 1982, in which she sees the drama as figuring a "cosmological epic having to do with the Fall of Man and the Christian themes of temptation, transgression, salvation and regeneration." She reads symbols of the Nativity and Eucharist into Roderick's encounter with the villager and his wife at the end of the second act, in an interpretation that is conformist and restricted to the confines of Christian morality, within which the king is a sinner in need of redemption. Even less persuasive is Ramón Araluce Cuenca's declaration that it is really Pelayo, not Roderick, who is the last Goth referred to in the title, an assertion that is not borne out by the text of the play, and is even more firmly refuted in Lope's *Jerusalén conquistada*, which clearly describes Roderick as "el último godo de España."

Upon closer reading, the dangers of royal immorality and absolutism that appear to be underlined in the play are subsumed by more compelling cultural tensions and anxieties pertinent to the relationship between Christians and Muslims, which are embedded in persistent ambiguities and subversions of plot and characterization. Again, Melveena McKendrick makes helpful comments, not in relation to cultural ambivalences, but in respect of countercurrents and subversion in Lope's kingship plays. She considers the plays to suggest "not an ideologically monolithic and complacent drama, but one which is multivalent and which potentiates ambiguities and subversive readings."[13] These readings evidently went unnoticed by inquisition censors, who were more concerned with representation than signification, and largely ignored ironies and contradictions. McKendrick acknowledges the importance of ambiguity in addressing delicate political issues in *El postrer godo*, claiming "the setting up of what amounts to an entire counter-text which creates a disjunction between what is said and what is seen to be the case, between the characters' expressed perception of events and the play as a whole, and which through this clash of perspectives speaks trenchantly to the nature of kingship."[14] This strongly refutes the conventional view of Lope's theatre as epitomizing seventeenth-century conformism, and while I am convinced of the subversiveness of *El postrer godo*, I diverge from the opinion that it is the theme of kingship that is central. Paradoxically, nowhere is this more apparent than in Lope's presentation of Roderick himself.

Professor McKendrick perceives Roderick as an out-and-out villain, incapable of self-governance, who breaks his word and commits treachery, selling his kingdom for a moment's pleasure. In line with the seventeenth-century view that history was a textbook in the art of government, Roderick's sexual misdemeanor is, she says, "a mis-use of the power invested in a prince for the protection, not the betrayal, of his subjects. The play dramatizes, early in a new king's reign, the dangers seen by political commentators in Spain to be inherent in absolutism."[15] This is perhaps what an audience might have been expecting on the basis of common knowledge of the medieval legend. Early Christian chroniclers had always blamed the Visigothic king for the invasion of the peninsula. However, this view is hard to sustain, in particular when Florinda declares at the end of Act 1: "El rey no tiene la culpa" [The King is not to blame] (Act 1, line 1040). She takes this no further, leaving an eloquent silence, in which we ask ourselves why the king should be blameless. Even Menéndez Pidal, in the throes of his outrage at the ghastly influence of Miguel de Luna, admits that Lope renders Roderick nobler than his source does. In the very first scene, the king acts to eliminate the corrupt monarchy that usurped his rightful throne by blinding Witiza in order to avenge Witiza's blinding of Roderick's father. When Roderick regains power by receiving the royal scepter, Teodoredo, his courtier, remarks on his clemency:

> no parece que castigas,
> mas que perdonas parece.
> (Act 1, 4–5)
> [it does not seem that you punish,
> you rather seem to pardon.]

Leosindo, another follower, praises his justice: "tu justicia conocemos" [we know of your justice] (Act 1, 62). The king is immediately beset by fate, for the crown and scepter fall from him, a bad augury borne out by the terrible revelations inside the enchanted cavern in Toledo. Roderick shows exceptional bravery in breaking the locks that no previous king has laid hands upon, to be confronted with the now familiar prediction of the Arab invasion depicted on canvases showing horsemen in Arab dress and headgear.

These visual representations of the Arabs are swiftly transformed into reality as a shipwreck brings the Moor Abembucar and Zara, daughter of the king of Algiers, to Roderick's court. Astonishingly unperturbed by the recent revelation of his destiny, Roderick proposes to marry the beautiful Zara on condition that she converts to Christianity. I will return to this conversion shortly, but wish to underline the wisdom and vision of Roderick as king in forging this alliance between Christian and Arab. This is not a monarch unfit to rule, but one who seeks to create a powerful allegiance between the two sides in a marriage preferable, he says, to that with a Christian woman, because

> no quiero hijos deudos de vasallos,
> No quiero suegro que me inquiete el reino;
> que tanta sangre cuestan a los godos:
> (Act 1, 574–76)
> [I don't want sons who are relatives of vassals,
> I don't want a father-in-law who will unsettle my kingdom,
> Which has cost the Goths so much blood.]

Harmony with honorable Arab neighbors is superior to the corruption of the Goths. Through this surprising scene, Lope presents a vision of how things might have been, or how they still might be.

But destiny prevails. Very soon after this marriage, Count Julian brings Florinda to the king's court, leaving her in good faith under Roderick's protection. The effect she has on him is immediate and overwhelming. No longer is he the strong, decisive leader, but trembling and uncertain, unable to believe the violent change in his feelings:

> "A hablarla voy; tiemblo, dudo,
> ¿Qué es esto? ¿De qué estoy mudo,
> si no de tanta mudanza?"
> (Act 1, 997–1000)
>
> [I will talk to her; I tremble, I doubt.
> What is this? Why am I struck dumb,
> If not at such a change?]

This final scene of Act 1 reveals the king as human, fallible, and beguiled by a clever, persuasive, and slightly teasing Florinda, in a touching, sensitive, and emotionally charged encounter that nevertheless ends with her sexual violation. Even his subsequent remorse and the painful realization of his betrayal are treated with sympathy. The devastating loss of kingdom and status, and Roderick's humility before destiny are symbolized in the peasant's clothes he swaps for his own garments at the end of Act 2.

It is not Roderick, but Count Julian, who is the real villain of the piece, and his role as the protagonist of Act 2 gives ample opportunity for Lope to set his actions against the comportment of the Moorish characters with whom he associates. The motif of the treacherous vassal or adviser, often a count, who intervenes in the action, as identified by Marcello Meli in similar legends of royal ruin, may have implications regarding the advisability of close relationships between kings and favorites, notably between Felipe III and Lerma, to which Lope wished to draw attention, but it also allows the treacherous Christian to be contrasted with the noble Moor. When Julian receives Florinda's letter he is in Tunis with Muza, the Arab ruler. Their dialogue in the first scene of Act 2 reveals the intimacy of their relationship and the trust between them, as Muza shares Julian's outrage, reading the letter aloud on his behalf. The count's idea of revenge for his dishonor is to betray Spain and hand it over to Muza and the Arabs:

> "quiero venderle su tierra,
> pues él me vende mi fama."
> (Act 2, 1304–5)

[I want to sell his country,
since he has sold my reputation]

he says of Roderick. Muza too is shocked at the king's behavior, but when Julian has left, he shows his scorn and dislike of Julian's treachery:

Ya temo su Guerra;
que hombre que vende su tierra,
no le oso llevar detrás.
         (Act 2, 1327–29)

[I already fear his war,
for a man who sells his country,
I dare not take with me.]

In the subsequent discussions between Tarife, Muza, and Julian regarding the invasion, Tarife too is distrustful of Julian, demanding a hostage in case he double-crosses them:

Que, aunque eres persona honrada,
en la guerra es muy usada
la traición.
         (Act 2, 1497–99)

[for, although you are an honored person,
betrayal is very common in war.]

Thus far, Lope's recreation of the Roderick legend presents a Visigothic, yet Moorophile, king who is powerless to escape destiny, and a Christian count who is on intimate terms with the Arabs, but whose legitimate desire for revenge is overshadowed by his treason and treachery. Corruption lies on the Christian side and is further blackened by the contrasting noble, dignified manners, and behavior of Muza as ruler and Tarife as soldier.

Ironic contradiction and cultural ambiguity are keynotes in the depiction of the other Moorish characters in the play. When Princess Zara converts to Christianity at Roderick's behest prior to their marriage, she technically becomes a *morisca*. Irony is poignant as Roderick offers her, as well as conversion, Spain itself:

RODRIGO   le ofrezco
                la salvación del alma, y después de ella
                a España, que es lo más que puedo dalla.
ZARA   !A España? ¿Cómo?
RODRIGO   Siendo mujer mía.
                      (Act 1, 496–500)

[RODERICK   I offer you
               salvation of your soul, and after that,
               I offer you Spain, which is the greatest thing I can give.
ZARA   Spain! How?
RODERICK   By being my wife.]

When her Moorish admirer Abembucar comes to save her during the invasion, she agrees to marry him if he too converts to Christianity. He does so willingly to win her, but their punishment for this conversion is death at the order of Tarife, for betrayal of Islam. This tragic circumstance could not have been lost on Lope's audience, watching at a time of interracial and religious tension, crisis, and doubtful conversions.

This is further borne out by Lope's use of dress change in the play, which touches upon seventeenth-century reality in an interesting way. When Zara becomes Christian, she wears "traje español" [Spanish dress] to denote her new status, similar to the way in which Roderick's loss of status after the battle is indicated by his adoption of peasant clothes. This theatrical device is effective, and must have been a reminder to contemporary audiences of the obligation of *moriscos* to change their clothes from Arab to Christian ones. Most telling, however, is the scene in Act 3 in which Pelayo is attempting to rescue his sister Solmira who has been captured by the Moors. He can only do so by wearing Moorish dress, but rather than seeing this as a metaphor for the clothes of the enemy Pelayo casts off in the equivalent of a classical *ekdysia* or divestiture ceremony after his symbolic baptism in the river, as Niehoff claims,[16] Pelayo seems elevated by his "alquicel" [Moorish cloak]. The future victor and king, uncouth and rough, is dignified and empowered by his change of clothes, taking on almost superhuman strength while wearing them, to ford the river and escape. His cross-dressing, like that of Zara, suggests on another level an interchangeability of cultural identity that negates perceived difference.

The 'complicitous subtext' that Melveena McKendrick points to in Lope's kingship plays does not, in this case, relate principally to issues of how a prince or king should rule, yet that subtext is, I feel, strongly political. It connotes, instead, contemporary struggles and religious conflicts in its implicit idealization of the Moorish characters. Luce López-Baralt discusses the enigmatic nature of Moorophile literature in inquisitorial Spain, noting the contradiction of the noble Moor of literature appearing at a time when real live Moors were forbidden their own cultural identity, and doubting the conventional view that idealization was conferred by the ultimate victors upon their former conquerors just prior to their expulsion.[17] With reference to the popular story *El Abencerraje*, which Lope used as a source for another of his Moorophile plays, *El remedio en la desdicha* [The Remedy in Misfortune], the critic Claudio Guillén feels that this apparently escapist literature alludes to the misery of *moriscos* at the time by means of silent contradictions.[18] Recent scholars echo this view, increasingly favoring the idea that much Moorophile literature in this era was a cleverly concealed literature of dissidence. Lope de Vega was noted as a Moorophile author, as his strong vindication of the Abencerraje nobility in his novel *La desdicha por la deshonra* [Misfortune through Dishonor], and his published defenses of the social dignity of the Moor reveal. It is also known that Lope was familiar with *aljamiado* texts, one of which actually uses a sonnet of his to illustrate erotic teachings.

In the light of these observations, the reading of *El postrer godo de España* against the grain uncovers ambivalences and inferences that constitute an interrogation of received interpretations of cultural and political events, both at the time of the Muslim invasion of Spain and in the early seventeenth century. The last Visigothic king is not a weak and cruel tyrant, but a man who seeks to merge his realm with that of the Arabs in a peaceful way, rather than to impose his culture upon another. His destined desire for Florinda again reveals ambiguity, for while she is a distant relative of his, she has been brought up in Arab lands, and even her ancient designation of La Cava comes from the Arabic.

Her inevitable dishonor allows her father to make the fatal choice of treason as his vengeance, a flaw of corruption that brings about death and the loss of the Visigothic kingdom. It is entirely fitting that the upright and just Tarife should kill him for his iniquity:

!Moros, corred tras él, sacad la espada,
o con lanzas le pasad el pecho;
que un hombre que vendió su patria amada,
no puede ser a nadie de provecho!
Castigaráme Alá si aquí le tengo.
Voy a matarle, que hoy a España vengo.
(Act 3, 2578–83)

[Moors, go after him, take out your swords,
or run your lances through his chest;
for a man who betrayed his beloved country
can be of benefit to no one!
Allah will punish me if I keep him here.
I am going to kill him, for today I come to Spain.]

The implication that, once purged of iniquity, a just and hopeful future awaits Spain under Islamic rule would have had special resonance for those *moriscos* in the audience, on the threshold of expulsion. A reading that focuses on the uncharted margins of the work shows *El postrer godo de España* to be essentially anachronistic in its metamorphosis of the Roderick legend into a vehicle that potentiates cultural and religious transformation. In a secular drama that would have spoken directly to an arguably far wider audience than that having access to previous versions of the story of Roderick and La Cava, Lope de Vega takes the most vibrant, long-lived, and resonant of all Hispanic legends and deploys it to unsettle the status quo, to subvert the traditional Christian interpretation that heaps guilt and blame upon the lovers, in order to hint at not only what might have been, if this Roderick's desire for harmony between Arabs and Christians had been fulfilled, but also to sow in the minds of his spectators the seeds of a utopic vision of what could be, in an alternative future in which *moriscos* might remain and flourish.

Transgression, Tyranny, and Treason: William Rowley's *All's Lost by Lust*

The English Jacobean dramatist William Rowley's little known play *All's Lost by Lust*, first performed about 1619 and published in 1633, is considered to be his most important sole work, described as a "romantic tragedy with a strong strain of dramatic morality." It is of great importance as the earliest example of an untransposed recreation of the legend outside Spain, in which Rowley focuses on the destructive effects of transgressive lust and monarchical tyranny when Roderick's rape of Jacinta, daughter of one of the King's generals, Julianus, leads the latter to avenge her violation by conniving with his own Moorish prisoners to oust Roderick from the throne. In terms of cultural transformation, Rowley's reworking of the story is fascinating, since his recreation of the medieval legend endows it special relevance for an English Jacobean audience, exposing powerful cultural anxieties and tensions through ambiguity and subversion.

William Rowley was born around 1585 and probably died in 1642. He had started acting before 1610, belonging to Prince Charles's Men as chief comedian, later joining Lady Elizabeth's Men, and then the King's Men in 1623, serving as both a playwright and actor. He is known to have written over fifty plays alone or in collaboration, most famously with Thomas Middleton, with whom he wrote *The Spanish Gypsy* and *The Changeling*, among many others. His practical stage experience probably contributed to the high demand for him as an associate, and it is recorded that he was beloved of Shakespeare, Fletcher, and Jonson. *All's Lost by Lust* was performed a number of times between 1619 and 1639 and Samuel Pepys notes that he saw it performed at the Red Bull Theatre. The sole authorship of the work and its categorization as a tragedy, rather than a comedy, for which Rowley had such flair, may indicate the importance of the subject to the playwright, although the details of his life are too sketchy to cast light on two significant questions—why he chose the story of King Roderick and what source he used.

The question of Rowley's source for the play is an intriguing one. According to Trudi Darby, editor of his comic history *A Shoemaker, A Gentleman*, Rowley inclined to use historical sources for the works he wrote alone, without other collaborators. She comments that it is clear from those sources that Rowley was widely read, familiar with Latin and Greek, and in her opinion, probably with some European languages as well.[19] In his 1910 edition of *All's Lost by Lust*, Charles Wharton Stork points to a possible source in a version of the thirteenth-century Spanish history by archbishop of Toledo Rodrigo Jiménez de Rada, in a Latin collection called *Rerum hispanicarum scriptores*, compiled by Robert Beale and printed in Frankfurt in 1579. This seems unlikely to me for two reasons. First, a principal innovation in the recounting of the legend by the archbishop of Toledo is that Roderick violates Count Julian's wife, not his daughter, which Rowley does not follow. Second, the story of Roderick and La Cava was evidently known in England as early as 1580, if not before, as a reference to it appears in Robert Greene's mirror for ladies of England, entitled *Mamillia*, printed in 1583, but written some years earlier, probably prior to 1580. The reference, "Roderick of Spaine lost his kingdom for Camma" (p. 82) comes in a work that shows "howe Gentlemen under the perfect substance of pure love, are oft inveigled with the shadowe of lewde luste" (title page). It is therefore used as an example of the destructive power of lust over men, which is the theme Rowley develops in his play. There is no hint of where Greene learned the story, but presumably he came across it in his extensive travels in Spain, and the frequency of diplomatic contact between England and Spain at that time and later would suggest that it could easily have been passed on either orally or in manuscript version, for there were a number of histories of Spain in vogue at the time.

Rowley's definitive source remains a mystery at present, but the issue is a vital one, for it constitutes the first of several unanswered questions posed by the play that destabilize its apparent agenda. In reworking his material, Rowley makes two notable alterations to the established legend of the Visigothic king. While retaining the names of the male protagonists, Roderick and Julian (as Julianus), he chooses the name Jacinta for the female protagonist, who is known in other versions as either La Cava (which Greene has as 'Camma') or Florinda, a name certainly known and used in other contexts by sixteenth-century authors such as George Pettie and William Painter. One possibility is that Rowley might have been working from an early version of the legend that does not name Julian's daughter, so he picked a Spanish woman's name with which he was familiar. The other significant change Rowley makes relates to the famous forced entry of King Roderick into the enchanted palace in Toledo. In this version, Roderick has a vision of his various victims, among whom, bizarrely, he himself is included. This change is easier to account for, as it indicates that the Muslim invasion of Spain is not the key issue for Rowley in this episode; instead, it is the consequences of the king's tyrannical lust that is the focus of the play's title.

A superficial answer to the question of why the Roderick story was used in this play might be that it chimed with one literary trend of the times. Moralizing works on the subject of lust, or mirrors of love, were clearly popular in the late sixteenth and seventeenth centuries, as the writing of the aforementioned Robert Greene, George Pettie, William Painter, and also John Hind shows. Rowley was tapping into a popular theme in his play, in which lust has three principal axes, transgression, tyranny, and the treason and betrayal that these bring in their wake, articulated through two parallel plots, which do not necessarily reinforce each other. By exploring and interweaving these three elements through the two plots, Rowley uses them as vehicles for a more profound interrogation of racial, religious, and social divergence, as well as querying the role of the monarch.

In both plots, the fundamental transgression lies in illicit sexual relationships, between the king and his general's daughter, which destroys the king-vassal relationship as well as that between himself and Jacinta, and in the soldier Antonio's bigamous relationship with the high-ranking and beautiful Dionysia. It is precisely the illicitness of his passion with which Roderick tries to tempt Jacinta:

> Do as your sex has done, tast what's forbid,
> And then distinguish of the difference.
> (2.1, 1114–15)

His transgressive desire identifies him as the lustful tyrant who was a frequent character in romantic plays of the time, yet Rowley renders him original, for Roderick is not entirely villainous. When Julianus tells him of the imminent Muslim invasion, his response is bold, fearless, and pragmatic: "Tut, feare frights us not, nor shall hope foole us" (1.1, 65). The king is portrayed as a victim of destiny, for his actions are already fated, as he himself admits when he describes: ". . .some saintish Infidell, / That prophesies subjection of our Spaine, / Unto the Moores" (1.1, 28–30). Yet his tyranny is an important issue in the play, in its implicit questioning of the nature of kingship. Roderick exerts his royal power over Julianus by sending him away to battle, thus allowing him unfettered access to Jacinta, addressing his general in words of great irony: ". . .in thy heart / be loyaltie and courage" (1.1, 85–86). It is precisely this loyalty that the king will abuse and which will turn to treachery later in the play. He asserts a veneer of authority over his base transaction with the bawd Malena, clothing an illegitimate act in the language of legality: "Thou must be my Lawyer (I'le fee thee well,) / And at the Barre of beauty pleade a cause, / Whether right or wrong, must needs be mine" (1.1, 150–55).

In the final act, as the king wrestles with his guilt, his servant Piamentelli urges him not to have such scruples over a maidenhead, and encourages him to assert his royal powers:

Stand on your guard, and royalize the fact
By your owne dispensation.
                    (5.1, 15–16)

Yet when Jacinta, in disguise, goes to break the news of her dishonor to her father, her question cuts to the chase: "Say a king should doo't? were th'act lesse done / By the greater power, does Majesty extenuate a crime?" (4.1, 86–89). These words and the depiction of the wielding of royal power must have struck a chord with an audience familiar with the contemporary debate over Common Law and with King James I's emphasis on royal authority in his published writing. It is interesting to note that in his *Trew Law of Free Monarchies*, James asserted that "the king is above the law, as both the author and giver of strength thereto." A good king, he added, would "frame all his actions to be according to the law, yet is he not bound thereto but of his good will and for good example-giving to his subjects."[20] While it seems unlikely that Rowley was having a dig at his own king, he may well have been making a statement about the nature of Spanish monarchy, carefully framed in a distant historical period that would safely circumvent the 1599 ban on satirical material that commented on contemporary politics. It is hard, however, not to see a comical topical reference to the insufficient funds in James's royal coffers to enable him to start a war with Spain in Julianus's remark to Roderick in Act 1: "But my dread liege, does not your treasury / Grow thinne and empty?" (1.1, 42–43).

In both main and secondary plots, illicit sexual desire is linked to the transgression of social rank. Clearly Jacinta is not a match for a king, a discrepancy tyranny ignores. In the secondary plot, Antonio distinguishes himself for bravery as a soldier in Roderick's army, though his dishonorable behavior in love does not match the honor won on the battlefield, for he marries Margaretta, an orange-seller far below him in social standing, before falling for the captivating Dionysia, who is of his own rank and whom he marries bigamously. Antonio's relationship with Margaretta parallels the unequal match of Roderick and Jacinta, an inequality feared by Margaretta's father Pedro, who has serious misgivings about the marriage, in vivid contrast with Julianus's blindness to the dangers hinted at by Jacinta when she warns him that Roderick has spoken to her of love. Julianus accuses her of treason, and takes no heed of her reminder that Tarquin was both a king and a ravisher.

But the apparent message that marriage only works among equals in rank is undermined by Antonio's startling suggestion that he could convert to Islam. In a play in which irony predominates, revealing the gap between the expectation or the ideal and its opposing reality, Antonio, who has just been commended for great bravery in fighting against the Moors, announces:

> Persuade me to turne Turk, or Moore Mahometan,
> For by the lustfull lawes of Mahomet
> I may have three wives more.
> (2.3, 42–44)

While the view of Moors as inherently lustful was a typical perception of the time, Antonio's attitude expresses an ambiguity toward his recent enemy that conveys a certain attraction or admiration, and implies that aspects of Islam might be preferable to or more desirable than Christianity.

The portrayal of Moors in *All's Lost by Lust* is a central aspect of the play. Conventional perceptions of the Moor are tested, as Rowley presents the infidel as an ambiguous character, both enemy and avenger, who reveals his Oriental perception of the white European as a counterprejudice. Jack D'Amico's study of the Moor in English Renaissance drama includes a discussion of *All's Lost by Lust*, which is illuminating in establishing the cultural context of such theatrical characterizations. He makes the useful point that the portrayal of the Moor as villain "becomes a convenient locus for those darkly subversive forces that threaten European society from within but that can be projected onto the outsider."[21] Because the Moor is opposite in race, religion, and character, he can confirm the superiority of Western values or on occasion allow conventional oppositions to be redefined.

D'Amico's discussion of the extensive contact between England and Morocco from about 1550 to the early 1600s in both trade and diplomacy is of direct relevance. There is evidence of continuous trade between England and Morocco as early as 1548, and the trade in arms was significant, since Queen Elizabeth overlooked the strict prohibition against a Christian nation providing munitions to the infidel due to the imminent threat of attack from Catholic Spain. D'Amico notes that anti-Catholic and anti-Spanish prejudice encouraged this relationship, and he feels it plays an important role in dramas that presented both Moors and Catholics, especially Spanish ones, to the English audience.[22] The situation was so sharply defined that two English merchants trading with Morocco, Hogan and Bodenham, independently made efforts to align Protestant and Islamic causes against what was perceived as the true enemy, Catholic Spain, indicating the extent to which prejudice against Islam could be set aside in face of the threat of Catholicism.[23]

In the light of this, Rowley's depiction of his Moorish characters can be seen as in some ways contrary to expectations, going against the stereotype. Although he makes use of standard epithets, 'hot', 'barbarous', 'tawney' to describe them, and Roderick instructs Julianus to "scourge back agen those halfe-nak't infidels / into their sun-burnt climate" (1.1, 84–85), expressing the familiar idea that great heat and nakedness cause backwardness or aberrant faith, there is a gap between the perception of the Moors in the play by the Spanish characters and their true condition. Early in the first scene, Roderick employs the cliché of comparing the black-skinned Moor with the devil, yet it is at once undermined by the hypothetical. He says:

> They would deter us with their swarty looks:
> Were they the same to their similitude,
> Sooty as the inhabitants of hell,
> Whome they neerest figure, cold feare should flye
> From us as distant as they are from beauty.
> (1.1, 31–35)

In reality, they are not actually devilish, it is merely an appearance, deftly indicated by the use of the subjunctive 'were.'

In the second act, the Moor's contrary view of the Spanish has no such nuance. The Moorish king, Mullymumen, expresses his repugnance at the white complexions of his adversaries:

> those smoothe white skins,
> That with a palsey hand she paints the limbes,
> Makes us recoyle.
> (2.3, 8–10)

This association of illness and corruption with white Europeans reflects their moral corruption in the eyes of the Moors. When Mullymumen learns of Margaretta's attempt to murder Antonio he remarks: "More fruits of Christians" (5.5, 56). Contrary to stereotyping and audience expectation, the lustful ways of Muslims are substituted by the lustful and destructive intrigues of Christians. In contrast, in Act 2 the Moorish king upholds honor and right action: "Who flies from honour, followes after shame" (2.3, 23). In his fatal act of treason, Julianus addresses the Moors as 'valiant' (4.1, 176), admitting to a closer link with them than he has with his own Christian king: ". . .I have no friends / But these my enemies, yet welcome, brave Moores, With you Ile parley" (4.1, 151–54). The conventional association of lust with the blackamoor is again subverted in this play, for it is Roderick who, in his sexual passion, takes on this characteristic and is equated with blackness. When Jacinta is disguised and describes her violation to her father in Act 4, Scene 1, she asks what he would do if the king had defiled "her white lawn of chastity, / With ugly blacks of lust" (4.1, 74–75).

The treason and betrayal that are the crucial consequences of transgression and tyranny lead to a revenge in both main and secondary plots that relies upon the agency of a Moorish character to mete out justice. The martial imagery connecting the invasion and violation of Spain by the North Africans with the violation of Jacinta by Roderick gives way to the ironic vocabulary of trust and honor that conceals Roderick's betrayal of Julianus and Antonio's betrayal of Margaretta. In both cases, the revenge of those betrayed fails, for Julianus' treason leads to the loss of his country and his own death, and Margaretta's attempted murder costs her her own life as well as those of Antonio, Lazarello, and Dionysia. Apprised of her husband's bigamy, Margaretta plans to murder him as he comes to pay her a prearranged night-time visit, but it is her aptly named servant Fydella, a Moor, who loyally resolves to stand by her mistress to the end. Margaretta asks her:

> . . .Suppose I went
> In the right noble way, to meet my foe
> I'th field, wouldst be my second.
> FYDELLA To my second life, Madam.
>   (3.2, 81–84)

Margaretta calls her "Thou little instrument of my revenge" (4.2, 39) after Fydella, who is prepared to kill for her, has strangled the person they think is Antonio (though it turns out to be Lazarello). She administers Margaretta's justice, though they are both the unfortunate victims of Lazarello's substitution trick, which costs him his life into the bargain.

In Act 5, Scene 5, Mullymumen is the bringer of justice as an avenger of both Julianus's treason and of Roderick's rape of Jacinta. He offers his love to her as her avenger in chasing Roderick from the land, but having sought vengeance for her dishonor, she fails to esteem the instrument of revenge. The dominant note of irony is sustained to the end, for Mullymumen is dishonored by her rejection of him, a feeling Jacinta cannot seem to appreciate, though suffering dishonor herself. The Moorish king must therefore seek his own revenge for her refusal, by cruelly cutting out her tongue to silence her abuse of him. Irony prevails once more, since initially Jacinta refuses to be won by language when Roderick and then Malena tempt her, and in the end has her ability to speak stripped from her.

Mullymumen's justification for killing Julianus is expressed in a fine speech in which he accuses Julianus of being a traitor:

> What art thou but thy king's and kingdom's ruine?
> Was it thy hopes, that ever I should trust thee?
> Traytors are poyson'd arrowes drawne to th'head,
> Which we shoot home at mischiefe; being struck dead,
> Then let the arrow be consumed in fire:
> Hast not betrayed thy King and Country basely?
> (5.5, 24–29)

This casts the blame squarely upon Julianus, not upon Roderick or the Moorish king. He is worthy of no man's trust, and his dishonor does not merit the treason he perpetrates. In the final cruel scene in which Mullymumen tricks Julianus into killing Jacinta and takes pleasure in it, it is hard to feel sympathy for the Spaniard, who is duly treacherously betrayed himself.

Interacting with the social, racial, and cultural differences that create dramatic tension through ambiguity and subversion of expectation, gender differences reinforce the didactic purpose of the play while hinting at alternatives to the established order. With the exception of Malena, who is an interesting comic character familiar to the Jacobean stage, with a celebrated Spanish counterpart in Fernando de Rojas's bawd Celestina, the female characters are notably virtuous and feisty. While Jacinta has only words with which to defend herself, and later devolves responsibility for revenge upon her father, Margaretta takes matters into her own hands, showing that low social rank is no impediment to courage and a sense of avenging honor:

> Spite of the low condition of my birth,
> High spirits may be lodg'd in humble earth.
> (3.2, 87–88)

Nor is Dionysia just a pretty face. It is the way that she speaks that attracts Antonio initially: "I see nothing in her face, / Prethee attempt to make her speak agen" (2.2, 44–45). In fact, her wit is so fast and sharp that Antonio cannot keep up with her, and her mental agility is only matched by her courage in the final tragic scene where she takes her own life to join Antonio in death. Her words are telling, for her desire is to join him in the heavenly marriage bed, alongside Margaretta: "I'll lie as close as shee on thy left side" (5.5, 114). This harks back to Antonio's earlier intimation of a secret yearning for the Muslim faith. What she is suggesting is that the triangular relationship that cannot be permitted for Antonio, Margaretta, and herself as Christians, she desires in an afterlife that reflects the Muslim idea of paradise. On this basis, it is hard to go along with the opinion expressed by Pilar Cuder-Domínguez that *All's Lost by Lust* is "meant to reinforce conventional values and mores, and the representation of the Islamic characters is thus conventional as well."[24] Her view that the Moors are portrayed as hellhounds dealing death and punishment to all involved may well follow the rules of the tragedy of blood of the 1620s, but Rowley's apparently didactic purpose is destabilized by the problematical implicit questions raised by the text, thereby elucidating the fundamental question posed earlier as to why William Rowley chose to use this story from medieval Spanish history and legend. What were the questions to which it was a response?

The scope of Rowley's innovativeness in this respect must be celebrated, for *All's Lost by Lust* is the first full version of the legend of King Roderick and La Cava to appear outside Spain. Two important aspects arise from this, which when considered together, cast significant light upon the issues raised above. First, there would have been little audience familiarity with the details of the story. Even though earlier brief references to it in England do exist, as mentioned, it could not have been known widely or in any depth. This suggests that Rowley wanted to present issues that he felt could be conveyed only by using new material, a different story, which would logically present a different way of looking at certain themes. Second, this first foreign version appears in England, not France, Germany, Italy, or elsewhere, presumably because Spain had greatest contact with England at that time, a fact that would have encouraged cultural exchange between the two countries. The first English edition of *The History of Amadis of Gaule*, the great Castilian chivalric romance, was also published in 1619, while Anglo-Spanish grammars and dictionaries began to appear in London shops around the 1620s. It is therefore plausible that the playwright wanted to present a potentially alternative view of Spain and the Moors to the dominant one of the day.

Just what that dominant view was is indicated by Wentworth Smith's play of 1614–15, *The Hector of Germany*, in which he depicts the involvement of the Palsgrave in the European wars after the deposing of King Pedro 1 of Castile by the usurper Enrique de Trastámara. Although in the view of Tristan Marshall the play treads a fine line between anti-Spanish narrative and a more cautious, balanced depiction of Spain,[25] the King of Spain is known throughout by his epithet 'the Bastard' and is described as follows:

> The Bastards but a Coward and a Spanyard,
> Coward and Spanyarde off-times goe together.
> (Sigs. A3v–A4)

Anti-Spanish feeling was clearly running high at the time Rowley wrote *All's Lost by Lust*. In 1618, James 1 had issued a proclamation pardoning an assault on the Spanish embassy in the Barbican, and Marshall notes that concerns about continued vigilance over potential Spanish aggression were reflected by dramatists, to the extent that after 1620 public theatre grew "more brazen in its depiction of martial themes and directly advocated a return to Elizabethan England's firm anti-Spanish stance."[26]

In Rowley's play, the depiction of invasion by an alien race and religion must have resonated with contemporary theatre-goers, who might have viewed Spain and Catholicism as a threat to the status quo. Yet his message is not a straightforward one. While the lust and betrayal of the Spaniards is undoubtedly at the heart of the play, revenge is not the answer, for it brings disaster. The story of King Roderick had of course been perceived by Christian historians up to this time as the fable of the disastrous loss of Spain to the Moors provoked by Visigothic lust and decadence. In this Rowley is spot on. However, Roderick is not a black-and-white character. He is in thrall to destiny and cannot escape his fate. The scene that Rowley radically reinvents, in which Roderick enters the enchanted castle where he faces not a proleptic vision of the Moorish invasion, but a vision of all his victims and a projection of his self, suggests that the king is a victim of his own passions, and shows resounding courage in facing his own conscience. Nor does Roderick meet death at the end, like the other Christian protagonists, for it is not he who is the true author of his country's invasion, but Julianus. The anticipated portrayal of a brutal Spanish tyrant is mitigated by other human qualities. In this nuanced depiction of the Spanish, Julianus's villainy suggests that the loyalty of subjects to their king is paramount.

So Rowley uses cultural, racial, and social difference to hint at new possibilities. The play is not unambiguously anti-Spanish and anti-Muslim/ Moor. It does not categorically uphold the social hierarchy, nor portray women solely as victims of male power. The creation of Moorish characters who have honor and dignity, and of English lovers who long for the Muslim paradise edge toward a vision of how things might be. The audience is also left to ponder what might have been if Antonio and Margaretta had not been forced apart by social rank; if kings were beholden to the law and not all-powerful; if women were not the victims of lust, but agents of their own destinies. On the title page of his play, Rowley quotes Juvenal's *Satires* 7.90, "Quod non dant Proceres, Dabit Histrio" [what great men do not give, the stage player shall give you]. The playwright is reiterating Juvenal's complaint about the neglect of learning and letters that caused writers to depend on the patronage of actors, not of wealthy men. Yet it is tempting to think that he may have had something else in mind too. The presentation of the legend of King Roderick on the English stage might be viewed as a response to pressing contemporary questions regarding the nature of religious, racial, and social difference. What the playwright can give, within the constraints of a theatrical convention that required the final reestablishment of order, is a glimpse of an alternative view of the world, in which the past can be harnessed in the present to show how the future could be.

Expanding Vitality and Variation

The development of the legend in the seventeenth century was not limited to poetry and drama. Three prose variations stand out in terms of diversity of authorial motivation and in the singularity of the appropriation of the storyline. The first two are historical or pseudo-historical works published within a year of each other, the earlier being the diplomat Diego de Saavedra Fajardo's *Corona gótica, castellana y austríaca* [Gothic, Castilian and Austrian Crown] of 1645, written while he was on extended government business in Munster. Saavedra Fajardo's reputedly finest work was his *Idea de un príncipe político cristiano* [Idea of a Christian Political Prince], published in Munich in 1640, a mirror for princes whose precepts are echoed in the dedication to the prince of Spain in the *Corona gótica*, in the form of a pointed request for the prince to consider his own actions in the light of those of his predecessors: "En ellos (los progenitores) se ha de mirar vuestra alteza para el conocimiento cierto de sí mismo y para el desengaño de los errores propios, presuponiendo que movió el dedo índice mi pluma, señalando en lo que fué lo que agora es"[27] [Your Highness must look upon them (the predecessors) in order to gain certain knowledge of himself and to see his own faults clearly, assuming that my index finger moved my pen, by pointing out in what was that which now is]. Fajardo appears to have consulted a large number of historical sources for his survey of all the Visigothic kings of Spain ending with King Roderick. In the tradition of Mariana and certain earlier historians, he lays the blame for the Muslim invasion at the feet of Witiza, given over to a sensual pleasure and libertinage that Roderick continues: "Era destemplado en la sensualidad, imprudente en sus afectos y pasiones"[28] [He was excessive in his sensuality, imprudent in his affections and passions]. Yet in this case it is a combination of the agency of Witiza's two sons and the ire of God that brought about Spain's downfall, not Roderick, nor his lover or her father.

The attachment to constituted history that Pidal notes[29] in Fajardo's work is illustrated in his openness to the authenticity of the story of the enchanted tower that Roderick breaks into. He states: "No lo afirmamos nosotros, pues el arzobispo de Toledo don Rodrigo lo dejó dudoso; solamente decimos que las historias romanas y otras contienen casos mas fuera del órden natural de las cosas, y no se les niega el crédito"[30] [I am not affirming it, since the Archbishop of Toledo, Don Rodrigo, left it in doubt; I am merely saying that Roman histories and others contain incidents even further from the natural order of things, and their credibility is not denied]. More importantly, Fajardo is prepared to acknowledge the existence of Florinda, criticizing those versions of the story that do not give credit to her existence. As he claims, "Si así se desacreditan las tradiciones antiguas heredadas de padres a hijos, y confirmadas con testimonios de escrituras, ¿en qué otros fundamentos podrá mantenerse el edificio de la historia?"[31] [If ancient traditions handed down from fathers to sons are discredited in this way, on what other foundations can the edifice of history be maintained?].

This stress on the continuity of historical records appears to be linked to Fajardo's intention of writing a history that underlines Spain's legitimacy as a monarchy at a time when the country's failure to maintain its empire was being questioned. He uses the familiar argument that although Roderick was the last of the Gothic kings, this was a question of title rather than of bloodline, since his successors were kings of Castile, Leon, and Asturias, thus maintaining the original royal line and continuing Spain's destiny, so rudely interrupted by the Hapsburg connection. If Fajardo's willingness to give credit to legendary elements as authentic historical records suited his purpose, it also lent legitimacy to the increasingly important figure of Florinda.

In stark contrast to Fajardo's efforts to provide a reliable historical account of the Visigothic kings, culminating in Roderick's reign, the apparently anonymous *Cronicón de San Servando* [Chronicle of Saint Servando], published in 1646, is an extravagantly fictitious document masquerading as the history of the canon and bishop of Orense in Galicia, starting with the creation of the world and relating how Spain was peopled by the descendants of King Tubal, including the reigns of the Caesars plus a list of various martyrs connected with each. It turns out, astonishingly, that Bishop Servando was Roderick's confessor, a role that gives him access to the intimate details of the king's private affairs and allows him to elaborate on the familiar story by developing the idea, probably taken from

Julián del Castillo's version, that Roderick has love affairs with both Florinda and her mother. The bishop describes events as follows: "Don Rodrico querie moito a o Conde don Juliao e a la Condiesa Fandina que era moito fermosa. E don Rodrico facia pecado co ela, e a tinha a mandar. Eo propio com unha Filha sua chamada Cava Florinda, que era de estremaida fermosura. Eo Rey ha persuadeu a seu amor. E non contento o que tinha com a may se deytou co ela, e fez nela un filho que se criou em Evora de Lusitania chamado Alterico. Ista malvada escreviou á seu Pay o que ficera com o Rey, e por isso tomou moito enojo. . ."[32] [Roderick was very fond of Count Julian, and of Countess Fandina, who was very lovely. And Roderick sinned with her, and held her in thrall. The same happened with a daughter of hers called Cava Florinda, who was extremely beautiful. The king persuaded her of his love, and not content with what he had with the mother, he lingered with her, and engendered in her a son called Alterico who was raised in Evora in Lusitania. But the wicked girl wrote to her father and told him what the king had done, and he became greatly enraged. . .].

In spite of the double crime Roderick commits in this account, Florinda is castigated for her betrayal of him to her father, and presumably the king is absolved by his confessor! The reasons behind this extraordinary account and behind the chronicle itself are clarified by its own lively history. The polymath and chronicler par excellence Joseph Pellicer de Ossau, a specialist in genealogies, had a copy of the *Cronicón de San Servando*, translated into Galician, which he published in 1646, and managed to convince a number of scholars and churchmen that it was genuine. However, much later, Pellicer admitted he had been given the original chronicle by one Pedro Fernández de Boán from Orense, who had forged the chronicle in league with his brother, in the same way that they had forged various other old documents. Their motivation was simple. They were of noble origins and wanted to prove their lineage by creating a written authority that could show the ancient origins of families as required. Who better than the first bishop of their home town to provide the historical authenticity? They gave the manuscript to Pellicer whose court connections and reputation as a researcher into genealogical documents made it easy to authenticate it for them.

Twenty-five years later in 1661, Cristóbal Lozano took up the story of the king and his lover in a prose work markedly different from its immediate predecessors. The three volumes of the *David perseguido* is not a historical text but a religious one, principally on the subject of the trials of the biblical king David. Lozano has what Menéndez Pidal calls the "extravagante idea"[33] [highly extravagant idea] of consoling David's daughter Tamar after she has been raped by Amnon by citing various examples of women aggrieved in a similar way, one of whom is La Cava.

However, the author also states that the examples he chooses are not so much to relieve Tamar as "para exemplo de Príncipes lascivos"[34] [an example to lascivious princes].

There are a number of particularly interesting aspects to Lozano's rendering of the legend of Roderick and La Cava. First, he underlines the continuing widespread currency of the story at this stage in the seventeenth century: "Ya veo que es esta una Historia tan sabida de todos, que no solo la antigüedad de mas de novecientos años no ha borrado sus noticias, sino que cada día refresca sus memorias, pues apenas quantos nacen llegan a edad de razon, quando tropiezan con ella"[35] [I realize that this is a story well known to everyone, and that more than nine hundred years have not only failed to erase its meanings, but refresh its memory daily, because as soon as the newborn reach an age at which they can reason, they come across it]. This indicates a familiarity with the story at all levels of society, not just among the literate and educated.

Second, Lozano is adamant in his defense of La Cava against the traditional ill-feeling arising out of her blame for the destruction of Spain. He notes this hatred for her in strong terms: "Sea la Caba, o Florinda la primera, tan odiosa, y tan aborrecible para España, que solo de su nombre abomina el mas piadoso, y el menos compassivo se reviste de furias, y despechos"[36] [La Cava, or Florinda is the first example, so hateful, so abhorrent to Spain, that the most pious person detests the mere name, and the least compassionate is filled with fury and indignation]. But Lozano does not share this hatred, for he believes that it was the religious laxity and general corruption of the Visigothic monarchies of both Witiza and Roderick that invoked the wrath of God in the form of the Muslim invasion: "¿Por qué alegan, pues, por causa de la ruina el quexarse la Caba de su agravio, y no el quebrantar sagradas Leyes? Tener irritado a Dios con la desemboltura, enojado al Cielo con la desobediencia, y ofendida hasta la tierra con tanta maldad, esto fue la causa que España se perdiesse, no que la Caba clamasse. Ella fue solo instrumento para tomar Dios el azote, y executar los castigos. Cúlpese a sí mismo el hombre quando peca, cúlpese a sí mismo el Reyno quando delinque, y no culpe al que ofendido acarrea los pesares"[37] [Why, then, is La Cava's complaint at the wrong she suffered alleged as the cause of Spain's ruin, and not the breaking of sacred laws? To have angered God with shamelessness, to have enraged the Heavens with disobedience and offended the earth itself with so much evil, these were the reasons why Spain was lost, not because La Cava cried out. She was only the instrument through which God lashed his whip and dealt out punishment. The man who sins should blame himself, the kingdom that breaks the law should blame itself, not the person offended who brings those sorrows with them].

In an intricate plot that draws on Julián del Castillo, Mariana, and certain ballads, Lozano weaves a complex web of relationships. Julian is married to Witiza's sister, Fraudina, and is the king's private adviser. Roderick's plans to marry La Cava are hindered by the arrival from Africa of the Infanta Egilona, apparently already promised to the king. Lozano notes that his sources do not clarify why Roderick would have chosen a Moorish princess over a Christian wife (although Egilona is a Visigothic name), but the marriage goes ahead, and leaves Julian and La Cava feeling scorned. Tiring of Egilona, Roderick turns again to La Cava, who understandably rebuffs his attentions.

To complicate matters further , Lozano suggests that La Cava's mother, Fraudina, takes a fancy to the king and may have slept with him when her daughter rejected him. But Roderick is not content with this and violates La Cava, precipitating Fraudina's anger over his preference for her daughter. She incites La Cava to take revenge on the king by writing yet another version of the letter to her father. This twist of the plot, similar to the double crime Roderick commits in Pedro Boán's account, greatly appealed to the nineteenth-century Spanish dramatist Zorrilla, who used it in his play *El puñal del godo*, discussed in chapter 9. In these circumstances, the faithful Julian is doubly dishonored, though Lozano insists that the rape was not the cause of the loss of Spain, which he explains was already predestined in the legend of the enchanted tower of Toledo, while Julian was already in Africa seeking to reinstate Witiza's banished sons prior to these events.

The third aspect of interest in Lozano's work is that he gives a second example of a Spanish woman wronged as Tamar and La Cava were. The daughter of the Duke of Favila, and sister of the legendary Pelayo, who is nameless in this story, is raped by a Christian, Munuza, who governs the city of Gijón for the Moors. Pelayo finds out and takes revenge, culminating in his election as king of Spain. This allows Lozano to conclude neatly: "mas se ha de reparar en una cosa notable, que ya que la fuerza de Florinda ocasionó la pérdida de España, la fuerza de esta hermosa Infanta. . ., fue el principal motivo de que se restaurasse"[38] [but a remarkable thing should be noted, that although the rape of Florinda brought about the loss of Spain, the rape of this beautiful Infanta. . ., was the main reason that it was restored].

Lozano's lively mixture of fact and fiction was extremely popular and widely read up until the nineteenth century. Nascent plot strands that bring La Cava and a mother figure into the limelight would be reworked more extensively in later times, but at the end of the seventeenth century the personage of La Cava was becoming more engaging and sympathetically drawn, amplifying the more favorable portrayal of her in certain ballads.

New Performance in Early Opera

The evolution of the legend in the seventeenth century takes on an entirely new dimension in opera. Coinciding with the early development of the operatic form, the dramatic qualities of the story of Roderick and La Cava found further expression in performance outside Spain, this time in Italy. How the legend was known in Italy is uncertain, though it may be as Menéndez Pidal suggests, due to the prestigious reputation and popularity of Spanish Golden Age literature. The first operatic version I have found, Giovanni Battista Andreini's tragedy *La Florinda*, is of enormous interest for this reason alone, although a detailed discussion of the work lies outside the scope of its book[39] due to the fact that the story is transposed into a different geographical and cultural context, that of Scotland. The work was performed in Florence in 1606, and consists of five acts, a complex tragic plot and a markedly pastoral setting.

By the end of the century, there existed a number of musical dramas in which the legend was reenacted, such as Giuseppe Malatesta Garuffi's musical drama performed in Rome in 1677, written for a single actor who appeared in all three acts, and Giovanni Battista Bottalino's *Il Roderico* of 1684. These operatic works, though popular at the time, are now obscure and virtually unknown. They herald the operatic developments of the eighteenth century, in which the story of the king and the whore weaves its inspirational magic on a grander scale.

The poetry, prose, theatre, and opera of the seventeenth century in Spain, England, and Italy embraced the legend of King Roderick and La Cava for diverse reasons, political, racial, religious, artistic, and even genealogical. The powerful dramatic qualities of the story that were apparent in the ballad cycle are intensified as the protagonists come alive on stage as complex and fascinating individuals caught inexorably in the web of destiny. The figure of La Cava begins to acquire prominence and to gain legitimacy as writers appropriate the story to explore issues of gender and individual responsibility, while the perceived Muslim enemy turns out to be not as black as he is painted in a number of cases. It is significant that the two major dramatists, Lope de Vega and William Rowley, use the legend to hint at more utopian visions of racial and social interaction. These elements combine with new aspects that come under close scrutiny in the eighteenth-century proliferation of the legend in theatre and opera.

CHAPTER 6

CENSORED!—THE EIGHTEENTH CENTURY

Roderick in Spain

In 1726, when Fray Benito Feijóo (1676–1764) began to publish his critical writings, Spain was still preoccupied with the themes of loss and restoration of its empire, and the contrast between intellectual conservatives and the innovators of the Enlightenment was sustained. Padre Feijóo, a Benedictine monk from Oviedo, was a much more revolutionary individual than many of his contemporaries, whose contribution to changes in Spain in the eighteenth century was widely recognized. Backed by the Benedictine Order and the king, and dedicating his work mostly to kings and princes, his awareness of cultural and scientific developments in the rest of Europe led to a departure from the seventeenth-century literary traditions still favored by his peers. His importance in the life of the legend of Roderick and La Cava lies in his reference to La Cava herself in his celebrated writings on theatre, *Teatro crítico universal*, where he devotes two paragraphs to the subject, in Volume 1 of 1726 and again in Volume IV of 1730. While the legend had spread to other parts of Europe, it had lain dormant in Spain for ninety years. Father Feijóo's defense of Florinda sets the tone for the evolution of the story during the eighteenth century in its focus upon the female protagonist and her rehabilitation, and in its equation with a classical legend.

In Volume I,[1] he argues against what he describes as the commonly held yet erroneous view that women are the source of all evil, epitomized in the popular belief that La Cava caused the loss of Spain, and Eve the loss of the entire world. He casts the blame squarely upon Count Julian, and upon men in other similar cases, a view he reiterates in Volume IV.[2] The pain occasioned by the loss of Spain is still uppermost: "Nunca puedo acordarme de la pérdida de España sin añadir al dolor de tan gran calamidad otro sentimiento, por la injusticia, que comunmente se hace al más inculpable instrumento de ella"³ [I can never recall the loss of Spain without adding to the pain of such a great calamity another feeling, arising from the injustice of blaming the least guilty instrument of its demise]. He likens Florinda to Lucretia, as the earlier ballad writer had done, asking why Lucretia is celebrated and Florinda detested. His answer is as follows: "Fue saludable a Roma la queja de Lucrecia; fue funesta a España la de Florinda. Pero del bien y el mal fueron autores únicos el esposo de una y el padre de otra, sin intervención, ni aun previsión de las dos damas"⁴ [Lucretia's complaint was favorable to Rome; that of Florinda was disastrous for Spain. But the sole authors of good and evil were the husband of one and the father of the other, without the intervention of the two ladies, nor even their anticipation of such outcomes]. Feijóo justified his digression on La Cava as a defense of an important yet anonymous Spanish woman who continued to be unfairly maligned, a defense that contributed strongly to the increasing momentum regained by the legend in the late 1700s. Renewed interest in the story brought female characters to the fore for certain specific reasons, and classical influences became apparent.

Although dramatists of the early eighteenth century continued to use the formulas and practices of the previous century, new developments arose that influenced the portrayal of the king and the whore. The theatre was seen as an instrument for expressing social and moral reform, while the first attempts to produce tragedies (a genre that foreigners believed Spaniards incapable of writing)⁵ were made in the 1750s. Yet moral reform alone could go only so far. The playwright Eusebio de Vela wrote *La Pérdida de España*,⁶ staged in Murcia in 1768 and according to Menéndez Pidal, based entirely on Miguel de Luna and inspired by Calderonian style; yet it was censored. In 1770 the Vicar of Madrid precluded it: "por indecorosa al rei que en ella se refiere de España, al obispo y su dignidad y a la misma nación española, pues aunque se hallen en algunos libros y en la Historia noticias de esta pérdida, no es justo renovarlas en el theatro, en el que no deben representarse obras que manifiesten conspiraciones ni traición alguna a los soberanos, cuio debido respeto i lealtad debe enseñarse, en cumplimiento de lo mandado y justamente prevenido; y más, en una ocasión en que se solicita reformar el theatre"⁷ [because it is indecorous to the king of Spain referred to, to the bishop and his dignity and to the Spanish nation itself; although accounts of this loss can be found in some books and in history, it is not right to revisit it in the theatre, where works presenting any conspiracies and betrayal of sovereigns should not be staged, for due respect and loyalty to these should be taught, in fulfillment of what is justly ordered and provided; and even more, at a time when the reform of the theatre is being sought].

A later play on the subject of King Roderick, Manuel Fermín de Laviano's *Triunfos de valor y honor en la corte de Rodrigo*, of 1779, was still restricted by censorship. Laviano was obliged to focus on the secondary Duchess of Lorena episode from Pedro de Corral's *Crónica sarracina*, and although of comparatively inferior quality, the play was performed for over forty years, largely because it did not deal blatantly with the Roderick legend. Although the action takes place at Roderick's court following his marriage to Eliaca, an African princess who has renounced Islam and converted to Christianity, Roderick is a dull, wooden, and stereotypical king. The Duchess is at court, but in disgrace following accusations that she has not observed the statutory two years of widowhood in a state of chastity after her husband's death. According to her evil brother-in-law, Lembrot, this means she will no longer be entitled to the dukedom, which will naturally be inherited by Lembrot instead if he can prove his case. Until the end, Roderick is totally deceived by the situation, believing the villains to be virtuous and vice versa. Count Julian, though not the familiar traitor, is ignoble and sides with Lembrot. Fortunately the day is saved by the nobleman Sacarus, taken from the *Crónica sarracina* also, the wicked plot is revealed, the villains are killed, and Julian is sent to Algeciras. The subject matter is certainly tangential to the core legend, and produces a slow, uninspired, and predictable play, making its success on the stage a mystery.

A further example of the effects of censorship upon the legend can be found in the dramatic monologue entitled *Rodrigo, scena trágica con intermisiones músicas* written in 1789 by Juan Hernanz Dávila. Although this could not be performed on the public stage, it lived in private theatre. It exists in a single manuscript in the library of Santander, which Menéndez Pidal managed to consult, and to report that Roderick is a figure full of remorse, based on Corral's work, while Florinda herself is never actually named in the text. Dávila modernizes the story by sending Roderick off to fight in another war, an idea also adopted by Southey in the next century.

An intriguing result of the prohibition of presenting King Roderick on the public stage was the consequent tangential remolding of the legend to focus on characters peripheral to Roderick and La Cava themselves, often shifting the subject matter from the loss of Spain to its restoration. In 1754, the count of Salduéñas wrote a drama entitled *Pelayo*, as did the more celebrated writer Jovellanos in 1792, the latter being concerned with the story not as the outcome of tyrannous love, but as a story of the infringement of human rights and absolutism. Glendinning points out that this play reflects the preoccupation of the Enlightenment with the rights of invaders, a sensitive subject at a time when Spaniards were often criticized for the treatment of the South American peoples by the conquistadors.[8]

Nicolás Fernández de Moratín's work *Hormesinda*, written in 1770, also centres on the legend of Pelayo, in which Hormesinda, Pelayo's sister, is portrayed as a rival of Florinda at King Roderick's court. The play was not a success, having only six performances, although it had a certain political relevance in its criticism of absolute power. It was perhaps limited by the extreme rigor of its composition as Moratín strove to comply with the rigid rules of composition of the eighteenth-century theatre. Although there was a definite tendency to favor the legend of Pelayo over that of Roderick at this time, this was not a new idea; it goes back to the earliest Asturian chronicles in the ninth century. What was new, however, was the dramatic exploration of the character of Roderick's Visigothic widow, Egilona.

As Pidal points out, she had been previously ignored, but her appearance was sudden and lasting, extending to the late nineteenth century. C.M. Trigueros published a play in 1760 entitled *La Egilona, viuda del Rey don Rodrigo*, in which Roderick's widow Egilona marries the Moor Abdalasis and is proclaimed queen of Spain, narrowly escaping the clutches of the lowly nephew and son of Pelayo, both of whom want to marry her. King Roderick is not mentioned. In 1785, a play along very similar lines by the prolific dramatist Antonio Valladares de Sotomayor was staged, entitled by Moratín *La Egilona, viuda del rey don Rodrigo*.[9] It appears to have been a play of little merit, described by Pidal as "un enredo disparatado y mareante" [an absurd and boring muddle] in which Abdalasis the Moorish ruler proclaims Egilona queen of Spain, with Valladares wildly extemporizing upon historical details, inventing two entirely different Rodrigos and Pelayos who bear no relation to those in the original story. During the coronation celebrations of Charles IV in 1788, another play, *La Egilona, drama heroica en prosa*, was put on. It was anonymous, perhaps because of its somewhat radical departure from Spanish theatrical tradition in its sentimental and terrifying aspects, with Julian dying drinking poison while Florinda falls in love with the Moor Abdalasis as they remove the count's body, invoking Egilona's jealousy. Pidal makes the wry comment that neither play draws upon Egilona's life as recorded by historians, though she cuts a potentially interesting figure as the originator of the Gothic-Arabic kingdom in Spain.[10]

If the Roderick legend was censored on the Spanish stage of the eighteenth century, there was no such prohibition in poetry and prose writing. José Cadalso, a cavalry officer who had traveled widely in Europe, wrote his *Carta de Florinda a su padre el conde D. Julián después de su desgracia* in 1773, a long epistolary poem that fuses the medieval and the contemporary, epitomizing the remarkable flexibility and creative potential of the legend. In parallel with eighteenth-century research into the early history of Spain, an increased interest in medieval poetry was growing in other European countries at the same time. The medieval axiom of blending didacticism with entertainment was echoed in the poet Luzán's view of the aim of poetry, to "aprovechar deleitando" [to be beneficial while giving delight]. Within this context, Cadalso's soldierly patriotism expressed itself in his liking for themes from national history, and the legend of King Roderick and La Cava fitted the bill perfectly.

In his poem, written in Italianate sextets of alternating hepta- and endecasyllables, Cadalso reworks the Ovidian tradition of heroic epistles on love themes exemplified by the *Heroides*. However, Florinda is not writing a love letter to Roderick, but a letter of vengeance to Julian, recounting how the king has wooed her, and in face of her apparent imperviousness to his advances, has seemed to admit defeat and comply with her wishes. Overcome by emotion at his forbearance, she faints, and Roderick seizes the opportunity to take advantage of her, raping her while she is unconscious. Roderick's suggestion that they should then be united for life is viewed with horror by Florinda, who longs to kill him in revenge, but does not dare to do so, believing that a king can be punished by only God.

While his classical background is in evidence, Cadalso's reinterpretation of the legend based on the famous letter first created by Miguel de Luna in the style of Arabic historiographers indicates a firm grounding in Spanish tradition in a period when Spain is often thought to have been dominated by French influences. Yet the poet succeeds in fusing these elements with other eighteenth-century literary trends. The critic R. Merritt Cox analyses the *Carta de Florinda* in such terms, claiming that Cadalso's treatment of the theme creates a new ambience for the legend in this century. In summary, he argues that the poem is an embryonic epistolary novel of the kind written in the pre-Romantic era. He points out the similarity in the languid sentimentality of Florinda to heroines like Clarissa and Julie in eighteenth-century novels, all of whom prefer tearful affliction to action. It is also interesting to note that the first-person narrative style and tragic tone of the poem resembles another popular eighteenth-century form, the melologue, or 'tragic scenario for one person,' similar to Hernanz Dávila's dramatic monologue mentioned above.

Merritt Cox is illuminating on a number of issues. He notes that the tendency in the late eighteenth century "to turn every situation into an emotional spectacle enhances the writers' or characters' ability to step outside himself, to become a spectator of his own personal drama."[11] Florinda takes pleasure in contemplating the heart-breaking drama in which she plays the role of the innocent victim, and establishes herself as a typical Rousseau-like pre-Romantic heroine, languid, yet more philosophical and anxious to enjoy every nuance of mental pleasure attending her affliction and anguish than her helpless descendant, the Romantic heroine.[12]

Cox also draws attention to Cadalso's innovativeness in literary technique. His use of the letter allows expression of a new aesthetic in eighteenth-century literature, the natural goodness of a girl's feelings, none of which is disdained, not even her tears. In this he is in tune with his century in its predilection for enjoying the outpouring of grief, affirmed by the poet Oliver Goldsmith: "the distresses rather than the faults of mankind make our interest in the piece."¹³ While Florinda's letter is a vehicle for tearful release, Cox may overstate her innocence in declaring that it is not an instrument of revenge. Her desire for vengeance is expressed strongly on several occasions, notably as she flees through the palace, crying: "Venganza," sí, "venganza," repetía, / "y al cielo y a la tierra la pedía" ["Vengeance," yes, "vengeance," I repeated / "and asked it of heaven and earth"] (l. 171–72). It is precisely her desire for revenge that prompts her to write asking her father to do that which she lacks courage to perform. Her plan to lure Roderick into the garden fails: "Ya me falta el aliento / para la grave empresa meditada" [Now I lack the strength / for the grave and meditated plan] (l. 197–98), while her letter is the means by which Julian will betray his country to avenge their dishonor.

The irony of Florinda's dishonor lies in the fact that it is her virtue and gratitude that lead to her undoing, again a fashionable theme then. Her contemplation of suicide at the end, echoing Florinda's suicide in Miguel de Luna's version, was also an ending characteristic of epistolary novels of the time. However, although the king is not portrayed initially as villainous, "El era rey y joven y era amante" [He was the king, and young, and acted with fondness] (l. 35), and Florinda is not unmoved by his attentions, his rape of her while unconscious introduces a macaber, blacker tone of sexual violence that is a new departure in the life of the legend.

Such elements of eroticism and ghoulishness also become more widespread in the Gothic novels of this era, a notable example of which is the English writer Matthew Lewis's *The Monk*, a supernatural and erotic satire of Jesuits, contemporary with an extraordinary novel entitled *El Rodrigo* [Roderick] published in Madrid in 1793 by Pedro Montengón, who was born in Alicante in 1745 and studied at the Jesuit college there before acting as grammar master. At the age of twenty-one Montengón became involved in the astonishing expulsion of the Jesuits from various European kingdoms that later resulted in the abolition of the Order itself. This had arisen because of hostility toward the Jesuits fostered by the conviction that they had become an independent power within the church, ruthless in their advancement and extremely wealthy, as well as proving themselves adverse to royalty and agents of papal interference in royal authority. Their control of education and teaching, their scandalous trading between South America and the East Indies, and their encouragement of disobedience to civil and ecclesiastical authority resulted not only in satire, but also in the enforced departure of all Jesuits from Spain. As a Jesuit novice, Montengón was exiled to Italy, where he left the Order, though he lived most of his life there with his wife and daughter, dying in Naples in 1824.

El Rodrigo was designated as a 'romance épico' [epic romance] by its author, apparently intended as a prose outline in twelve books of a poem Montengón did write later, although he in fact followed a very different plan. The poem *La pérdida de España reparada por el rey Pelayo* [The Loss of Spain Restored by King Pelayo], written in 1820, is tangential to the legend in so far as it concerns restoration rather than loss. Julian is a furious avenger and Witiza and Roderick are both tortured, wild, and prey to desperation, while Florinda is a *femme fatale* who arouses uncontrollable passion in Tarif and the caliph as well as Roderick, and is a dark and tormented character in comparison with her counterpart in the novel, which deserves more detailed consideration.

El Rodrigo is based on the historical events surrounding King Witiza and his sons, out of which Montengón identifies the three causes of the loss of Spain—Visigothic decadence, love, and fate. Roderick is doomed from the very first day of his reign, coming to the throne as a man of "humanidad, justicia y clemencia"[14] [humanity, justice, and clemency], yet alarmed and saddened by an evil portent in the form of a comet that appears on his coronation day. Montengón makes a number of compelling innovations to traditional material, one of which is Florinda's love for Evanio, eldest son of Witiza. In addition, the initially heroic Roderick is demeaned by his villainous adviser Guntrando, an almost Iago-like figure who plots the death of Witiza's sons as an act of revenge because the king banished him from his court. Guntrando tries to manipulate Roderick to persuade him to wield his royal authority over the princes: "El poder y la autoridad del soberano no deben avasallarse a ninguna ley: su querer es la suprema ley en tierra"[15] [The sovereign's power and authority should not be in vassalage to any law: his wish is the supreme law on earth]. However, Roderick will not comply, claiming that kings who abuse their authority degenerate into tyrants.

Guntrando taps into Roderick's Achilles' heel, his passion for Florinda, to achieve his aims, when the king, who is prey to the conflicts and torments of his feelings, resorts to his adviser for help. At this point the quasi-incestuous theme latent in Pedro de Corral's version reemerges as Roderick pretends to take on the role of substitute father to Florinda: "encubriéndole su ardiente pasión y ostentando cariño de padre"[16] [hiding his fiery passion from her and giving an appearance of fatherly affection]. New to the legend is the moral conscience Roderick reveals as he realizes not only the baseness of what he is planning, but also what his violation might lead to. He anticipates the invasion at this early stage, whereas in all other versions, he has no idea of what will follow. Yet Guntrando manages to persuade him to take Florinda out into the country to better achieve his ends. The classical influence on Montengón is evident in the innovatory grotto scene in which Florinda is tricked by a servant girl in Guntrando's pay into bathing naked in a grotto with a crystal fountain, watched by several prostitutes wearing wood-nymph costumes. Roderick arrives as arranged to take full advantage of her. This scene, probably inspired by the description of the Emperor Tiberius's retreat on Capri by Suetonius or Tacitus,[17] is striking in its fusing of the erotic and tawdry with purity and innocence.

Later, as Florinda flees from the fight in which her cousin Atanagildo kills Guntrando, she finds herself in another *locus amoenus*, the paradise setting of trees, silence and running water beloved of classical, biblical, and medieval writers. In this happier version of the grotto scene, by unconvincing coincidence Florinda happens to meet her fiancé Evanio, now living as a shepherd. Reunited, they vow vengeance on Roderick and apprise Count Julian of what has happened. The king finds out and swears to have Julian's throat cut. In another new episode, while out hunting in a forest, Roderick comes upon Adenulfo, a two-hundred-year-old magus who is the guardian of a secret temple and the urn it shelters: "la guarda de la urna de cuya conservación dependía la de la nación goda"[18] [guarding the urn upon whose preservation depended that of the Gothic nation]. Montengón combines the legend of the enchanted tower of Toledo in which Roderick discovers the depiction of the Moorish invasion with elements from Grail legend, fusing medieval religious and historical myths to conform to his story structure. Adenulfo tells the king that if the urn is broken or opened, the nation and monarch will both perish. Inside the temple, a cave taken from Grail stories, carved with alarming effigies and lit by lamps, Roderick overcomes the magus, breaking the urn to reveal the canvas depicting the imminent Arab invasion. His reason struggles with his emotions as he persuades himself that the canvas was a trick contrived by the old man.

He soon has reason to believe Adenulfo's prediction, for meanwhile, Julian, Evanio, and Florinda are heading a fleet of Moorish soldiers bent upon the invasion of Spain. At this stage, Florinda has serious doubts about the outcome of their revenge, which will bring devastation, fire, and the destruction of her own people, but her fears are dismissed as unworthy by Evanio. Astonishingly, Florinda rides into battle on horseback dressed as a warrior, fighting as part of the Moorish army! Montengón's alignment of his heroine with the militant Muslim warrior is a huge leap onward from the association of Julian's daughter with the Moors by virtue of her name La Cava evident in earlier reworkings. But her triumph in this guise is short-lived. Her lover Evanio dies, and Roderick, victorious in this initial battle, orders all Muslim enemies to be killed. In a scene taken from Tasso's *Jerusalén libertada*, the king fails to recognize the disguised Florinda on the battlefield and tragically kills her with his own hand.

Montengón concludes his story by presenting a very favorable view of the caliph: "su ánimo, superior a cualquier adversidad, y su mente, impertérrita en sus grandiosas miras, no se acobardan enteramente"[19] [his spirit, greater than any adversity, and his mind, imperturbable in its grandiose designs, showed no trace of cowardice]. He visits Mecca, where the miraculous voice of the prophet tells him he must conquer Spain, and as the Moors defeat Roderick at the River Guadalete, the king sees in the Moorish vanguard the replica of the image depicted on the canvas in the urn. The prophecy is fulfilled. True to the earliest versions of the story, no one knows if Roderick escapes or dies at the end.

Montengón used themes from national and particularly, medieval, history in his poetry as a patriotic exercise, and he combines this in *El Rodrigo* with a plot that appeals strongly to the senses, and to imaginative pleasure, in which the prophetic elements echo those of the earliest Arabic accounts. Those elements of religious tolerance and the dominant power of fate that were criticized by the inquisition in his novel *Eusebio* are present too, as are bloody and macabre events such as Guntrando's gruesome death and Florinda's rape, laced with frequent supernatural happenings in the form of comets, the magical urn, and the voice of Mohammed among others. One of the strengths of the novel, of considerable interest in the evolution of the story, is the psychological depth of Roderick, described by Carnero as a Byronic hero with an ambiguous and split personality.[20] He is certainly a desperate man, whose feelings fluctuate as his reason and goodness battle with his overwhelming sexual desires. He is to a large extent a fusion of the Romantic hero with classical and medieval elements, and he does not emerge as the villain of the piece.

Montengón's achievement lies in his innovations to the plot, introducing a number of new scenes that revitalize the legend. The work is marred not only by what Menéndez Pidal describes as linguistic errors and vulgarisms, but also by over-contrivance, unsophisticated use of coincidence and the excessiveness of melodrama. In spite of this, it is important as the first historical novel of Spanish Romanticism,[21] earlier even than the great historical novels of Sir Walter Scott, and reaffirms the regenerative power of the legend that once more is the vehicle for evolution of literary form.

The development of the legend of Roderick and La Cava in eighteenth-century Spain thus reveals an expansion of the basic story to include peripheral figures, as well as more finely tuned psychological development of characters in line with the sensibility of the time. As in earlier centuries, the legend shows flexibility in its ability to adapt to the dominant trends of the time, in this case focusing upon feelings and senses, in combination with eighteenth-century interest in classical traditions. The figures of

Florinda and Egilona come to the fore as the legend grows in scope and diversity of interpretation.

Roderick Abroad: England

The first manifestations of the legend outside Spain in dramatic and operatic forms, as it was embraced by William Rowley in England and by early Italian librettists, were regenerated in both countries in the early eighteenth century. Nearly one hundred years after *All's Lost by Lust* was written, English audiences were treated to a new version of Rowley's plot in the form of a five-act play entitled *The Conquest of Spain*, by Mary Pix. The first woman writer to tackle the theme, Mrs. Pix burst onto the London stage in 1696, having published a novel and two plays in one year. The daughter of a vicar, she was born in Nettlebed in Oxfordshire in 1666, and married George Pix, a merchant tailor from Kent, when she was eighteen. They had a daughter who died in 1690. Very few details of her life are known beyond these, though her writing career spanned ten years during which her output was steady. Her debut novel, *The Inhumane Cardinal, or Innocence Betrayed*, warns women to be aware of deceivers of their own sex, and has many aspects later apparent in her plays, including characters that are either supremely good or supremely bad, a plethora of violent deaths, bloodshed and murder, conflicts of love and honor, and sentimentality. An enthusiasm for Oriental and Spanish themes is evident in the titles of her first two plays, *Ibrahim, the Thirteenth Emperor of the Turks*, acted in Drury Lane in 1696, and a farce called *The Spanish Wives*. They were a success, and encouraged her to write five more plays by 1700, prior to which she had come under the influence of William Congreve. In her edition of Mary Pix's plays, Edna Steeves remarks that "Like many a minor writer, Mrs Pix more faithfully mirrors the taste of her age, whatever its failures, than many of her contemporaries whose works time has judged of greater artistic worth."[22] This comment has relevance to the nature of the evolution of drama at the time, and also to the political situation, both of which bear upon the deployment of the Roderick legend in *The Conquest of Spain*.

In the decade of her writing, 1696–1706, there were significant changes in the London theatrical world. The playhouse audience consisted mainly of nobility and royalty, and it expected wit and polish, and relished bloodthirsty scenes. As a result, the preferred types of play were heroic tragedies with themes of love and honor, and licentious comedies. The censorship of plays in eighteenth-century Spain had a parallel in England in the Lord Chamberlain's call in 1695–96 for stricter licensing of plays on moral grounds, reflecting an upper middle class morality stricter than that of audiences in Charles V's time.

The presence of women was becoming an increasingly influential factor, both as members of the audience and as playwrights themselves. Steeves points out that between 1695 and 1696, five new plays written by women appeared on the stage.[23] Yet few women writers dared claim their works because of the prevalent satire and prejudice against their sex, though Mary Pix, "a feminist before feminism became trendy,"[24] sought to defend women against attacks upon character and intelligence, serving as a model for other women to aspire to in her success as a playwright.

So it was within this context that *The Conquest of Spain* was the first fresh play performed at the new Queen's Theatre in the Haymarket in May 1705, lasting only six days. Although based on *All's Lost by Lust*, Mary Pix made substantial alterations to the plot and rewrote most of the dialogue in blank verse. Her prologue excuses the choice of tragedy, slates contemporary French and Italian drama as "far-fetch'd Trash" and uses the male voice throughout, the latter indicating the diffidence she felt in presenting the play as a woman dramatist, even as late as 1705. This diffidence does not extend to the portrayal of the play's two female heroines, Jacincta and Margaretta, who demand maximum sympathy on account of their abuse and betrayal by men.

As the scene is set in Act 1, we discover that both Antonio and Margaretta are linked by family to Julianus, Antonio as his nephew, and Margaretta as the daughter of a dear deceased friend, whom he brings up as his own child alongside his daughter Jacincta. Nephew and ward marry in secret, in collusion with a new and evil character, Alvarez, purportedly Antonio's lifelong friend, who has lustful designs upon Margaretta, later inventing Antonio's bigamous marriage to a noblewoman in order to achieve his ends. There is no Dionysia in this plot, an omission that ennobles Antonio, who is beyond reproach as a lover and soldier. Margaretta's social status is also raised in the play in its insistence that she is Antonio's equal in birth, not the lowly orange-seller she was in Rowley's version.

Again in contrast with the earlier play, King Rhoderique is thoroughly corrupt and decadent. Antonio describes him as "the Inglorious King, / Who wastes his life in Luxury and Ease," a comment borne out in Act 2 when Rhoderique sends Julianus to war and remarks to his servant Clothario: "Let Heroes mind the Business of the War, / To love and to possess is all my Care." If monarchy is vice-ridden, Julianus as patriarchal figure is its antithesis, "A rough, unpolish'd, perfect Soldier," whose loyalty to the king is stronger than anything else. The king has recalled his general from retirement to counter the Moorish invasion of Spain, the cause of which Julianus identifies as the decadence of the Visigothic court: "'Tis from our Wantonness, our slothful Ease, / From our Neglect of Arms, the Moors presume / Thus to defy us at our very Gates."

As her father departs for war, Jacincta is full of a foreboding entirely justified in Act 2, when Rhoderique has her forcefully separated from Margaretta and taken to his chambers, where he rapes her. Twice in this act, Margaretta voices her bitter criticism of the Spanish, which she calls "this barbarous, infernal Race," aligning herself for preference with the Moors when her friend is so violently snatched away by the king's servants: "Inhuman Monsters, Fiends of Hell, / Better the Moors shou'd be our Lords than you." To intensify Jacincta's suffering, Mary Pix makes an important innovation to the plot in introducing Theomantius, a nobleman betrothed to Jacincta but believed to have been killed during a prior battle. In Act 3, the consequences of the king's violation lead on inexorably to the tragic end. Julianus makes a victory speech against the Moors that is disappointingly trite and conventional in its prejudice, employing familiar imagery to assert his military superiority. As Mullymumen and other Moorish prisoners are brought before him, Theomantius unexpectedly appears among them, having escaped from Moorish capture while wrongly assumed to be dead. Amid Julianus's joy at his return, Jacincta arrives at the camp, having escaped from court by stealing a servant's keys, as in Rowley's play. In a scene taken from the Jacobean play with one important difference, Jacincta reveals the terrible truth of her violation to her father. Interestingly, Pix disguises her as a Mooress when breaking the news to Julianus. While Pilar Cuder-Domínguez suggests that this Moorish costume hints at the defilement and alienation she has undergone and projects a symbolic image of the future of Christian Spain,[25] in my view Jacincta needs to take on Moorish identity in order to convey the truth. It is what gives her words authenticity in Julianus's eyes, before she reveals her actual identity to him. It is one of the few instances in the play, as in Margaretta's vitriolic words in Act 2, where Moors are aligned with an authenticity, nobility, and honor that the Spanish king and his court lack.

What happens next exonerates Julianus of the treacherous betrayal so often attributed to him in past and future versions. Theomantius and Antonio enter and discover Jacincta's plight. In a passion of revenge, Theomantius urges Antonio to join him against the king: "What is it guards our Arms from just Revenge? / Come on, and let us rush upon the Tyrant, / Tear him from his voluptuous Seat of Power, / And show the Monster bare, the Beast of Rapine." To make matters worse, they take Julianus's Moorish prisoners to fight on their side against Rhoderique. At no point will Julianus concur with this behavior, declaring: "Forbear, forbear, / Nor ever let such Sounds approach my Ears," before rushing after them in an attempt to restrain the rebellion, to no avail. Theomantius therefore has an important purpose in this play, which is to redeem Julianus from blame.

Act 4 is given over to the denouement of the parallel plot, in which Margaretta plans to kill Antonio (without the help of a Mooress, in this case) when Alvarez tells her that he plans to visit her that night. He intends to take Antonio's place in her bed, as in a similar scene in *All's Lost by Lust*, but in the nick of time, Antonio himself appears, discovers the betrayal, and kills his erstwhile friend on the spot. In this secondary plot, the lustful transgressor is foiled, in contrast with Rhoderique in the main narrative, though not before the dying Alvarez has accused Antonio of conspiring to murder the king, resulting in the lovers' imprisonment.

The final act descends into melodrama, as most of the Spanish characters die or are killed. In a touching scene between the king and Julianus, the latter upbraids him for his lustful tyranny, but refuses to injure him, assisting him to escape the clutches of the approaching victorious Moors. Jacincta, mortally wounded by accident, accuses Julianus of treason (unjustly in my view), declaring that even her rape by the king does not justify such treachery. Through Jacincta's speech, Mary Pix expresses an aspect of the legend previously identified as problematical, namely that violation is not sufficient reason to betray one's country, when it could have sufficed to kill Rhoderique alone to avenge dishonor. Fortunately Jacincta forgives her father before she dies, upon which Theomantius also kills himself by falling on his sword. Julianus, also dying, begs Mullymumen to allow Antonio and Margaretta free passage out of Spain, to which he agrees before proclaiming himself king of Spain.

Mary Pix's presentation of the unfailing purity of her heroines, and the crude parallel drawn between Jacincta's body and the Spanish nation underline the two main axes of her play. The first, the vulnerability of the female sex and its natural goodness, to which the playwright alludes in the epilogue, clearly become powerful destructive forces when abused by men. The second axis, the violation of Spain by the Moors which mirrors that of Jacincta, exploits contemporary political issues for dramatic purposes. The subject of Spain was no less engaging in Mary Pix's time than it had been in William Rowley's. Her play was written during the War of the Spanish Succession (1702–13), in which the English supported a rival candidate to the Spanish throne in order to prevent the French grandson of Louis XIV, Philip, from becoming king and thereby cementing an alliance between two powerful Catholic kingdoms threatening to England. The ambivalent feelings of the English toward Spain seemed even more acute. It has been suggested that England defined itself and the character of its overseas expansion in relation to Spain, as a nation with strong similarities to itself, but also with crucial differences. England prized its nobility and power, like Spain, but was a free Protestant country dependent on trade as opposed to an absolutist, Catholic one.[26]

Mary Pix, a strong Whig supporter, chose to depict the story of Spain's defeat in a play whose very title, *The Conquest of Spain*, intimates a certain allegiance with the power that conquers tyranny, rather than conveying sympathy in loss, as Rowley's title does. Spanish imperialism would have been morally and politically repugnant to her as a Whig, and also as the protégée of Congreve. His critique of absolute power in both State and family in *The Mourning Bride* are issues also addressed in Pix's play. Patriarchy and monarchy are forms of tyranny that fail in each case. Rhoderique is uncompromisingly villainous, and undeserving of his throne, and of Julianus's old-fashioned loyalty. His decadence is a sign of internal disorder and external weakness to attack, giving the Moors a victory that must have had a resonance for theatre-goers immediately after England's recent capture of Gibraltar. The religious conflict between Catholicism and Islam is never referred to in *The Conquest of Spain*, as it is in William Rowley's work. There is no hankering after an Islamic future, for the religious dimension is absent from the play. Nor are Mary Pix's Moors much more than conventional representations of contemporary prejudices.

The failure of patriarchy mirrors that of monarchy. Although Julianus is frequently referred to as 'God-like' in his role as father and protector, he is ultimately disempowered in spite of his unflinching virtue. Courtly vice and corruption is contrasted with the honorable life of the soldier, but Julianus fails as the guardian of Rhoderique's throne, "thou Guardian Genius of my Throne" (Act 1) as well as in his role as the father of Jacincta. The links of legitimate family are broken, while the adopted children triumph through Julianus's guardianship of them, by escaping to freedom. In the same way that the legitimate royal Catholic line must make way for the unlawful invader, the true family line perishes and gives way to the assumed family, which will have a future in Margaretta's unborn child. That such issues were at the heart of Mary Pix's recreation of the Spanish legend is borne out by her epilogue, again written in the male voice, in which she marks the difference between England's beloved ruler, Anna, aided by the triumphant Marlborough who led British troops against France and Spain, and King Rhoderique, who loses his throne. As Orr points out,[27] imperialism is defined negatively as an immoral pursuit of power productive of tyranny, without any admiration for the achievements of Catholic expansionism. The future in her play lies in a new, non-Catholic regime, and in the life of her heroine Margaretta and her child.

Roderick Abroad: Italy

The most outstanding reformulation of the legend in the eighteenth century was created out of an astonishing conjunction of circumstances and people. Italian interest in the story combined with exciting new developments in opera to inspire a brilliant librettist, Francesco Silvani (d. 1728/44?) and one of the greatest composers of all, Georg Friedrich Handel (1685–1759), to construct the masterly opera known by the title *Rodrigo*. The potent dramatic interest of the Roderick legend made it the subject of a remarkable number of Italian operas of the late seventeenth century, whose composers included Gasparini (1694) and Bassani (1696).[28] The story lent itself in a variety of ways to the manner in which opera was evolving at this time, in particular in relation to the creation of *opera seria*, devoted exclusively to sublime topics and thereby eliminating the comedy of the Venetian style. Meaningful delivery of significant verse in grand productions chimed with the demands of the audience for visually spectacular works and for the vocal virtuosity of solo singers. This built on the increasing emphasis in the late seventeenth century upon solo singing and the *aria*, partly due to less demand and less available money for large choruses, and partly to the limited musical dimension of the recitative, used as a vehicle to tell the story expressively. It is this use of the *aria* as a focus of musical interest Handel exploits so successfully in *Rodrigo* to develop his characters while allowing the singers to display their technique without compromising on dramatic impetus.

This was the operatic climate at the time Handel arrived in Italy from Germany in the autumn of 1706, aged twenty-one, after acting as a composer and orchestral player for the Hamburg opera house in 1704 and 1705. It was essential for ambitious composers of the time to make their mark in the field of opera composition, and since Italy was the center of European opera and Venice was at its heart, it was a natural choice to make. Early on Handel must have met the abbot Francesco Silvani, about whose life very little is known beyond his virtuosity as a librettist. Between 1691 and 1716 Silvani collaborated with nearly all the leading opera composers, particularly Gasparini, producing librettos for various theatres in his birthplace of Venice almost every year, and serving Ferdinando Carlo, Duke of Mantua, from 1699 to 1705. He was identified with reform librettists such as Zeno and Pariati, whose movement toward a limited rationalism was reflected in clearly motivated and historically based plots, elevated diction, and extensive passages of recitative, from which comedy and subplots were excluded. Silvani's work enjoyed high literary esteem, borne out by the exquisite poetry of the *Rodrigo* libretto.

It appears that Silvani's heroic plots often had historical characters, while their contexts were fictionalized. This tendency was consonant with the popularity among audiences of plots drawn from history, especially from the classical and Roman periods, and the opera scholar Winton Dean notes that political themes with a moral flavor were often grafted onto the purely erotic motivation of older dramas.[29] As has so often been the case in the course of its history, the legend of Roderick and La Cava fitted this bill perfectly. His musical drama, *Il duello d'amore e di vendetta* [The Duel of Love and Revenge], was performed during the carnival season of 1699–1700 in Venice at the Vendramino theatre, and was set by M.A. Ziani, with the famous castrato Nicolini singing the part of Rodrigo. In it he adapts a version of the Roderick legend taken, he states in the plot summary, from the Italian historian P. Foresti, presumably Jacobus Philippus Foresti, a late medieval historian.[30] An opera on a Spanish theme would have been significant to audiences at a time when Italy was in the throes of the war of the Spanish succession (1700–1714), which arose from the dynastic rivalry between the Bourbons and the Hapsburgs. The Austrian Hapsburg Archduke Charles, proclaimed Charles III of Spain, had allies in Venice, but was opposed by Florence and the Papal States who sided with France and the Bourbons. In this era, opera texts regularly hinted at political events, and Reinhard Strohm[31] notes that such themes became obsessively frequent in Italian opera, especially those of the librettist Silvani. In this case, *Rodrigo* alludes to the strictly contemporary events of the War, evidently from a Francophile viewpoint, since the opera was written for performance in Florence.

This libretto was in turn adapted for Handel's purposes, though not radically altered. Strohm remarks that the most striking constant in Handel's operatic writing is that he never set new texts, only those already in existence. His starting point was always something given, which caught his imagination.[32] One important change was the title, which became *Vincer se stesso è la maggior vittoria* [To Conquer Oneself Is the Greatest Victory], taken from the end of the libretto and epitomizing the moral of the work. However, this title was no less cumbersome than the original one of Silvani, and the shorter form of *Rodrigo* came to be used. Handel's performance score is no longer in existence, though it is known that he composed it in Rome between the adapting of the libretto and the production version for Florence, where the opera was first performed in 1707. The composer was presented with one hundred sequins and a service of plate for his efforts, which indicate that the work had a positive reception. It is interesting to note that the overture to *Rodrigo* was the first music by Handel to be heard in London, in January 1710, where it was played as incidental music at a revival of Ben Jonson's *The Alchemist* at the Queen's Theatre. The work was deemed incomplete until the discovery in 1983 of the entire Act 3 in a long lost copy among the Earl of Shaftesbury's collection. Only one small gap now remains, which is the opening of Act 1. The opera was not performed again until 1984, 270 years later, although it was deemed by Reinhard Strohm to be ". . .the most 'modern' opera Handel wrote before *Radamisto* in 1720" on account of its elements of heroic determination and sentimentality.[33]

In terms of story evolution, *Rodrigo* is a milestone in the life of the legend. The dictates of the musical genre significantly affect the story and foster its growth and originality, for they define plot development. In this most elaborate of art forms, the presence of music strengthens, inflects, or renders words more subtle, intensifying the relationships between individual characters. While the opera has a historical setting and basis, it is the legend itself, the fiction, that facilitates the exploration of character psychology and enables individuals to be transformed. In a work in which set and background events are pared down to a minimum, with no diluting subplot, the conflict between characters is paramount. In accord with classical unity, all the action stems from the confrontation between Rodrigo and Florinda, which in turn affects his wife Esilena, the heroine of the piece. Two other characters are also affected, Giuliano, Florinda's brother in this version and not her father, apparently because at the time the part was played by a tenor, unsuitable for a paternal role, and the king of Aragon, Evanco, usurped by Rodrigo, who is in love with Florinda.

Nominally, the opera centers upon Rodrigo, who undergoes a character change of a different kind from any previous versions, in which at most he repents as a good Catholic. For reasons related to the plot and to the operatic conventions of the time, his tyrannical side is not dominant. As Hicks points out,[34] on the whole, Baroque music did not lend itself to the depiction of tyranny. Although he is accused of being a tyrant by Florinda and Evanco, he has the virtue of courage under attack, and latterly, of true affection under the influence of Esilena's love. His villainy is also mitigated in so far as he has only usurped the kingdom of Aragon in the opera. Evanco here is the rightful king, whose father Witizza has been betrayed by Rodrigo. While there is some historical accuracy in the notion that the two sons of Witizza, named as Evanco and Siseberto in the opera, bore a grudge against King Roderick for claiming the Visigothic crown in their place, Evanco was never a monarch nor had any connection with Aragon. However, in this reworking, Evanco undertakes a civil war against Rodrigo, thus bypassing the whole issue of the Moorish invasion of Spain, and siding with Florinda and her brother against him. Handel also added extra scenes at the start of Acts 1 and 3 that are important in rendering Rodrigo a more credible character. As Dean observes, "In Act 1, feeling free to repudiate Florinda now that Giuliano's victory has secured the kingdom, he exasperates her beyond endurance by his callousness. This makes a stronger motive for her implacable resentment than a seduction several years earlier."[35]

The secondary male characters have essential traits sharply drawn but are on the whole unconvincing. Evanco, as indicated, is vital to the plot, and shows himself to be defiant and brave when captured by the king. Yet the audience is told none of the backstory that would explain his professed love for Florinda and her rejection of him in the past. He is oblivious of her faults and of her dishonor by Rodrigo, pledging himself to her wholeheartedly as they unite against him, but one is left with the feeling that after Florinda's rebuff by Rodrigo, Evanco is a port in a storm, and ultimately plays the role of second best.

Florinda's dishonored brother Giuliano has none of the venom of earlier Count Julians, and his treachery is in a minor key. Staunchly loyal to Rodrigo and victorious in the Castilian battle with Aragon, he is duly outraged when Florinda reveals her betrayal by the king for whom he has just risked his life. In a complete volte-face, he immediately sides with Evanco, whom he has just captured, and with his sister, heading a rebellion against Rodrigo. His defection to the Aragonese is underlined by his proclamation of Evanco as rightful king of Castile, but his betrayal does not have the far-reaching consequences of his predecessors' betrayal of Spain to the Moors. In fact, he could be seen as a somewhat gullible character, unaware in his loyalty to Rodrigo of the king's lustful nature, and too honorable to refuse a meeting with Rodrigo's general Fernando, who tricks and captures him. Giuliano is saved from death only at the last minute by an arrow from Evanco which kills Fernando on the spot.

The adopted title of the opera, *Rodrigo*, belies the supremacy of the two female characters, Florinda and Esilena. They hold the power in the plot, and are set in opposition to each other in character and position. Florinda is an energetic, dynamic personage, to a far greater extent than in any of her previous incarnations. She is angry, passionate, cruel, and prey to ambition. As the curtain rises, Rodrigo and Florinda are in the middle of a confrontation which launches the action and establishes the central plot theme, her betrayal by the king. She is furious with Rodrigo for not fulfilling his promise to marry her and make her queen. As in the English plays by Rowley and Pix, the king claims that he is above the law, that a different set of rules apply to him as opposed to the common people: "Florinda, ha varia legge / il re dal volgo" [Florinda, the king has a different law / from that of the common people] (Act 1, Scene 1). He goes on to accuse her of "blind ambition," insulting her by suggesting she was too easy a conquest and that he has lost interest. The accentuation of her desire for personal gain and power is a new departure in terms of her development within the legend; she was clearly not unwillingly seduced by Rodrigo, a possibility only hinted at in earlier versions.

It is as if her feelings of guilt and repentance fuel her furious desire for revenge. She is implacable when Esilena offers her the throne and her husband too, and the queen describes her as "Qual baccante megera" [That shrewish bacchante] Act 1, Scene 10. Even Giuliano accuses his sister of committing a crime, from which he largely absolves her on account of her repentance. Her cruel, demonic fury, as Esilena puts it, is ironically rewarded at the end, for her ambitions to become queen are fulfilled in her marriage to Evanco, whom Rodrigo reinstates as king of Aragon.

A further innovation to the legend is the baby son born illegitimately to Florinda and Rodrigo, an element important in the musical version of the legend performed in London in 2001. The child saves Rodrigo's life, for Esilena arrives with him in her arms when Florinda is on the point of killing the king. Her maternal instinct proves stronger than her hatred, for as a mother poised to kill the father of her child, she relents and allows Rodrigo his life. In the end, Rodrigo makes his son heir to the throne of Castile.

The irony of this scene and its outcome is strong, for Esilena, the king's lawful wife, is barren, and can never be the mother that Florinda has become unwillingly. Yet Esilena is undoubtedly the heroine of the opera. She wields extraordinary power on both personal and political levels, is skilled in diplomacy, noble, selfless beyond the norm, devoted to her undeserving husband, and the source of wisdom and rationality. Rodrigo, initially lustful, tyrannical, hasty, and injudicious, is saved on every level by Esilena, and is transformed into a repentant, just, and loving man by her constancy and devotion. The parallel established between conflicts among individuals and wars between rival states is reinforced by Esilena's role as adviser to the king. When Rodrigo announces the Castilian victory over the Aragonese rebellion to her, she hints at both the earlier title and the denouement of the opera when she praises his victory: "Molto vincesti; un più sublime e degno / triunfo ancor ti resta" [Much you have conquered; but a more sublime and worthy triumph awaits you] (Act 1, Scene 4). His success on the battlefield is of less moment than his personal success in conquering his lustful nature.

Esilena further shows her power and authority over Rodrigo by pleading successfully for Evanco's life when her husband threatens to kill him in Act 1, Scene 5. Again, in Act 2, Scene 8 she advises Rodrigo that killing Giuliano will merely fuel the rebels' rage, and Fernando agrees with her. Again, the king follows her advice. This political and diplomatic skill is matched by her power to change her husband for the better on a personal level. As early as Scene 11 of Act 1, Rodrigo is beginning to repent and acknowledge the importance of her love: "Ma in me più può la fiamma / del pudico amor tuo, che del suo sdegno" [but in me the flame of your chaste love / counts for more than all her (Florinda's) wrath]. In a very noble action, Esilena suggests that he leaves her and makes Florinda queen, as she can provide heirs to the throne. Moved by her devotion, he begins to see the error of his unfaithfulness. In the beautiful aria at the end of Act 1, Esilena speaks of her example of sublime faith to Spanish wives, in which, though she may cede her husband, she will resign herself to loving without hope.

But her selflessness is rewarded. In the exquisite duet in Act 3, Scene 2, Rodrigo swears his devotion to her, and again she encourages him before the battle against the rebels headed by Evanco and Giuliano. Esilena's sudden appearance with her husband's baby by another woman in Scene 7 is so powerful a demonstration of her love, and so painful to Florinda that she gives in to the queen. Giuliano and Evanco are appalled at this, but Esilena uses her negotiating skills in reminding them that since Rodrigo spared their lives, they should spare his in return. Evanco rightly praises her as a great queen: "deh tu, che sola puoi / le menti, e l'alme a tuo voler piegare" [O you, who alone / can bend minds and souls to your will]. As Rodrigo returns the throne to Evanco, installs Giuliano as regent of Castile until his son is of age and retires to live in peace with Esilena, Florinda finds a positive outcome in her own sins: "O qual gloria risulta ai miei delitti, / se son d'essi gran pregi / rendere i regni, e migliorare i regi" [O what glory results from my sins, / if they have the great premium of having / restored kingdoms and corrected kings] (Final scene). But Esilena has the final word in repeating the original title: "Vincer se stesso è la maggior vittoria" [The greatest victory is to conquer oneself].

Winton Dean notes that it is a peculiarity of Handel's early work that the women characters are much more vividly realized than the men,[36] an aspect reinforced by the composer's emphasis on the higher voice registers. This is certainly true of *Rodrigo*, in which the strength and impact of the female characters is reinforced further by the operatic convention that obliged heroic male parts in *opera seria* to be sung by sopranos and altos. With rare exceptions, tenors and basses were confined to old men and servants, and were regarded as subsidiary in status both on and off stage. In addition, many male parts were written for women, who often specialized in what were known as 'breech roles'.

The renovation and development of the legend in *Rodrigo* went hand in hand with the innovation of Handel's musical style. As Alan Curtis comments in his notes to the libretto, the composer arrived suddenly during his stay in Italy from 1706–10 at a style that though Italianate, was strikingly his own. Some musicologists believe he was at his best during this early period. He built on established style and traditions, focusing on principal characters and themes by sweeping away the convention of ending intermediate acts with arias for secondary characters, giving the final say to a major personage and concentrating on the crucial issues of the story. The centering of *Rodrigo* upon the melodrama of the characters' emotions reflects this process, and also harks back to those earlier performance texts, the ballads, in which a similar focus exists. It is important to note that unlike previous versions of the legend, including those of the eighteenth century previously discussed, there is no trace of any religious or racial tension in this opera. There is no reference to Islam or Christianity, and in fact it is firmly set in a pagan, classical context, in which the setting of Act 3 Scene 1 in a temple of Jupiter was an anachronism required by ecclesiastical censorship. The setting is within Spain, and the conflicts are all internal ones, the civil war on a military level reflecting the inner strife of the individuals.

As a contribution to the life of the legend, Handel's *Rodrigo* is unique in its concentration upon a sentimental theme, that of self-mastery, unique in excluding race and religion, and unique in giving such imposing roles to its female characters, in particular to the king's wife, Esilena, who takes the leading role for the first time in the history of the legend. At the same time it reflects the rising star of opera in this era, and echoes features of the legend, already discussed, that typify the *zeitgeist* of the eighteenth century, particularly an emphasis upon sentiment, and the prominence of the female protagonists of the story.

The dominance of gender issues and of the performance dimension of the legend were intimately linked to political and generic concerns and developments during this era. Within Spain, the clash between the desire to express moral and social reform through theatre, and theatrical censorship that deemed the depiction of King Roderick himself as a sensitive issue led to a kind of liberation in which protagonistic characters peripheral to the king, and female characters in particular, came into the limelight, simultaneously shifting the focus in some recreations onto the restoration of Spain instead of its loss.

The rehabilitation of La Cava was growing not just in drama but also in poetry and prose, which combined an increasing renewal of interest in medieval subjects and a strong sense of patriotism with a new strain of eroticism, the supernatural and the violent that created greater psychological depth and dynamism of characterization.

This mingling of innovative expression with strong classical influences and analogies in the legend of King Roderick and La Cava produced Spain's first historical novel in the Romantic style.

Outside Spain, the legend was once more at the heart of generic development in the case of Italian opera, as Handel's *Rodrigo* strongly foregrounds its female cast, and notably Queen Egilona for the first time, while in England the female voice dominates in both author and text in Mary

Pix's play, which reveals the close links between political and gender concerns in its condemnation of patriarchy and tyrannical monarchy. These general issues in the life of the legend were also prominent at the start of the following century as the imaginative boundaries of the story widened even further.

CHAPTER 7

ROMANTICISM AND RENEWAL

The legend of King Roderick and La Cava took flight in the nineteenth century, borne on the wings of politics and poetry. The interest in the subject outside Spain that had found expression in Jacobean theatre and early opera intensified with the development of Romanticism and the accompanying nineteenth-century fascination with the medieval world. In England and France, the story was rewritten in quite divergent modes, both of which have something to say about the involvement of those two countries in the Spanish peninsular war. While the reworkings of the legend in ballad form by Abel Hugo and Émile Deschamps introduce translation and adaptation and avoid any political reference to a subject that was perhaps perceived as being too fraught, three giants of English Romanticism took up the political gauntlet to recreate powerful new readings of the story in poetry and drama, which underlined their anxiety over and commitment to the Spanish cause in the peninsular war. Sir Walter Scott's narrative poem *The Vision of Don Roderick*, Walter Savage Landor's drama *Count Julian*, and Robert Southey's epic poem *Roderick, the Last of the Goths* manifest the unique genius of their authors in harnessing pressing contemporary issues to the medieval legend to create three outstanding works that raise the Roderick narrative to new literary heights. While all three English authors were writing on the subject contemporaneously during the second decade of the century, Walter Scott was the first to publish his version in 1811, and it is with him that this chapter begins.

Politics and Prolepsis in Walter Scott's *The Vision of Don Roderick*

"We are inclined to rank *The Vision of Don Roderick* not only above the Bard, but (excepting Adam's vision from the Mount of Paradise and the matchless beauty of the sixth book of Vergil) above all the historical and poetical prospects that have come to our knowledge." Praised as of Shakespearan stature in this quotation by William Erskine, and simultaneously damned as negligible by Grierson, Walter Scott's narrative poem reinvents the medieval Spanish legend of Roderick. The striking divergence in contemporary and later critical views of the poem discloses a fundamental ambiguity and lack of clarity in the work, attributed by some reviewers to its hasty execution. In his preface to the poem, Scott himself admits it has "an appearance of negligence and incoherence," yet it is precisely this incoherence that reflects underlying but important discordances and ambivalences that convey meanings that are at cross-purposes with the apparent intention of the work.

The Vision of Don Roderick, published in July 1811, was the only major work Scott wrote in that year. Robert Southey and Count Landor were attracted to the same subject, but the *Vision* stole the thunder from Southey's own poem *Roderick, the Last of the Goths*, not published until 1814. Southey, an expert Hispanist, had discussed his planned theme with Walter, but both he and Landor proceeded at a slower pace than Scott. However, there seemed to be no ill feeling between them, since there was no real conflict. *The Vision of Don Roderick* presents a wholly different interpretation of this foundational legend of the Spanish people from those of either Southey or Landor, and marks a further turning point in its lengthy evolution since the eighth century. In contrast with the numerous earlier interpretations in drama, and in opposition to the French recreations of the story of the Visigothic king in ballads by Abel Hugo and Émile Deschamps a decade or so later, Scott chooses a distinctive form, the Spenserian stanza, to relate medieval history directly and significantly to the contemporary political situation in Britain, Spain, and Portugal.

Basing his reworking on the late-sixteenth-century Spanish source written by the notorious *morisco* Miguel de Luna, Scott focuses upon the ancient tradition that narrates King Roderick's temerity, against all good advice, in forcing an entry into a mythical, enchanted vault in Toledo. Once inside, the king sees images of Saracens depicting the impending Arab invasion of Spain, and knows that his fate is sealed. The poem, which consists of ninety-three stanzas, is divided into three sections, preceded by a fantasy Introduction where the poet invokes the muse of the mountain spirit, which advises him to seek beyond Scottish shores and look to Spain for inspiration. Each of the subsequent three sections represents a different period of historical time, beginning with the invasion of Spain by the Moors, and the defeat and death of Roderick in 711. The second period embraces the sixteenth and seventeenth centuries, when Spain has been reconquered by the Christians, who have discovered and colonized South America, but are sullied by the superstition, greed, and cruelty of the

Catholic church. The last historical section describes the invasion of Spain by Napoleon in the peninsula war of 1810–14, culminating in the recent victories of the combined British and Spanish troops. There is a Conclusion, which comprises a eulogy of the British, and particularly the Scottish, soldiers who fought in Spain to overcome the French.

Scott evokes this pageant of Spanish history in a highly inventive and original manner. Once Roderick has entered the ancient vault where his fate is to be revealed, a colossal statue of Destiny smashes a hole in the wall with his mace to reveal a series of visions of the future, which Roderick is compelled to watch. The king foresees his imminent destiny and that of his country in the future, from the eighth century up to the time of writing in the nineteenth. The theme of invasion is anchored to predestination as Scott remolds Roderick's story using the major trope of prolepsis to bring to light its relevance to the ongoing Napoleonic war. The French invasion of the Hispanic peninsula and the ensuing battle against Spanish and Portuguese forces, with the support of British soldiers, was of enormous interest at the time. Landor had actually gone to fight with the Spanish army, while for Southey the peninsula war exemplified a struggle in which good and evil were clearly defined. The conduct of the war became an obsession for Scott, born, I think, of his deeply entrenched admiration for soldiering, which he felt was the ultimate occupation, and one from which he was excluded due to his physical disability. As John Sutherland observes, no other nineteenth-century poet until Kipling was so fond of battle, as the scenes of combat that form the climaxes of all his major poems show, and the reviewer of the *Vision* in *The Eclectic Review* of August 1811 berates Scott precisely for taking up the ancient function of the bard "to celebrate military prowess, and set off pride, ferocity and revenge."[1]

At first glance, *The Vision of Don Roderick* purports to eulogize the Duke of Wellington and Scottish soldiery, betraying the excessiveness of Scott's fierce patriotism in his disproportionate stress on the triumphs of the Highland Scots regiments in the poem's conclusion. By reaching back into the historical past and gazing proleptically forward from that vantage point, Scott seems to celebrate the liberation of the much-invaded Spanish from the horrors of a tyrannical leader. However, there are significant aporias in the text, which cannot merely be attributed to the characteristic speed of execution that Sutherland had already criticized in the earlier *Lady of the Lake* of 1810, in which Scott's "helter-skelter" mode of writing "results in gaping holes in the poem's narrative."[2]

From the first, ambivalence and paradox surround Scott's portrayal of the Arab invasion of Spain, and of King Roderick himself. Roderick's portentous phrase in Part I, stanza 8, "All is not as it seems," when describing his relationship with La Cava, has strong resonances for the text as a whole.

The very opening line of the poem formulates a question, striking a note of uncertainty that predisposes the reader to wonder why Scott sets an exotic, almost glamorous tone in his prefatory allusions to Moorish influence and custom, considering the conventional view of Christian historiographers who perceived the invasion of Spain by the Arabs as catastrophic. In stanza 12 of the Introduction, the poet describes the mingling of Christian and Arab cultures as follows:

> Of strange tradition many a mystic trace,
> Legend and vision, prophecy and sign;
> Where wonders wild of Arabesque combine
> with Gothic imagery of darker shade.

The allure of the Middle East conveyed here is betokened by the vivacity of the prior "wild morisco measure" in stanza 9 and is curiously echoed in the proleptic Arabization of Roderick's soldiers as they wait for him outside Toledo cathedral, adorned with the opulent gold helmets, silver-studded belts, and ivory quivers that set them apart from their Gothic forebears (Part I, stanza 3). That simultaneous attraction and fear that is woven into Western literary and artistic representations of the Orient emerges in Scott's depiction of the Moorish invaders, who wear white turbans (stanza 20), in an intriguing inversion of the common use of white and black to symbolize good and evil, while it is the Christian Gothic king Roderick who is cast into darkness and shadow.

The poetic depiction of Roderick himself is also essentially ambiguous. So frequently cast as the villain of the piece, Scott unexpectedly treats him with some sympathy. In an evocative scene of confession before the bishop of Toledo in the cathedral, Roderick seeks to excuse his sexual passion by implying that La Cava may have encouraged him. Historically accused of conniving to murder his predecessor Witiza, Scott mitigates Roderick's crime as the king explains: "Oh! rather deem 'twas stern necessity! / Self-preservation bade, and I must kill or die" (Part I, stanza 7). After Roderick orders the prelate to open the secret vault so that he can learn his nation's "future fates," in a magnificently evoked Gothic scene of candlelight, winding staircases, dark aisles, and secret nooks, the mighty figure of Destiny in the forbidden chamber reads from a book describing lost empires and fallen kings of the past, which prefigure the narrative present. Destiny's mace then unveils "new sights of fear and wonder" but it is not until Roderick looks into the future and sees himself deserting the battlefield that he is described with scorn. It seems consonant with Scott's idealistic view of soldiery that cowardice, rather than murder or rape, should be the king's worst sin.

After the Christian defeat, the portrayal of the Arab occupation destabilizes the negative cadence of the theme of invasion, for peace and prosperity flourish:

> Far to Asturian hills the war-sounds pass,
> And in their stead rebeck or timbrel rings;
> And to the sound of the bell-deck'd dancer springs,
> Bazaars resound as when their marts are met,
> In tourney light the Moor his jerrid flings,
> And on the land as evening seem'd to set,
> The Imaum's chant was heard from mosque or minaret.
>
> (Stanza 25)

The unsettling ambiguity inherent in this description is further intensified in the second sequence, as the visionary scene is obscured by smoke, which serves to advance Roderick's proleptic view of Spain's future. As the smoke clears, the king now gazes upon the time when "The Christians have regained their heritage" (stanza 27), having overcome the Arabs, and colonized the Americas. However, the reestablished Catholic order and the wealth of the colonies do not present the expected or desired picture. Surprisingly, Spain is ruled by an anachronistic knight, Valour, who is dressed in medieval garb, and by a hermit who represents Bigotry. Scott picks up the old medieval debate between the knight and the priest by vilifying the hermit who makes the knight his slave and evilly indulges in the newly gained riches of the Americas in a shocking mix of false piety and violent cruelty: "And at his word the silver censer sways, / But with the incense-breath these censers raise, / Mix steams from corpses smouldering in the fire" (stanza 32). Scott's poem was the only English version of the Roderick legend translated into Castilian at this time, and it is a measure of how critical of Spain this depiction is that the Spanish translator saw fit to omit the offending sections and alter the text in order to glorify his countrymen instead. The Scottish poet draws on his early love of Spenser in referring to the Spanish hermit as the Archimage, mirroring the false vision and hypocrisy of Spenser's Archimago, with all the negative connotations of the deluding power of magic and the idolatrous worship of saints and images with which Catholics were associated in the Protestant view. Spenser's knight of truth, Red-Crosse, also casts a long shadow in the form of the knight Valour, with whom Scott clearly identifies in the *Vision*.

So the defeat of the Arab invaders and the reassertion of Catholic supremacy leads, paradoxically, to an even more corrupt and oppressive regime. From this highly undesirable state of affairs, the scene moves seamlessly to nineteenth-century Spain, the two eras melding together to form a continuum, which both distinguishes and conflates the characters in the new vision before Roderick's eyes. The "sad pageant of events to be" (stanza 50) becomes the war between the invader Napoleon and the Spaniards and Portuguese. Amid the climactic, extended battle scenes and the eulogies of Scottish troops and officers, Napoleon is predictably described as a ruthless tyrant obsessed with ambition, whose troops are routed by the allied forces in a number of important battles. For a second time on Spanish soil, the invader suffers defeats, and the reinstatement of the previous order is heralded and hoped for. At the end of the third vision the poet declares: "King, Prelate, all the phantasms of my brain, / Melted away like mist-wreaths in the sun" (stanza 63), in a way akin to Prospero's vision in *The Tempest*. What does not melt away is the anxiety and uncertainty the poet conveys in *The Vision of Don Roderick*. Its confusions and paradoxes suggest a conflict within the poet that is reflected in the narrative structures and in the very language and meter of the work.

If the original Arab invasion prefigures the Napoleonic invasion, and the Christian reconquerors anticipate a later conquest by the combined peninsula and British troops, the analogy casts both French invaders and the allies in an ambiguous light, due to the notably sympathetic portrayal of the Arabs, set against the very negative evocation of the Catholic colonizers. The implications are that an allied victory might potentially have undesirable disadvantages, and that perhaps Napoleon, like that other alleged villain, Roderick, might not be as black as he is painted. *The Vision of Don Roderick* is therefore contradictory, as it posits one thing, while the proleptic visions suggest the opposite.

These fundamental paradoxes at the heart of the poem are reinforced by the lexis and verse form. The "collection of new compound words and outlandish phrases" for which Scott is criticized in *The Monthly Review* of July 1811, neologisms such as "incense-breath," "gore-moisten'd," "land-flood," "mountain-rage," strain forward as if Scott were reaching out into the future to create new words to grasp ideas still elusive or repressed. Napoleon's invading might is captured in one such Manley Hopkins-like phrase, "He clutch'd his vulture-grasp, and call'd fair Spain his prize" (stanza 37), in which the compound word "vulture-grasp" fuses linguistic innovation with a kind of figurative prolepsis, for Napoleon metaphorically circles his prey and anticipates the fall of Spain, in the manner for which the bird itself is notorious.

The archaic Spenserian stanza Scott chooses for his verse form predates Byron's use of the measure in 1812 in *Childe Harold's Pilgrimage*. Harking back to Spenser's sixteenth-century innovation of this stanza of nine iambic lines, the first eight in pentameters and the last a hexameter or alexandrine, Scott adopts the poetic form in order to address contemporary politics, and also to cast a glance into his own future. His choice is inspired, for the very nature of the Spenserian stanza, as described by MacLean and Prescott in their edition of Spenser's verse, relates to "the play of analogy, pattern, and discontinuity or deferral."[3] They claim that its exaggeratedly alliterative language, which Scott exploits to the full, stresses discordancy,[4] while the longer ninth line invites a pause for reflection. Interestingly, Scott's contemporaries saw it as a verse form of gravity, well suited to express grandeur and magnificence. All these elements, analogy and pattern, discontinuity and discord, even grandeur, each play a part, as the successive and apparently analogous visions of momentous invasion and battle uncover the profound dilemmas ingrained in their ambivalence and indistinction.

Scott's debt to Spenser does not lie in the verse form alone. At the end, Walter also aligns himself with Spenser's knight Red-Crosse, who represents truth and chivalry in the *Faerie Queene*, as he announces "I strike my red-cross flag" in the last line of the *Vision*. The nature of truth is at the nub of the poem, for Scott's blending of fiction and history was not to the taste of his contemporaries, and it is this very dimension that Scott questions in stanza 61 when he asks: "Hath Fiction's stage for Truth's long triumphs room?" as if querying his whole undertaking. Yet Spenser's influence may be crucial here too, for in his letter to Sir Walter Raleigh that prefaces the *Faerie Queene*, he sets out his view of poetic renderings of historical material: "For the Methode of a Poet historical is not such, as of an Historiographer. For an Historiographer discourseth of affayres orderly as they were donne, accounting as well the times as the actions, but a Poet thrusteth into the middest, even where it most concerneth him, and there recoursing to the things forepaste, and divining of things to come, maketh a pleasing Analysis of all."[5]

As if picking up Spenser's gauntlet, Scott has turned his historical theme into one of urgent popular interest, in which the Vault of Destiny invoked in stanza 63 allows a glimpse, not only of Spain's future for Roderick, but also of the possible future for Scott and his contemporaries. As the poet concludes his work, he openly expresses the deep anxiety he feels about his own future: "O vain, though anxious, is the glance I cast, / Since Fate has mark'd futurity her own" (stanza 63). A double prolepsis suggests the uncertainty of what lies ahead, as he questions whether he dare ". . .stretch a bold hand to the awful veil / That hides futurity from anxious hope" (stanza 62).

Such anxiety may well reflect the concern with which the British people watched events in Spain, fearing a possible invasion by Napoleon themselves. But *The Vision of Don Roderick*, with what the reviewer in the July 1811 edition of *The Portfolio* described as its "train of jarring, discordant sensations," may well reflect conflicts within the poet he did not admit even to himself. The evil of invasion becomes a two-edged sword in this work, and Scott might also have felt ambivalent toward Napoleon. The arch-villain was in fact just the kind of powerful, ruthless soldier and leader Scott might have admired, and a pair of whose pistols decorated the walls of Scott's Abbotsford home. It is a hypothesis corroborated by his *Life of Napoleon* written much later, in 1827, that extended to nine volumes. Scott's official hatred of the French may have been in conflict with his inner feelings, perhaps more partisan than he dared to admit, for he was also married to a French woman, his son and heir was half-French, and he wrote the novel *Waverley*, whose ideologically unsettled hero Edward shows marked support for the Chevalier, soon after *The Vision of Don Roderick*, although he had begun the novel as early as 1808. Scott's striving for an elusive truth in his poem problematizes both Spanish history and the contemporary historical and political situation the legend of Roderick and La Cava anticipates. The trope of prolepsis works on linguistic, structural, and interpretative levels to create a narrative poem that, in its very uncertainties and equivocalness, strives to express ideas and feelings, both personal and political, as yet not fully formulated, and that belie Scott's perceived conservatism, hinting at a latent radical tendency, which if it could not find expression on the battlefield, does so emphatically in this complex and illuminating work. In the light of contemporary wars and instabilities in Europe and current tensions between Arab and Western cultures, Scott's well-founded anxiety for the future acquires great poignancy. As such, Scott's recasting of the story of Roderick and La Cava was unique in both the innovativeness of its literary form and concept and in the truly visionary manner in which its relevance to nineteenth-century European politics and history is revealed.

A Story 'Wrapt in Gigantic Mists': Walter Savage Landor's *Count Julian*

"May every Frenchman out of France perish! May the Spaniards not spare one!...I am learning, night and morning, the Spanish language...I hope to join the Spanish army immediately on my landing, and I wish only to fight as a private soldier."[6] Landor wrote these valiant, vehement words to his friend Southey prior to his departure for Spain in 1808 to fight in the peninsular war. While Scott and Southey remained at home, Landor fought for Spanish Independence on Spanish soil, where his gallantry and his gift of 20,000 *reales* to the cause were gratefully acknowledged by the Madrid government. His experience as a soldier, and the passionate feeling and heroism his words convey lie at the heart of his depiction of Count Julian, the dishonored father of La Cava, in the tragedy of that name, published finally and anonymously in 1812. With thoughts of Spain strong in his mind upon his return to the British Isles, Landor had also been reading installments of Southey's poem *Roderick*, which his friend sent to him for comment. Inspired perhaps by Southey's project, Landor brought great innovation to the legend in his conception of a five-act tragedy in verse whose subject was Count Julian.

As the prior history of the legend indicates, the blame or exoneration of either Roderick or La Cava had been a theme in various literary forms, but no one had previously attempted the protagonistic portrayal of Julian. Menéndez Pidal[7] astutely observes the Romantic spirit underlying the neoclassical form of the play, suggesting that it was Romanticism's inclination toward people debased or not understood by the poetry of earlier ages that led Landor to favor Julian, traditionally loathed in both history and poetry. His choice of protagonist was inspired, and the significance of his play within the evolution of the story is radical, as in a sense *Count Julian* epitomizes the whole project of this book, constituting a kind of mise en abyme of the development of the legend itself in its confluence of classical, medieval, Renaissance, and Romantic literary and historical elements with the personal conflicts of the author and contemporary political issues of the utmost import.

Such complexities are both revealed and illuminated by contemporary and later critical opinion of the play, within which Landor's dialogue with Southey on the subject is of crucial importance. In spite of confessing to his friend that he had "not seen a play acted a dozen times in my life,"[8] he conceived the story as a play, closely following Aristotle's precepts on classical drama, citing his models as Sophocles and Euripides and applauding his own achievement of unity of action: "the events of the first act lead naturally to the last, and every scene is instrumental to the catastrophe." As soon as Southey read the play, he commented: "It is too Greek for representation in these times."[9] The remark sets the tone for the numerous criticisms of *Count Julian* then and since. Landor's work appears to displease because it is at once too rooted in the theatrical conventions of the past and too experimental to be fully appreciated yet. On the first score, Landor's biographer, Malcolm Elwin observes: ". . .*Count Julian* presents a psychological study so unrelievedly tragic that no practical dramatist of either Shakespeare's or Dryden's age would have considered submitting it for stage production."[10] Several critics do not even consider it as a play in a theatrical sense, but as a series of imaginary conversations in verse whose characters are stark representations of overwhelming emotions, with every incidental detail pared away. Elwin felt that this demanded too much of the reader's imagination, while Waterman Evans commented in his 1892 study of Landor's work that his Greek models required him "to pitch his theme in an ideal key," impossible to sustain without drowning the human interest necessary to the harmony of the whole. Julian's magnificent speech standing before Roderick was praised by Southey as "the grandest image of power that ever poet produced," yet Evans feels such passages lose much of their force because Landor is striving to maintain too continuous a level of sublimity, with no light relief, or balancing human touches.[11]

In spite of the many perceived faults of the drama, Thomas De Quincey saw to the heart of Landor's achievement. He stated that Landor was "...probably the one man in Europe who has adequately conceived the situation, the stern self-dependency, and the monumental misery of Count Julian." His appreciation of the depth and power of Landor's work is brilliantly expressed in his comparison of *Count Julian* with Shelley's *Promethus Unbound*: "There is in this modern aërolith the same jewelly lustre which cannot be mistaken, the same *non-imitabile fulgur*, and the same character of 'fracture' or *cleavage*, as mineralogists speak, for its beaming iridescent grandeur, redoubling under the crush of misery. The colour and the coruscation are the same when splintered by violence; the tones of the rocky harpy are the same when swept by sorrow."[12] Landor was so absorbed in his creation of Julian that he shed tears over it, linking Julian's fears about the future of his country to the author's own anxieties about the Napoleonic invasion of Spain. Elwin feels that Landor had the hated Bonaparte in mind when describing Roderigo as a despised tyrant who brings a curse upon his people.[13] There is also an apparent suggestion of Bonaparte's then recent divorce from Josephine to marry the younger Marie-Louise in Roderigo's casting off of his barren wife Egilona in order to marry Julian's daughter. Landor clearly hoped not only that the comparison with contemporary politics might be acknowledged, but also that the originality of his work would be appreciated. He remarked to Southey: "if *Count Julian* is endured it will be because it is different from anything of the day, and not from any excellence."[14]

Critical opinion reveals divergent responses to this work, whose imaginative conception is strained to breaking point by the tension between its classical form and tenor and its radical originality. Too different, intellectually demanding and innovative to appeal to the many,[15] Landor had great difficulty in finding a publisher for what he tellingly described as "my *Lear*."[16] This comparison by the author with Shakespeare's play has gone unnoticed by commentators and critics, yet upon examination of the text of the drama, the importance of the analogy becomes crucial in its divulgation of significant new dimensions in both play and legend. Whether Shakespeare's *King Lear* was one of the dozen or so plays Landor had actually seen on stage, or whether he knew it through reading alone, it was evidently a powerful model for *Count Julian* in its portrayal of a tormented father whose daughter disrupts the paternal fantasy of her purity and inviolability.

Given the intensely tragic tone of Landor's play, it appears surprising that its ending lacks the deaths on stage of father and daughter we see in the case of King Lear and Cordelia. However, in the oldest dramatic version of the story, *The True Chronicle History of King Leir*, of unknown authorship and published in 1605, though probably written in the sixteenth century, Leir is reconciled with his daughter Cordella, unlike Shakespeare's version. The Gallian king who is Cordella's husband invades and defeats Cornwall and Cambria, reinstating Leir. Importantly, in all Shakespeare's known sources except this old play, Cordelia commits suicide. This aspect has special relevance to Landor, since the notorious adaptation of Shakespeare's *King Lear* by Tate after 1681, which adopted the happy ending, continued to be performed until 1823, when Kean restored the version with the tragic ending. Landor would therefore have known Tate's version, which may account for Julian remaining alive at the end of the play, while his daughter flees.

In his introduction to the play, Landor emphasizes the enormous significance of the story, noting its fundamental irony: "It is remarkable that the most important era in Spanish history should be the most obscure."[17] But it is precisely this obscurity that the playwright values, as it allows him plenty of poetic license. His sources appear to have been Corral, and whatever other historical versions were available to him, including Portuguese accounts, from which he chooses the name Covilla for Julian's daughter instead of La Cava or Florinda, deeming the latter unsuitable for the person and the period. The resemblance in sound between the word 'Covilla' in its Spanish pronunciation, and the name Cordelia is striking, and serves to illustrate Landor's preoccupation with *King Lear* at the lexical level as well as in terms of plot and tone.

In the very first scene, as Julian expresses his anguish over the loss of Spain to the Muslims, the bishop Opas counsels him to feel pity both for the Spanish people and for his daughter: "See her, Count Julian, if thou lovest God, / See thy lost child" (l. 1–2). His words at once echo Lear's loss of Cordelia, and alert us to the importance of sight so pertinent in Shakespeare's play, while Lear's torment has a parallel in Julian's plight, described again by Opas:

> . . ., when thy Covilla stands
> again an outcast, and a suppliant at thy gate,
> why that still stubborn agony of soul,
> those struggles with the bars thyself imposed?
> Is she not thine? not dear to thee as ever?
> l. 11–14

Julian hopes that ". . .I shall see again / My own lost child" (l. 28–29), and in Scene 2 of Act 1 stresses what is the crux of this play in his hope that others "...might perceive some few external pangs, / Some glimpses of the hell wherein I move, / Who never have been fathers" (l. 10–12). Yet while this may be the dominant idea of the play, the causes and motivations are vexed and complex. In his essay on *King Lear*, Harry Berger Junior asks a pertinent question: "How do characters use the roles and relationships of love, courtship and marriage, of family, court and kingdom, of race, religion and gender, to validate their pursuit of power or pleasure or pain or self-interest or love?"[18] In the case of *Count Julian*, the protagonist's tortured state of hatred arising from the dishonor of his daughter's rape by King Roderigo, a crime never alluded to directly, perhaps in order to observe what Menéndez Pidal calls "la correcta etiqueta moral"[19] [the correct moral etiquette] is part of a dense web of conflicting desires and pressures, not least of which is the relationship between king and vassal. In his dramatic revenge upon Roderigo by defecting to the side of the Moors, Julian is acting above his station as the king's general. In Act 1, Scene 1 Opas reproaches Julian: "I never yet have seen where long success / Hath followed him who warred upon his king" (l. 42–43), while Roderigo himself turns the tables upon his vassal in Scene 3 by accusing him of being an equal sinner himself: "Thy violence and fancied wrongs I know, / And what thy sacrilegious hands would do, O traitor and apostate" (l. 8–9). A paradox lies in Julian's love and loyalty to his country, which he has violated by allowing the Moors to invade Spain, in order to avenge Covilla, and it shows that he is both sinned against and sinning. He will allow no prince to ruin Spain, but ruins it himself.

A further irony is manifest in the damaging interpretations of his actions by both the king and the king's wife Egilona. In the bitter Scene 3 of Act 1 between Roderigo and Julian, the king accuses him of mad ambition and a desire for regicide, asking whether he plans to murder him and conquer Spain to rule it himself. Later, in Act 2, Scene 3, Egilona asks him: "Can it be true, then, Julian, that thy aim / Is sovranty? not virtue, not revenge?" (l. 33–34). Even Covilla's suitor Sisabert, whose father Witiza was blinded by Roderigo, and who looked upon Julian as his second father, accuses him of usurpation when he speaks to Covilla: "Thy father comes to mount my father's throne" (3.2, l. 46). Julian denies these accusations hotly, but seeds of doubt have been sown. Viewed as a father-figure and king by his soldiers, "Father, and general, and king, they shout" (3.3, l. 218), he in turn sees Spain as a mother he has lost: "And Spain! O parent, I have lost thee too!"(1. 3, l. 18), recalling the lost mother Covilla hopes to see again but never does. The loss of his daughter is transposed into the loss of his figurative mother. Yet his fury and hatred is such that he goes against Covilla even when Roderigo, accusing Egilona of barrenesss, offers Covilla his crown, his love, and his repentance. Julian refuses to accept this way out of his dilemma, and turns against his daughter in a Lear-like rage: "Covilla should not be the gaze of men, / Should not, despoil'd of honour, rule the free" (1. 3, l. 93–94). In an ironic confession to Roderigo, the perpetrator of his anguish, he reveals his changed feelings toward his daughter, akin to Lear's changed feelings for Cordelia:

> . . .One I thought
> As every father thinks, the best of all,
> Graceful and mild, and sensible and chaste:
> Now all these qualities of form and soul
> Fade from before me. not on any one
> Can I repose, or be consoled by any.
>   (1.3, l. 121–26)

He justifies his assertion of patriarchal authority over both daughter and country through his immense outrage at Roderigo's betrayal of his trust, worse, in his view, than war itself: ". . .crimes are loose / At which ensanguin'd war stands shuddering" (2.1, l. 30–31). Yet this authority has an element of egotism about it when he confides in Covilla:

> I am the minister of wrath, the hands
> that tremble at me, shall applaud me too,
> And seal their condemnation.
>   (2. 1. 36–38)

Julian's ironic tragedy is that he is the agent of his own destruction, as well as that of Spain. In seeking to restore his honor and save his country from tyranny, he is painfully aware that he has destroyed both: "I have, alas! myself / Laid waste the hopes where my fond fancy strayed" (2. 1, l. 98–99). His idyllic vision of leading a rustic life in some remote corner of Spain with Covilla "Amongst those frank and cordial villagers" (2. 2, l. 188) is reminiscent of King Lear's dream of a simple future with Cordelia, "so we'll live, / And pray, and sing, and tell old tales, and laugh / At gilded butterflies" (5. 3, l. 11–13), but can never be realized, since Julian has brought invasion and war upon the land. The tragic paradox is emphasized in the spirited scene between Julian and Roderigo in Act 4 where once more he continues to denounce the king vigorously and justify his action, perceiving himself to be truly great, and better than the king: "The truly and the falsely great here differ" (4. 1, l. 27). Ironically, Julian accuses Roderigo of the crime he has committed himself, that of betraying his people, but Julian is forced to acknowledge his own criminality: "I stand abased before insulting crime, / I faulter like a criminal myself" (4. 1, l. 120–21), his guilt and sin sitting uneasily with his avowed greatness and virtue.

Whether Julian is trapped by his roles of patriarch and vassal into seeking revenge, or whether he is using these roles to validate his pursuit of power is ambiguous. However, what is clear is that racial and religious relationships serve not to bolster the virtue of his actions but to undermine them. Julian's treachery in siding with the Moorish leader Muza and his son Abdalazis against his own king and people is not applauded by the Muslim side, but is a source of suspicion. Muza's early doubts are confirmed in Act 5, when he learns that Julian has finally allowed Roderigo to escape from his tent:

> That Julian, of whose treason I have proofs,
> That Julian, who rejected my commands
> Twice, when our mortal foe besieged the camp.
> (5. 1, l. 9–11)

The Moorish soldier Tarik continues to defend the count against rumours until in Act 5, Scene 4, Julian himself admits that he has helped the king escape. Tarik is appalled: "...Who is safe! a man / Arm'd with such power and with such perfidy!" (5. 4, l. 47–48), and again the count is accused of desiring the Spanish crown for himself, this time by the Muza: "Thou camest hither with no other aim / Than to deprive Roderigo of his crown / For thy brow!" (5. 4, l. 77–78). Julian is a traitor to both Muslim and Christian alike.

Though Julian and Covilla remain alive in the final act, akin to the original King Leir story, Julian's personal tragedy is overwhelming. Covilla survives, to live in shame, but while her father has been obsessed with his daughter in Spain, Muza's troops have captured Ceuta from him as its governor, killing both his sons in that city, following which his wife dies of grief. Julian vows vengeance upon Muza, but the final impression is one of a ruined man, as his soldier Hernando's earlier words to Tarik echo in the reader's mind: "Now plainly see I from his alter'd tone, / He cannot live much longer—thanks to God!" (5. 2, l. 30–31).

De Quincey was acute in his perception of the importance of *Count Julian*. His reference to the story as one "wrapt in gigantic mists" pertains not only to the intractable uncertainties surrounding it historically, but also to the perplexing motivational ambiguities of the characters, expressed often in a fractured, awkward language, as if Landor were grasping at the inexpressible. The critic cuts to the chase in his analysis of the play's moral meaning: "...it is the most fearful lesson extant of the great moral that crime propagates crime, and violence inherits violence, - nay, a lesson on the awful *necessity* which exists at times that one tremendous wrong should blindly reproduce itself in endless retaliatory wrongs."[20] In this respect,

Landor's interpretation of the legend of Roderick and La Cava raises it to another level in adducing this new, powerful meaning. He also moves into uncharted territory in terms of characterization, not least in his creation of Covilla, neither the evil temptress, nor entirely good in her temptation by power and wealth, of Roderigo, a sinner, but also a dignified and repentant king who to some extent foreshadows Southey's reformulation of his character, and of Egilona, torn between love and hate, who flees to the Muslim side and finds happiness with Abdalazis. But Landor's monumental achievement lies in giving Count Julian center stage, hitherto unprecedented, and there casting him in the mould of Shakespeare's arguably greatest tragic protagonist. Not only does his creation of the character of Julian focus upon the dangerous and overwhelmingly destructive power of a father's love, but in doing so elevates the story to perhaps its highest level by virtue of its Shakespearean echoes. Landor's play blends past concerns, both literary and historical, with those of the time he lived, and the final words of the play, spoken by Julian, could not fail to have moved readers who were following events in the peninsular war: ". . .– years shall roll / And wars rage on, and Spain at last be free" (5. 5, l. 33). Simultaneously the play reaches into the future, toward Spain after the civil war and Juan Goytisolo's own, brilliant rendition of Count Julian.

Roderick, the Last of the Goths: Robert Southey's Monument to Medievalism

Robert Southey (1774–1843), Poet Laureate and member of the Royal Spanish Academy, plays a part in the evolution of the legend that places him under a spotlight apart from his contemporaries or predecessors, on account of his renown and expertise as a Hispanic scholar. While sharing the concern for the invasion of Spain by Napoleon in the peninsular war with his friends Walter Scott and Landor, and aware, like them, of the contemporary political relevance of Spain's foundational story, his profound knowledge of Spanish and Portuguese literature and history and his feeling for its medieval manifestations lend an authority and rare poignancy to his versions of the tale. During his extensive travel in both Spain and Portugal as a young man,[21] where he immersed himself in the language and literature of both countries, he must have encountered Miguel de Luna's *Historia verdadera del Rey Don Rodrigo*, upon which he founded a monodrama of seventy-two lines in free verse entitled *La Caba*, written in 1802. In Longman's edition of Southey's poetical works, it appears as one of a series of dramatic monologues on the theme of rape and adultery that give the female victim a powerful voice, and is immediately preceded by a monodrama on the rape of Lucretia. Southey appends substantial notes to the text, notes clearly written much later, for he states that in this case he has taken a very different view of his subject from that adopted "when treating it upon a great scale,"[22] referring to his later epic poem on Roderick. Southey states that Miguel de Luna's history was "translated from the Arabic,"[23] suggesting that he erroneously perceived his source to be authentic, although he chooses to use the name La Caba after Fray Luis de León's ode, thus casting her as the culpable whore, and to call her father Illan as in the *Crónica de España de 1344*, thus differentiating them from the names used in his later poem and also from those of his source, which are respectively Florinda and Julián.[24]

In the monologue, Southey takes the scene in Miguel de Luna's work where La Caba is about to commit suicide by throwing herself from a high tower, before which she addresses her distraught father on the ground below. Her speech in this masterfully paced poem artfully conveys Illan's terrible predicament and his reactions to her speech. Her first words, "Father! Count Illan!" (l. 1), at once establish and emphasize his status as patriarch and aristocratic vassal of the king, encapsulating the two dimensions in which his honor is offended. La Caba's abrupt phrases, "here— what here I say, / Aloft. . .look up!. . ." (l. 1–2) show that initially Illan has no inkling of her suicidal intention or of where she is. The nine repetitions of the word 'here' in the first thirty lines not only underline her terrifying physical situation but also produce a pun on the word 'hear,' as if she is desperate to make her father listen. The very sparseness of her speech makes the reader work to imagine Illan urgently attempting to reach her as she insists that "The way is barr'd; / Thou need'st not hasten hither!—Ho! Count Illan, / I tell thee I have barr'd the battlements!" (l. 3–5). His efforts are vain, for La Caba is determined to take her own life, an appalling act through which she finally controls her destiny and becomes "free mistress of myself" (l. 9). Her powerful assertion of female independence in line 11: "I command my destiny!" combines with equally powerful blame of her father, first for bringing her back to Spain from Africa to witness the awful consequences of her violation, "where every Moorish accent that I hear / Doth tell me of my country's overthrow, / Doth stab me like a dagger to the soul" (l. 27–29), and second, for being the perpetrator of treacherous revenge.

There is an important emotional transition from victimizer to victim expressed in lines 32–34, in which she describes the "slaughter'd sons of Spain" (l. 31) as "My victims; —said I mine? Nay—nay, Count Illan, / They are thy victims!" before proclaiming "I am thy victim too, —and this death more / Must yet be placed in Hell to thy account" (l. 37–38). Her proleptic view of her future reputation, "I shall be written in thy chronicles / The veryest wretch that ere yet betray'd / Her native land!" (l. 43–45) will be redressed by Southey in his later epic poem, but here La Caba is resolute in blaming her father, in particular for taking his revenge through betrayal to the Moors, expressed through the metonym of weaponry: "Thou hadst a sword, / Shame on thee to call in the scymetar / To do thy work!" (l. 61–62). She picks up the thread of her first reference to Illan's identity from the first line of the poem in her assertion of what Illan has lost: "Thou wert a vassal" (l. 56) and "Thou wert a father" (l. 59), accusing him of betraying both roles by turning African: "Moor! turbaned misbeliever! renegade!" (l. 69). Illan has betrayed rank, race, religion, and family in her eyes and finally shame and sorrow overcome her as she leaps to her death.

La Caba's physical and psychological destruction matches that of her country, rendered martyrical by this speech of self-exoneration in which the injustice of her name blackened for posterity is forcefully presented as she wreaks her own vengeance in turning the tables and blaming her father unreservedly. Southey's presentation of the opposite portrayal of La Caba from that of his source is an eloquent statement of support for female oppression and victimization, further strengthened by his omission of the famous letter from La Caba betraying her violation to her father that is so important in Miguel de Luna's version because it precipitates the count's dreadful vengeance.

Six years later in 1808, Southey published his *Chronicle of the Cid*, a work that is both a translation and a compilation of various sources of material on Spain's greatest hero, the eleventh-century Castilian Rodrigo Díaz, El Cid, and that was very widely admired at the time. Southey's espousal of things medieval was pervasive. As Pidal notes, the poet's engagement with contemporary events in Spain was framed in medieval terminology. In his eyes those events brought back to life "the best times of chivalry, as we poets represent it; ancient honour, ancient heroism and ancient generosity have been reborn."[25] Infused with the medieval spirit, Southey began work on what would be the last of four epic poems in 1809, finally publishing *Roderick, the Last of the Goths* in 1814. The length of this endeavour meant that he was overtaken by both Scott and Landor, who published their versions in 1811 and 1812, but this did not bother him, as he realized that each poet had adopted a totally different approach to the legend. In his rather lukewarm letter to Scott about *The Vision of Don Roderick*, Southey comments: "It is remarkable that three poets should at once have been employed upon Roderick. . . .Differing so totally as we do in the complexion and management of the two poems, I was pleased to find one point of curious comparison, in which we have both represented Roderick in the act of confession, and both finished the picture highly. Our representations are so totally different, as to form a perfect contrast."[26] Southey was convinced of the uniqueness and distinctiveness of his *Roderick*, as he remarks in his letter to John May in January 1813: "My poem is of a perfectly original character,"[27] claiming that it was unlike anything attempted before in prose or verse. As early as 1809 he wrote to his relative Lieutenant Southey that the whole interest of the poem was to be derived from human character and the inherent dignity of the story.[28] It turned out to be financially his most successful poem, and by 1818 had made him the considerable sum of £700, despite his initial feeling that the work would not be well-received: "It is in too deep a strain of passion to become popular till the opinion of the few shall become that of the many. . ."[29]

While Southey thought of the poem as a cathartic tragedy, the very fact that he identifies himself on its title page as a 'Member of the Royal Spanish Academy' emphasizes its political nature. In his life of Robert Southey, Mark Storey comments that the poet was well aware that the work might have an effect on public attitudes toward the Spanish war. In the poet's view, a defensive war was not enough, and what was needed was more pugnacity, including training of the Portuguese army by the British. Southey's fascination with the very violence he appears to condemn is manifested in the hero of his poem who becomes an avenging angel wielding extreme violence to achieve the end it appears to justify.[30]

The unexpected success of *Roderick* may in part have been due to its fashionable appeal to popular nineteenth-century taste for things medieval, fused with its clear engagement with the political and military events of the time. However, Southey's initial reservations about its success might well have been more than an expression of the modesty topos. Beneath the superficial veneer of the Gothic, *Roderick, Last of the Goths* proves to be an intractably medievalized work on every textual level, displaying a degree of erudite knowledge and sympathetic reconstruction of medieval style and techniques, characterization and themes that render it a poetic tour de force. Southey remedievalizes the legend unlike anyone before or since, and as such his poem may well be viewed as the apogee of the literary recreation of the story of Roderick and La Cava. While this very aspect of the poem in combination with its length and its extensive scholarly notes could have led Southey to doubt that his work would be properly appreciated, it is precisely these elements that raise the life of the legend to new heights.

Roderick, Last of the Goths consists of twenty-five cantos of free verse that begin where most versions of the legend end, with the battle of Guadalete in which Roderick and the Goths are defeated by the Moors. His poem creates an imagined future in which the consequences of Roderick's actions for both himself and his country form the focus of the action. Through true repentance, the king is transformed from his initial solitary desolation, despair, and abandonment after the battle into a hero reborn, who is reconciled with himself, with Florinda and with her father, and ultimately joins with the Asturian leader Pelayo to fight again and win back Spain from the Moors. The conception of the poem is one of heroic grandeur, through which Southey remedievalizes Roderick as an epic hero with appropriate virtues of piety, courage, and hope to create a Cid-like, almost supernatural figure who conquers against all odds. This marks another unique moment in the history of the legend, for Southey is the first (and last?) person to convert Roderick into a hero, presenting a portrayal of the king unprecedented in the evolution of the narrative.

The nature of this portrayal is fundamentally linked to the medieval ethos of the work on both thematic and stylistic levels, and those links are divulged through a more detailed exploration of the text. Southey's preliminary quotations from Tacitus's *Histories* and from Wordsworth reveal his essential plan, since the former describes the value of virtue and penitence in conjunction with the exemplary value of stories of former times, and the latter addresses the power and beauty of Virtue and its growth out of despair. While the use of quotations from both ancient and contemporary writers underlines the universal and enduring nature of the theme, the poet has alighted upon virtue as a quintessentially medieval concept, enshrined in the chivalric ideal of valor and moral excellence, and which formed one of the orders of the medieval celestial hierarchy. Virtue is key to this poem, in particular in its dimension as the central chivalric aspiration, which was achieved through suffering. In addition to alerting the reader to the perennial relevance of medieval concepts and stories, the poet also points obliquely in his preface to a centuries-old source of tension in the recreation of the legend, the interaction between fiction and history. He notes the obscurity of the history surrounding the Muslim invasion of Spain for his readership (in contrast with the attitude of Jacobean writers, who supposed a certain familiarity with it), yet while indicating that he is using real events from the past, he presents the reader with a long cast list for the poem, as if it were a play, clearly denoting those characters that are imaginary and those that are historical.

These two facets are evident in the first two cantos in Roderick's meeting with the priest Romano, one historical man, the other imaginary, and representing the typically medieval dualism of secular power and religious power, monarch and clergyman. Romano comforts the desolate king after a defeat described by Southey in a way that is critical of both Christian and Islamic religions. The "inhuman priests" (1. 4) of the Goths are no better than the Muslims with their "impious creed" (1. 22). The poet attributes the fall of the Gothic kingdom to Julian's vengeful treason, not to sexual corruption, thus mitigating Roderick's act of violation. This is further reinforced by the supernatural protection the king receives in battle. While both sides in the battle believe him to be dead, he escapes miraculously uninjured to wander in grief until he meets the priest. The presentation of a dream vision of Florinda, a technique characteristic of medieval epic, and the frequent parallels made between Roderick's suffering and that of Christ, heighten the spiritual and miraculous dimensions of the work.

The third and fourth cantos of the poem introduce another imaginary character, Adosinda, daughter of the governor of Auria, who is sole survivor of a Moorish raid on her town. Roderick's encounter with her is crucial in transmuting his identity within the poem, and also crucial to his personal salvation. Adosinda is a powerful, courageous woman with an invincible spirit, whose stirring words rouse him from his desperation. In a magnificent speech, Southey presents a highly sympathetic portrait of an independent woman suddenly deprived of husband, child, and parents:

> What else of consolation may be found
> For one so utterly bereft, from Heaven
> And from myself must come. For deem not thou
> That I shall sink beneath calamity.
> (3. 293–96)

When the king hears her moving story of murdering a Moor who had taken her captive, he is transfigured emotionally, stirred to revenge for his people. But it will be a revenge attained through violence and bloodshed:

> . . .in the invader's blood
> She (his soul) must efface her stains of mortal sin.
> (4. 15–16)

Southey paints a portrait of a man both destroyed and redeemed by woman; although his passion for Florinda brought catastrophe, Adosinda's courage has saved him in order to fight for Spain that will "arise regenerate" (4. 45). Naming him Maccabee after a Jewish freedom fighter, Adosinda and Roderick make a pact to fight for Spain, and by the end of the fourth canto, Roderick has renounced his royal status and, ironically, assumed the role of priest conferred on him to his horror at the monastery of Saint Felix. The king alias Maccabee laments for Spain as a country that has always been prey to foreign invasion:

> Here in their own inheritance, the sons
> Of Spain have groan'd beneath a foreign yoke,
> Punic and Roman, Kelt, and Goth, and Greek.
> (4. 272–75)

Although Roderick's words relate to Spain's plight in the eighth century, it is not hard to infer a parallel with the Napoleonic invasion of Southey's time.

The poet introduces yet another imaginary character in cantos Five and Six in the form of Roderick's foster-father, the elderly Siverian. Though unconvincing in his failure to recognize his adopted son, Siverian's role at this point is to vindicate Roderick and to establish him firmly in a heroic mould. In his encounter with the incognito king, the old man claims that the fall of the Visigothic kingdom was predestined:

> The evils which drew on our overthrow
> Would soon by other means have wrought their end,
> Though Julian's daughter should have lived and died
> A virgin vow'd and veil'd.
> (5. 66–69)

Praising Roderick's courage, Siverian roundly criticizes his wife Egilona, who cast a shadow over the court and drove her mother-in-law from the palace. As he recounts the tale of his foster-son's vengeance upon King Witiza for blinding his father, he gives Roderick the qualities of a hero for the first time:

> Roderick,...oh when did valour wear a form
> So beautiful, so noble, so august?
> Or vengeance, when did it put on before
> A character so aweful, so divine?
> (6. 146–49)

Upon entering the church where his father is buried, they are challenged by a man "clad in sackcloth, bare of foot" (6. 221) yet "of majestic form / And stature" (6. 220–21). In this depiction of Roderick's first encounter with Pelayo (which never happened historically), the Asturian mirrors Roderick's dual status as holy man and king in his garb and stature. In canto Seven the two men join forces and espouse what Roderick describes as "The work/of holy hatred" (7. 119–20) that is the Catholic purpose in the form of a holy war akin to *jīhad*. Southey really beats the drum for Spain as Roderick inspires Pelayo to fight:

> Of that most ancient and heroic race,
> Which with unweariable endurance still
> Hath striven against its mightier enemies,
> Roman or Carthaginian, Greek or Goth;
> So often by superior arms oppress'd,
> More often by superior arts beguil'd,

> Yet amid all its sufferings, all the waste
> Of sword and fire remorselessly employed,
> Unconquer'd and unconquerable still;. . .
> (7. 142–51)

No doubt the poet once more had contemporary events in mind.

Florinda does not appear in the poem until virtually the mid-point, in the very brief canto Nine, which condenses an account of her fate since the battle of Guadalete. The apostate priest Orpas has claimed her for his bride in connivance with her father who seeks to preserve his ancient line. Pelayo's pity for her leads him to take her with him as he escapes from Cordoba, paving the way for the encounter with Roderick, which is a climactic point of the poem.

Canto Ten, entitled "Roderick and Florinda," functions by virtue of Roderick's disguised identity. Thinking he is a priest, with Roderick hidden in his hood in the darkness, Florinda asks him to hear her confession in a profoundly ironic and poignant scene. He is deeply moved as she pleads for him unawares, and takes the blame herself: "I come a self-accuser, self-condemn'd / To take upon myself the pain deserved" (10. 138–39). Recounting the story of their love that he knows only too well, she confesses her passionate feelings for him thinking she is talking to Maccabee. For the first time in the evolution of the legend, Florinda expresses a desire equivalent to that of the king for her, describing him as "My hope, light, sunshine, life and everything" (10. 245). Yet her rejection of him, even after he tells her the church will free him from his "unfruitful bed" (10. 332) with Egilona and make her his queen, seems perverse, as she herself admits, being in that

> . . .desperate mood
> Of obstinate will perverse, the which, with pride
> And shame and self-reproach, doth sometimes make
> A woman's tongue her own worst enemy,
> Run counter to her dearest heart's desire. . .
> (10. 337–40)

Southey is very vague, almost coy, about the violation itself, if it can be called that in this case, but the oblique reference to a "transitory wrong" (10. 358) must be the reason for Florinda's desire for revenge. She asks Roderick, as Maccabee, to forgive her for her "wicked vengeance" (10. 381) at the end of a profoundly moving scene that pivots on the question "what if. . .?" that pervades this poem, made powerful by irony, pathos, and disguise.

In the following four cantos, as Roderick and Pelayo arrive in Asturias to muster the troops there, the references to "an impious foe" (12. 170) that oppresses Spain and brings "strange laws, / strange language, evil customs, and false faith" (12. 171–73), plus Pelayo's description of "Our portentous age" (12. 185) that he says "Hath loosen'd and disjointed the whole frame / of social order" (12. 187–88) resonate with relevance to the Napoleonic war. By canto Fifteen, Roderick is reunited with his mother, though still incognito as Father Maccabee, enabling Southey to pursue his strong ironic strain, while in the succeeding canto, Pelayo is reunited with his family. These two family units parallel the country itself and the region of Asturias, united again under Christian leadership.

Count Julian makes no appearance until canto Twenty, when he sends a missive to his daughter from the Moorish camp to ask her forgiveness and forbearance. They meet in a beautiful *locus amoenus*, by a fountain in the forest, where Julian makes a surprising speech to Florinda and to Maccabee, showing an openness to all religious creeds that is at once generous and moving, and calls into question the consequent purpose of all the fighting:

> Of one great Father, in whatever clime
> Nature or chance hath cast the seeds of life,
> All tongues, all colours. . .
> (21. 173–76)

and

> As every clime, there is a way to Heaven,
> And thou and I may meet in Paradise.
> (21. 194–96)

Interesting too are the opposing views of women expressed by Julian:
"Still to the Goths art thou the instrument / Of overthrow; thy virtue and thy vice / Fatal alike to them!" (21. 141–44) and by the renegade bishop Orpas: ". . .Allah thus / By woman punisheth the idolatry / Of those who raise a woman to the rank / Of Godhead" (21. 144–49). Destroyer of the Christian side and facilitator of the Muslim one, woman remains the catalyst in the dance of power between both sides in the history of the legend.

By canto Twenty-Four, the Moors have turned against Julian, despising his traitorous nature, and attempt to kill him "To punish treachery and prevent worse ill" (24. 85). The lance impaled in his side is reminiscent of the Cid's death in a similar manner in Arab legend, and like the Cid with Jimena, the dying Julian is laid at Florinda's knees. At the last moment, Julian asks Maccabee to reconvert him to Christianity, and in a moment of extreme irony, Roderick absolves him before revealing his true identity and asking Julian's forgiveness. Once he is forgiven, he dies, followed immediately by Florinda, overwhelmed by events.

In the final canto in which Roderick reveals himself and rides into battle at Pelayo's side wielding Julian's sword, he again manifests superhuman powers and is immune to death by arrows and spears. With the battle won and Pelayo set to be the new king of Spain, Roderick once more forsakes his beloved horse Orelio and disappears. Southey skillfully fuses the unknown fate of Roderick in the original story with this second invented battle and closure, relating ultimately how Roderick's tomb was found at a future time, in Viseu.

This superb poem both poses and responds to a series of unanswered questions relating to the legend of King Roderick and La Cava. The fantasy meetings after the battle of Guadalete between Roderick and Florinda and Roderick and Julian constitute visions of what might have occurred if they had met on those occasions in reality, and more fundamentally, if Florinda had indeed loved Roderick and become his queen. These visions contain implicit queries over whether history would have changed as a result, and whether the course of history truly depends upon the fragile and transient emotions of its protagonists. Such queries maintain the creative momentum of the legend, but Southey's genius lies in the construction of the poem's neomedieval framework, which forms a bridge from the past over the present and into the future. It is precisely the envisioned encounters between the protagonists that act as vehicles for the medieval themes the work espouses. The personal conflicts between Roderick, Florinda, and Julian reflect the conflicts of a national, political, and moral nature taking place within Spain at that time, and these echoed Southey's own project to express faith in the glorification of man, in a new form of nationalism and in historical transcendence. Considered one of the foremost poets of his time, he helped shape Victorian attitudes toward political revolution, social change, and morality,[31] issues that are at the heart of *Roderick, the Last of the Goths*.

Contemporary critics' perceptions of the main theme of the poem vary from the connection between violence and morality to the confidence in Faith.[32] In Kenneth Curry's discussion of the work in his book *Southey*, certain words stand out. He describes it as a poem marked by reconciliation, affirmation, truth, and justice in the righting of wrongs,[33] and in my view these are key aspects of the predominant theme of virtue that Southey points to at the outset. The epic hero, Roderick, is inherently virtuous from the start, falls from grace then regains his virtue through suffering and atonement as he follows the characteristic questing journey of the medieval knight. The pervasive medieval dualism of church and monarchy is present at every step along the king's way, from the monk Romano's power to comfort the anguished monarch at the start to Roderick's relinquishment of his kingly status to assume that of a churchman and create a hero in whom church and state are joined and free from conflict. Yet God plays little or no part in the work or in Roderick's salvation, which he achieves himself, with the help of Adosinda. His triumph is a human one.

The issues of racial and religious difference arising from Roderick's crime and punishment are notably ambiguous. While Moors are demonized, a number of Christian Goths such as Orpas and other priests, and Pelayo's sister Guisla are portrayed as corrupt. Neither is Catholicism presented in a favorable light. Julian's words in canto 24 imply that the Catholic faith, and Christianity itself, formed one of several mythologies, a notion that Meachen points out was heretical and would have alienated Southey's readers if expressed in anything but poetical form.[34] Nevertheless, it is militant Christianity that supports the king's aspiration to a virtue that is in part achieved through the violence of battle, as in all medieval European epic. The ambivalence toward Roderick and racial and religious matters that has been evident in many earlier manifestations of the legend continues in this nineteenth-century epic poem.

The neomedieval themes of this work are upheld through characterization. Brian Wilkie notes that the Romantic poets used the epic tradition much as earlier poets had done, but in a radically original way, finding the seeds of the present in the past.[35] As he states, usually the epic hero "has a divinely sanctioned mission to accomplish that requires fortitude and resistance to temptation, including sensual temptation," with the action often concerning some crucial historical episode of a nation.[36] Clearly Roderick matches this definition and is the central character of the work, although initially Southey agonized over whether the king or Pelayo should be the main protagonist, and in fact used the working title of *Pelayo* for some time. He must have ultimately perceived that Roderick was a much more interesting character to develop, cleverly using Pelayo to highlight the king's virtue consistently, so that even in the final scene when Pelayo is about to be crowned king of Spain, this is made possible only because of Roderick's heroic actions. His characterization and that of others is also strengthened through the use of biblical typology, for example, in his portrayal as a Christ-like figure on occasions, as is Pelayo later, while Adosinda is likened in her ferocious courage to the biblical Judith. The powerful female characters Southey draws in this poem, Adosinda, Florinda, Rusilla, and even the corrupt Guisla, build on and extend epic characterization, where typically women are present but not dominant.

The poetic tools Southey uses to construct his characters and build themes draw extensively not only on the techniques of medieval learned epic but also on those of oral epic. Brian Wilkie's observations on the presence of familiar epic patterns and details in Southey's long poems including *Roderick*, such as the ordeal journey, the purposefulness of the action, and the presence of supernatural agencies are based on the premise that the poet's literary ambitions were molded by classical and Renaissance literary epics and romances.[37] What he does not take account of was Southey's expertise as a Hispanist who had translated the famous oral epic *Cantar de mio Çid*. While the elements noted above are evident in learned epic, they are also present in oral forms, as is the comparative lack of narrative unity that was persistently criticized in all Southey's epic poems. In *The Spirit of the Age*, Hazlitt compared their structure to "the unweeded growth of a luxuriant and wandering fancy,"[38] but failed to note that such absence of formal harmonious composition inheres in medieval romance and in oral epic itself. This informality of structure is mirrored in Southey's choice of verse form. Although he believed that regular blank verse was "the noblest measure...of which our admirable language is capable,"[39] he chose irregular blank verse for *Roderick*, a meter admired for its variety by some of his nineteenth-century critics,[40] which much more naturally lends itself to recitation as it reflects the natural rhythms of speech to a greater degree than regular verse. Allied to this is the frequent use of alliteration, at times to extremely powerful effect. In canto One, the stirring description of the Moors on the battlefield creates a dynamic, vibrant image of their magnificence: "White turbans, glittering armour, shields engrail'd / With gold, and scymitars of Syrian steel" (1. 38–39), accentuated by the alliteration on the letters 'g,' 'd,' and 's' and the assonance of 'i'. In canto Twenty-Four, as Julian sits in his tent with his men they see the approaching Christians caught in the heat of battle:

> In the distant vale a rising dust was seen,
> And frequent flash of steel,...the flying fight
> Of men who, by a fiery foe pursued,
> Put forth their coursers at full speed, to reach
> The aid in which they trust.
>
> (24. 48–52)

The complex sound effects of these lines, largely achieved through alliteration on the letters 'd,' 'f,' and 'r,' with assonantal emphasis upon 'i' and 'e,' serve to emphasize the noise and haste of war. Such forceful alliterative and assonantal effects are akin to those of the assonantal rhyme that typified oral Romance epic, notably in the *Cantar de mio Çid*, in that both devices enhance the spoken dimension of the poems.

One further unique aspect of Southey's style in *Roderick* is of interest in this regard, namely his constant use of ellipsis. This syntactical figure appears regularly throughout the twenty-five cantos of the poem, often during direct speech, with the effect of creating a pause or hesitation in the delivery. In canto Two, "Roderick in Solitude," the king longs to hear his mother's voice: "Oh, might he hear / That actual voice!and if Rusilla lived,. . ./ If shame and anguish for his crimes not yet / Had brought her to her grave,. . .sure she would bless / Her penitent child" (2. 238–42). Here the use of ellipsis for hesitation leaves the reader to imagine the unspoken words that might fill the gaps. Adosinda also speaks with ellipsis as she strives to express her anguish in canto Three: "There,. . .with firm eye and steady countenance, / Unfaltering, she addrest him,. . .there they lie, / Child, Husband, Parents,. . .Adosinda's all!" (3. 252–54). The gaps in the text are eloquent in conveying her grief. An equivalent effect is achieved in canto Nineteen, when Rusilla recognizes her son: "Still, still, my Son!. . ./ Changed,. . .yet not wholly fallen,. . .not wholly lost, / He cried,. . .not wholly in the sight of Heaven unworthy, O my Mother, nor in thine!" (19. 18–21), where ellipsis reveals her profound emotion and also facilitates a subtle yet natural transition in speaker, to leave us momentarily unsure as to who is talking. The presence of this device is indicative of Southey's supreme craftsmanship, since on a technical level it reinforces the sense of orality of the work, while on the interpretative level, the feeling of omission or implication intrinsic to ellipsis subtly underlines the significant ambivalences of the work.

If Southey shows himself to be a masterful poet in *Roderick, Last of the Goths*, he also proves that he is an equally excellent scholar in the forty-six pages of notes (some of which have footnotes themselves) of remarkable breadth and erudition written in Spanish, Portuguese, and Latin appended to the poem. From a purely scholarly point of view, the notes are of outstanding interest for Hispanism even today, showing that Southey drew upon a wide range of sources including Saint Isidore, Saint Julian, Ambrosio de Morales, Britto, whose inventiveness in his *Monarchía Lusitana* of 1609 was used by the English poet to locate the first two cantos at the monastery of Alcobaza in Portugal and incorporate the monk Romano into the plot, Pedro de Corral to a great degree, Lope de Vega, Juan de Mena, Mascarenhas, and Miguel de Luna, regarding whom Southey has a fascinating opinion on the latter's forgery, putting forward sound and interesting reasons for absolving him from fakery (Note 21). Southey's translation of Roderick's final penance from Corral's *Crónica sarracina* must still be the only English version in existence.

The purpose of such a daunting body of commentary is essentially to clarify, justify, explore, and expound, and as such, Southey is continuing a long-standing medieval tradition of glossing the text. Some nineteenth-century critics complained about the fashion of encumbering a poem with notes, a precedent set by Erasmus Darwin's *Botanic Garden* of 1791,[41] though Southey would have been well aware of the much earlier exegetical notes and commentaries upon biblical and other texts in the Middle Ages. Diego Saglia makes the point that the notes to *Roderick* constitute what he calls "virile factual concerns that establish the poem's credibility, the value of its historical reconstruction and its antiquarian status,"[42] thereby asserting the authority of the poet. Saglia also quotes Derrida's claim that notes can also work against textual unity and signification, multiplying the latter and undermining authorial control,[43] although he does not add that this was an aspect also evident in medieval glosses. The apparent conflict between poem and notes is acknowledged by Southey, who clearly states in Note 1 that the truth or falsity of the story is immaterial to his poetry. What he does use the notes for to some degree is to reinforce the ideology or morality of the poem, for example, in his scathing attack on Catholicism in note 13, which he accuses of producing more "practical evils" than any other system, and in his claim in Note 2 that "Never has any country been so cursed by the spirit of persecution as Spain."

Southey's notes to *Roderick*, while extensive, are valuable and important, not least because they complete the remedievalizing of the legend in their exegetical dimension that anchors the imaginary narrative in the historical and literary reality of the Middle Ages. While the conflict between fiction and history has been ongoing since the inception of the legend, the notes mitigate that conflict because they allow Southey to present two different kinds of truth, one in poetry and one in prose, one emotional and subjective, the other scholarly and more objective. In this poetic tour de force, Southey has recreated the legend by infusing his poem with medievalism from the grammatical level of the text upward. He has succeeded in writing the epic poem with Roderick as its hero that Spain has never had.

The Legend in English Prose

Over a decade after the publication of *Roderick, Last of the Goths*, two prose versions of the narrative appeared in English, one in 1829 penned by the American writer of legends Washington Irving, best known today for *The Legend of Sleepy Hollow*, and the other in 1830 by Telesforo de Trueba, a Spaniard from the region of Santander who wrote in English. Irving's interest in Spain and its literature grew during his period of residence in Paris in 1824, where he studied Spanish, which he described as a language "full of power, magnificence and melody."[44] In 1827 he visited Toledo, the legendary site of the enchanted cave or palace he incorporated into his *Legends of the Conquest of Spain*, finishing the sections on Roderick whilst in Granada in 1829.

Irving appears to have consulted many sources of the legend and mistakenly believed Corral's *Crónica del Rey don Rodrigo* to be a translation of the version by Rasis. He was also aware of Lope de Vega's *Jerusalén Conquistada* and *El último godo*, as well as Scott, Landor, and Southey's reworkings, for he comments somewhat negatively that the story "has been so much harped upon by Scott and Southey as not to possess novelty with literary persons."[45] This remark begs a question: why, therefore, did Washington Irving decide to use this material himself? It is a question that has not been addressed before, since, as Dahlia Kirby Terrell points out in her edition of *The Crayon Miscellany* in which the legends appear, critics of the American writer have paid very little attention to his *Legends of the Conquest of Spain*, though historians and critics have at times pointed out his factual or linguistic errors.[46] One such is S.P. Scott, who states in his *History of the Moorish Empire in Europe, Vol. 1* that Irving's quotations indicate a surprising want of familiarity with the Castilian language.[47] In contrast, the New York Mirror of 1835 called the *Legends* a "*chef d'oeuvre*" though without stating the basis for such an accolade. Such divergent views may in part stem from the vexed nature of Irving's narrative, which is perplexing on account of the author's vacillating relationship with his source materials and his equivocal purpose.

In his Preface, Irving convincingly expounds the importance of the circumstances of 711: "Few events in history have been so signal and striking in their main circumstances, and so overwhelming and enduring in their consequences as that of the Conquest of Spain by the Saracens; yet there are few where the motives and characters and actions of the agents have been enveloped in more doubt and contradiction." He goes on to make the ironic and incisive point that such apocryphal sources as those, albeit unidentified, "which savor of the pious labors of the cloister, or those fanciful fictions that betray their Arabian authors' have been appropriated to create 'the most legitimate and accredited Spanish histories.' "[48] This candid opinion of the merit of his sources as history led to the decision to construct "a short chronicle or legend, containing the most striking scenes at full length and with full effect,"[49] yet his stated wish not to claim for them "the authenticity of sober history, yet giving nothing that has not historical foundation"[50] contains a contradiction that obscures Irving's reinterpretation and restates the profound tension between history and fiction that lies at the heart of the reception of the legend.

From the outset the American echoes Southey in noting Spain's perpetual predisposition to invasion up to the time of Witiza, whom he suggests used the precepts of Islam as an excuse for his licentiousness. Irving writes as if Witiza set up a liberal, Muslim-style sexual regime in absolute opposition to the Catholic one, defying the pope and readmitting the banished Jews into Spain. His glowing portrait of the youthful Roderick is gleaned from unspecified "ancient writers," and his account of the love affair between Roderick and Princess Elyata are drawn from "the details of an Arabian chronicler, authenticated by a Spanish poet" who turn out to be Miguel de Luna's Abulcacim Tarif Abentarique and Lope de Vega respectively. His ironic remark that "the sober pages of history should be carefully chastened from all scenes that might influence a wanton imagination, leaving them to poems and romances and such like highly seasoned works of fantasy and recreation"[51] is further evidence of his confused approach. He is torn between writing a chronicle and writing fiction, and the above statement clearly does not square with his subsequent use of the historically unconfirmed character of Florinda, without discussing sources, origins, or other possibilities.

The status of the text becomes even more puzzling for the reader in Chapter 7, the "Story of the marvellous and portentous tower," in which Irving recounts Roderick's forced entry into the "necromantic tower" after Florinda's rape. The source for the episode in this case is a friar named Agapida, who is in fact a character invented by Irving himself and whom he used in another account entitled *The Conquest of Granada*. The author's technique of authenticating information by the use of a footnote, in this case relating to the fictitious Agapida who states that the marvellous should not be discounted, is exactly parallel to Miguel de Luna's use of footnotes in his *Verdadera historia del Rey don Rodrigo*. Other points of interest in this engaging and powerfully written chapter lie first in the depiction of Roderick as Janus-faced in his role as guardian of the doors of the tower, looking back on the past and into the future as he did in the very earliest visual image of the king at Qusayr 'Amra, and second in Irving's description of the images on the linen cloth the king finds inside the tower, which become a moving vision of the future and indicate the strong influence of Walter Scott's *Vision of Don Roderick*.

There are further chapters on the "Legend of Count Julian and His Family" in addition to those details elaborated in the chapters on Roderick, which solidify Julian's background and noble status as the royal swordbearer and exemplify the new nineteenth-century interest in the figure of the count already examined in Landor's work. If the pseudo-historical nature of Irving's legends proves to be unsatisfactory for the reader, his choice of material indicates a moral and even political purpose that shores up his overall project. From his depiction of Roderick as a virtuous monarch led astray by sensual temptation, Florinda as a guiltless victim and Julian as an ambitious and power-hungry villain, he extracts a clear didactic message: "It is a story full of wholesome admonition, rebuking the insolence of human pride and the vanity of human ambition, and shewing the futility of all greatness that is not strongly based on virtue."[52] This is a rather more extreme position than that of Southey's, and Irving also makes it clear that the sections on Count Julian are to act as a warning against the fate of the traitor. Mary Weatherspoon Bowden casts interesting light on these aspects in her study of Washington Irving, adducing a parallel between the legend of Roderick and La Cava and contemporary events in the United States, relating principally to Vice-President Calhoun, who fell out with President Jackson over the apparent affair Calhoun was having with the wife of one of Jackson's cabinet advisers. Earlier in their political careers Calhoun and Jackson had also clashed when the latter had misinterpreted Calhoun's orders regarding the repression of an Indian uprising in Georgia, invading Florida against Calhoun's wishes.[53] It is impossible to know whether Irving had such specific matters definitely in mind, but it is clear that he rewrote the old stories for didactic and political reasons, whether general or specific. Beyond this, Irving added nothing new to the development of the legend, and his uncertain relationship with his source material may well have contributed to the poor reception of *Legends of the Conquest of Spain*, which was far less popular than his *Tales of the Alhambra*.

Telesforo de Trueba's *The Romance of History: Spain*, published in London in 1830 contains the familiar merging of fiction and history in its very title. The author on the one hand reassures the reader in the preface that the tales presented are "founded on events admitted as authentic by Spanish historians," while on the other he states that the poetry he borrows from Lockhart's ballad translations is used to "throw a glowing charm over my illustrations of romantic history."[54] This "glowing charm" involves the addition of elements to the legend that range from being inventive and full of potential to being wildly fanciful and bizarre. In "The Gothic King," which starts with a quotation relating to Julian from Southey's *Roderick* and is replete with archaisms such as "Prythee" and "thou," Florinda is demonized for apparently giving in to Roderick's persistence because she is dazzled by his court and by the promise of becoming queen. Trueba is highly castigatory of women: "Florinda at length became the victim of her love—the dupe of her vanity—and she soon, too soon, alas! received the award that generally attends a deviation from female purity,"[55] although he praises Egilona's strength of mind. In this rendering, the evil Oppas is Julian's brother and Pelayo becomes Roderick's cousin, an invention that allows Trueba to contrast Pelayo's nobility and heroic integrity with Roderick's debauched licentiousness.

Although Trueba indicates that his inclusion of the episode in the enchanted palace of Toledo is taken from the historian Mariana, he embellishes it with fantastical descriptions of a palace with gold, silver, and iron locks on it that fly open at Roderick's mere touch, and in whose environs supernatural events take place at night, including a vision of a vast crimson banner emblazoned with a fiery crescent. At the climax of the account,

Roderick tries to escape in the dark but unluckily meets Count Julian, who fights and kills the king. This interesting interpretation of the story might have made a satisfactory ending to the legend, though it again becomes wildly fanciful, as Moors arrive to take the spoils, sever Roderick's head and place it on a spear, which they then carry to Tarif, who has it embalmed and sent to the Caliph of Damascus. In the final scene, Florinda wanders onto the battlefield searching for Roderick, never finding out that her father has killed the man she loved. Trueba launches another attack upon her: "Cursed by thy father, and pursued by the maledictions of a whole nation, whose misery thou has accomplished; spurned,despised, hated by all. . ."[56] before summarizing Arab rule in a few lines and moving on to Pelayo's victory in "The Cavern of Covadonga."

After reading these two prose works by Irving and Trueba, one is left with the feeling that history is used as a masquerade for the invention of fictional developments that lend nothing to the reception of the legend, and present it as a remote curiosity employed as a mere vehicle for the articulation of the authors' preoccupations and prejudices.

Translation and Adaptation: The Roderick Legend in Nineteenth-Century France

The development of the legend in nineteenth-century France bore no resemblance to its evolution in England, an aspect vividly exemplified in its reformulation in 1801 by the Marquis de Sade in his *Crimes de l'amour* [Crimes of Love], a collection of stories apparently intended to persuade women to hate those who deceive them by portraying what he describes as his "heroes" as men who ". . .suivent la carrière du vice, tellement effroyables, qu'ils n'inspireront bien sûrement ni pitié ni amour"[57] [. . .follow the path of vice, and are so appalling that they could inspire neither pity nor love]. Such is the basis for his depiction of Roderick in the allegorical story entitled "Rodrigue ou la Tour Enchantée," whose historical foundations the Marquis acknowledges, although he draws on the work of Abulcacim as a source, erroneously believing him to be a historian, unsurprisingly ". . .inconnu des spécialistes que nous avons interrogés"[58] [. . .unknown to the specialists consulted]. The Marquis boasts that he has added such a wealth of new events and material to the story that he has created an anecdote that truly belongs to him.

The resulting tale remorselessly demonizes Roderick, who is thoroughly bad, unscrupulous, sybaritic, and ruthless, if fearless. The narrative begins in a familiar enough manner, depicting a sixteen-year-old Florinde who writes the famous letter to her father and in this case, dies before she receives a reply. At this point, Rodrigue enters the enchanted tower in order to avail himself of the fortune he believes it conceals, upon which the story becomes a fantastical fairytale. A giant leads the king up 800 steps to reach a torchlit chamber where all the unfortunate souls sacrificed by Rodrigue reside. The giant asks the king to consider "...les ruisseaux de sang répandus par ta main, seulement pour server tes passions"[59] [...the rivers of blood spilt by your hand, merely to serve your passions]. In a further room, Rodrigue is faced with all the young girls he has dishonored, and is addressed by Florinde, who announces that it is her task to avenge all the disgraced women around her. A third room contains a huge statue of Time, and a prediction of the invasion of Spain as a punishment for his crimes. The Marquis de Sade thereby espouses the conventional Christian view of the invasion as divine retribution, but there is nothing conventional about what follows. The king is magically transported to the top of the tower to see the approaching Moors, but unmoved and emboldened, he demands to be returned to the tower to seize its treasure. He is at once precipitated, not into the tower, but into Hell, where he must cross a river to reach a desert where the treasure lies.

Once in the desert, an eagle flies with him to the sun and finally leaves him on a mountain top, which Rodrigue must descend, killing six giants on the way, to reach the untold riches inside a cave. The king awakes or regains consciousness at this point to find himself among his friends outside the enchanted tower, with fifteen cartloads of gold! But his trials are not over, as he must wage battle against the Moors and enter into single combat with the Moorish leader, who at the last moment turns out to be Florinde in disguise. She takes her vengeance and kills him as she says: "Ne t'avais-je pas dit que tu reverrais Florinde au dernier instant de ta vie?"[60] [Didn't I tell you that you would see Florinda again at the final moment of your life?].

This is a simplistic story, unsophisticated and overexaggerated, though intense, powerful, and highly imaginative, lending Roderick an enhanced mythical status. His visions in the tower predate those in Walter Scott's poem, and interestingly, the ending in which Florinda appears as a Moorish warrior suggests that de Sade may have known Montengón's *El Rodrigo*, the only prior version to use this particular disguise. The tale is certainly a unique vision of the legend and perhaps the only one that condemns Roderick so completely.

The French reworkings of the ballad cycle a decade or so later seem tame in comparison with "Rodrigue ou la Tour Enchantée," though these French poetic rewritings may well address the legend in such a distinct manner largely because of the nature of France's involvement in the peninsular war.[61] Émile Deschamps verse interpretations avoid any political reference to a subject that was possibly uncomfortable to confront, and allows free reign to the spirit of French Romanticism. Creuzé de Lesser's *Romances du Cid* of 1814 set the precedent in France for the romanticizing of Spanish balladry, while Victor Hugo's brother Abel established French interest in the Roderick ballads in his edition entitled *Romancero e historia del rey de España don Rodrigo, postrero de los godos, en lenguaje antiguo* [Ballad Collection and History of King Roderick of Spain, Last of the Goths, in Ancient Language], published in Paris in 1821.[62] While J.G. Lockhart's translation of Spanish ballads including several on the Roderick legend appeared in England the following year, Émile Deschamps went a step further in his adaptations of the story to create what he described as "mon oeuvre la plus importante" [my most important work], entitled *Romances sur Rodrigue, dernier roy des goths, imités de l'espagnole* [Ballads of Roderick, Last King of the Goths, Imitated from the Spanish], which appeared in 1828. His prefatory essay is full of enthusiasm and admiration for the Spanish ballad tradition, "ces admirables romances espagnoles, qu'on a si bien nommées une Iliade sans Homère"[63] [those admirable Spanish ballads, so aptly described as an Iliad without Homer]. He continues: "J'en ai traduit quelques-unes, j'en ai developpé ou inventé entièrement quelques autres, en m'inspirant de toutes les chroniques du temps, et en me servant surtout de l'excellent travail de M. Abel Hugo sur la poésie espagnole. J'ai conservé la forme lyrique des romances, en ayant soin de varier continuellement les rythmes comme les tons et j'ai tâché de coordoner tous ces matériaux de manière à présenter un intérêt suivi, une espèce d'action dramatique ayant son exposition, son noeud et sa catastrophe"[64] [I have translated some, developed or completely invented others, using the inspiration of all the chronicles of the time, and above all the excellent work by Mr. Abel Hugo on Spanish poetry. I have preserved the lyrical form of the ballads, taking care to vary rhymes and tone continually, and I've tried to coordinate all these materials so as to present a consistent idea, a kind of dramatic action with exposition, crux of the plot and catastrophic dénouement]. This outline of his intentions is enlightening, revealing in particular the desire to blend translated source with poetic invention and highlighting his focus upon the form and emotional texture of the work. He translates seven ballads from Abel Hugo's collection, though even a brief comparison of the ballad *Despues que el rey don Rodrigo* discussed in chapter 4 with Deschamps' version of the king's encounter with a shepherd who directs him toward the hermitage where he suffers his final penance shows the extent to which the poet has elaborated on the old poetry. Deschamps works three complete sections of poetry out of one ballad, including a prayer of penitence, retaining details such as the frugal meal the shepherd offers Roderick, who gives him his gold chain and ring in exchange, and God's revelation to the hermit of the king's dreadful penance of entombment with the snake, desexualized in the French version, in which the creature sucks his liver, instead of eating his genitals as it does in the Spanish ballad. However, the spectral, crazed king who wanders, tearing at his neck with his nails, through burning sun and icy nights, and the dull-eyed shepherd who lives in a threatening "pays des ours" [land of bears] play upon the reader's emotions of pity and fear more obviously than the characteristically understated Spanish original. In Section XI "Pénitence et mort de Rodrigue," Deschamps develops the encounter between the king and the hermit, during which the latter offers him a coin for his journey. As Roderick takes the money, he recognizes with horror his own image on the coin, which leads him to confess his identity to the cenobite. This dramatic deployment of coinage links Deschamps' poetry with the earliest known visual image of King Roderick dating to 710 or 711.

In addition to these very free translations, Deschamps also adds a letter from Florinda, and the episode of her suicide, both of which are taken from Miguel de Luna, a section about the fugitives of the battle of Guadalete entitled "Bertrand Inigo" that Pidal notes is a paraphrase of the Carolingian ballad "Con la mucha polvareda perdimos a don Beltrán"[65] [In the Great Dustcloud We Lost Beltran] and a new section, "Les Brigands" [The Bandits] in which Roderick is assailed by renegades on his way to the hermitage. The poet's stated design of exposition, crux, and catastrophe follow the familiar pattern in which a carefree Florinda is violated against her will by Roderick, and writes a letter to her father telling him of her disgrace and demanding that he take revenge, with the inevitable consequence of Julian's treason, the loss of the battle of Guadalete and Roderick's flight and penitence. In this version, both the king and Florinda die, but Julian falls into madness instead.

Despite the added secondary episodes, Deschamps' version of the legend contributes nothing new in terms of its narrative evolution. There are nevertheless some effective touches in relation to setting and characterization. The poem starts and ends with Florinda, whose initial purity and innocence is reflected in a stylized description of nature with its "ruisseau d'argent qui roule / Des sables d'or" [silver river which flows / Beside golden sands] (1: 8–9). As the girls play in the garden, Roderick watches "Ces nymphes d'Andalousie" [those Andalusian nymphs] (1: 34), in a pastoral idyll reminiscent of Garcilaso. Deschamps' Count Julian is a poor figure, "Pauvre vieillard, sur qui tous les yeux son ouverts!" [Poor old man, upon whom all eyes have fallen!] (3: 16), in total contrast with Landor's majestic depiction of the traitor, and seemingly unworthy of Florinda's deference in her letter to "Vous, mon prêtre et mon roi" [You, my lord, my priest and my king] (4: 15.) The incitement to treason is located in Florinda's words to her father: "Dites à l'étranger / De nous venger" [Tell the foreigner / To avenge us] (4: 119–20), and orientates the attribution of blame in the poem. Deschamps translates the old ballad lines to render the subject contemporary "Qui fut le plus coupable, en sa faute mortelle, / De Florinde ou du roi?. . .Comme alors, aujourd'hui / Les hommes disent que c'est elle, / Les femmes disent que c'est lui" [Who was more to blame in their mortal sin, / Florinda or the king?. . .Then, as now / The men say it was her, the women say it was him] (2: 57–60), and clearly aligns himself with the male point of view in his conclusion, in which he describes women as beguiling temptresses who ensnare the finest men: "Toujours un vague instinct, un charme involuntaire, / Un céleste besoin sauront, avec mystère, / Aux bras de la moins tendre enchaîner le plus fier" [Always some vague instinct, some involuntary charm, / A heavenly need will, mysteriously, / ensnare the noblest man in the arms of the least tender woman] (12: 19–21). This belies Julian's description of Roderick as "Voluptueux tyran, de tes désirs esclave" [Voluptuous tyrant, slave to your desires] (3: 20), and the "Philtres d'enfer, nocturne embûche, et sourde intrigue, / Et violence" [Infernal filters, nocturnal trap and muffled intrigue, / And violence] (2. 51–52) that surround Roderick's violation of Florinda are mitigated by his depiction as a hero with supernatural qualities during his attack by bandits, who are horrified to find that their victim "n'avait pas d'un mortel l'attitude ordinaire" [did not have the ordinary bearing of a mortal man] (8: 40), with a voice that "comme un tonnerre / Mugissait dans son sein" [like thunder / Roared within his breast] (8. 41–42). This newly added scene acts as part of his penitential purification, and is much more effective than the earlier added section on Bertrand Inigo, which sings the noble courage of an old retainer to no apparent purpose.

As he indicates in the Preface, Deschamps does vary the form and rhythm of the poem, though not always to good effect. The poetry is a blend of elements that typify the *romancero* with much more formal techniques. Section 5, "Rodrigue pendant la bataille," contains the lists, numbers, and repetition that are characteristic of oral poetry, but is on the whole a poor, uninspiring piece, with a doggerel effect in the rhyme scheme. The octosyllabic line of the ballad is often employed for narration, along with alexandrines and shorter hexa- and hendecasyllabic lines to create striking changes in pace and to reflect direct speech, though lines which imitate the direct orality of the ballad, such as "Mais attendez; les rois sont cruels par nature, / Et ce n'est pas ainsi que finit l'aventure" [But wait; kings are cruel by nature, / And the love affair doesn't finish there] (1. 54–55), are at times banal and anticlimactic. On occasions the rhyming to intensify Florinda's extreme agitation in Roderick's presence is overexaggerated: "Sous des pleurs sans nombre, / Ses regards dans l'ombre / Jetant une sombre / Et morne lueur" [With countless tears, / Her glances in the shadows / Casting a sombre and dismal light] (2. 5–8), to the extent that it is almost comic. Deschamps ends his work on a note of optimism for the future in his conjuring of Pelayo who will save Spain. In this respect there is a point of contact with Southey's *Roderick*, but it is the only one. The French reception of the legend in the nineteenth century was in a minor key in comparison with its counterparts written in England. It is less evolved in the sense that it refers more directly to a specific written source via translation and adaptation and lacks the forceful political agenda of English versions.[66]

The espousal of the legend by three major English poets in this century is a remarkable testimony to its dramatic power, interest, and adaptability, a factor reinforced by the sheer number of recreations of the story not only in England but also in France and the United States. The pivotal issues involved were precisely its political dimension in nearly all cases, the emergence of Count Julian as a major protagonist, an increasing sympathy for the female characters and the Romantic medievalization of the story, elements that lift the legend to a new level and accentuate its regenerative power.

CHAPTER 8

MULTIPLE PERSPECTIVES IN HISPANIC ROMANTICISM

The legend of King Roderick and La Cava prospered in nineteenth-century Spain in a manner quite divergent from its evolution in England and France during that century. Various features characteristic of its eighteenth-century manifestations continued to be explored in drama, poetry, and prose, in particular the theme of patriotism, the interest in the female protagonists of the story, and the dominant focus upon sentiment, though these are revealed in literary works diverse and unpredictable in their sequestration of the elements of the legend. This kaleidoscopic dimension creates an overall impression of fragmentation in presentations of the story that are partial and incomplete, as if posing more unanswered questions than they respond to themselves and indicate the persistently problematical nature of the narrative for Spaniards. While interest in the legend was unabated, a good number of capriciously imaginative and often unfinished renderings suggest their writers were reaching out toward an as yet uncharted future that might provide solutions to the complexities and problems the story had clearly created for Hispanic writers of the 1800s.

A recurrent feature in the reception of the legend is its capacity to be in tune with contemporary events, and this is no less the case during this era. The political and monarchical instability leading up to and during the War of Independence, when the threat of invasion by Napoleon was turned into reality, recalled the inexorable invasion of Spain by the Moors Roderick was helpless to prevent. When the Spanish Parliament, the Cortes, was summoned in 1809 to organize a war effort to drive out the French from Spain, its members created a constitution affected in its very form by the constitutional tradition of medieval Spain, which in 1812 became the 'sacred codex' of nineteenth-century democratic liberalism.[1]

This grounding of aspects of contemporary legalities in the Middle Ages had a parallel in the development of Romanticism in the peninsula. The Prussian consul in Cadiz, J.N. Böhl von Faber, worked hard to acclimatize the new aesthetic ideas emanating from Germany that embraced a return to national traditions, and to a literature that was heroic, monarchical, and Christian, while still reflecting popular ideals. It was in this way that Romanticism in Spain and Portugal came to center upon nationalism and religion, and implicitly attacked the literary and philosophical culture of eighteenth-century France, by then perceived as the invader.[2] The prevalent definition of Romanticism among leading intellectuals and writers was of a literature founded upon the ideals and world-view of the chivalric Middle Ages, aided and abetted by the influence of Byron and Scott in the early 1820s.

However, in his survey of Spanish literature after 1700, Geoffrey Ribbans notes that instead of bringing Spain into prolonged contact with contemporary artistic currents, Romanticism caused it to look backward and imitate its own literary past.[3] With its concerns over patriotism and treachery, Christianity and Islam, monarchy, heroism and invasion, and its origins in the earliest medieval period, the legend of Roderick and La Cava encapsulated the *zeitgeist* of nineteenth-century Spain perfectly.

The Legend in Nineteenth-Century Hispanic Drama

Early Works

In 1799–1800, the body of theatrical censors published long lists of old and new plays prohibited by Royal order, encouraging the idea of a regulated theatre. At last, the subject of King Roderick, categorized as a classical tragedy, found some favor with the censors after its years of restriction to private performance,[4] though in spite of this, difficulties still arose over performance in the public domain. The exploration of the rich vein of dramatic interpretations of the legend in nineteenth-century Spain must begin with a neoclassical, rather than Romantic, play by an exceptional woman, María Rosa Gálvez de Cabrera, born in Malaga in 1768, who lived as the adopted daughter of an army colonel and a mother who was the niece of Jose de Gálvez, one of the ministers of Carlos III. The known details of her life are of special interest in so far as they have a direct bearing upon her writing. Her privileged family circumstances allowed her to benefit from an excellent education at a time when the education of women was gaining momentum. It was only in the year of her birth that Carlos III introduced normative measures for the schooling of women without financial resources. María Rosa was clearly well read and a good linguist, for she translated plays from French into Spanish before embarking on her own writing, which shows influence of both classical and French literature. In the "Advertencia" that precedes her *Obras poéticas*[5] she refers specifically and sympathetically to Racine and Corneille as examples of great dramatists who did not achieve perfection from the outset of their writing careers.

She married José Cabrera Ramírez, a government attaché. They moved to Washington on account of her husband's diplomatic work, but the marriage did not last and María Rosa returned to Madrid where she became involved in a scandalous affair with Manuel Godoy, the prime minister of Carlos IV, at the time when Spain's destiny lay largely in his hands, for it was Napoleon's distrust of Godoy that caused him to intervene in the affairs of the Spanish monarchy and eventually establish his brother Joseph upon the Spanish throne. María Rosa Gálvez appears to have been cruelly scorned by authors and critics of the early nineteenth century because of this involvement, although her association with Godoy was very beneficial to her writing, as he used his influence to have her works published by the Royal Press. Although she wrote a number of poems, her real vocation was for drama, and between 1801 and 1805 she produced a remarkable number of plays, though sadly her death at the age of thirty-eight in 1806 deprived the Spanish theatre of a major dramatic talent. The range of her playwriting is extraordinary, and includes classical tragedy, moralizing, and also sentimental comedy, historical drama, *zarzuelas*, and musical monologues. In spite of constant attacks from critics, and prohibitions by ecclesiastical censors, her work continued to be staged until late in the nineteenth century.

This is the context within which María Rosa published her three-act tragedy in verse entitled *Florinda* in 1804, in the second volume of her *Obras poéticas*. It is a play that was never staged, written in hendecasyllables, and, in accordance with classical unities, lasts from dawn until midnight, taking place in the Visigothic camp on the banks of the river Guadalete. One is struck immediately by the title, which places Florinda at the heart of the plot and action in an unprecedented way. Gálvez also introduces the major innovation of a love affair between Florinda and Pelayo, to whom she has been promised in marriage, and in doing so poses two crucial questions. What might have happened to the destiny of Spain and to Florinda herself if she had in fact married Pelayo as planned? And what was Florinda's true status in this tragic and passionate tale?

A glance at the cast list is revealing in this respect. In addition to the three main protagonists, Rodrigo, Florinda and Count Julian (who does not make an appearance until scene 6 of the final act), Pelayo is present as Rodrigo's cousin, with the addition of the soldier Tulga, who is Florinda's uncle. The courtier Egerico is Rodrigo's confidant and a supporter of Bishop Opas, who is present in the play in name only in spite of being the arch-traitor in the plot. Tarif, as Moorish conqueror of Spain, has a small but vital role in handing Florinda the dagger belonging to Rodrigo with which she kills herself in the last scene. Two things stand out in this cast; first, the fact that Florinda is the only female character, and second, that family ties between certain characters are emphasized. It will be precisely Florinda's aloneness in this male world, and the vexed question of family honor, which will be instrumental in the heroine's tragic downfall.

The relationships between these characters are fraught with intrigue and deception. This is immediately plain in the initial conversation between Tulga and Pelayo that sets the scene in Act 1. Tulga's patriotism is at war with his sense of honor, since he is fighting for a king who has committed a crime brought about by Tulga's own niece, who is "causa de nuestro daño" (1. 59). Her uncle's honor means more to him than her life, and he is vicious in his desire for vengeance upon her. She must die for Roderick's crime:

> . . .¡Ah cuánto anhela
> mi corazón su muerte! Sí; su sangre
> solo puede lavar de mi nobleza
> la mancha que mi honor ha mancillado
> por la infame passion y por afrenta
> con que sació Rodrigo su apetito.
>
> [. . .Oh, how my heart
> desires her death! Yes; her blood
> alone can wash clean the stain upon
> my honour besmirched by
> the infamous passion and affrontery
> with which Roderick satiated his appetite].
> (1. 62–67)

In one of the many asides in the play, Pelayo, "héroe de España" [Spain's hero] (1. 29), reveals that he is secretly keeping Florinda prisoner in his tent, while pretending to agree with Tulga. In the same act, the friction between Tulga and Egerico is established, the forthright soldier loathing the king's unctuous adviser for his smooth tongue and partisanship with the evil bishop Opas, and making no bones about the fact that he distrusts the priesthood: "yo la lealtad dudo de un Prelado" [I doubt the loyalty of a Prelate] (1. 101). The first dialogue between Pelayo and Rodrigo also has deception at its heart. Pelayo defends Tulga against the king's criticism of him, while Rodrigo defends himself by accusing Florinda of greed for power: "...¿Esa Florinda / que pretendió ceñir mi Real diadema?" [...The same Florinda who aspired to bear my Royal diadem?] (1. 215–16), an insult that is shown to be blatantly untrue shortly after, when Rodrigo laments to himself:

> ¡Ah si hubiese podido mi diadema
> de Florinda ceñir la hermosa frente,
> menos su ultraje y mi delito fuera!
> Mas no pude romper el yugo impío
> que a Egilona me unió
>
> [Oh, if only my diadem had
> framed Florinda's lovely brow,
> her outrage and my crime would be the less!
> But I could not break the impious bond
> That united me with Egilona].
> (1. 324–28)

The sympathy for the king that permits the suggestion that he might divorce Egilona comes later, in the work of Southey and Landor, but does not suit the tragic purpose of this drama.

By the end of Act 1 all the characters involved are prey to dissimulation conveyed through tense undercurrents and shocking asides. Pelayo is hiding the fact that he is Florinda's lover and has her under his protection, Rodrigo is hiding the fact that he knows that Pelayo is his rival, Egerico is plotting to destroy the king while pretending to support and help him, and Tulga is hiding his hatred and suspicion of Egerico and Opas.

Florinda appears in the penultimate scene of Act 1, appropriated, like an item of property, from Pelayo's tent at Rodrigo's command. She expresses her desperate aloneness and sense of abandonment in strong terms:

> ...Abominada
> del universo, odiada de la mesma
> patria que me dio el ser, aborrecida
> aún de mi propia sangre,
>
> [...Detested
> by the universe, loathed by the same
> homeland that gave me being, abhorred
> even by my own blood].
> (1. 361–64)

Her words fill the king with compassion and a desire to make amends. Resisting his declarations of love, she describes the ultimate betrayal, that of her own mother, who cruelly berates her on her deathbed:

> ...¡oh nunca yo te concibiera
> para que me cubrieses de ignominia,
> para que de tu padre la nobleza
> por tu venganza manchen las traiciones!
> Vive, y que las edades venideras
> como yo te maldigan...
>
>   [...Oh that I might never have conceived you
> for you to cover me in ignominy,
> for your father to stain his nobility
> with betrayal, to avenge you!
> Live, and may future times
> Curse you as I do...].
>
>   (1. 418–23)

When she tells Rodrigo that she begged Pelayo to shelter her, he becomes furious and orders her imprisonment in his own tent. In the last scene of Act 1, the traitorous Egerico, who has been listening, pretends that he is on her side and that his plot to remove the king will end her troubles. Surrounded by betrayers, Florinda longs for death.

    The dominant feature of Act 2 is its prefiguration of the tragedy in the final act. Florinda is overwhelmed by the abuse and scorn of the men that surround her, and she is harshly critical of her father, whom she describes as "ambicioso, soberbio y agraviado, / contra su misma patria" [ambitious, proud and aggrieved, / at his own country] (2. 12–13). Pelayo totally rejects their former betrothal, declaring himself "muerto para el amor" [dead to love] (2. 77) and choosing his country over all else. Alone and tormented by his contempt, she is next assailed by Tulga, who accuses her of prostitution, calls her "Oprobio de mi honor y de mis años" [Opprobrium of my honor and of my years] (2. 133) and finally attempts to kill her with his dagger. He is restrained at the last minute by Rodrigo, who asserts his power and authority over his soldier and over Florinda, who is placed under armed guard in his tent.

    On the battlefield things are going badly for Rodrigo, himself assailed by a mob of Visigothic soldiers apparently incited by Tulga. He dons his royal cloak and crown and takes his scepter as he awaits a visit from Tarif, who asks him to surrender all power to the Moors and to Opas, and hand over Florinda. The Moorish commander perceives the corruption and deception in the Visigothic camp, warning Rodrigo that "infinitos traidores y ambiciosos / están contra tu vida conspirando" [an infinite number of traitors and ambition-seekers / are conspiring against your life] (2. 441–42). Yet Rodrigo shows himself to be brave, noble, and resolute in this encounter, refusing to surrender and swearing to overcome his adversaries in battle.

In Act 3, Rodrigo's love turns to hate as he cruelly and unfairly blames Florinda for the loss of the battle to the Moors, accusing her "Del funesto / destino de la España; tú eres causa / de mi desdicha y de su baldón eterno" [Of Spain's ill-fated destiny; you are the cause of my misfortune and of her eternal disgrace] (3. 77–79). When her father Julian finally appears in Scene 6 to liberate her, he cannot understand why she fails to rejoice with him in Rodrigo's downfall and defeat by the Moors. By this time, Florinda is tormented by her emotional afflictions, now convinced that the massacre of unwitting inhabitants has been her fault alone: "que por mi causa sufren sin remedio / millares de inocentes" [that thousands of innocent people are suffering / helplessly because of me] (3. 248–49). Pelayo arrives to find her with Julian and Egerico, and at once condemns her as a traitor too: "Me admiro el veros / con vida, cuando ya por vuestra causa / religion, patria y Godos fenecieron" [I am amazed to see you still alive, when because of you / religion, country and Goths have perished] (3. 310–12). As the scene darkens with nightfall, Pelayo launches a scathing attack full of hatred upon her, damning her with the proleptic curse of future generations: "maldecirán [sic] el detestable nombre / de la odiosa Florinda" [they will curse the detestable name / of loathsome Florinda] (3. 371–72). Florinda's pathos is excessive and exaggerated as she describes her "vida criminal" [criminal life] (3. 391) prior to Tarif's arrival with Rodrigo's cloak, crown, and dagger, found at the supposed site of his drowning in the Guadalete. In total darkness, Florinda is prey to horrifying visions of suffering, and seizing Rodrigo's dagger, kills herself before her father can prevent her.

This play is an unforgiving depiction of Florinda's awful downfall at the hands of implacably cruel men and family members. Although the most significant blame for the defeat of the Visigothic army is attached to the absent bishop Opas, all the male characters of the play are severely flawed. Rodrigo does show some compassion and love for Florinda, but cannot sustain it and remains tyrannical and licentious, if courageous and loyally patriotic. Pelayo's initiation of the reconquest of Spain is noted by Pidal and Hormigón[6] as the basic theme of Spanish tragedy written by Enlightenment dramatists, in line with the theory that tragedies should deal with matters of national history and with the kind of patriotism epitomized by Pelayo. However, it is hard to agree with Hormigón[7] that Pelayo is the hero of the play. Regardless of his prior love for Florinda and his loyalty to

Rodrigo in spite of their jealous rivalry, his exceptionally cruel treatment of Florinda diminishes his stature and cannot be excused. Even her father Julian remains a traitor whose actions she abhors. Florinda is cast as the victim of seduction, rape, betrayal and unjust accusation from which she derives great pathos. It is the question of rape that Daniel Whitaker addresses in his article on Gálvez's tragedies, an aspect *Florinda* shares with two of her other plays, *Amnón* and *Blanca de Rossi*, and which constitutes a familiar eighteenth-century theme exemplified in Samuel Richardson's *Clarissa*. Noting the relation between masculine power, war, and rape that has often served to reinforce masculinity and victory, Whitaker points out that Rodrigo's rape of Florinda has actually brought about the downfall of his people, and underlines the importance of the play: "...Gálvez's tragedy is remarkable for being the first major work on the subject which highlights the physical suffering, mental anguish, and the unwarranted guilt of a woman who is both a victim of her abductor and of her family."[8]

Equally remarkable, and of great importance in terms of the development of the legend, is the dramatist's elevation of *Florinda* to an almost Racinian level of tragedy, with which it shares austerity and intensity of emotional focus, and a set of characters who are ruthless and extreme. As is the case in Racine's tragedies, the play presents the working out of an inexorable series of events, which lead to a predictable catastrophe. Like Racine's work, the action is already at a crisis point when the play starts, with the tension mounting until one or more of the protagonists is destroyed. Gálvez uses the same combination of historical theme and tragic fatalism, since all events, including the rape, are predestined and ill-fated, as the prediction in the Toledan tower described by Tulga proves.

Similar to Racinian protagonists, Rodrigo and Julian are perverse, wilful, and controlled by their passions. Florinda's desperate predicament is reminiscent of Phèdre, punished by the gods, and the victim of predestination. Only when she, like Phèdre, has sunk to the deepest humiliation is she allowed to die. The dreadful "lamentos de un pueblo desolado" [lamentation of a devastated people] (3. 448–49) and the bloody ghosts Florinda envisions, "errantes sombras, que a la luz del fuego / vuestras heridas me enseñáis sangrientas" [wandering shades, who show me your bleeding wounds / in the light of the blaze] (3. 456–57) echo the terrible Trojan war in Racine's *Andromaque*, described by Andromaque herself as "cette nuit cruelle / Qui fut pour tout un peuple une nuit éternelle" [that cruel night / which was an eternal night for a whole people] (3. viii), and recall the flames Oreste describes to Andromaque as Greece burns, or the "fleuve teint de sang" [river stained with blood] (1. ii) that Pyrrhus sees as he contemplates the ruins of Troy.

While there are political undertones to *Florinda* in the implications for her era of a flawed monarch who loses his nation through betrayal, and an overt criticism of the political power and corruption of the church in Gálvez's insistence upon the evilness of Opas, these are secondary to the instatement of Florinda as a tragic heroine who is the victim of sexual violence, family treachery, and cruelty, which constitutes the response to the unanswered question regarding her status within the story. It is significant that the first published woman dramatist in Spain should place the female protagonist of the legend on center stage at a time when Enlightenment women were beginning to make an impression on the political and cultural hegemony enjoyed by their male counterparts. Whether her depiction had a parallel with María Rosa's own personal situation and the unnecessary scorn and criticism she suffered because of it is impossible to say. Whatever the case, she firmly establishes the female protagonist of the legend in a powerful central position at the start of the nineteenth century.

In complete contrast, an undated dramatic work from the early 1900s, *Perder el reino y poder, por querer a una muger*, by Josef Concha, introduces a comic note in the legend for the first time in its history. Describing himself as a "cómico español" [Spanish comic actor], the author explains beneath the title that this is a one-act play "fácil de executar en casas particulares por estar arreglada para seis hombres solos" [easy to perform in private houses, as it is arranged with six male parts]. Evidently the threat of censorship still weighed upon Concha in relation to his choice of subject, possibly more so because of its humorous element. Perhaps for practical reasons of availability of actors, Florinda is absent from this short play, whose six characters are Rodrigo, Pelayo, Julian, Tarif, and Monuza, who are Moors, with a new addition, Bato, a shepherd. In a tour de force of concision, Bato plays a key role in events, that move from an encounter between Julian and Tarif in which the former explains his treacherous plan for vengeance, to the forcing of the locks in the forbidden tower in Toledo to reveal a bronze statue beating a globe with a mace, to the final battle of Guadalete in which Rodrigo flees. Bato enters on two occasions to complain strenuously about the shepherd's way of life in an amusingly ironic, antipastoral manner. Bato is central to the ending of the play, since Rodrigo meets the shepherd as he flees from the battle scene and exchanges clothes with him. This is reminiscent of Lope de Vega's *El último godo*, in which Rodrigo swaps his royal clothes with a poor man he meets. In this case, Bato provides simple humor in his delight with his king's outfit: "Quanto más me miro, más / me parece que estoy bello" [The more I look at myself, / the more I think I look handsome]. Tarif and Julian also come upon Bato, and Tarif mistakes him for the king until Julian recognizes the error. When Bato explains what has happened, he ends by asking them: "¿No es verdad que estoy muy majo?" [I do look splendid, don't I?]. Concha's brief but humorous interpretation of the story brings a new and welcome lightness to it.

A second single-act work, this time a tragic monologue of over three hundred lines entitled *Florinda*, was written about a decade later in 1817 by an anonymous Valencian author, who undertakes to rewrite the ending of María Rosa Gálvez's play by having Florinda die of anguish on the battlefield. The implicit question in Gálvez's work regarding what might have happened had Florinda married Pelayo is verbalized in this monologue when the protagonist wishes she had sealed the reciprocal love between herself and in this case Turismundo, not Pelayo. If she had, "No se vería atravesado ahora / mi tierno corazón de agudas flechas" [My tender heart would not now be pierced by sharp arrows]. Nor would she have become the curse of the Spanish people.

The Height of Romanticism

In the period from 1825 to 1845 four new plays by renowned authors were written in Spain on the legend of King Roderick and La Cava. In 1825, Antonio Gil y Zárate (1793–1862), described by David Gies as "one of the most prolific, interesting and nearly forgotten dramatists of his generation,"[9] presented his first original tragedy *Rodrigo*, but its performance was at once prohibited by the notorious censor Padre Carrillo, who claimed that he was repulsed by the play, whose subject matter was not suitable for the Spanish stage. Carrillo decreed: "Aunque en efecto haya habido en el mundo muchos reyes como don Rodrigo, no conviene presentarlos en el teatro tan aficionados a las muchachas"[10] [although in reality there may have been many kings like Roderick in the world, it is not appropriate to present them in the theatre with such a liking for young girls]. This appears a particularly harsh and unreasonable judgment since the king does not actually commit a rape in this play, and is truly repentant of his base desires by the final act, although its prohibition underlines Menéndez Pidal's comment that during the era of Fernando VII, censorship suffocated not only comedy, but also the incipient revival of tragedy.[11]

Gil y Zárate's play is unashamedly similar to María Rosa Gálvez's *Florinda*, and includes characters identically named Egerico and Tulga. However, Gil y Zárate's adjustments are more than nominal. The play is a five-, rather than three-act tragedy, perhaps in order to contain the whole of the action, including Rodrigo's attempted seduction of Florinda and Julian's betrayal, within the confines of the classical unity of time. The title indicates that the king is the focus of the play, not Florinda, possibly consonant with Gil y Zárate's espousal of the German Romantic ideal of a literature that was heroic, monarchical, and Christian, which the dramatist rehearses in his later *Manual de Literatura* of 1842.

Florinda has a lover, as she does in Gálvez's drama, though not Pelayo but Teodofredo in this play, and in contrast with the earlier work, the young Visigothic hero remains constant to Florinda as his betrothed and to Rodrigo as his king throughout. The suggestion of hope and renewal implicit in the presence of Pelayo in the plot is absent from *Rodrigo*, which ends with a sense of tragic doom for Spain, though it may be that Gil y Zárate felt too strongly the inconsistency of allowing Pelayo and Rodrigo to coexist within the same time frame. In contrast with *Florinda*, Egerico has a minor role as Julian's supporter, while it is Tulga in this case who is the evil adviser to the king. He suggests that Rodrigo can easily get rid of Egilona by divorcing her and making Florinda queen, and then contrives a plot to kidnap the girl at dead of night to enable Rodrigo to seduce her. This scheme fails, as in true Romantic fashion, a bolt of lightning strikes the tent and destroys it as Florinda beseeches Rodrigo to spare her, leaving her unconscious as the king flees into the night.

Although the first scene of the play takes place, identically to Gálvez's work, on the banks of the river Guadalete, Gil y Zárate makes the notable change of introducing Julian in the first act (unlike his appearance in the last three scenes of *Florinda*) and allowing him a much more substantial presence in the drama. Although the characterization is on the whole sketchy, Julian is drawn in the most detail as a complex man fraught with conflicting feelings who is ultimately overcome by his implacable desire for vengeance. He abhors the corruption of the Visigothic monarchy under Vitiza:

> ...vicios, licencia,
> Cobarde olvido del honor primero
> Y torpe corrupción, la herencia es esta
> Que nos dejó al caer
>
> [...first, vices, licentiousness,
> cowardly forgetfulness of honour
> Then lewd corruption, this is the inheritance
> He left us when he fell].
> (1. i, 63)

By Act 4, Julian realizes the extent of his betrayal: "...¡Todo un pueblo / Víctima habrá de ser de mis rencores!..." [...An entire people / Must be the victim of my rancor] (4. ii, 4–5), but his remorse is not stronger than his obsession with revenge, which he attempts to justify as a kind of heroic act: "...si es crimen, solo / cabe tal crimen en heróicos pechos" [...if it is a crime, such a crime can only lie within a heroic breast] (4. iv, 3–4).

Rodrigo, who overcomes his passion and frees Teodofredo from prison to allow him to marry Florinda, dies as they do at the end of this tragedy, but Julian does not. In a final scene reminiscent of that in Landor's *Count*

Julian, Florinda expires in her father's arms blaming him for her death, but when Julian goes to take his own life he is scornfully prevented from doing so by the Moorish victor Tarif, who loathes his treachery and insists on making him live on in order to suffer for his treason.

Rodrigo lacks dramatic power, partly due to the excessive pace at which the action moves. Several scenes are just a few lines long, as if Gil y Zárate were hastening through the plot and straining to encompass the narrative within five acts, and the language is not memorable, although Tulga and Julian have a few stirring lines. There is also an impression of uncertainty on the part of the dramatist as to which character to place center stage, regardless of the title, and a sense that in spite of the formal adherence to classical form, Romantic elements such as pathos and the pathetic fallacy destabilize the dramatic structure and compromise both styles, accentuating the feeling of vacillation that drains away dramatic impact.

This tension between neoclassical and Romantic styles was resolved in Miguel Agustín Príncipe's espousal of a comparatively restrained Romantic mood in his intriguing play *El Conde Don Julián*, written in 1838 and performed at the end of that year. Príncipe was born in Zaragoza in 1811 and died in Madrid in 1866, where he went to work as a lawyer and later a librarian, after holding a chair in literature at the University of Zaragoza. His prolific talent manifested itself in histories, legends, narratives, and poetry as well as drama, and deserves an attention as yet unbestowed. His work was much admired by his friend Cayetano Balseyro y Goycochea, who described *El Conde Don Julián* in a review as ". . .sustituyendo a la frialdad y a las travas del clasicismo caduco, el movimiento, la animación y una racional independencia" [. . .substituting for the coldness and encumbrances of outmoded classicism a sense of movement, animation, and rational independence] while avoiding the ". . .estravíos y la anárquica licencia de un romanticismo frenético"[12] [. . .the bad ways and anarchical license of the frenetic style of Romanticism']. In spite of this, Príncipe's historical verse drama written in seven scenes casts the spotlight upon Julian, whom the dramatist compares in the opening poem to a classical subject, Tarquino Colatino, the Roman whose wife Lucretia was raped by Tarquin the proud in the sixth century BC. This act determined the fall of the monarchy, which was replaced by government under the two consuls Colatino and Brutus. The dishonorable rape of a subject's wife by a licentious monarch is as far as Príncipe takes the analogy. According to Menéndez Pidal, the Spanish dramatist used Landor's tragedy as a basis for his play, possibly via an unknown translation. This is plausible, as Landor had Spanish connections, and Pidal lists a number of parallels between the plots of the two works.[13] Julian's vacillating emotional states in Príncipe's version, ranging from delirium, calm, fury, tenderness, anger, and desperation are akin to the emotional extremes of his counterpart in Landor's work, although the Spaniard's purpose is to exonerate the count entirely from the betrayal of his country, unlike Landor, who presents the complexities of his plight rather than passing judgment upon his actions. Also unlike Landor's play, Julian dies at the end in this case.

Landor is not the only influence apparent, as Príncipe's Florinda is betrothed to Pelayo as in Gálvez's play. Her father's hint that she may be pregnant with Roderick's child is a story element first introduced in Handel's Rodrigo, also used in Juan de Dios de Mora's slightly later novel and also more recently in the twentieth-century musical, *La Cava*. Egilona, who is the most dignified and moving character in the drama, showing her nobility and forgiveness of Rodrigo in her devotion to Florinda and offering the latter to her husband as his queen instead of herself, is strongly reminiscent of Handel's Egilona. It seems unlikely that Príncipe could have known Handel's work, particularly since it was not performed at that time, but whatever the degree of influence, Príncipe works these elements into a truly striking contribution to the evolution of the legend. His tour de force lies in his creation of an entirely new interpretation of the episode of the enchanted palace near Toledo. In Scene 2, a Gothic atmosphere is evoked as Julian and the superstitious and terrified Count Requila arrive at the ruined palace amid a mighty storm. To their horror two ghosts materialize to inform them that Rodrigo already has Florinda and is on his way to Toledo with her, making it too late for Julian's revenge. The ghosts disappear before Roderick arrives to discover the canvas bearing the infamous predictions of his destiny, but return again in increased numbers to prevent Roderick and Julian fighting a duel.

It transpires that the dead are really the living, as the ghosts turn out to be two Jewish characters, Tobías and Jehú, and their followers, who have conspired to betray the Visigoths to the Moors. When Egilona is imprisoned in Roderick's palace, Tobías acts as her guard, and the queen cannot conceal her hatred for his race. However, the Jew's story elicits compassion, as it appears that his wife and son have been taken away from him, despite Julian's virtuous protection of him in the past. His own hatred for the Visigoths is stronger than his loyalty to Julian, so he mixes a narcotic drink for the count upon Roderick's orders, and awaits his revenge:

¡Alégrate, Sion! pueblo judío,
¡alza la frente de temor agena!
tus viles opresores se dividen,
¡y tú, Tobías, el momento acecha!

[Be joyful, Sion! Jewish people,
raise your forehead indifferent to fear!

> Your vile oppressors are divided,
> and you, Tobías, must choose the right moment!].
>   (3. 2)

Tobías and the other Jews will exact a vengeance against the Visigoths that parallels Julian's vengeance against Roderick. The Jewish plot to turn the sons of Witiza (in this case Sigiberto and Azasuldo) against Roderick fails, as Pelayo heroically rouses them to fight against invasion. However, Tobías brings the chest containing the portentous canvas depicting the Arab invasion to show Tarif, who makes a pact with the Jew to fight against the Goths on the basis of concessions to be given to the Jewish people after the battle. In a scene that stretches the imagination, Tobías speaks before the Ark of the Covenant, of which he has secret charge, of the vengeance of the Jews upon centuries of slavery under Gothic rule:

> ¡Reyes difuntos!, mirad,
> esprimid, saboread
> el fruto de la opresión
>
> [Deceased kings! Look,
> squeeze out, savour
> the fruit of oppression].
>   (7. 8)

But the Jews do not live to see the glory of Israel, as they so desired, for when the betrayer is betrayed, Julian is so horrified at Tobías's treachery that he kills him with a dagger. In an ironic and highly poignant ending, Witiza's sons accuse Julian of betraying the Goths, and realizing that posterity will see him as a traitor, he screams: "¡MIENTE LA TRADICIÓN! ¡MIENTE LA HISTORIA!" [TRADITION HAS LIED! HISTORY HAS LIED!] (7. 15), before taking his own life. This would have made a magnificent ending, if Sigiberto had not announced: "¡¡¡¡AUN VIVE PELAYO!!!!," [PELAYO STILL LIVES!!!!], which creates a bathetic, almost farcical effect far from the one intended.

In this play, Roderick is portrayed as deeply repentant of his violation of Florinda, and actually contrives to release Pelayo from imprisonment to allow him to marry her. However, it is the vindication of Julian that comes to the fore. If, as Goycochea maintains, Príncipe's purpose was to fight against eleven centuries of tradition and erase the stain on Julian's character cast upon it by history, he does so at the expense of the Jews, who are the villains of this piece. There is some historical evidence to suggest that the Jews may have been heavily involved in the invasion of Spain. In the Visigothic legislative document promulgated after *Concilio XVII* [Council XVII] of 694, during the reign of King Egica, it is noted that certain Jews wanted to usurp the throne, thus provoking the ruin of their people and their country. According to Pilar León Tello, the Acts of the Council also claim Jewish intrigues contributed to the events of 711: "se cree tramaban con sus correligionarios de África la invasion de los árabes que tuvo lugar diecisiete años después"[14] [it is believed that they connived with other Jews in Africa over the Arab invasion that took place seventeen years later]. It is not possible to say to what extent Príncipe was familiar with the details of Visigothic history, though Julian's anguished words at the end of the play indicate the playwright's skepticism over traditional historical interpretations of the invasion of Spain. Yet it would not be fair to say that this is an antisemitic work, for the Jewish characters are portrayed with considerable sympathy, and as Goycochea points out, their actions "demuestran las consecuencias de la tiranía y de la oppression" [demonstrate the consequences of tyranny and oppression].

Although Miguel Agustín Príncipe is outside the literary canon of today and is not mentioned in the Cambridge History of Spanish Literature, his play met with unbridled enthusiasm when it was staged in Zaragoza. The Aragonese playwright was dragged from his sick bed onto the stage amid rapturous applause, perhaps more exuberant precisely because Zaragoza had been attacked by the Carlists early in 1838 and had driven them back, this constituting yet another setback for the faction that wished to place Fernando's brother Carlos on the throne instead of Queen Isabella. Goycochea's comment in his celebratory review of *El Conde Don Julián* that the end of the play reveals "los riesgos a que se esponen los partidos y las naciones que fían a los estrangeros su salvación y su futura suerte"[15] [the risks to which parties and nations expose themselves who rely on outsiders for their salvation and future fate] suggests that the play's reenactment of the medieval story with a surprising new twist that turned history on its head may have been highly pertinent to contemporary Spanish politics.

If Príncipe's play interrogates history and tradition in relation to the legend of King Roderick and La Cava, the famous Romantic playwright José Zorrilla's diptych of one-act dramas on the theme of the Visigothic king explores what might have happened to Roderick, Julian, and Florinda after the defeat at the battle of Guadalete. The first play, *El puñal del godo* [The Goth's Dagger] of 1842 was written in just twenty-four hours for a bet, as the dramatist indicates in his dedication. Menéndez Pidal has much that is interesting to say about this frequently performed drama,[16] including the anecdote that in true Romantic fashion, Zorrilla wrote the play without a break all day and night without any sustenance other than coffee and hot chocolate. In spite of his claim to spontaneity of writing, Pidal points to a number of earlier versions of the legend that must have influenced the composition, such as Brito, from whom the Portuguese setting and the monk Romano derive, Southey, who also uses Romano and whose Roderick similarly joins Pelayo in battle at Covadonga, possibly Corral, and also Espronceda, whose poetic work *El Pelayo*, discussed below, contains a scene in which Roderick dreams of a dagger. The play has an all-male cast of four, due to the fact that no actress was available for the first Christmas performance, and also because a limited cast enabled the work to be performed in private houses with ease. Despite this, the drama was written in 1842 but did not get the approval of the censors until 1849.

The characters in question are Rodrigo, the monk Romano, Julián, and the new invention of a Visigothic soldier, Theudia, who is the voice of reason and saves the king's life. The action takes place entirely inside Romano's simple hut at the top of a mountain, on the anniversary of the defeat at the Guadalete. Rodrigo has been sheltered there for five years by Romano, and has lived the life of a penitent recluse, often displaying symptoms of psychological derangement, part of which is an obsession with his obviously phallic Gothic dagger. This obsession is the result of what the king believes was a vision of a monk who warns him that Julián will seek him out and kill him with his own weapon. Theudia, who is loyal to Rodrigo and saved his life in the battle, when once reunited with his king encourages him to cast aside his fantastical imaginings and take practical action by fighting with him and Pelayo in the impending battle in Asturias. Lifted from his moroseness and depression, the king agrees, and invokes the name of Julián, whom he longs to kill.

At this point the door bursts open amid the storm that is raging, and the count himself appears. He and Rodrigo have an interchange in which each statement is mirrored exactly by the other character so that their situation and feelings appear identical, an obvious piece of stagecraft that might be thrilling or amusing depending on its interpretation. Once they recognize each other, Rodrigo's fear looks set to be justified as Julián seizes the eponymous dagger, but Theudia steps in and slays Julian just in time.

In this highly imaginative and emotionally compressed play, the two male protagonists of the legend are placed upon an equal footing in their suffering and dishonor. Neither is entirely vindicated, nor entirely demonized, though there is no redemption for the count, only death. Their encounter is an acting out of a longed-for scenario, and one that has been mooted in the past, notably in the ballad where Roderick suggests Julian might have killed him, rather than betray a whole country. But here Julián does not get his revenge, and his death at the hands of Theudia underlines in simple terms the values of loyalty, courage, and rationality, for the soldier is the real hero of the drama, whose status as such is reinforced in Rodrigo's last lines, when he equates the soldier's honor with royal status: "siempre ha de ser, para quien muere honrado, / tumba de rey la fosa del soldado" [for one who dies much honored, the soldier's grave must be / the tomb of a king] (lines 902–3).

The second play of the diptych, *La Calentura*, was written five years later in 1847, again with a cast of four, with Julian substituted by Florinda. Menéndez Pidal's scathing comment on its inferiority fails to take account of the imaginative excellence of the drama. Zorrilla describes it as a "drama fantástico," which could mean "a fantasy drama" or a "phantasmal drama," either of which would fit the bill, as Roderick, who has returned to Romano's hut following the battle of Covadonga, is plagued by the fear of a "sombra maldita" [cursed shadow] that follows him each time he ventures outside. Zorrilla writes two scenes exactly parallel to those in *El puñal del godo*, starting with the first scene in which Theudia appears in Romano's hut and the hermit invites him to warm himself by the fire, as before. He offers him food, better fare of cake and wine this time, and tells him of the king's return. In the statutory violent thunderstorm, Roderick enters and recounts how Pelayo would not believe he was the king and accused him of being an impostor. In despair, Roderick has made his way back to Portugal, though his beloved horse dies on the way.

Several of the subsequent sections of dialogue between Roderick and Theudia were not performed, possibly because of aspects relating to kingship and the clergy that might not have been deemed appropriate. As Roderick describes the ghostly vision that torments him, Theudia once more adopts the voice of reason, telling him it is all a fantasy and giving him courage to carry on. The climax of the drama lies in the sudden and melodramatic entrance of Florinda, wild and feverish, demanding water to drink. She and Roderick have a mirroring dialogue identical to the one between Julian and Roderick in the previous play, in which they both express similar feelings of dishonor and despair, until the truth of their identities is obvious to each of them. During Florinda's account of her violation, which bears a similar terrible irony to the dialogue between Florinda and Roderick in Southey's poem, she reveals that it was her mother who was really to blame in secretly desiring the king herself, and then luring him to Florinda's apartments with a letter, intending to substitute herself for her daughter. Having thus exonerated Rodrigo, she dies, and the king goes out into the night also to die, inconsolable in his disgrace.

As in *El puñal del godo*, Zorrilla compresses powerful emotion to create scenes of great dramatic impact. By means of the rather obvious, though probably effective stagecraft, the playwright poses the question "What if

Rodrigo had met Julian and Florinda after the events of 711?" and presents the audience with his vision of what might have happened after the battle of Guadalete. In this vision, Rodrigo is a penitent, not a hero. None of the three main noble protagonists of the legend is heroic in these dramas; there is no redemption for them, just death. It is the hermit and the common soldier who are good, strong, and morally upright. What is particularly interesting is Zorrilla's depiction of the absolutely identical emotions of Rodrigo, Julian, and Florinda. They are all equally dishonored, emotionally destroyed and cursed by future generations. One is not more to blame than the others for their actions. Zorrilla's achievement in addressing a previously unexplored aspect of the legend within the scope of two one-act plays is considerable, and goes far beyond what Ribbans describes as the playwright's characteristic use of Castilian historical subjects "to extol, at the most superficial level, national qualities of bravery, honour and religion."[17] In this insight into the hearts of the three protagonists, Zorrilla invents a new fragment of the legend that looks beyond the nominal end of the story and provides fresh insights into their feelings in a way that both finishes the unfinished and hints at new possibilities in the future of the legend.

The last nineteenth-century dramatic work I wish to discuss in any detail was written by the Cuban poet and novelist Gertrudis Gómez de Avellaneda, better known for works such as *Sab*, a novel that movingly portrays the evils of slavery in her native country. In fact, she wrote sixteen full-length plays, the first of which, *Leoncia*, was staged in Seville in 1840. Like María Rosa Gálvez, she brings one of the female protagonists of the legend to the forefront, not Florinda in this case, but Egilona. In doing so she harks back to the powerful portrayals of Egilona in eighteenth-century versions of the legend,[18] this time placing her in the limelight as the heroine, rather than in the background as she is in Gil y Zárate's drama, in which Roderick is willing to abandon her because she is sterile. While Miguel Agustín Príncipe is sensitive toward her plight in his play and portrays her as a noble and generous character, Gómez de Avellaneda's *Egilona*, written in 1845, centers upon the terrible dilemma in which Roderick's queen finds herself in Seville at the end of 715 AD, after the defeat of the Visigothic army. In this three-act tragedy written in hendecasyllables, the apparently widowed Egilona marries the Moorish emir Abdalasis, only to find that Roderick is still alive.

From the first Act, Egilona is beset by guilt because she loves Abdalasis, but feels she is betraying her country and Rodrigo, speaking of her "criminal amor" [criminal love] (1. 2, 92) after a vision in which the former king chastises her. The emir is portrayed in a highly favorable light throughout the play. The more conventional depiction of Moorish characters as cruel and alien is turned on its head in the case of Abdalasis, who is praised by Egilona's friend Ermesinda:

> Su mano por la tuya dirigida
> mil beneficios próvida derrama
> sobre el pueblo español, que fiel amigo
> y no opresor le juzga.
>
> [Guided by yours, his provident hand
> showers a thousand good things
> upon the Spanish people, who judge him
> to be a loyal friend, not oppressor].
>   (1: 2, 174–77)

The jealous and treacherous Berber Caleb remarks that the emir is rather more Christian than Muslim: "y más que el alcorán se reverencian / en su palacio los cristianos ritos" [in his palace Christian rites are more revered than the Koran] (1: 4, 50–51). Although this renders him slightly ambiguous by aligning him with the religion of the people he has conquered, the dramatist has clearly wished to create a character of great religious tolerance and beneficence. This generosity of spirit is evident when he reproaches Caleb for his intolerance with the three Visigothic prisoners in his charge:

> Omnipotente Dios, ser infinito,
> que acoge grato los sinceros votos
> con cualquier culto que le son rendidos.
>
> [Omnipotent God, infinite being,
> who is pleased to welcome sincere vows
> from any cult from which they are offered]
>   (1: 6, 60–62)

Abdalasis magnanimously releases the Christian prisoners, but Gómez de Avellaneda creates a masterly twist in the plot that shocks in its unexpectedness and its power to wreak havoc. One of the prisoners is Rodrigo. The latter asks the emir about the fate of Egilona, and upon discovering that she now has a new husband, he reveals his identity and claims his lawful wife. Abdalasis is greatly disturbed but reaches the conclusion that the prisoner is a madman, and sends him back to jail.

From Act 2 onward, the plot becomes highly complex as those on stage hatch different plans, both good and evil. Abdalasis orders Caleb to enter the prison and kill Rodrigo, but the Berber has his own agenda, which is to murder the emir. Egilona meanwhile discovers this reimprisonment of one of her countrymen, and resolves to release the captive herself and find out what has angered her new husband so greatly. By the start of Act 3, Caleb has Rodrigo in a trap. Instead of following the emir's orders to kill him, he gives Rodrigo a dagger, and a letter that has come secretly from Muza in Syria, ordering Abdalasis' death. If Rodrigo kills the emir, he will go free. Rodrigo sees through the plan, at which point Egilona arrives and discovers that her first husband still lives. At this crucial dramatic point, Abdalasis himself arrives in the dungeon amid the noise of the mob outside demanding Egilona's death, and attempts to kill his wife and Rodrigo with a hatchet, but cannot bring himself to do so.

The second part of Act 3 is unusually set in a mosque in which the emir has sought a haven. At another moment of high drama in a deeply moving scene, Abdalasis makes an almost superhuman sacrifice and says he will allow Rodrigo to go free, and take Egilona with him. Although Rodrigo forestalls Caleb's attempt on the emir's life, Abdalasis is killed according to Muza's orders. Unable to overcome her feelings for him, Egilona kills herself to be with him, rather than leave with Rodrigo, and the play ends on an upbeat note for the Christians, with the familiar refrain that Rodrigo and Pelayo still live.

Egilona is powerful and original, addressing the kind of question repeatedly posed by nineteenth-century Spanish writers as to what might have happened to Roderick and in this case, Egilona, after the defeat in 711. It is interesting that neither Julian nor Florinda is mentioned and plays no part whatsoever in the proceedings. Although Egilona is the pivot of the action and the title suggests she is the central protagonist, she is overshadowed by the character of Abdalasis, who is sensitively portrayed as a noble man brought down by destiny. His greatness of spirit and tolerance are unappreciated by both the Visigoths and his own people, and one is left with the impression that Spain might have been a much better place had he lived than it was before and after his brief rule in the play. As a woman dramatist, Gómez de Avellaneda's evident sympathy for her main female character ultimately gives way to her sympathy for a man both racially and religiously maligned by tradition, like the Cuban slaves about whom she writes so tellingly in her prose works.

The dramatic recreations of the legend in the second half of the nineteenth century were comparatively lacking in depth and substance, though there was a distinct movement from theatre to light opera. The focus was shared between Roderick and Florinda, the former portrayed by Antonio Arnao in a lyrical drama of 1857, *Don Rodrigo*, whose libretto was based upon the Duque de Rivas' poem *Florinda*, and a slight drama of 1886 by Florentino Molina Acosta, *Rodrigo*. Florinda appears in two late-nineteenth-century *zarzuelas*, one by J.J. Jiménez Delgado dated 1880 and another by Salvador María Granés, both entitled *Florinda*, and in a more serious operatic work, *Florinda* (1189–92) with the libretto by Angelo Bignotti and F. Ximénez de Embún.[19]

The legend found fullest expression in drama in nineteenth-century Spain, through which important questions regarding Spain's early history and its defining narrative were articulated in kaleidoscopic ways that brought new elements into more dominant focus, in particular the portrayal of female characters, and the years after the defeat in 711. At the same time, Spain's finest Romantic poets also took up the challenge in what constitutes the most extensive poetic exploration of the legend within Spain since the ballads.

The Legend in Spanish Romantic Poetry

The self-styled Spanish Byron, José de Espronceda (1808–42), is the earliest Spanish poet of the nineteenth century to find inspiration in the love affair of Roderick and Florinda. The publication by Durán of a collection of Spanish ballads in the early 1800s and the fashionability of historical themes due to the influence of Walter Scott combined with the perception that Spain's past should be defended and learnt from, as manifested in the drama of the era. However, Espronceda's poem *El Pelayo* does not reflect contemporary problems through earlier historical events. It is incomplete, fragmentary, and experimental, a work begun as a sixteen-year old in Guadalajara under the tutelage of the poet Lista y Hermosilla, though he reworked it while in London in 1828, and still had a mind to finish it in 1840.

Espronceda's precocious genius is evident in his experiments with style and structure in the poem, by means of which he evolves a new poetic idiom through the fusion of neoclassical and Romantic elements. The presence of the definite article in the title indicates a desire to write an epic poem, of which the historical theme, the verse form of *octavas reales* and the staging of set pieces from classical epic, such as the meeting of a council, and a portrait of hunger, are evidence. In this respect he is akin to Southey, who also entitled his poem *Pelayo* until he realized that Roderick was a far superior poetic subject. It is quite possible that Espronceda knew Southey's poem, published ten years before *El Pelayo* was started, although Menéndez Pidal makes reference only to its similarities to Byron's *Sardanapolos* in its depiction of Roderick as a feminized, orientalized monarch.[20] At the beginning of the Fragmento Primero, the third person narrator, like Southey, focuses on virtue: "Virtud contemplo, libertad y gloria, / Crímenes, sangre, asolación, ruina" [I contemplate virtue, freedom and glory, / crimes, blood, devastation, ruin] (1: 1, 5–6), but in this case it is juxtaposed with the horrors of war and crime.

Juxtaposition, disjointedness, and inconclusiveness characterize *El Pelayo*, due in part to the fact that during Espronceda's short but tumultuous life some of the manuscripts were lost, leaving only fragments of fragments. But fragmentation and incompleteness are recognized characteristics of the poet's later works, and aspects he appeared to favor. The extant poem consists of six fragments, but Pelayo makes an appearance only in the final section, although in a confusing change from third person to first person narrator, he actually narrates the central episode of the battle of Guadalete. In addition to this narrative confusion, the chronology is also unclear. The initial setting is Roderick's court at Toledo, where the king is "alegre y descuidado" [happy and carefree] (1: 4, 6), longing for the "dulce, bella, celestial Florinda" [gentle, lovely, heavenly Florinda] (1: 4, 8), all couched in a Gongorine pastoral idyll amid emerald green grass (1: 8, 3). Fate and lust drive the king to rape, upon which the landscape changes dramatically in sympathy with events as the predictable storm blows up as a symbol of divine anger. The image of fallen leaves after the hurricane of wind, a frequent one in Espronceda's verse, poignantly expresses Florinda's dishonor, and the fragment ends with the typological prefiguration of Roderick in a comparison with King Balthasar in the biblical Book of Daniel, who profaned the sacred vessels of the Jews, and was warned of his punishment in the inscription of three Hebrew words on the wall by an invisible hand, echoing the Arab figures etched on the canvas in the legendary Toledan tower.

Roderick's dreadful dreams in the second fragment, in which both Death and Julian assail him, the latter in the form of a fiery dragon with a three-pronged tongue, presage the terrible defeat in battle that constitutes the central episode in the Fragmento Tercero, consisting of fifty-eight verses. Nearly all of this fragment is devoted to the newly invented character of Sancho, Roderick's son, a "mancebo hermoso, intrépido y Lozano" [a handsome, intrepid and robust young man] (3: 14, 8), who fights bravely in battle and shows himself to be a fearless hero in contrast with the atmosphere of Gothic terror evoked by ghouls and specters around the soldiers' campsite. Interestingly, it is Sancho, not Pelayo, who is designated as "Héroe del español" [the Spaniard's hero] (3: 34, 1), yet the age and origins of this young fighter remain unknown, leaving the reader to speculate as to whether his mother was Florinda or Roderick's queen.

Continued fighting in the fourth fragment contrasts strongly with the sensual luxury of the seraglio described in the fifth, itself juxtaposed with a ghastly description of the death and hunger after the battle, which is not individualized. In the Fragmento Sexto, Pelayo finally rallies a dying people to save Spain. The conquering hero is thereby reduced to a shadowy presence in the poem, mentioned in almost anecdotal episodes, while the focus is upon Rodrigo, his son Sancho, and upon a number of impersonal and disjointed descriptions that underline the dissonant nature of the piece. Ynduráin, editor of the 1992 edition of Espronceda's poetry, feels that the ruptured nature of *El Pelayo* marks a rupture with classical order and balance.[21] As such it marks the experimental nature of the poem, which is manifested in its imprecision and sense of mystery. There is no depiction of the fate of Rodrigo or Florinda in this unfinished work and the presence of an invented character, Sancho, is puzzling, since Espronceda could have used Pelayo as a figure antithetical to Rodrigo without further fictionalization. As well as reaching for new forms of poetic expression, Espronceda also renders the legend itself fragmented and disjointed, and in doing so reflects a similar tendency already identified in nineteenth-century dramatic representations of the story.

The fragmentary is also a feature of *Florinda*, a narrative poem published by Ángel Saavedra, Duque de Rivas (1791–1865) in 1834. The poet describes it as a work that "debe mirarse como fragmentos, no como una obra completa"[22] [should be viewed as fragments, not as a complete work], and is a further instance of imaginative reinterpretation of the legend and its aftermath that places Florinda at the heart of the action in a surprising manner. It is a poem written during an exile imposed by an ill-fated king, Fernando VII, perhaps akin in Saavedra's mind to Roderick, part written in England, Gibraltar, and Malta, which might account for its fragmentariness to some degree. The stay in England must have influenced the poem, for Menéndez Pidal again points to similarities with Byron's *Sardanapolous* of 1821,[23] while he rejects any influence by Landor or Southey. Nevertheless, Saavedra uses scholarly notes in the same way as Southey and Scott, quoting detailed sources for aspects of the legend such as the episode of the enchanted tower. This attention to historical verisimilitude (which the Duque took seriously, for he refers to Miguel de Luna's *Historia verdadera* but agrees with Conde that it is absurd) reflects his characteristically Romantic desire to glorify Spain's past, particularly that of the Middle Ages, an aim in tune, as Gerald Brenan points out,[24] with the ideology of the Spanish Liberals who hoped to restore the greatness of Spain, and whose views Saavedra shared as a young radical abroad.

As a soldier who fought in the War of Independence, the Duke of Rivas was a man of deep political and national feelings, and the poet may well have had the contemporary situation in mind when he describes the Visigothic people as foolish and decadent:

> ¡Triste del pueblo a quien su triste suerte
> tanto a la infamia y corrupción prosterna,
> que necio ríe y necio se divierte
> con los vicios de aquel que lo gobierna,

[Sad the people whose sad fate
prostrates them before infamy and corruption,
who foolishly laugh and foolishly amuse themselves
with the vices of he who governs them].
(Canto 2, v. 3)

Saavedra also had his finger on the pulse of contemporary literary developments. Like Espronceda's poem, *Florinda* has one foot in the neoclassical past and one foot in the Romantic present, and is constructed using the classical meter of epic poetry, *octavas*, with a corresponding classical division into *cantos*. The ten thousand–line poem also shows strong influence of Pedro Montengón's *El Rodrigo* in certain plot details, though this is not acknowledged by Saavedra. Blended with these echoes of the eighteenth century are specific features that came to typify Romanticism, notably effects of horror and mystery. In his short, helpful discussion of the poem, Allison Peers emphasizes that these elements marked an important stage in the Duque de Rivas' poetic development, that he was breaking new ground.[25] Canto 1, "El banquete y la prisión" [The banquet and the prison] is one of the two most successful scenes in the poem in its powerful theatricality. As Florinda and Rodrigo enjoy a magnificent banquet in the king's palace, an unknown stranger enters and watches the scene unnoticed. In the midst of the feasting, an elderly Jew, Rubén, introduces elements of shock and horror as he announces that his wine cup is full of blood and throws it over the table. Upon hearing these premonitory words, the mysterious stranger draws his sword and attempts to stab Rodrigo in the chest, describing himself as a messenger of divine wrath: "la celeste ira, / que mi brazo terrible está animando" [the heavenly anger / that my dreadful arm gives life to] (1: v. 20). His blow misses the king, and upon immediate arrest, he is revealed to be Count Julian, in elemental fury at the scene he has witnessed.

But Julian has arrived too late to save his family honor, because Florinda has already fallen for Rodrigo, and refuses to kill him at her father's behest. He is appalled, and curses her before joining with the evil bishop Opas to seek vengeance. The lovers' passion continues unabated, and Rodrigo goes to the ancient Toledan tower to consult the learned Rubén. After a very protracted description of the ghastly Gothic tower, Rodrigo has a vision similar to the one in Walter Scott's *The Vision of Don Roderick*. In this case, "el encantado alcázar se estremece / y como polvo y humo desaparece" [the enchanted fortress shudders / and like dust and smoke, disappears] (2: v. 39). It is replaced by a gruesome vision of a "tropel innumerable de escuadrones / de extrañas y fierísimas naciones" [an innumerable throng of squadrons / of ferocious foreign nations] (2: v. 41), and a second vision of the king's Visigothic ancestors who curse him.

In a strongly contrasting scene, Florinda ponders the beauty of the Toledan night and wonders if her ill-fated love can be blamed upon the corruption of court life, compared with the purity of the rustic idyll. The frightening figure that approaches her in the gloom is revealed as her lover the king, struck dumb with the horror of his recent vision. In Canto Three, "La Venganza" [Vengeance], the narratorial viewpoint changes to the first person, as Julian laments his fate as he sails to Africa to enlist the help of the Moors. Saavedra's second master stroke comes in the fourth Canto, "La Batalla" [The Battle]. Florinda, protagonist of the poem, is tormented by her terrible destiny, and the poet touchingly teases out the conflict in her heart between her love for her father and her love for Rodrigo, a conflict reminiscent of Doña Jimena in certain versions of the Cid legend in which the Cid kills her father. She has a premonitory vision of the two men in mortal combat and the poet asks:

> En lucha tan fatal, ¿a quién intenta
> ayudar la infeliz? ¿Por cuál envía
> su voto al cielo? De las dos, ¿qué espada
> de funesto laurel querrá adornada?
>
> [In such a deadly fight, who should the
> poor girl try to help? For whom should she
> send her vows to heaven? Of the two, which sword
> would she see adorned with ill-fated laurel?].
>
> (4: v. 32)

Her vision becomes reality as Rodrigo and Julian fight each other amid the raging battle, but they are interrupted by a figure whose face is hidden behind a visor, who is revealed to be Florinda in battle dress, come to separate them. In this reformulation of Florinda's disguise as a Moorish warrior used by Montengón and the Marquis de Sade, Saavedra has Julian flee the scene, while Rodrigo rides into battle with Florinda at his side.

In the final Canto, the poet composes a stirring description of the battle, befitting an ex-soldier. The poem ends inconclusively, for the reader does not know the ultimate fate of the protagonists, although the poet concludes that death would be the kindest end for the king. While the themes of love, patriotism, and religion that shine bright in this work are akin to those of Southey in his *Roderick*, it is Florinda who embraces passion, courage, and uprightness, and Florinda who saves the two men she loves from destroying each other, rising above her fate to take on an almost manly role on the battlefield. This portrayal of the bravery and compassion of his heroine is a stroke of genius by Saavedra in a poem that has its *longueurs* and mediocre, prosaic descriptions. Her unabashed passion for

Rodrigo is a step removed from the chaste love of Southey's Florinda, and her redemptive agency in the poem as a warrior on the battlefield is unprecedented in the history of the legend.

Three further poetic versions of the story of the king and the whore appeared around the middle of the nineteenth century in Spain. A poem entitled *Don Opas* by José Joaquín de Moras, a Bolivian expatriot, was written in 1835 and published in 1840. It is entirely different in character from all that has gone before, because for the first time in its long evolution, the legend is satirized. The poet adopts an arch, wry tone that is pure burlesque in his creation of Rodrigo, who is cynical and disenchanted, preferring to enjoy orgies rather than fight with his men:

¿Qué me importa la hazaña o la proeza,
en que esta gente la existencia funda?
Este casco me parte la cabeza;
y esta maldita y ponderosa espada
me tiene la cintura derrengada.

[What do I care about the heroic deeds and exploits
these people base their existence upon?
This helmet is killing my head;
and this damned weighty sword
strains my waist.].

(IV: v. 108)

As the title suggests, de Moras presents the destruction of Spain as the work of a priest, Opas, and a young girl, Florinda, the former adopting a flippant tone once his treacherous betrayal of his country has been achieved. He says to the Moor Tarif: "Ya todo se acabó: toca esos cinco," / diz el malvado. "El moro apenas osa / tocar aquella mano ignominiosa" [It's all over now, give me a high five, says the wicked one. The Moor hardly dares / to touch that ignominious hand] (IV: v. 122, 6–8). De Mora combines down-to-earth, colloquial language with obscure, poetic vocabulary (for example, the juxtaposition of the terms 'proeza' and 'hazaña' with a phrase such as "me parte la cabeza" in the quotation above), and his rhyme scheme is complex. The poet is also mordant in his view of the events of 711 as "...rico tesoro / de mentira o verdad, que las abuelas / bordan a su solaz" [...rich treasure of lies or truth, which our grandmothers / embroider for their pleasure] (IV: v. 123, 4–6).

In contrast, the priest J. Arolas wrote a dull short poem entitled "Florinda," that is undated but appeared in 1850, in which Florinda is a mythical creature, "Náyade medio desnuda, / que al margen del río llora" [Half-naked naiad, / who weeps by the riverbank] (v. 7: 1–2), chastised by

Heaven and condemned to be called La Cava. There are some awful rhymes (such as "dejarme a solas / con las olas" [leave me alone, with the waves] (v. 3: 2–3) in a weak poem that is unsympathetic toward its subject.

The latest Romantic poem that reworks the legend is an ingenious and interesting three-part work by Ramón de Campoamor, entitled *Los dos cetros* [The Two Scepters], written in 1860 and dedicated to His Royal Highness the Prince of Asturias. The poet is the narrator in Part I, basing his plot on the Viseu legend in describing how he inherited a convent with a half-ruined temple, where he finds an ancient holy man beside an ancient altar. Hidden inside the elderly saint's walking crook is a piece of papyrus upon which none other than Pelayo has inscribed a narrative. Part II is devoted to telling Pelayo's ballad-like story, and the reader is addressed directly as the account starts with a note of sympathy for Rodrigo:

y a los que amengüen su gloria
les ruego que hagan memoria
que hay manchas hasta en el sol.

[and I ask those who diminish his glory
to bear in mind that even the sun
has dark shadows.].
(II: 3. 5)

Like the poet after him, Pelayo finds himself before this altar, where he encounters the king "llevando cetro de caña, / pobre pastor solitario, / rey de una pobre cabaña" [bearing a cane scepter, / poor lonely shepherd, / king of a poor hovel] (II: 13–15). As his rightful heir in this version, Rodrigo leaves Pelayo to choose between the scepter and the shepherd's crook before he leaves to take "...el camino / de la eterna soledad" [...the road / of eternal solitude] (II: 44–45). Pelayo of course chooses the scepter, which is why the poet finds the crook in the keeping of the old man.

In Part III, the poet addresses his dedicatee, the prince of Asturias, linking poet and monarch as inheritors respectively of the pastoral life epitomized in the shepherd's crook and the throne of Spain (belonging to Roderick and Pelayo before him). The poet uses the comparison to idealize the simple rustic life of a shepherd, superior in his view to the life of care the prince will inherit as future king, and preferring his own "cetro de caña" [cane scepter] to the prince's "cetro de oro" [gold scepter].

Again the focus of the legend is the time after the defeat at Guadalete, once more addressing the uncertainty surrounding Roderick's fate, and again linking Pelayo to him through an imagined inheritance that allows the prince of Asturias to whom the poem is dedicated to appear the inheritor of the heroic Pelayo, who also took on the onerous mantle of kingship. Campoamor's poem cleverly reinforces the Romantic ideal of the simple, pastoral life, while simultaneously reinforcing the continuity of the Spanish monarchy through its perceived link with the Asturian leader Pelayo.

The evolution of the legend in Spanish Romantic poetry parallels its development in theatre at that time in the generally sympathetic attention paid to Florinda and to Roderick to a lesser degree, and in its concentration upon events after the defeat by the Muslim invaders. The metaphors and style of Romanticism intensify the inventiveness of the reworkings and emphasize the fleeting, fragmentary, and uncertain, at the same time adding elements of melodrama that are so fundamental to the performance dimension of the story.

The Legend in the Nineteenth-Century Peninsular Novel

Although the title of the Portuguese novel by Alexandre Herculano (1810–77) published in 1844, *Eurico o presbítero* [Henry the Priest], does not appear to relate to the story of King Roderick and La Cava, the work itself is absolutely fascinating in its incorporation of the story of the Muslim invasion of Spain into the plot of a novel about the celibacy of the priesthood. Its author was an extraordinary figure in the life of his country who created a kind of Renaissance in Portuguese letters, and was renowned as a historian, journalist, and politician. When his death was announced in 1877, there was spontaneous national mourning.

Written at the apogee of Portuguese Romanticism, *Eurico o presbítero*'s dominant plot is the love affair between Eurico, a priest, and Hermengarda, sister of Pelayo, whom he cannot marry because of his vow of chastity, although their love predates his entry into monastic life. The backdrop to this ill-fated passion is the Muslim invasion of Spain, and Pelayo's organization of Christian resistance while in hiding in Covadonga. As such the historical and legendary events are not the main focus of the work, a new aspect in itself with additional interest because of the way in which Roderick and Julian are presented. It is significant that Herculano did not know how to classify his own novel. In his Introduction he states that it is not a poem in prose, nor a historical romance in the style of "o imortal Scott"[26] [the immortal Scott], though he does explain that the Gothic Empire in this work is analogous to the heroic times of Greece. His uncertainty as to the nature of his writing is another manifestation of the potential for the legend to inspire experimentation, to engender the innovative and previously undefined.

In contrast with his uncertainty over generic categorization, Herculano shows a historian's concern with factual accuracy which, I surmise, is the explanation for the complete absence of any reference to Florinda in the narrative. At the start, the author highlights the decadence and moral dissolution of the Visigoths, noting the corruption of the Visigothic clergy against whom Eurico stands apart as morally pure and incorruptible. Herculano introduces "o célebre Roderico" [the famous Roderick] who disputes the Visigothic throne with Vitiza's sons Sisebuto and Ebas, who succumb not to Roderick's usurpation, for the Gothic throne was not legally hereditary, but to the "fortuna e ousadia do ambicioso soldado, que os deixou viver em paz na própria corte e os revestiu de dignidades militares"[27] [good fortune and daring of the ambitious soldier, who let them live in peace in his own court and endowed them with military dignities]. Herculano identifies the conspirators against the new king as "Ebas e Sisebuto filhos de Vitiza, Opas, seu tio, sucesor de Siseberto na Sé de Híspalis, e Juliano, conde dos domínios espanhóis nas costas de África, do outro lado do Estreito, eram os cabeças dos conspiradores"[28] [Ebas and Sisebuto, sons of Vitiza, Opas, their uncle, successor to Siseberto on the See of Seville, and Julian, count of the Spanish dominions on the coast of Africa, on the other side of the Strait, were the leading conspirators]. Count Julian is therefore identified as a traitor to his king, but not for reasons of avenging his dishonor due to his daughter's violation. The reader learns Julian's motivation via Eurico himself, whom Herculano imaginatively places in a key position as a witness of the first invasion of Arabs into the peninsula. One night he creeps down to the beach camp where he overhears Julian talking to Tariq, later reporting the conversation by letter to his friend the Duke of Cordoba. Eurico asks: "Como e porque atraiçoou a terra natal? Ódios civis o levaram a tanta infâmia, segundo entendi das suas palabras. Parricida e fratricida a um tempo, busca vingar-se, talvez de bem poucos de seus irmãos, esmagando-os debaixo das ruínas da patria. A memória deste malaventurado sera réproba e maldita das gerações remotas!"[29] [How and why did he betray his native land? Civil enmities led him to such infamy, as far as I understood from his words. Parricide and fratricide at the same time, he sought vengeance, perhaps for a good few of his brothers, crushing them beneath the ruins of his homeland. The memory of this poor soul will be damned and cursed by generations far into the future]. There is no mention of Florinda, and later, Julian describes the reason for his anger at Roderick as being due to the failure of God's justice in allowing Roderick to live licentiously on Vitiza's rightful throne.

In this novel, Roderick is a token presence in the narrative, the Visigothic figurehead who is dissolute yet courageous in battle. Julian acquires the status of a criminal who unleashes the invasion, thereby allowing Eurico, disguised as a black knight, to save Hermengarda from the clutches of the emir. Tragically for him, however, he refuses to break his priestly vows and abandons her to die in battle, while she goes mad with grief. *Eurico o presbítero* contains powerful and ghastly scenes of self-mutilation and death, of a kind of Christian sadism and masochism to which Eurico falls victim in the end, and these Romantic elements contrast strongly with the author's desire for historical verisimilitude in terms of context. Herculano marshals the events of 711 to present a horrifying picture of the individual destruction caused by imposed celibacy, rendering the legend at once tangential and incomplete while inventing yet another interpretation within its multifaceted evolution in the nineteenth-century Spanish peninsula.

In 1853, a decade after the publication of *Eurico*, Juan de Dios de Mora published his serialized novel *Florinda o La Caba* in Castilian. The work is viewed very unfavorably by Menéndez Pidal, who dismisses this extensive novel of almost seven hundred pages, claiming that "su mal escrita prosa nos recuerda a veces de lejos la literatura"[30] [its badly written prose often bears a vague semblance to literature]. Undoubtedly this is not a literary masterpiece, for it suffers frequently from banal dialogue, excessive and contrived use of coincidence that is beyond credibility, numerous and lengthy subplots involving a host of secondary characters, an exaggeratedly melodramatic Gothic mood and repeated cliff-hangers at the end of chapters, the latter presumably a function of its publication in installments. Nevertheless, it has more virtues than Pidal gives it credit for, as it makes up for stylistic and structural deficiencies by the ingeniousness and complexity of the plot.

De Mora draws heavily upon the plot of Agustín Príncipe's drama in the crucial role played by Jewish characters in the narration. Unlike the play, which centers upon Julian, the focus of the story is Florinda, as the title suggests, who is the inevitable catalyst of the action and an entirely innocent victim of Rodrigo's lust. Pelayo is once more Florinda's betrothed, and Julian kills himself at the end as in Príncipe's play. However, the conspiratorial and ambitious Jewish doctor, Daniel, who loves the king's wife Egilona and doses Florinda with a strong narcotic to allow Roderick to rape her, turns out to be the son Julian never knew he had as the fruit of an adulterous love affair, and consequently Florinda's half brother. Doomed never to enjoy Pelayo's love because of her dishonor, even worse befalls Julian's daughter as she finds herself pregnant and gives birth to a boy named Chindasvinto.

The melodrama of the passionate relationships between Florinda, Pelayo, Rodrigo, Egilona, and Daniel is interwoven with an intricate pseudo-historical plot in which the famous letter from Florinda to her father and his subsequent betrayal of his country to the Moors is almost a detail in the plot already instigated by the Jews to avenge the treatment of their race by earlier Visigothic kings and collude with the Moors to invade Spain. The Jewish high priest Samuel's double deception of Daniel by manipulating the situation to force Julian to kill his own son unwittingly also reveals a motive of personal vengeance upon Julian for his own past dishonor and the death of Samuel's son at the hands of the unfortunate count. But the Jews are not the only conspirators, for the bishop Oppas and the sons of Witiza long to overthrow Roderick. Samuel double crosses both the Moors and Daniel by secretly coordinating the defection of the Jewish men to those Visigoths fighting against their king.

The explanation for this is extremely inventive and ingenious. Samuel reveals that the strange parchments Roderick finds in the enchanted palace alongside those depicting the overthrow of Spain by Arab soldiers have been placed there to protect the secret hiding place of the Ark of the Covenant in the locked chamber. The Jews have built up and exaggerated the old legend of the curse on the king who breaks the locks in order to deter entry to the chamber and the discovery of their priceless relic "...sin que jamás les revelásemos que el arca sagrada del Viejo Testamento era la que allí se ocultaba"[31] [...without us ever revealing to them that the sacred Ark of the Old Testament was what lay hidden there]. When Roderick profanes the palace, he must be dethroned to protect the Ark's future. The demystification of the legend as a cunning Jewish trick is intriguing, and more plausible than many elements of the story. Less convincingly, prior to the battle of Guadalete, Daniel runs off with Egilona, who is not dead as believed, but merely drugged, then Samuel kills himself dramatically once he has seen Julian kill Daniel. More familiarly, Pelayo is the great hero of the battle, and flees to find Florinda, too late, for she has taken the veil, allowing the lovely Gaudiosa to be betrothed to Pelayo, who then leads the incipient reconquest. Roderick escapes to Portugal, but in a complex twist at the end, crime is shown to generate crime, one of the stronger messages of the novel, since Julian's ghastly desire for vengeance outlasts him. Living as a hermit in Viseu, Roderick is provoked to fight to the death by his own son, Chindasvinto, whom he does not recognize. The king kills him, only to be given a parchment revealing Julian's evil plot to lead his grandson to his own father unawares and then be slain by him. Not surprisingly, Roderick dies at the end of this extraordinary narrative.

Florinda was designated as a historical novel, yet it is historical only in the vaguest terms. While it may owe a debt to Walter Scott in its complex narrative of individual conflicts set against a vast historical backdrop, it undoubtedly has many features of the modern-day soap opera, as well as certain scenes, when Daniel is forced to undergo a series of trials by his Jewish compatriots, which are reminiscent of Indiana Jones, though they have little to do with the legend itself. Although Juan de Dios de Mora's historical details are strange (the events are set in 713 and 714), he elaborates upon ideas from Príncipe, Zorrilla, and even the Duque de Rivas to create an imaginative tour de force. Clearly the issue of Jewish relations with Christians and Moors was of great interest to the author, as a large proportion of the story is devoted to this aspect, although the Visigothic Christian characters are ultimately equally culpable, and Roderick is presented as a tyrannical king who is God's vessel through whom evil is punished with evil. The Visigothic line is extinguished in the deaths of both Roderick and his son, and both Jewish protagonists die. Only Pelayo, Gaudiosa, and Florinda survive, although the latter is dead to the world in her convent. Yet in spite of certain brief reflections upon the nature of history, kingship, and the plight of Jews, what stands out is not a moral message, nor the contemporary relevance of this novel, but rather the sheer joy in storytelling that prevails.

The keynote of the extensive development of the legend during this century in the Spanish peninsula is fragmentation, indicating a degree of disintegration of the legend in its essential outlines. The multifaceted productions in all major genres, encompassing both popular literature and works of higher artistic quality, reveal the extent to which the story of the king and the whore appealed to Romantic writers in Spain and Portugal as a vehicle to experiment with new literary forms, techniques, and sensitivities, in which the female protagonists find new voice and are drawn with deeper sympathy, achieving evolution through the fusion of the neoclassical with the Romantic. The identification of the legend with contemporary politics is less marked than is the case in non-Hispanic versions of this era. The splintering of the storyline into an incompleteness at times accompanied by fantastical imaginativeness suggests queries and contradictions within the authorial mind, whose resolution is sought through these fragmentary and often exaggerated reworkings. While such contradictions and uncertainties may relate to literary expression, they appear to me to convey an increasing dissatisfaction with the traditional legend and its conventional interpretations that herald certain more radical departures within twentieth-century postmodernism.

CHAPTER 9

THE ONCE AND FUTURE KING

The extraordinary longevity of the legend of King Roderick and La Cava, manifest in its recurrent and widespread transformations in the twentieth century in Spain, France, England, Latin America and the United States, positions the Spanish medieval narrative firmly within contemporary culture. In this century, however, there is a dynamic change in generic focus as prose takes precedence over poetry and musical forms take precedence over drama. Menéndez Pidal identifies the lack of interest in narrative of early-twentieth-century poets as the explanation for the absence of any poetic version of the subject in the peninsula at this time.[1] The only verse interpretation in this era was written by the Belgian poet Jules-Joseph Leclercq, whose *Rimes Héroïques* were published in France in 1922. While Leclerq's reinterpretation of certain Spanish ballads, including "Despues que el rey don Rodrigo," seems similar to that of his French counterparts a century earlier, Pidal notes what must constitute a radical metamorphosis of Corral's benign hermit who helps Roderick to die a gruesome death at the mercy of the serpent into a demonic Julian, disguised as the hermit, who exults in his vengeance and laughs at the dying king.[2] Leclerq is the sole author to permit Count Julian an unabashed revelry in his revenge.

The paucity of poetic interest in the legend in the twentieth century is counterbalanced by its regeneration in prose. Yet the legendary story narrated by Esteban Moreu in 1904 entitled *La Cueva de Hércules* [The Cave of Hercules], and Florentino Soria López's two-volume historical novel *Los Titanes de la Raza* [The Titans of the Race] published in 1925 are tangential to the principal storyline, the former because it focuses on the legend of the enchanted cave and the latter because Roderick is a minor character in a work protagonized by Pelayo. Soria's work is of interest in its aims, which are in opposition to the kind of historical novel made famous by Walter Scott, denigrated by Conde de X in the prologue for their lack of historical veracity, in which he claims that Soria's novel excels, elevating it to ". . .la verdadera y hasta el presente, no escrita epopeya nacional"[3] [. . .the true and until now unwritten national epic]. With their concentration on subject matter peripheral to the central legend of Roderick and La Cava, these two works are further evidence of the fragmentation of the legend in Spain, at this time perhaps at its lowest ebb since its beginnings. The tide did not turn until the decade between 1960 and 1970, when the story rebounded with renewed vigor.

Sodomizing the Myth: Juan Goytisolo's Mudejarism

"Sin duda las dificultades entrañadas en un suceso de edad tan remota, difícil de comprender y de reconstruir, son los prohibitivos candados que cierran la puerta de este palacio encantado de la invención. Todavía esperamos al artista fuerte en osadía que quebrante los cerrojos y penetre en el recinto para revelar los viejos misterios imaginativos allí celados por Hércules"[4] [Undoubtedly the difficulties inherent in an event from such remote times, hard to understand and to reconstruct, are the prohibitive bolts that lock the door to this enchanted palace of invention. We still await an artist bold and daring enough to smash those bolts and penetrate the enclosure to reveal the old imaginative mysteries hidden there by Hercules]. Menéndez Pidal's challenge to future Spanish writers to create a worthy contemporary version of the legend was met in the strongest possible terms when Juan Goytisolo picked up the gauntlet in his novel *Reivindicación del Conde don Julián* [Vindication of Count Julian] published in 1970. Goytisolo is widely acclaimed as Spain's greatest living novelist, whose self-imposed exile in Morocco combined with his fascination with Islamic culture, his solidarity with the marginalized, his extraordinary learning and knowledge of the Spanish literary tradition, and the powerful influence upon him of Edward Said and Américo Castro came together in the construction of a work that he hoped would constitute an act of treason as significant and enduring as Julian's original treachery: "anulando de golpe el orden fingido, revelando la verdad bajo la máscara, catalizando tus fuerzas dispersas y los donjulianescos proyectos de invasion : traición grandiose, ruina de siglos : ejército cruel de Tariq, destrucción de la España sagrada :"[5] [annulling the feigned order in one blow, revealing the truth beneath the mask, catalyzing your dispersed forces and Don Julianesque plans for invasion : grandiose betrayal, ruin of centuries : Tariq's cruel army, destruction of holy Spain :].

This brilliant novel has received a critical attention worthy of its complexity and importance, though little has been written upon the relationship of the legend of King Roderick and La Cava to Goytisolo's text.

My concern here is to focus upon the evolution of the legend in *Count Julián*, whose unprecedented form in this novel may well constitute its zenith. As its title suggests, Count Julian is central to the narrative as the arch-criminal whose treachery is vindicated as a regenerative act of transgression. None of the other players in the legend appears on stage. The novel is "sin Rodrigo, ni Frandina, ni Cava : nuevo Conde don Julián, fraguando sombrías traiciones"[6] [without Roderick, without Frandina, without Cava : new Count Julian, forging somber betrayals]. This new Julian is identified with the anonymous narrator, addressed as 'tú' throughout, ambiguously present in both twentieth-century Tangiers and in North Africa just prior to the Muslim invasion of 711. During the course of a single day the reader follows the narrator as he performs certain acts of violation, first in the library of Tangiers where he fills the volumes containing the works of celebrated Spanish authors with dead insects and spiders, then killing off his youthful self as he is sodomized and sadistically murdered by Count Julian in disguise as the wolf in a reworked version of Little Red Riding Hood, before the narrator finally metamorphoses into a new Muslim Messiah. The outrageous subversiveness and transgression of these events stem from thematic strands addressing fiction, history, truth, and the political regime in contemporary Spain, which are informed by a pervasive and fundamental Mudejarism at the heart of the novel and of Goytisolo's mindset.

The author is his own best critic and elucidates his motivation and inspiration for the novel in a number of essays, which merit detailed discussion. In his collection of essays *Saracen Chronicles*, Goytisolo notes the central position occupied by the Muslim world in relation to the Christian one because of the threat posed to it by Islam, whether Arab or Turkish, from the eighth to the seventeenth centuries. He claims that in *Count Julián*, he set himself the task of undergoing a national psychoanalysis through a reading of the collective traditional discourse on Islam embedded in Spanish literature and history. The new figure of Count Julian/anonymous narrator is a reincarnation of the original Julian, who dreams of another invasion of his country whose effects will last for another eight centuries, notably "the destruction of the values and symbols on which the Spanish personality has been constructed through opposition to the threat and rejection of the temptation of Islam."[7] In expounding his understanding of Mudejarism, a term coined by Américo Castro to describe Hispano-Arabic intercultural cross-fertilization, Goytisolo explains the importance of myth for modern-day Mudejares: "...pueden servirse de ellos con fines *mitopoiéticos* pues todo texto literario rico, profundo y complejo no se compone sólo de ingredientes racionales sino que cala en las honduras y entresijos del subconsciente individual y colectivo en donde se esconde el mito"[8] [...they can use them (myths) for *mythopoetic* purposes, since all complex, profound, and rich literary texts consist not only of rational ingredients but also probe the depths and mysteries of the individual and collective subconscious where myth lies hidden].

While Goytisolo stresses the connection between myth and Mudejarism, *Count Julian* also lays bare the aporia between history and myth that so exercised earlier writers of the legend of Roderick and La Cava. The introductory quotations in Section 1 of the text show history to be unreliable. In the first citation Valdeavellanos indicates the uncertainty surrounding Julian's name, position, and race in his history of Spain, and the second, from Alfonso X's *Primera Crónica General*, paints a black picture of Julian, "...destroidor de su tierra, culpado et alevoso et traidor contra todos los suyos"[9] [...destroyer of his country, guilty and perfidious and a traitor to his own people]. Not only has received history blackened the name of Count Julian, it has also, as Goytisolo points out,[10] blamed the greatest historical tragedy of the peninsula on a sexual crime, forging a tradition composed of hundreds of different kinds of text that interpret the collapse of the Visigothic monarchy on the basis of a hostile, condemnatory attitude toward sexuality, and a demonization of the Moorish invader as ferocious and lustful. This discourse of many centuries' duration actually forges the "historical facts" themselves.

In recreating the myth, Goytisolo reworks elements drawn from such discourses, as other writers had done before him. The most significant of these elements is his appropriation of the story strand of Roderick's penance and the introduction of the snake into the legend, initially in the *Refundicion de la Crónica de 1344*, and then more fully in Pedro de Corral's *Crónica sarracina*. It is curious that Goytisolo does not mention the development of the penance episode by Pedro de Corral, although he points to its introduction in the earlier text of the *Refundicion*, yet he was clearly aware of Corral's importance, mentioning his name in the list of authors he has drawn on at the end of the novel, and naming a collection of his essays after Corral's work. The function of the powerful sexual symbol of the serpent is inverted in *Count Julián*, where it becomes a symbol of salvation rather than of punishment. Aligning the serpent with Julian rather than with Roderick, the Count's transgressive sexual crime regenerates and renews rather than destroys Spain. As Goytisolo explains,[11] the sodomization of the Christian boy/younger narrator, the symbol of Catholic Spain, represents the author's desire to use the "robustas sierpes" [strong serpents] of the Arabs to sodomize all the Old Christian myths and "poseer la leyenda por detrás" [possess the legend from behind].

This violent reformulation of the legend also has a political motive, as so often the case in earlier versions. It is striking that the title of the novel is reminiscent of, though in opposition to, the well-known plea for Spanish imperial expansion in North Africa entitled *Reivindicaciones de España* [Vindications of Spain] published in 1941 by the Nationalist diplomats Aveilza and Castiella.[12] Goytisolo's mythologizing opposes that of the Spanish regime that suddenly updated the story in 1936 to justify what was termed the African punishment inflicted on a republic guilty of crime and excess. Goytisolo points out how the Spanish Left espoused legend, fantasy, and stereotype in their xenophobic, openly racist propaganda, tarring all Moroccans with the same brush.[13] In a similar way to Américo Castro, Goytisolo equates the Arab presence with the essence of Spain, subsequently betrayed by Castilian domination and by the forging of a national character based on Castilian and Catholic purity. As Alison Ribeiro de Menezes observes, for Goytisolo, both the reconquest and the civil war were not events of salvation, but deviations from a desired cultural promiscuity that draws on all available influences to build an open-minded society.[14] The new Count Julian is thus exalted as a traitor in the spirit of Jean Genet's statement quoted at the start of Section 1, in which he glorifies treason as a route to freedom.

However, unlike the original Count Julian, the new narrator/Julian cannot destroy people and towns with his invasion. His most powerful vehicle of betrayal is therefore language, which must be violated in order to violate: "...para violar la leyenda y los mitos y los valores hispánicos tenía que violar asimismo el lenguaje"[15] [...to violate Spanish legend and myths and values I had to violate language itself]. Despite the narrator/Julian's first act of betrayal in the virulent attack on the works of other Spanish authors in Tangiers library, including surprisingly, Lope de Vega, a known Moorophile, *Count Julián* is inspired by four muses in the form of Fernando de Rojas, with whom the author claims to share a subversive soul, Fray Luis de León, whose *Profecía del Tajo* is used thematically to reiterate the legend of Spain's destruction, Cervantes, whom Goytisolo wishes to emulate in creating a work that is at once literature and literary criticism, and fourth, Luis de Góngora, whose influence upon the author's use of language is fundamental: "idioma mirífico del Poeta, vehículo necesario de la traición, hermosa lengua tuya : instrumento indispensable del renegade y del apostate, esplendoroso y devastador a la vez :"[16] [marvelous language of the Poet, necessary vehicle of betrayal, your beautiful language : indispensable instrument of the renegade and apostate, magnificent and devastating at the same time]. At first it appears inconsistent that Goytisolo should elevate Góngora above all other writers in this context, considering that the poet might be viewed as the epitome of Spanish Renaissance erudition whose arcane and convoluted complexities render him inaccessible to many. Yet upon closer consideration, certain aspects of narrative and linguistic structure that Goytisolo declares to be at the core of his Mudejarism, for example, the fundamental value conferred upon the linguistic sign and its potential variations, euphuistic preciosity, and frequent recourse to polysemy,[17] coincide with features that Colin Smith identified as characteristic of Góngora's work,[18] such as its nature as poetry that is metaphor, rhythm, linguistic magic, dimensions, objects, light, and shade. Goytisolo's novel also shares with Góngora a Baroque feeling of movement and conflict, clashes and contrasts of "monstruosidad" [monstrousness] and "belleza" [beauty], violence and tenderness, hyperbole and dramatization. But above all it is the radical innovation in Góngora's structure and style that transcends the real and inspires Goytisolo, an idea that the narrator/Julian expresses with energy and brilliance at the end of Section 1 of *Count Julián*: "con los versos miríficos del Poeta incitándote a la traición : ciñendo la palabra, quebrando la raíz, forzando la sintaxis, violantándolo todo : a un paso del tentador Estrecho : a punto de cruzarlo ya : inclinando también la cabeza y cerrando, sí, cerrando los ojos"[19] [with the marvelous verses of the Poet inciting you to betrayal : tightly encircling the word, breaking the root, raping the syntax, violating it all : one step away from the tempting Strait : on the point of crossing it now : lowering your head and closing, yes, closing your eyes]. Roderick's rape of La Cava has been transferred to language, which violates everything. The narrator/Julian is poised to invade.

At the start of Section 3, the second epigraph from Saavedra Fajardo's *Corona gótica, castellana y austríaca* refers to the African "sierpes" let loose upon Spain during the 711 invasion. In the following text, the anonymous narrator/Julian, now convinced of the urgent need for betrayal, "por el simple, y suficiente, placer de la traición : de liberarse de aquello que nos identifica, que nos define"[20] [for the simple, and sufficient, pleasure of betrayal : to be liberated from what identifies us, from what defines us], incites the Arabs to invade, using Saavedra's image of the serpents to equate sexual and political power: "que vuestra sierpe sediciosa se yerga en toda su longitud y, cetro soberbio y real, ejerza el poder tirano con silenciosa, enigmática violencia"[21] [may your seditious serpent swell up to its full length and, proud and royal scepter, may it exercise tyrannical power with silent, enigmatic violence]. The original legend is inverted, as Roderick's sexual crime is substituted by the Arab penis/scepter that now violates. The narrator/Julian reveals his hatred for the heroic Christian Spain of El Cid, which will be swept aside in eight centuries of "un desorden sin fin, una corrupción general"[22] [an endless disorder, a general corruption]. The narrator/Julian will uncover the hybrid roots of the supposedly pure Castilian language, to reveal that it too is mudejar: "el olé, Julián, el olé! : el bello y antiquísimo wa-l-lah! : saca el adocenado orín que lo cubre, restituyéndole el lustre original"[23] [the *ole*, Julian, the *ole!* : the beautiful and very ancient wa—l—lah! : remove the everyday rust that covers it, restoring its original luster]. Finally, the Christian story that is demythified as the antithetical version of Christ's nativity becomes the epiphany of the new Muslim Messiah. As the narrator/Julian/Messiah returns to his room at the end of the day, he acknowledges that the invasion will start all over again tomorrow and the next day, repetitively, and the text ends where it began.

Reivindicación del Conde don Julián was described by the Spanish critic Pere Gimferrer as the most radically subversive masterpiece in Spanish literature. Its recreation of Count Julian is a far cry from the tortured and guilty protagonist of Landor's play, as Goytisolo turns centuries of narrative back on itself to respond passionately and vituperatively to that age-old implicit questioning and problematizing of the legend surrounding the Muslim invasion of Spain in 711. The tentative reaching toward unconventional readings evident in certain versions of the legend from the late Middle Ages onward, the latent leanings toward an alternative view of Catholic Spain and its Arab intruders, find explosive expression in this novel, which for the first time openly and exuberantly welcomes the Arab presence in the Hispanic peninsula and applauds the 711 invasion.

Roderick and La Cava are absent from the narrative because it suited Goytisolo's purpose to use Julian as a traitor-figure whose age-old disgrace could be turned into an exaltation of his crime. This joy in corruption is fundamental to Goytisolo's conception of literature as a criminal act, of art as dissidence, of the creator as transgressor. That it fulfils these roles is borne out by the fact that *Count Julián* was banned in Spain until Franco's death. The novel stands as a powerful statement upon the unreliability of history, and by extension, upon the importance of myth in revealing truth. It is a scathing indictment of twentieth-century Spain both politically and in literary terms, as well as constituting an exceptionally innovative work of literature in its own right, a work that answers Menéndez Pidal's challenge so eloquently in writing the alternative version of the legend of the Muslim invasion. Its particular brilliance lies in the way in which Goytisolo unites themes with style and structure. In an interview with Julio Ortega, he explained that the fundamental objective of the novel was "lograr la unidad del objeto y el medio de representación, la fusion de la traición-tema y la traición-lenguaje"[24] [to achieve the unity of purpose and method of representation, the fusion of the betrayal theme with the linguistic betrayal]. All levels of the text are infused with Mudejarism, a concept that would not have existed if the invasion had never taken place, revealing the undiminished power of the legend of King Roderick, La Cava, and of course, Julian, to forge lasting works of art. This novel is in its essence and conception a testament to that defining moment of Hispanic culture in 711 and to its repercussions both artistic and political.

The Legend in Contemporary Musical Form

If the keynotes of Goytisolo's interpretation of the legend were innovation and renovation, the musical manifestations of the story in the twentieth and twenty-first centuries are more closely characterized by restoration, both in the sense of a reliance upon the more traditional format of events, and in returning to the musical roots established first by the ballads in the late Middle Ages, and by Handel in the eighteenth century. During the same decade that Goytisolo was writing *Count Julián*, the legend was being rekindled as far afield as Argentina. The close literary relations between Spain and Latin America were signaled by Menéndez Pidal in his comments on the drama *Muza* written by the Argentinian Claudio Cuenca in 1850 at the height of Romanticism in that continent, and apparently showing strong influences of Agustín Príncipe.[25] Thirty years later in 1880 the Colombian poet Rafael Pombo composed the libretto for the second opera to be written in that country, *Florinda*, a work indicating some knowledge of Arnao, though with more lyrical and dramatic value than the earlier model.[26] As in the case of Handel two hundred and fifty years before, operatic form dictated the evolution of the Roderick legend in ways that reflected the avant-garde nature of the enterprise. In 1962 the municipality of Buenos Aires commissioned Argentina's greatest composer, Alberto Ginastera (1916–83), to write an opera for the Teatro Colón, the civic opera house of a country claiming the most intense operatic activity in Latin America. In collaboration with the Spanish dramatist Alejandro Casona (1903–65), living in self-imposed exile in Argentina following his flight from Spain in 1939, Ginastera wrote his first opera, *Don Rodrigo*, a work in three acts, each with a corresponding musical imprint, namely heroic, lyrical, and tragic. The opera requires a monumental stage setting and huge orchestra, including twenty-five bells that ring out from different areas of the auditorium at the stunning conclusion of the work. Ginastera's musical idiom is ultramodern, comprising a 12-note serial structure that varies constantly in contrasting rhythmic planes, while still upholding the traditions of grand opera in the tragic and fantastic elements of the work, and in old forms such as the madrigal and canon. His use of the final sequence of twenty-five bells harks back to the *Refundición de la Crónica de 1344*, written around 1440, where it is recorded that upon Roderick's death in Viseu, all the bells rang miraculously.

After success in Buenos Aires in 1964, *Don Rodrigo* was then performed to inaugurate the new premises of the New York City Opera in 1966, with

Plácido Domingo in the starring role. Reviews in the *New York Times*, *New York Post*, and *Opera News* of that year highlight the adventurous, experimental nature of the work, and its impact as a stunning visual spectacle of medieval pageant. However, in *Opera News*, Frank Merkling identifies an absence of emotional warmth, which he claims is overridden by the powerful symmetrical structure of this "twelve-tone *Otello*" in which the hero's tragedy unfolds ritualistically.[27]

According to Ginastera, it was precisely this ritualistic, symbolic quality that he wished to exploit in order to convey the archetypal nature of his subject. As Juan Orrega-Salas observes, "el antiguo romance de Don Rodrigo se desliga de toda amarra a una época determinada para proyectar ciertas esencias perdurables"[28] [the old ballad of Roderick liberates itself from all connections to a specific era, to reveal certain enduring essences]. Ginastera, reported as saying that sex, violence, and hallucination are three of the basic elements of grand opera, makes use of all three to create an experience in which, he says, "se confunden lo real y lo irreal, lo verdadero y lo imaginario, lo humano y lo divino" [the real and the unreal, the true and the imaginary, the human and the divine are blurred], affirming that *Don Rodrigo* "recoje las violentas pasiones humanas y las presenta dentro de un marco inmutable y eterno"[29] [gathers together violent human passions and presents them within an eternal and unchanging setting]. Ginastera has seen to the emotional heart of the legend, perceiving those elements of the story that have endowed it with enduring creative vitality. Outside any temporal context, its violent, grand passions and conflicts confer a mythical status upon it.

The emphasis upon irreality and symbolism serves to dehumanize the characters, transforming them into almost Wagnerian, god-like personages. Examination of Casona's libretto exposes the grand scale of the story structure, whose minimalism strips the protagonists bare and uncovers their essence. Casona, born in 1903 in Asturias, was a successful and innovative playwright in both Spain and Argentina. His nostalgia for his homeland, and his familiarity with the myths and legends of his native Asturias are both vital elements in his version of Spain's foundational story. In Act 1, the key traits of Rodrigo and Florinda are exposed through their initial meeting. Irony is strong at the outset, for Rodrigo returns to Toledo victorious in avenging the violent blinding of his father, fulfilling his wish to "lavar un ultraje" [avenge an outrage], not yet knowing that he himself will commit an outrage demanding revenge. From the start, Florinda appears excessively keen to encounter Rodrigo, pleading with her father to be allowed to meet the future king. Rodrigo is immediately attracted to her and agrees to act as her surrogate father in Julian's absence. The ambivalence of Florinda's racial identity is disclosed as she insists she is

Spanish: "Mi única patria es España. África sólo es mi tierra" [My only homeland is Spain. Africa is only where I live], yet Rodrigo describes her using Arabic imagery of lion and gazelle. In the coronation scene, Casona hints at tragedy in employing Florinda to hand Rodrigo the crown of Spain, which she lets fall at his feet, firmly establishing her as the potential cause of the king's downfall. The motif of prefiguration is repeated in the third scene, in which Rodrigo breaks open the magical cave in Toledo to find the prophesy of the Moorish invasion written upon a canvas that Julian alone can decipher. In this first triptych, victory, coronation, and impulsive boldness characterize Rodrigo as heroic king, but the sexual attraction to Florinda, while mutual, strikes an ominous note.

In the first scene of Act 2, "El Amor," Casona crystallizes the scene, taken from Pedro de Corral, in which the king watches Florinda and her friends bathing naked in the garden, and is filled with uncontrollable passion for her. Scene 5, "El Ultraje," is the central point of the drama, in which the king enters Florinda's private apartments and violates her. In an emotionally charged interchange, she begs him to master himself: "!Defiéndete de tí!" [Guard against yourself], echoing the central preoccupation of Handel's opera, the need for self-mastery, though with the opposite outcome. In Scene 6 in which Florinda, violated and now abandoned by the king, sends the famous message to her father aprising him of her rape, the ambivalence of her Spanish/Moorish identity is paralleled by her ambivalence of feeling as she asks herself whether her desire for vengeance comes from her dishonor or from her subsequent rejection by Rodrigo: "¿Es honra o es amor?" [Is it honor or is it love?].

At the start of Act 3, the phrase "Toda la escena debe producir un efecto de obsesionante surrealismo" [The whole scene should create an effect of obsessive surrealism] sets the mood as Rodrigo has a dream in which a mysterious voice blames Florinda for the imminent destruction of Spain: "!Unos ojos de mujer te quemaron las entrañas! / !Una mano de mujer prenderá fuego a tu España!" [A woman's eyes burnt you to the core! A woman's hand shall set fire to your Spain]. The voice is subsumed in a vast chorus that mounts a terrifying verbal attack on the king. In Scene 8, as the battle rages, Rodrigo poignantly asks the treacherous Julian the familiar question from the ballad cycle: "Si querías vengar a una hija, ¿por qué has vendido a una patria?" [If you wanted to avenge a daughter, why have you sold a country?]. In the concluding scene, as the defeated king is wandering as a beggar, Casona uses another ballad line "Ayer era rey de España / hoy no lo soy de una villa" [Yesterday I was king of Spain, / today I don't have a town to my name] to emphasize his plight and set the scene for Rodrigo's powerful confession. At the last minute, Florinda appears, bringing hope for Spain born anew in Asturias, and Rodrigo dies redeemed, amid the miraculous pealing of bells.

Casona has taken the barest, most powerful bones of the medieval story to present a picture of an ambivalent and highly guilty Florinda, who instigates the downfall of Spain then implemented by her father. Certain elements personal to Casona give the text a unique flavor. The interest in dreams, death, and myth apparent in his theatre are manifest in the libretto, as are echoes of exile and phrases showing the marked influence of Lorca. Casona's nostalgia for Asturias is strong in the last beautiful song Florinda sings to give Rodrigo hope, "!allá en las verdes Asturias se alzan tu cruz y tu espada!" [there in the green lands of Asturias your cross and your sword are raised!], alluding to the legend of Pelayo, the Asturian leader who was believed to have saved Spain and renewed the Visigothic line.

So, the key new operatic work of Argentina harks back to Spain and the shaping of its history through the Arab invasion. In a country and continent obsessed with forging identity, the implication may be that the new must spring from the old and traditional, and this is certainly borne out by Ginastera's music, which blends Argentinian folkloric motifs with European operatic tradition. Alejandro Casona's theatre consistently displayed a moral message, and one wonders whether the experiences of the playwright and Ginastera, who both fled from dictatorships (Ginastera leaving Argentina for a number of years when Perón came to power), point in this opera to an implicit warning against the abuse of that power, despite Ginastera's resolute rejection of didactic or ideological elements in art.

The opera demonstrates a variable equilibrium between the demands of genre and the urge to redesign the legend in a fresh, topical way. While allusions to the abuse of power, and to the tension between the barbarism of war and rape and the civilization of the Toledan court echo Argentinian preoccupations, the emotional power of *Don Rodrigo* is privileged over and above contemporary associations. The performative nature of opera foregrounds the dramatic, human elements of the eighth-century story that Ginastera and Casona brought vividly into focus in their own time. Their interest in doing so is a further measure of the profundity and compelling qualities of the legend, whose universal nature is paramount in Ginastera's own description of *Don Rodrigo* as "una fantasía que tiene una existencia permanente y actual, eterna y viva, ya que los sentimientos que de ella emanan son los sentimientos universales del alma humana, el amor, el deseo, los celos, la venganza, el odio y el perdón" [a fantasy that has a current and permanent existence, eternal and living, since the feelings that emanate from it are the universal feelings of the human soul, love, desire, jealousy, vengeance, hatred, and forgiveness].

The operatic form constitutes a musical spectacle in which the relationship between Roderick and La Cava is revitalized in a way relevant to audiences of the past and present, and tends to elevate the human, universal qualities of the story above the religious, political, and cultural dimensions that often predominate in literary versions. The two most recent manifestations of the legend draw on precisely those qualities, thereby creating popular, accessible versions of the ancient storyline.

"Big Themes, Grand Passions, Epic Story"

In the previous century, the American writer Washington Irving had discovered the legend during his travels in southern Spain. In 1967 his countrywoman, Dana Broccoli (1922–2004), was similarly intrigued and inspired when she in turn discovered the story during a trip to Toledo. Married to the film producer Cubby Broccoli who created the James Bond films, Dana accompanied her husband as his assistant, and it was when they were on a location search in Spain for the film *Chitty Chitty Bang Bang* that she was told of the legend by a guide. Her resulting novel *Florinda* was published in New York ten years later in 1977. To dwell upon the considerable stylistic inadequacies of the work would be unproductive. It is aimed at a popular readership and its 180 pages make fast reading. It is written largely from Florinda's point of view, and she exerts considerable personal power over events in a way that the earlier popular writer Juan de Dios de Mora's Florinda did not. While Dana Broccoli follows a trite, well-trodden path in her portrayal of Spain beset by ". . .moaning in the darkness which was to persist for seven centuries"[30] following the Moorish invasion, she makes the significant plot innovation of creating a Moorish lover, Somail, for Florinda, whom the girl is forced to leave behind in Ceuta. This new element in the story is vital to the storyline, for Somail braves the odds to enter Spain, reach Toledo, and reclaim Florinda as his bride, but he is caught as a spy and cruelly killed upon Rodrigo's orders before Florinda's very eyes. The author shows none of the sympathy and compassion for her female protagonist that had been growing since the early ballad versions in the late Middle Ages. She transforms her into a cunning, scheming minx who is wild, irresponsible, and headstrong and who manipulates her father emotionally from the very first scenes where they are traveling to the king's court in Toledo. Julian cries "I fear for you, child. You have sparks in the brain. I fear that one day they will consume you. . .,"[31] and his fears are well-grounded, for Florinda vows to avenge Somail's death by betraying Rodrigo's passion for her to her father. However, although she writes him the traditional letter that reveals her dishonor, she does so, unprecedentedly, before any sexual act has taken place, enlisting the help of Sancho Ramirez, the man Julian has chosen from the Goths to be her husband, to act as her messenger. It is her wicked plan to lure Roderick into a sexual liaison with her after she has sent the letter, thereby vindicating her deception. Yet things do not go according to plan, because she and Rodrigo fall in love.

While the African queen Exilona whom Rodrigo has married languishes on her deathbed, Florinda and the king grow increasingly intimate. Dana Broccoli renders the legend of the enchanted palace more plausible by converting it into a recurring dream that plagues the king, prefiguring the imminent invasion. Overcome with guilt, Florinda half confesses to her dreadful act of betrayal, and Rodrigo is beside himself with fury as he leaves for battle. Beginning to realize the enormity of her deed, Florinda finds she is pregnant, and is then summoned to the dying Exilona who insists that she goes to find Rodrigo on the battlefield to warn him that the evil bishop Oppas has conspired against him. In the last dramatic chapter, Florinda finds Rodrigo severely wounded, tells him of their child and swears to save him. The novel ends ambiguously as the author evokes the earliest accounts that describe the discovery of the king's horse, cloak, and boots, but not of Rodrigo himself.

In this short novel, Rodrigo is portrayed as a victim of Florinda's fatal charms, and as a good, even idealistic, king, whose desire to build a Visigothic Empire by peaceful means, without battle and conquest, is somewhat anachronistic. Julian is not a well-rounded character, who is easily manipulated both by his daughter and by the Moors, and acts in a very predictable way. However, his bigoted view of Islam expressed in conversation with Sancho on the subject of the impending battle is not without resonance: "These Moslems are taught that to die in battle is the only sure promise of immediate entrance into Paradise. They are mad with the will to die. It is their fanaticism which terrorized their enemies and saves them from their own madness. Look at their empire since the death of Muhammed...it is greater than was once Rome. It is my belief that they wish to conquer the world in its entirety."[32]

Dana Broccoli's husband Cubby admired the dramatic qualities of the story and encouraged his wife to find a composer and convert it into a musical. Happily, her talents for performance adaptation were greater than her novelistic ones and resulted in the highly successful production of *La Cava*, first performed in Bromley in May 2000, from where it was transferred to the Victoria Palace Theatre, London, later in the month, and then to the Piccadilly Theatre in August of the same year, running until 2001 and starring Oliver Tobias as Roderic and Julie-Alanah Brighten as Florinda. The plot is essentially the same as in the novel, with a noticeable softening of the characterization of Florinda to make her less selfish and spiteful, more regretful, and guilt-ridden. The title of the musical is taken from Exilona's solo in the second act in which she accuses Florinda of stealing her husband and calls her by her ancient epithet, defining her role in terms of her sexual misconduct.

The musical is a triumph in terms of its direction, with lightning changes of scene praised by the Sunday Telegraph: "Steven Dexter's direction whisks us from battlements to dungeons to bazaar. There are reversals, escapes and intrigues in the spirit of Scott and Dumas."[33] This allusion to Scott is picked up in the theatre program that contains a quotation of three stanzas from Scott's *The Vision of Don Roderick* in which Florinda shrieks in alarm and begs the Prelate to spare her from punishment. Scott may well have approved of the London Theatreguide's description of the production as a ". . .big musical in the mould of Les Mis: a grand romantic story, lush music and ambitions towards opera."[34] The reviewer ranks it among grand-scale semioperas in second place only to *The Phantom of the Opera*, far ahead of *Les Miserables* and others, and other reviews are very favorable. The aspects identified as most striking are revealing in indicating the appeal of the story to contemporary audiences, namely, its unbridled passion and political intrigue, ". . .a cracking tale—that rare thing in a musical of girl power, of passion, of forbidden love, of vengeance and heroism, of religious bigotry and betrayal."[35] Florinda's legendary power, expressed musically in her solo "A Woman's Hands" in Act 1, is emphasized in the theatre program in a four-page spread placing her at the head of a series of women who have changed history, namely Cleopatra, Helen of Troy, Delilah, Agrippina the Younger, Eleanor of Aquitaine, Lucrezia Borgia, and Anne Boleyn.

This "thrilling theatrical spectacle"[36] fully exploits the human interest and drama of the legend as its musical predecessors did before it. The two most recent versions of the story, novel and musical, revisit the first portrayals of Florinda as the cause of the invasion of Spain, partly demonizing her, partly exalting her, rendering her as complex and ambiguous as she has ever been. In a video excerpt of the production, Oliver Tobias speaks of the spellbinding effect of the story upon the audiences he played to, a further testament to its perennial appeal. As the publicity brochure produced by the Piccadilly Theatre claims, "The eternal themes of passion, loyalty and betrayal mixed with sex, politics and power, make for a tale as relevant today as it was all those centuries ago." No audience could fail to observe the contrasting elements of Christian Gothic origin and those of an Arabic flavor, notably in the lively scenes at the bazaar and during the Berber dance, nor could they miss the relevance of relations between the medieval Muslims and Christians of the legend to those vexed relationships today.

CONCLUSION

Since its inception almost thirteen hundred years ago, the legendary story of King Roderick and La Cava has been recounted by historians, dramatists, composers, novelists, poets, and scholars in its place of origin in the Hispanic peninsula, in Europe, and as far afield as the United States and South America. The extent of its historical and geographical spread is a measure of its enduring power as a source of creative inspiration, akin in its longevity and regenerative force to the most familiar classical and biblical legends. Yet it paradoxically remains a legend largely unknown to people outside Spain who may well have encountered other legendary narratives such as those of Homer and of the Old and New Testaments. This book has sought in some measure to redress this imbalance through delineating the history of the reception of the legend and in doing so, uncovering the process of repeated appropriation of the story at the heart of what are, in my opinion, unquestionably the most important events in the history of the Spanish peninsula.

In doing so, I salute the magisterial achievement of Ramón Menéndez Pidal, the only previous scholar who has considered the legend of Roderick and La Cava extensively and diachronically. His three-volume *Floresta de Leyendas Heroicas* on the subject, with its scholarly survey of many versions of the legend and accompanying textual excerpts, has been of fundamental value in the preparation of this monograph, both in its basic spadework of enumeration of texts, and in its insights. This study has built on Menéndez Pidal's indispensable work, expanding it through the discovery and exploration of additional as well as new versions of the story, and also providing detailed critical analyses and interpretations of major reworkings within their political, religious, and cultural contexts. In charting the evolution of the legend chronologically, it has been possible to grasp its organic growth over the centuries, a growth that indicates its importance as a cultural entity in itself while simultaneously illuminating the issues tested and challenged at different historical times through its reception.

The status and nature of truth forms the kernel out of which the legend of the king and the whore unfurls, and is manifested in the quintessential tension between history and fiction that is present from the outset. In his Conclusion, Menéndez Pidal notes what he considers an outstanding innovation, that while it is a common tendency in historical legends to attempt to correct poetic fiction by adjusting it to historical reality, in this case many eminent historians have without precedent sought to do the reverse in their fictionalization of history.[1] The fusion of history and fiction that constitutes the story of Roderick and La Cava engenders its vital force. Lévi-Strauss's distinction between history and myth, which admits the former's dependency upon and responsibility to those dates that make up its objective framework,[2] is debatable in this instance. If we accept the hypothesis that Julian invented the account of his daughter's violation as a motive for his betrayal of Spain to the Arabs, then fiction shapes history and brings the narrative into being prior to the events of 711. It is as if this primary act of weaving a story predicates the preferred paradigm of the future.

This idea is reinforced by Hayden White's discussion of historiography in which he observes that historical narratives exploit metaphorical similarities between sets of real events and the conventional structures of our fictions. He claims that "histories should never be read as unambiguous signs of events they report, but as symbolic structures that 'liken' the events reported in them to some form with which we have already become familiar in our literary culture."[3] He explains that "the historical narrative thus mediates between the events reported in it on the one side and pregeneric plot structures conventionally used in our culture to endow unfamiliar events and situations with meanings, on the other."[4] These comments theorize the parallels drawn by Krappe between the Roderick narrative and those in Scandinavian and Germanic legend, and invoke the power of interpretation to appropriate historical events in order to bestow specific desired meanings upon them.

In this sense the story of Roderick and La Cava acquires mythical status as an ancient, traditional story that offers an explanation of events or phenomena. In the introduction I referred to Ricoeur's view of myth as both foundational and liberating in so far as it is transcendental and strives toward a future perfection through the revelation of previously undisclosed possibilities. This drive toward completion that pushes the boundaries of the legend ever outward is a characteristic of the development of the story throughout its lifetime, a drive possibly at its strongest in the provisional and incomplete versions of nineteenth-century Spain that found a degree of resolution in the work of Juan Goytisolo.

The three modes of interpretation of historiography designated by Hayden White[5] as epistemological, ethical, and aesthetic are helpful in the evaluation of the central issues arising from this study. In epistemological terms, the choice of an explanatory paradigm for the invasion of Spain

CONCLUSION

divides in the primary textual dialogue between medieval Arabic and Christian historiographers into one of conquest or of divine punishment for corruption. The idea of conquest is framed within the context of eighth-century Islamic expansion policy, prefigured visually in the Qusayr 'Amra frescoes, in which the ambivalent personage of Roderick serves as a vehicle for genealogical reinforcement and legitimation of the Islamic regime. The opposing Christian peninsula view that establishes the story as a foundational narrative of Spain holds a paradox within it, shrewdly observed by Mary Gaylord in her essay on Spanish Renaissance conquests, where she makes the point that the legend is not really a story of foundations or origins, but of unfounding, unsettling, usurpation, and loss, structured as a kind of secular scripture.[6] She comments that the events of 711 consequently created a need for repeated reenactment both in action, and in discourse by means of rewriting, in turn fabricating the reconquest as the privileged trope of Spanish national, racial, religious, and cultural unity.[7]

Medieval Hispanic historiography up to and including the *Refundición de la Crónica de 1344* explains the invasion of Spain as retribution for sexual licentiousness, firmly linking punishment and destruction with sexual misdemeanor according to the prescriptions of Catholicism. Alfonso X and the authors of both the *Crónica de 1344* and its *Refundición* also use this history to highlight dilemmas in their contemporary environments and to explore personal issues and circumstances. The two latter chronicles mould new perspectives within the legend for future writers to build on, until Pedro de Corral challenges the nature of chronicle writing in his overt fictionalizing of the story of Roderick and La Cava in the *Crónica sarracina* and hints at the veracity of fiction while addressing contemporary political issues within a text that subtly introduces ideas of cultural ambivalence. The discrepancy between title and content is even greater in Miguel de Luna's *Historia verdadera del rey don Rodrigo*, a blatantly false history with a strongly political and racial agenda that illustrates the vexed nature of historiography in the peninsula during the sixteenth and seventeenth centuries. In the nineteenth century, Robert Southey underlines the differences between poetic and historical truth in his poetic reworking of the legend set against his scholarly notes that draw upon historical evidence and texts, while his literary counterparts in Spain use the story of the king and the whore to envisage post-711 Spain in terms of a mythical 'other' world in which things might have been different, thereby demonstrating Ricoeur's proposition that mythical narratives can elicit liberating potentialities.

The dichotomy between history and fiction therefore offered new creative scope to question the meaning of the legend of Roderick and La Cava within the context of Spanish history and historiography. The same dichotomy had a strong and persistent influence upon the aesthetic interpretation of the story as manifested through genre. The regenerative power of the legend is not evident in terms of longevity and narrative vitality alone; it also has the recurrent and noteworthy ability to revitalize creative strategies and inspire new forms. The subject matter often seems to require new modes of expression, as if old ways are not adequate to convey the momentousness, power, or complexity of the content. In Corral's great work of 1430, history and fiction combine to create Spain's first historical novel and one hundred years later Palau's *Santa Orosia* becomes Spain's first historical drama. Twenty years or so after, in 1551 or 1552, Fray Luis wrote *La Profecía del Tajo*, the first ode in classical style on the subject. Poetry is again at the forefront of generic innovation in the late eighteenth and nineteenth centuries, when Cadalso's *Carta de Florinda* of 1773 introduces a new early Romantic aesthetic to Spain, soon followed by Espronceda's innovative and fragmentary poetic style in *El Pelayo*. Just two decades later, Montengón's novel *El Rodrigo* takes the honors as the first historical novel of Spanish Romanticism. Within established literary genres, two outstanding contributions to the life of the legend are radical in their innovation. The first, Robert Southey's *Roderick, the Last of the Goths*, of 1814, which begins in the imaginary future after the invasion of 711, embodies a brilliant and unique poetic remedievalization of the legend generically, thematically, and stylistically, while Juan Goytisolo's *Reivindicación del Conde don Julián* published in 1970 violates form and language to match Julián's violation of self and country in an unparalleled act of literary subversion. Conversely, on occasion genre bears upon plot evolution, notably in the case of opera. Although Handel renovated the legend in parallel with innovation in his musical style, the dictates of voice and casting affected gender issues to be discussed below, as did theatrical censorship in eighteenth-century Spain. There is an evident symbiosis between generic development and the evolution of the legend that points to the latter's enduring profundity and creative energy.

Genre, whether innovative or traditional, had a strong influence upon developments in the characterization of protagonists and occasional minor players, leading to a marked focus upon issues of identity and gender, which in turn constitute ethical interpretations of the legend in so far as they pertain to ideology and politics. Once again, Pedro de Corral sets the tone in his sympathetic portrayal of Roderick overcome with passion, tortured by temptation in the form of a demonic La Cava and cruelly punished through his penitence. This is the first psychological portrayal of the king, the first fleshing out of his character. The balladeers were quick to perceive the human interest and dramatic potential of Corral's storyline, presenting the characters as individuals acting out the destructiveness of sexual desire against a historical background of impending invasion. As the ballad cycle evolves, La Cava is portrayed increasingly as a victim, rather than as a temptress, while judgment of Roderick is kind. Julian takes the stage in the ballad cycle, and is presented with rather more understanding than he is in Alfonso X's chronicle.

As the central figure of the legend, the portrayal of Roderick becomes divergent and his actions also vary to suit authorial purpose. While Lope implies Roderick's racial and religious tolerance in *El último godo*, Pidal observes the late-seventeenth-century interest in the idea that the king seduces both La Cava and Julian's wife,[8] hinted at centuries before by Jiménez de Rada, taken up by Pedro Boán in his *Historia de San Servando* and then by Cristóbal Lozano in *David perseguido*. This element accentuates Roderick's lustful side, developed in a more extreme way by Cadalso, whose poem depicts the king committing an act of considerable violence in his rape of Florinda while she is unconscious. His sexual force is nuanced in Montengón's novel, which presents a portrait of great psychological depth, a Roderick torn in two by feelings that fluctuate as his reason and moral goodness fight his overwhelming sexual desire. The two nineteenth-century writers who focus on Roderick create entirely opposing interpretations of the last Visigothic king. For the first time, he becomes a great epic hero in Southey's long poem, while the Marquis de Sade is the only writer to condemn Roderick entirely.

The fluid nature of Roderick's depiction throughout the corpus of writing on the legend indicates his ambiguous status within the narrative. Although the initial point of reference is always the king's sexual act, which instigates the inexorable sequence of subsequent events, surprisingly little blame is laid upon him throughout the centuries. It may be that for complex reasons sexual misdemeanor in a man and in a monarch has been easier to absolve than in a woman. It may also be that illicit sexual passion is generally perceived as a lesser crime than treason. Certainly Roderick is depicted often as a man who suffers greatly, but he is not on the whole demonized for his role in the invasion of his country, being more often viewed as destiny's pawn. The ambivalent status of the king, as it was perceived by the eighth-century artists of Qusayr 'Amra albeit in political terms, has been a fundamental source of creative fecundity down the centuries, and also reflects, and has reflected, the uncertain and problematical status of the Muslim invasion of Spain for future generations.

The forgiving view of Roderick's sexual passion that permits his liberation through penitence and remorse exists alongside an equal and opposite condemnation of La Cava's actions during the first centuries in the life of the legend as well as in some later narratives. However, the nascent questioning of her culpability in the ballad cycle grows into a much more complex portrayal as victim, or as a woman with equivalent feelings to the king, and later as one who shares a mutual and deep love. Unlike Roderick, or Count Julian, the identity of La Cava is enigmatic from the outset, because there is no authentication of her existence. She therefore has a stronger fictional dimension than the male protagonists, which seems to have encouraged the mapping of legendary identities onto her persona, such as that in the biblical scenario in which she is an Eve-like figure who evilly tempts Roderick/Adam and causes Spain to fall from its Edenic state, or where she represents the Body Hispanic, which the king violates through corruption, laying his country/La Cava open to invasion. This legendary quality is also evident in the generic name transliterated from the Arabic word 'whore' by which she is described up to and after the time of Miguel de Luna, who liberates her from her shameful title by providing her with the old Visigothic name of Florinda. Yet as La Cava, she is at once a type, whose negative cadence defines her perception for centuries. Her chastisement through patriarchal discourse promotes an opposite reaction in a number of reworkings of the story from the late seventeenth century onward, further intensified due to specific external circumstances, and that enriches and fertilizes the ever-evolving storyline.

Cristóbal Lozano's spirited defense of La Cava against the traditional hatred of her in his *David perseguido* of 1661 is echoed in the eighteenth century by Father Feijóo. They perceive her as a helpless victim of the king's lust who has been unfairly condemned and their vindication of her coincided with the refocusing of the protagonism of the legend due to the constraints of theatrical censorship in the 1700s, when it was prohibited to publicly reenact the story with King Roderick as the central character. This resulted in the rise of the female characters in the story, including the king's wife, named as Esilena in Handel's opera, whose enormous courage and emotional strength saves the king, and also Florinda, who is not cast in the libretto as an evil seductress, but is nevertheless ambitious and hard-headed, seeking only her own gain. The importance of the king's wife is developed in a different way in Gertrudis Gómez de Avellaneda's play *Egilona*, in which she creates an interesting, powerful character in love with the caliph who is enemy to the Christians and to her previous husband. The sympathy of women writers for their female characters is ultimately manifested in María Rosa Gálvez's feeling for Florinda in her play of that name, which highlights for the first time Florinda's enormous suffering as a lone victim of family and patriarchy. A similar support for female oppression and victimization is conveyed in Southey's dramatic monologue *La Caba*, where he returns to her former designation to underline her unjust treatment at the hands of her father. Yet La Caba's only recourse at the end of this speech is to die. It is not until she swaps her female, Christian identity for a male, Moorish one in the Duque de Rivas' poem *Florinda* that she can truly exert power and influence. But she has no agency as a woman until Dana Broccoli gives her the opportunity to right her wrongs by giving Roderick an heir in the most recent version of the legend, the musical *La Cava*.

The ambivalence of the figure of La Cava is even greater than that of Roderick, and similarly provides a source of creative interpretation within the evolution of the legend. While her depiction fluctuates according to literary sensibility, not even those writers, both men and women, who espouse her cause can truly free her from the stigma forged by patriarchal discourse, that remorselessly associates her sexual relationship with the king with licentiousness and corruption. Within her artistic development to date, she has been unable to stand proud and free herself fully from the shackles of her medieval reputation.

The third protagonist of the legend, Count Julian, is a less ambiguous persona in so far as he is, with two notable exceptions, unrelentingly charged with treason and treachery and perceived (along with the evil Bishop Oppas, who is not a protagonist) as the arch-betrayer of his country. The vituperative attitude of posterity as revealed through the mouths of both Christian and Moorish characters alike (albeit with Christian authors) suggests the enormity of Julian's crime and its perception as worse than sexual crime and corruption. The first exception to this is Walter Savage Landor's play *Count Julian*, in which the count is the central character for the first time, and is raised by Landor to the status of a great Shakespearian tragic hero. The English Romantic writers' contribution to the development of the legend is crucial in its dimension as the epitome of its evolution, merging manifold literary and historical elements with both contemporary political conflicts and personal ones of the author. Like Landor, the second exception to Julian's demonization, the *Reivindicación del Conde don Julián* by Goytisolo, also presents the count as the hero of his text, viewing his act of betrayal to the Moors for the first time in the history of the legend as a force for good, which the anonymous narrator wishes to recreate in his own time. In this reconstituting of Count Julian, he is not only the perpetrator of treason, but also of the most extreme form of sexual perversion, through which Spain is ultimately liberated from its oppressors.

The unstable status of identity in the case of the three protagonists of the legend, as at once heroes and antiheroes, gives rise to a kaleidoscopic proliferation of variants that lend depth and richness to the ancient story. The complexities and perplexities of their dilemmas indicate the trenchant human interest of the story that so greatly favors its performance in oral poetry, drama, and opera, which exploits plot interest and character to the full. The drama and at times melodrama of the individual lives portrayed, with its essential ambiguity and difficulty of interpretation, mirrors equivalent situations on the broader stage of political, religious, and racial conflict that are addressed and interrogated through the vehicle of the story.

The significance of Roderick as a political figure is apparent from that first visual image in the palace of Qusayr 'Amra, where his presence in the fresco reinforces the political and genealogical claims of the Ummayad dynasty. His political significance is also apparent in Western accounts of the legend from the time of Alfonso X onward. In the earliest vernacular versions of the legend there exists an inclination to perceive the figure of Roderick metonymically as representing the Iberian peninsula itself. This is in turn associated with the quest for Spanish identity that informs Alfonso X's thirteenth-century drive to define a Castilian national purpose, and may explain why in Alfonso's chronicle Roderick is largely exonerated of his crime, thus easing the Learned King's alignment with the Visigothic monarchical line that he so desired and establishing the continuity and domination of the Castilian throne in face of the Islamic presence.

Under the influence of Alfonsine historiography, Pedro Afonso similarly harnesses the legend in the *Crónica de 1344* to emphasize the importance of Portugal as an independent area of the peninsula by enhancing the status of Portuguese history writing, while the fifteenth-century *Refundición* provokes an ethical response linked to the social and religious problems of the Jewish population in Spain in his time. Pedro de Corral also alludes to the contemporary political situation in his latent querying of the wisdom of the imminent expulsion of Moors and Jews from the peninsula. While Corral and the anonymous author of the *Refundición* have the courage to use the Roderick legend as an implicit criticism of the political and religious regimes current in their time, in the sixteenth and seventeenth centuries the urge to reformulate the legend to legitimize Spain's monarchy is evident in Palau's play, which reinforces the link of Spanish kings to the Visigothic line while acting as propaganda for Aragon, and upholding Catholicism. Both Saavedra Fajardo and Boán use the legend as history with the aim of validating the contemporary Spanish monarchy through lineage and genealogy, as does Brito in his *A Monarchia Lusitana* in order to reinforce Portuguese royal genealogy in a manner akin to his predecessor Pedro Afonso.

A more critical view of Spanish politics and monarchy prevails in the dramas of the two women playwrights who employ the legend, Mary Pix in the early eighteenth century and María Rosa Gálvez in the early nineteenth, both of whom present King Roderick as an example of the failure of monarchy, and use the legend to attack patriarchy and religious corruption. In Spain in the later part of the nineteenth century, the political dimensions of the legend were expressed in a more subdued manner, perhaps due to the aftereffects of censorship that had so dogged the eighteenth-century dramatists. An exception to this is the strong pro-Zaragozan stance taken in Miguel Agustín Príncipe's play *El Conde don Julián*, with its implicit criticism of the contemporary monarchy, a dissatisfaction echoed in the Duque de Rivas poem *Florinda*. Political interpretations of the legend tend inevitably to focus upon Roderick as monarch, although Washington Irving's rewriting of the legend also has a strong political and moralizing dimension in its concentration upon Count Julian as a salutary lesson against treason. The forceful effect of the Napoleonic War upon the development of the legend in England renders its political value paramount in the work of Scott, Landor, and Southey. Scott's interpretation of the story challenges the political situation of the time and questions the nature of invasion itself, while Landor views the urgent need for Spain's liberation through the lens of Count Julian's moral dilemma. Southey's long poem presents Roderick as the means through which he addresses both the original invasion and the Napoleonic War as national, political, and moral conflicts.

In the twentieth century, two political exiles rework the story in terms of the contemporary Francoist regime in Spain. In the case of Casona's libretto for Ginastera's opera *Don Rodrigo*, distance arouses nostalgia in the Asturian dramatist, whose restitution of Spain at the end of the libretto takes place within the Asturian region that is both Casona's native land and also the source of Pelayo's rebellion against the Moorish invaders, and suggests that cultural memory is persistent and long. Juan Goytisolo's vituperative attack on Franco's political regime in *Reivindicación del Conde don Julián* indicates the sustained ability of the legend to enshrine present-day relevance, in this case in the brilliant conversion of that original act of political, national, and moral treason into an act of political, national, and moral regeneration.

The capacity of the legend to constitute a commentary upon and interpretation of changing political events and regimes from its beginnings up to the present, in both national and regional terms, inheres principally in the fluidity of King Roderick as an ambiguous and polyvalent icon, and to a lesser degree in the moral degeneracy that Julian represents. Its political dimension is fundamental and crucial in its questioning of kingship, tyranny, treason, invasion, power, hierarchy, and licentiousness. That the issues of history, fiction and genre, gender, identity, and politics are central to the evolution of the legend is indisputable. However, its vitality also depends upon aspects that might be described as silent and repressed, which often lie hidden in the margins, or in the subtexts of the story, and that concern the racial and religious conflict that underlies the important dialogues between successive versions.

Invasion is by nature an act of violation. In the case of the invasion of the Iberian peninsula in 711 AD, that act of violation has been rewritten countless times through the trope of Roderick's violation of La Cava, whose alleged rape opened the way for the rape of the country. In fact, La Cava's shame and dishonor is often portrayed as that of the peninsula itself. Yet the trope is not entirely satisfactory in the sense that Roderick as the violator, a Visigoth and Catholic, is aligned with the Berber/Arabic/Muslim violator of his own country, rendering him both the Violator and the Violated, an image captured by the artists of the Qusayr 'Amra frescoes that suggests the king is Janus-like, looking back into the Christian Visigothic and Roman past and forward into the Muslim future. It may be this fundamental paradox that, albeit subliminally, has made the legend of the king and the whore so variable and perturbing down the centuries. As Visigothic king of Spain, Roderick simultaneously bears the characteristics of the invading Other, even in his notorious lustfulness, a character trait that the Christians associated with the fiery, black-skinned Saracen, and from which they created a discourse of demonization that has lasted for centuries. Roderick, as one man, one king, suggests both the native Hispanic self and that of the feared yet desired Muslim invader. He epitomizes the dilemma surrounding Spain's cultural identity that has manifested itself in a fervid effort to rewrite history so as to diminish the importance of its Islamic past, to carve out a pure Catholic heritage and Spanish lineage, and deny Islamic origins, to write and rewrite the legend of Roderick and the Muslim invasion in endless reformulations which seek to explain, justify, and in many cases query the validity of the old story and set it in new and radical contexts that might lay the specters of the past to rest. Its very survival reveals a continuing need to revisit the cultural and emotional site of invasion in an attempt to confront and resolve the tensions arising from the encounter between Christianity and Islam, between Europe and Arabia.

The writers of the legend who have engaged with these tensions have on the whole explored them in the uncharted margins of their works, hinting at an agenda at odds with the purported one. In the significantly titled *Crónica sarracina*, Pedro de Corral not only uses eroticism and violence to undermine the power structures of Catholic ideology, but hints strongly at the attraction of the Orient in his Arabic-hued narrative that seems to uphold the official line of hostility between Christian Spaniards and Moors while subtly suggesting the unofficial fascination with Moorish culture. Miguel de Luna carries this mixed message even further in his blatant invention of a historical text that upholds the legitimacy and claim of the Muslims to Spanish territory just prior to the expulsion of *moriscos* from the peninsula. In doing so, he sought to modify the perception of Spanish historians and religious leaders of the time by espousing mutual tolerance between Moors and Christians. Lope de Vega, contemporary with Miguel de Luna, gives dramatic expression to Roderick's questionable status discussed earlier. In his play *El último godo* he hints at what might have happened if the king's desire for harmony between Moors and Christians had been achieved, and the *moriscos* left to flourish. In England, William Rowley also presents a utopian idea in *All's Lost by Lust*, in which he responds to contemporary concerns over religious, racial, and social difference with a vision of a more harmonious future.

It should be noted at this point that the desire for racial and religious harmony in the evolution of the legend has not been limited to that between Muslims and Christians, but also relates to Jews in some versions. As early as the *Refundición de la Crónica de 1344*, the anonymous *converso* author used the legend in part to vindicate the role of the Jews in the Muslim invasion and liberate them from opprobrium. Much later, Jewish characters play important parts in the legend as interpreted by Montengón, Agustín Príncipe, and Juan de Dios de Mora, as well as in Gómez de Avellaneda's *Egilona*. Their presence is important in these works in terms of plot development and interest; at the same time there is a strong sense of a need to avenge their treatment at the hands of Christians that often manifests itself as treachery in the plots. In *Egilona*, sympathy for the racially and religiously marginalized is expressed in Gómez de Avellaneda's interpretation of the Jewish characters and particularly in her creation of a noble, generous, and good character in the Moorish ruler Abdalasis whom Queen Egilona marries.

Yet the question of racial and religious identity does not become central until Juan Goytisolo has the courage and boldness to write *Reivindicación del Conde don Julián*. He taps the regenerative power of the legend to right an ancient wrong, which was the perception of the Muslim invasion as a disaster of the greatest proportions for Spain. He sweeps away the centuries-old discourse that has molded negative Spanish feelings about the Muslim Other, to embrace the richness and diversity of the mudejarism arising from the interaction of Islamic culture with that native to Spain. This paradoxical regeneration of Count Julian's treason reflects the regenerative power of Islam, which produced a unique cultural and ethnic mélange in the Hispanic peninsula. Goytisolo's text responds to the questions posed overtly and implicitly in the repetitive reformulation of the legend down the ages by acknowledging the invasion of Spain not as a disaster but as a felicitous opportunity for renewal and growth.

The recurrent appropriation of the legend of the king and the whore to confront issues relating to political crisis, national identity, gender, and the nature of history and fiction has fostered a story of perennial relevance and value both inside and outside Spain. The desire of successive generations of creative artists to listen to ancient voices has established a vivid, living cultural entity of unique regenerative stamina in terms of its own revitalization and also in its illumination of the cultural issues tested and challenged through its reception. Not only has it grasped the attention of major writers and composers, but also transformed the perception of seemingly dull or mediocre documents and writing and magnetized their implications. The legend of King Roderick and La Cava was created out of the cooperation of the three great civilizations of the Spanish peninsula, Christian, Islamic, and Mozarabic,[9] and thus presents a fruitful way of rewriting the prehistory of our present cultural crisis. Its paradigmatic nature has permitted renovation and innovation that has opened up new possibilities of interpretation, pushing the boundaries of meaning ever outward toward its potential perfection. From our position in the present it is incumbent upon us to ask whether this series of dialogues with the dead answers questions about us now, about our current stance upon racial and religious issues between Europe and the East. In doing so, it may be prudent to bear in mind the growing transition in the European perception of the Muslim invasion of 711 as disclosed through the reception of the legend of Roderick and La Cava, from one of apocalyptic destruction and assault to one of retrospective acknowledgment of the fertilization and enrichment born out of conquest.

APPENDIX 1

GENEALOGY OF THE *CRÓNICA DE 1344* MANUSCRIPTS (ACCORDING TO CINTRA)

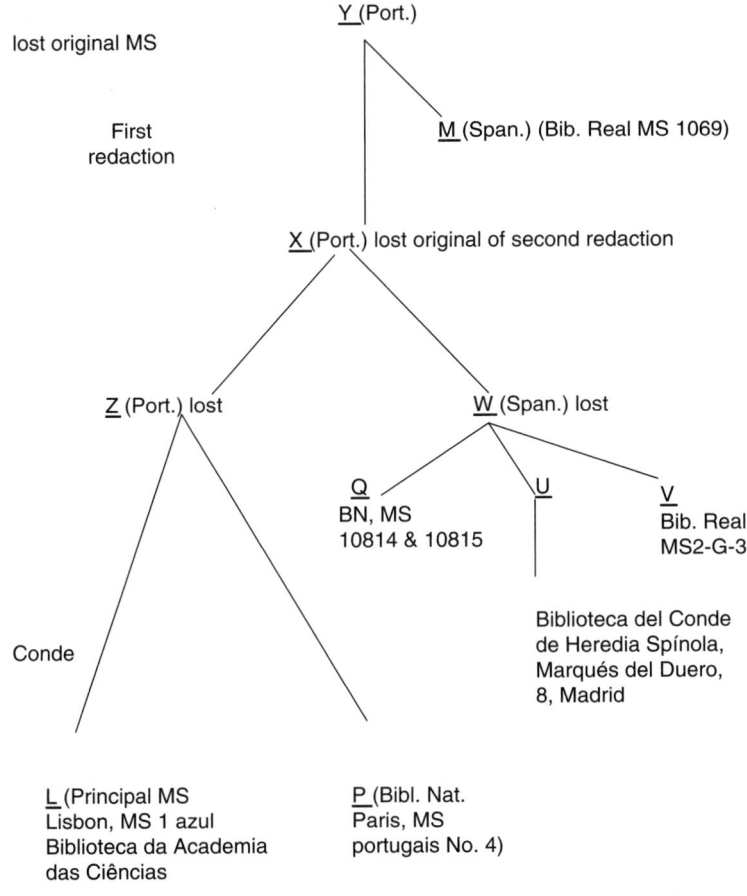

APPENDIX 2

VISUAL IMAGES OF KING RODERICK AND LA CAVA

An extensive investigation into visual images of King Roderick and La Cava has been beyond the scope of this book, although the limited exploration I have managed to undertake indicates a paucity of visual representations that is surprising in the light of the diversity of interest in the subject in other creative arts. The depiction of King Roderick in the frescoes of Qusayr 'Amra, which predates written records of the invasion of Spain, appears even more unique in view of the apparent lack of later portraits of the monarch. The image of Roderick also occurs on the coinage of Visigothic Spain discussed by Alois Heiss, but I have not found any other visual reference to the king until 1681, when his full face bust with armor and helmet illustrates Diego Saavedra Fajardo's *Corona gótica castellana* printed in Amberes.

To date, I have encountered just three visual images relating to the legend from the nineteenth century. While the Bridgeman Art Library database yields nothing more specific than a rather indistinct battle scene showing the Battle of Guadalete, Juan de Dios de Mora's novel *Florinda* contains a series of attractive black and white prints signed "Carnicero," depicting Roderick and the other characters in his story. However, the nineteenth-century German artist Franz-Xaver Winterhalter painted a lavish and voluptuous image of Florinda surrounded by ten ladies-in-waiting in a rural setting by a pool, which now hangs in Buckingham Palace. The president of Evyan Perfumes, Dr. Walter Langer, adapted the famous painting *Florinda* that he commissioned as a mural produced by the artist Alton S. Tobey, to advertise his perfume White Shoulders. It became one of the most admired examples of classic art as a medium for advertising.

If other visual images relating to the legend exist, then they are well hidden from view, and one might speculate as to the reasons for such an absence in contrast with such a prolific afterlife in literary, musical, and dramatic forms. Perhaps the subject proved too uncomfortable for Spanish artists more used to the portrayal of glory and victory through historical paintings, though this could not entirely account for the apparent disregard of the theme, especially by artists from other countries. It is even more surprising given the visual and dramatic potential of the story, which would be very well suited to a cinematic reworking, also lacking so far.

NOTES

Introduction

1. See Alan Deyermond, "The Death and Rebirth of Visigothic Spain in the *Estoria de España,*" *Revista Canadiense de Estudios Hispánicos* 9 (1985), p. 357 [345–67].
2. See Richard Fletcher, *The Cross and the Crescent: Christianity and Islam from Muhammad to the Reformation* (London: Allen Lane, 2003), pp. 158–59.
3. Fletcher, *The Cross and the Crescent*, p. 24.
4. Citation from Andrew Wheatcroft, *Infidels: The Conflict between Christendom and Islam 630–2002* (London: Viking, 2003), p. 55.
5. See Roger Collins, *Medieval Spain: Unity in Diversity, 400–1000*, New Studies in Medieval History (London: MacMillan, 1983), p. 151.
6. Roger Collins, *Medieval Spain*, p. 152.
7. Roger Collins, *Medieval Spain*, pp. 152–53.
8. Roger Collins, *Medieval Spain*, p. 150.
9. For example, W. Montgomery Watt, *A History of Islamic Spain* (Edinburgh: Edinburgh University Press, 1965), pp. 13–14 and E. Lévi-Provençal, *Histoire de l'Espagne musulmane* (Paris: G.P.Maisonneuve, 1950), Introduction and Translation by Emilio García Gómez in *Historia de España,Vol. I*, compiled by Ramón Menéndez Pidal (Madrid: Espasa-Calpe, 1987), pp. 12–16.
10. Citation from Paul Ricoeur, *History and Truth* (Evanston: Northwestern University Press, 1965), p. 490.
11. See Ramón Menéndez Pidal, *Floresta de Leyendas Heróicas Españolas: Rodrigo, el ultimo godo, Tomo 1, La Edad Media*, Clásicos Castellanos 25 (Madrid: La Lectura, 1925), p. 8.
12. Menéndez Pidal, *Floresta*, I, pp. 6–11.
13. Menéndez Pidal, *Floresta*, I, p. 12.
14. Menéndez Pidal, *Floresta*, I, p. 13.
15. See John Tolan, *Saracens: Islam in the Medieval European Imagination* (New York: Colombia University Press, 2002), p. xviii.
16. *The Independent*, 13 March 2004, p. 7.

Chapter 1   The Birth of a Legend

1. See Richard Ettinghausen, Oleg Grabar, and Marilyn Jenkins, *Islamic Art and Architecture 650–1250* (New Haven and London: Yale University Press, 2001), p. 48.
2. David Talbot Rice, *Islamic Art*, 2nd edn. (London: Thames and Hudson, 1975), p. 9–11.
3. K.A.C. Creswell, *Early Muslim Architecture: Ummayads A.D. 622–750*, 2 vols. (Oxford: Clarendon Press, 1969), p. 406.
4. Creswell, *Early Muslim Architecture*, p. 406.
5. For example, on the occasion of the marriage of the Persian emperor to the daughter of the Turkish king, Mas'ūdī notes that the kings of China, India, and possibly Tibet all call the emperor their brother. For further details, see Mas'ūdī, *Murūj al-dhahab*, ed. and trans. C. Barbier de Meynard and A. Pavet de Corneille (Paris, 1861–77), vol. 2, pp. 200–203.
6. See Oleg Grabar, "The Paintings of the Six Kings at Quṣayr 'Amrah," *Ars Orientalis* 1 (1954), p. 186 [185–87].
7. Grabar, *Ars Orientalis*, pp. 185–87. Richard Ettinghausen takes this further in his discussion of the six kings in his 1962 work *Arab Painting*. Like Grabar, he feels the fresco does not stress the defeat of the kings by Islam, but rather shows acclamation, in line with examples in Persian iconography in which kings greet their master in a similar manner. He also notes a similar gesture in some representations of the Apostles greeting Christ. Ettinghausen stresses the unusual and topical nature of the painting, which, he says, served a definite Ummayad purpose. In his view, the enthroned figure represents the caliph, who regards the six rulers as members of the family of kings of which he is now the commanding member. The consequently friendly association of the caliph with figureheads of long-established dynasties usefully legitimizes his new regime. It therefore combines conciliation with caliphal power. See Richard Ettinghausen, *Arab Painting* (Geneva: Editions d'Art Albert Skira, 1962), p. 30.
8. Creswell, *Early Muslim Architecture*, pp. 390–449.
9. Creswell, *Early Muslim Architecture*, pp. 400–401.
10. Both art historians Talbot Rice and Manuel Almagro, who led extensive renovations of the frescoes in 1975 espouse the conquered kings theory to explain the fresco. Papadopoulo, writing in 1976, turns these theories on their head by insisting on the total lack of Muslim character to these paintings and claiming that a proposed interpretation of a symbolic peaceful coexistence of world rulers does not fit historical reality nor the triumphant ideology of the Caliphate at that time. Such an interpretation depends, he says, upon identifying the enthroned individual as the caliph, when he believes it represents the Christ Pantocrator, in the Byzantine style, which would explain the respectful attitude of the six rulers. See Alexandre Papadopoulo, *Islam and Muslim Art*, trans. Robert Erich Wolf (Paris: Mazenod, 1976; trans. London: Thames and Hudson, 1980), pp. 70–71. The scholar Blázquez likes Grabar's theory of the family of kings, but sees no Persian influence in the fresco, and admits to some justification for Papadopoulo's suggestion regarding the Christ

Pantocrator, on the basis that Christian figures appeared in early Muslim buildings, notably the Dome of the Rock and at Kaaba.
11. Garth Fowden, *Empire to Commonwealth: Consequences of Monotheism in Late Antiquity* (Princeton: Princeton University Press, 1993), p. 143.
12. Fowden, *Empire to Commonwealth*, p. 144.
13. Garth Fowden, *Qusayr 'Amra: Art and Ummayad Élite in Late Antique Syria* (Berkeley and London: University of California Press, 2004), pp. 197–201.
14. Fowden, *Qusayr 'Amra*, pp. 224–25.
15. See *Fatho-l-Andaluçi*, ed. and trans. Joaquín González (Algiers: Leon Remordet and Co., 1889), p. 2.
16. See chapter 2 for a fuller discussion of these chronicles.

Chapter 2   Cultural Filters: Roderick and La Cava through the Eyes of Medieval Historians

1. Also known as *Chronica postbiclarense, Continuatio bizantina-arabica, Crónica arabigo-bizantina de 741, Chronica byzantia-arabica.*
2. Pedro Chalmeta, *Invasión e Islamización: la sumisión de Hispania y la formación de al-Andalus*, Colección Al-Andalus (Madrid: Editorial Mapfre, 1994), pp. 32–33. The text of the chronicle may be consulted in J. Gil, *Corpus scriptorium Muzarabicorum*, 2 vols. (Madrid: Consejo Superior de Investigaciones Científicas, Institutio Antonio de Nebrija, 1973), pp. 7–14.
3. Also known as *Continuatio Hispana* and *Chronica pacense*, among other titles.
4. Chalmeta, *Invasión e Islamización*, p. 33.
5. Aureliano Fernández Guerra discusses the Visigothic monarchical system in Spain in some detail, underlining the fact that the crown was elective, not hereditary, although Spanish nobles maintained that it ought to be, and fought to change it. When Witiza died, Roderick had been Duke of Bética province (contemporary Andalusia) for a number of years. The senate did not want the sons of an unworthy king to reign, and Roderick was thus anointed king in the basilica of San Pedro y San Pablo.
   See his *Caída y ruina del Imperio Visigótico español: primer drama que las representó en nuestro teatro* (Madrid: Manuel G. Hernández, 1883), pp. 38–45.
6. To read the full discussion, see Maravall, *Clavileño* 34, 1955, pp. 28–34.
7. The full text of the *Crónica mozárabe de 754* may be consulted in the edition and translation by José Eduardo López Pereira (Zaragoza: Anubar, 1980).
8. Georges Martin, "La chute du Royaume Visigothique d'Espagne," *Cahiers de Linguistique Hispanique Médiévale* 9 (1984): 211–12.
9. Roger Collins, *The Arab Conquest of Spain 710–797* (Oxford: Basil Blackwell, 1989), p. 59.
10. López Pereira, *Crónica mozárabe de 754*, pp. 70–72.
11. Martin, "La chute du Royaume Visigothique d'Espagne," p. 225.
12. Fred Donner, *Narratives of Islamic Origins. The Beginnings of Islamic Historical Writing*, Studies in Late Antiquity and Early Islam 14 (Princeton: Princeton University Press, 1998), pp. 117–118.

13. Collins, *Early Medieval Spain*, pp. 146–48.
14. There is an interesting discussion of this legend in R. Basset, "Légendes Arabes de l'Espagne: la maison fermée de Tolède," *Bulletin de la Société Géographique d'Oran*, 1898, pp. 42–58.
15. For a full account of Collins' interpretation of the Arab invasion and its historical records, see in particular Chapter 5 of *Early Medieval Spain*, and *The Arab Conquest of Spain 710–797*.
16. Chalmeta lists all known Arabic sources in great detail in *Invasión e Islamización*, pp. 33–44.
17. Chalmeta, *Invasión e Islamización*, p. 113.
18. Chalmeta, *Invasión e Islamización*, p. 119.
19. Menéndez Pidal, *Floresta*, I, p. 42.
20. Lucasde Túy, *Crónica de España*, ed. Julio Puyol (Madrid: Real Academia de la Historia, 1926), pp. 266–67.
21. Chalmeta, *Invasión e Islamización*, p. 47.
22. Alexander Haggerty Krappe, *The Legend of Rodrick, Last of the Visigothic Kings and the Ermanarich Cycle* (Heidelberg: Carl Winters Universitätsbuchhandlung, 1923), p. 10.
23. Krappe, *The Legend of Rodrick, Last of the Visigothic Kings*, p. 60.
24. Menéndez Pidal, *Floresta*, I, p. 125.
25. Menéndez Pidal, *Floresta*, I, p. 134.
26. Hayden White, *Tropics of Discourse: Essays in Cultural Criticism* (Baltimore and London: Johns Hopkins University Press, 1978), pp. 54–56.
27. *Crónica general de España de 1344: edición crítica del texto español de la Crónica de 1344 que ordenó el Conde de Barcelos don Pedro Alfonso*, eds. Diego Catalán and María Soledad Andrés (Madrid: Editorial Gredos S.A., 1971), p. xxxi.
28. Menéndez Pidal, *Floresta*, I, p. 81.
29. Menéndez Pidal, *Floresta*, I, p. 85.
30. *Livrod as Linaghens*, p. 230. Fred Donner describes a similar desire for genealogical legitimization in medieval Arabic historiography. Genealogy became a fully fledged science giving rise from the second century of the Hegira onward (ninth century AD) to vast genealogical works whose aim was to establish the legitimacy of the ruling elite. See *Narratives of Islamic Origins*, pp.105–6.
31. Thomas A. Lathrop, *The Legend of the Siete Infantes de Lara*, Studies in Romance Languages and Literatures, 122 (Chapel Hill: University of North Caroline Press, 1971), p. 15.
32. David Pattison, *From Legend to Chronicle: The Treatment of Epic Material in Alphonsine Historiography*, Medium Aevum Monographs, New Series XIII (Oxford: The Society for the Study of Medieval Languages and Literature, 1983), p. 148, n. 12.
33. Quoted in Menéndez Pidal, *Floresta*, I, p. 292 and p. 296.
34. Menéndez Pidal, *Floresta*, I, 95–96.
35. Lathrop, *The Legend of the Siete Infantes de Lara*, p. 16.
36. Both quoted in Menéndez Pidal, *Floresta I*, p. 295.
37. White, *Tropics of Discourse*, p. 56.

38. Quoted in Menéndez Pidal, *Floresta*, I, p. 295.
39. Pedrode Corral, *Crónica del rey Don Rodrigo, postrimero rey de los Godos (Crónica sarracina)*, 2 vols. ed. James Donald Fogelquist (Madrid: Clásicos Castalia, 2001), vol. 1, p. 9.
40. Juan Manuel Cacho Blecua, "Los historiadores de la Crónica sarracina," in *Historias y ficciones: coloquio sobre la literature del siglo XV*, ed. R. Beltrán, J.L. Canet, and J.L. Sirera (Valencia: University of Valencia, 1992), p. 55 [37–55].
41. Corral *Crónica del rey Don Rodrigo*, I, p. 48, n. 41.
42. Corral, *Crónica del rey Don Rodrigo*, I, p. 176.
43. Corral, *Crónica del rey Don Rodrigo*, I, p. 176.
44. Corral, *Crónica del rey Don Rodrigo*, I, p. 448.
45. Corral, *Crónica del rey Don Rodrigo*, I, p. 49.
46. Corral, *Crónica del rey Don Rodrigo*, I, p. 449.
47. Cacho Blecua, "Los historiadores de la Crónica sarracina," p. 48.
48. Corral, *Crónica del rey Don Rodrigo*, II, p. 391.
49. Corral, *Crónica del rey Don Rodrigo*, II, p. 394.
50. Corral, *Crónica del rey Don Rodrigo*, II, p. 395.
51. Corral, *Crónica del rey Don Rodrigo*, II, p. 396.
52. Gloria Álvarez-Hesse, *La Crónica sarracina: estudio de los elementos novelescos y caballerescos*, American University Studies Series II, Romance Languages and Literatures, vol. 124 (New York: Peter Lang, 1990), p. 129.
53. Anthony Weir and James Jerman. *Images of Lust: Sexual Carvings on Medieval Churches* (London: B.T. Batsford Ltd., 1986), p. 74.
54. Corral, *Crónica del rey Don Rodrigo*, II, p. 402.
55. Corral, *Crónica del rey Don Rodrigo*, II, p. 403.
56. Corral, *Crónica del rey Don Rodrigo*, II, p. 403.
57. Corral, *Crónica del rey Don Rodrigo*, II, p. 404.
58. Julie B. Miller, "Eroticized Violence in Medieval Women's Mystical Literature: A Call for a Feminist Critique," *Journal of Feminist Studies in Religion* 15:2 (1999), pp. 39–40 and p. 40, n. 62 [25–49].
59. Ian Moulton, *Before Pornography: Erotic Writing in Early Modern England* (Oxford: Oxford University Press, 2000), p. 9.
60. Corral, *Crónica del rey Don Rodrigo*, I, p. 72.
61. Menéndez Pidal, *Floresta*, II, p. 117.
62. Corral, *Crónica del rey Don Rodrigo*, I, p. 54.

Chapter 3 True and False Histories: The Case of the Master Forger Miguel de Luna

1. Juan María Laboa, *Rodrigo Sánchez de Arévalo, Alcaide de Sant'Angelo* (Madrid: Fundación Universitaria Española, 1973), p. 296.
2. Menéndez Pidal, *Floresta*, II, p. 47.
3. Juliándel Castillo, *Historia de los reyes godos que vinieron de la Scitia de Europa, contra el Imperio Romano, y a España: y la succession dellos hasta el Catholico y potentissimo don Philippe segundo Rey de España: a quien va dirigida* (Burgos: Philippe de Junta, 1582), p. 3.

4. Castillo, *Historia de los reyes godos*, p. 4.
5. Castillo, *Historia de los reyes godos*, p. 5.
6. Castillo, *Historia de los reyes godos*, p. 2.
7. Castillo, *Historia de los reyes godos*, p. lii.
8. Castillo, *Historia de los reyes godos* p. lvj.
9. Alan Soons, *Juan de Mariana* (Boston: Twayne Publishers, 1982), p. 39–40.
10. Soons, *Juan de Mariana*, p. 41.
11. Soons, *Juan de Mariana*, p. 105.
12. The case of the Lead Books is still of enormous interest and importance and the Arabic texts still remain largely unpublished. A team of researchers led by Professor Mercedes García-Arenal of the Consejo Superior de Investigaciones Científicas in Madrid is currently investigating the *plomos*, which were only returned to Granada from the Vatican by Cardinal Ratzinger just prior to his election as pope. The great irony is that the Granadans are not convinced by the authenticity of the artefacts returned to Spain, and fear they may be copies of the originals.
13. Menéndez Pidal, *Floresta*, II, pp. 49–50.
14. Miguelde Luna, *Historia verdadera del rey Don Rodrigo, compuesta por el sabio Alcayde Abulcácim Tarif Abentarique* (Valencia: en casa de Pedro Patricio Mey junto a S. Martín, 1606), p. 4.
15. Collins, *The Arab Conquest of Spain 710–797*, p. 1.
16. Collins, *The Arab Conquest of Spain 710–797*, pp. 4–5.
17. Donner, *Narratives of Islamic Origins*, p. 206.
18. Donner, *Narratives of Islamic Origins*, p.177.
19. Donner, *Narratives of Islamic Origins*, p. 210–11.
20. Luna, *Historia verdadera del rey Don Rodrigo*, p. 7.
21. Leonard Patrick Harvey, "The Moriscos and Don Quixote," Inaugural Lecture in the Chair of Spanish delivered at University of London, King's College, 1974, pp. 7–9.
22. Harvey, "The Moriscos and Don Quixote," p. 33.
23. Albrecht Noth, *The Early Arabic Historical Tradition: A Source-Critical Study*, 2nd edn, with Lawrence I. Conrad, trans. Michael Bonner (Princeton: The Darwin Press Inc., 1994), p. 80.
24. David Lowenthal, "Authenticity? The Dogma of Self-Delusion," in *Why Fakes Matter: Essays on Problems of Authenticity*, ed. Mark Jones (London: British Museum Press,1992), p. 186.
25. Menéndez Pidal, *Floresta*, II, p. 57.
26. Menéndez Pidal, *Floresta*, II, p. 58.

Chapter 4 Metamorphosis into Song

1. For a fuller account of the origins and features of the Spanish ballad, see Colin Smith's excellent introduction to his *Spanish Ballads*, 2nd edn. (Bristol: Bristol Classical Press, 1996) on which I have drawn.
2. Smith, *Spanish Ballads*, p. x.

3. Menéndez Pidal, *Floresta*, II, p. 7.
4. Smith, *Spanish Ballads*, p. xx.
5. Barbara Weissberger, *Isabel Rules: Constructing Queenship, Wielding Power* (Minneapolis: University of Minnesota Press, 2003), p. 111.
6. Menéndez Pidal, *Romancero tradicional de las lenguas hispánicas: Romancero del Rey Rodrigo y de Bernardo del Carpio* (Madrid: Editorial Gredos, 1957), p. 130.
7. Cervantes, *Don Quijote, Part II*, ed. Luis Andrés Murillo (Madrid: Clásicos Castalia 77, 1978), pp. 245–46.
8. Weissberger, *Isabel Rules*, p. 107.
9. Weissberger, *Isabel Rules*, p. 111.
10. Menéndez Pidal, *Romancero tradicional*, p. 59.
11. Menéndez Pidal, *Romancero tradicional*, p. 31.
12. Menéndez Pidal, *Romancero tradicional*, p. 19.
13. Menéndez Pidal, *Romancero tradicional*, p. 56.
14. Menéndez Pidal, *Romancero tradicional*, p. 106.
15. Michel Moner, "Deux figures emblématiques: la femme violée et la parfaite épouse, selon le 'Romancero General' compilé par Agustín Durán," in *Images de la femme en Espagne au XVIe et XVIIe siècle*, Colloque International, ed. Augustin Redondo (Paris: Presses de la Sorbonne Nouvelle, 1994), pp. 77–90.
16. Menéndez Pidal, *Floresta*, II, p. 39.
17. Menéndez Pidal, *Romancero tradicional*, p. 129.
18. See Pedro Correa, *Los romances fronterizos, Vols I and II*, edición comentada (Granada: Universidad de Granada, 1999), vol. 1. p.85.
19. Smith, *Spanish Ballads*, p. xxxviii.
20. For an opposing, if unconvincing view, see John R. Burt, "The Motif of the Fall of Man in the 'Romancero del Rey Rodrigo," *Hispania* 61 (September 1978), pp. 435–42.

Chapter 5 New Life in Drama and Music: From Poetry to Theatre

1. See *The Original Poems of Fray Luis de León*, ed. Edward Sarmiento (Manchester: Manchester University Press, 1953), p. 77.
2. For example, Cervantes also personifies the river Douro in his work *Numancia*.
3. Bartolomé Palau, *Historia de la Gloriosa Santa Orosia*, ed. Oleh Mazur, Colección Nova Scholar (Madrid: Editorial Playor, 1986), p. 37.
4. Menéndez Pidal, *Floresta*, II, p. 43.
5. See Lope de Vega Carpio, *Jerusalén conquistada, epopeya trágica*, edición y estudio crítico de Joaquín de Entreambasaguas, 3 vols. (Madrid: CSIC, 1954), vol. 3, p. 137.
6. Melveena McKendrick, *Theatre in Spain 1490–1700* (Cambridge: Cambridge University Press, 1989), pp. 74–76.
7. Henry Kamen, *Spain 1469–1714: A Society of Conflict* (London and New York: Longman, 1983), p. 219.

8. Menéndez Pidal, *Floresta*, II, p. 69.
9. Lope de Vega Carpio, *El Último godo*, ed. Marcelino Menéndez y Pelayo, *Obras de Lope de Vega XVI*, Biblioteca de Autores Españoles (Madrid: Ediciones Atlas, 1915, repr. 1966), p. 19 [345–93].
10. Menéndez Pidal, *Floresta*, II, p. 69–70.
11. Melveena McKendrick, *Playing the King: Lope de Vega and the Limits of Conformity* (London: Tamesis, 2000), p. 51.
12. McKendrick, *Playing the King*, p. 52.
13. McKendrick *Playing the King*, p. 2.
14. McKendrick *Playing the King*, p. 109.
15. McKendrick *Playing the King*, p. 51.
16. Susan Niehoff, "The Unity of Lope de Vega's *El Último godo*," *Kentucky Romance Quarterly* 29:3 (1982), p. 269 [261–72].
17. Luce López-Baralt, *Islam in Spanish Literature from the Middle Ages to the Present*, trans. Andrew Hurley (Leiden: E.J. Brill, 1992), pp. 209–10.
18. Quoted in López-Baralt, *Islam in Spanish Literature*, p. 210.
19. William Rowley, *A Shoemaker, A Gentleman*, ed. Trudi Darby (London: Nick Hern Books, 2002), p. xi.
20. Quoted in Roger Lockyer, *Tudor and Stuart Britain 1471–1714* (Harlow: Longman, 1964, 2nd edn. 1985), p. 211.
21. Jack D'Amico, *The Moor in English Renaissance Drama* (Tampa: University of South Florida Press, 1991), p. 2.
22. D'Amico, *The Moor in English Renaissance Drama*, p. 7.
23. D'Amico, *The Moor in English Renaissance Drama*, pp. 21–22.
24. Pilar Cuder-Domínguez, "The Islamization of Spain in William Rowley and Mary Pix: The Politics of Nation and Gender," *Comparative Drama* 36:3–4 (2002), pp. 333–34 [321–36].
25. Tristan Marshall, *Theatre and Empire: Great Britain on the London Stages under James VI and I* (Manchester: Manchester University Press, 2000), p. 158.
26. Marshall *Theatre and Empire*, p. 150.
27. Diegode Saavedra Fajardo, *Obras de Don Diego de Saavedra Fajardo y del licenciado Pedro Fernández Navarrete*, Biblioteca de Autores Españoles desde la Formación del lenguaje hasta nuestros días (Madrid: M. Rivadeneyra, 1853), p. 269.
28. Saavedra Fajardo, *Obras*, p. 374.
29. Menéndez Pidal, *Floresta*, II, p. 74.
30. Saavedra Fajardo, *Obras*, p. 376.
31. Saavedra Fajardo, *Obras*, p. 375.
32. José Godoy Alcántara, *Historia crítica de los falsos cronicones* (Madrid: Real Academia de la Historia, 1868), p. 285.
33. Menéndez Pidal, *Floresta*, III, p. 7.
34. Cristóbal Lozano, *David Perseguido y alivio de lastimadas: Historia sagrada parafraseada con exemplos, y varias historias humanas y divinas*, vol. 3 (Barcelona: Pablo Campius, 1745), p. 14.
35. Lozano, *David Perseguido*, p. 14.
36. Lozano, *David Perseguido*, p. 14.

37. Lozano, *David Perseguido*, p. 15.
38. Lozano, *David Perseguido*, p. 27.
39. A number of other works that recreate the legend are also outside the scope of this book either because the legend itself is subordinate to another main plot or idea, or because the original cultural context is changed. An example of such a work is André da Silva Mascarenha's Portuguese poem in nine cantos, *A destruiçam de Espanha e restauraçam summaria da mesma* of 1671, set on Mount Olympus among the classical Roman gods.

Chapter 6 Censored!—The Eighteenth Century

1. Discurso XVI, numbers 7 and 8, quoted in Menéndez Pidal, *Floresta*, III, p. 134.
2. Discurso XIII, number 53, quoted in Menéndez Pidal, *Floresta*, III, p. 135.
3. Menéndez Pidal, *Floresta*, III, p. 135.
4. Menéndez Pidal, *Floresta*, III, p. 135.
5. See Nigel Glendinning, *The Eighteenth Century, A Literary History of Spain* (London: Benn, 1972), p. 92.
6. The manuscript now resides in the Biblioteca Municipal, Madrid.
7. Quoted in Ramón Menéndez Pidal, *Boletín de la Real Academia Española* XI, December 1924, p. 554, as the censure of Doctor Francisco de la Fuente, in one of the copies of the Vela manuscript. Pidal also includes an outline of Vela's play.
8. See Glendinning, *The Eighteenth Century*, p. 102.
9. It is not clear whether the anonymous manuscripts of the same title held by the Biblioteca Municipal and the Biblioteca Nacional can be identified with Valladares' work. See Menéndez Pidal, *Boletín de la Real Academia*, p. 560 n. 2 for further details.
10. Menéndez Pidal, *Boletín de la Real Academia*, p. 561.
11. R. Merritt Cox, "A New 'Novel' by Cadalso," *Hispanic Review* 41 (1973), p. 658 [655–68].
12. Cox, "A New 'Novel' by Cadalso," p. 661–62.
13. Quotedin Cox, "A New 'Novel' by Cadalso," p. 659.
14. See Pedro Montengón, *El Rodrigo*, ed. Guillermo Carnero (Madrid: Cátedra, 2002), p. 125.
15. Pedro Montengón, *El Rodrigo*, p. 135.
16. Pedro Montengón, *El Rodrigo*, p. 158.
17. Pedro Montengón, *El Rodrigo*, p. 79.
18. Pedro Montengón, *El Rodrigo*, p. 206.
19. Pedro Montengón, *El Rodrigo*, p. 282.
20. Pedro Montengón, *El Rodrigo*, p. 80.
21. In an interesting article on *El Rodrigo*, José Juan Berbel Rodríguez argues that the novel is closer to an epic in prose than to a historical novel, on the basis that the work provokes a model of identification with the hero based upon catharsis, although Berbel Rodríguez also acknowledges the fantastic

elements of the novel such as Florinda's conversion into a she-devil. He does not refer, however, to Pedro de Corral, who did this long before Montengón. The author concludes that *El Rodrigo* is a firmly political novel, in which he claims that Montengón wonders ". . .si habrá alguien que encabece las tropas en una nueva Covadonga, en el inicio de una época que él intuye oscura y llena de dificultades y peligros" (. . .if anyone will lead the troops in a new Covadonga, at the start of an era which he senses to be dark and full of difficulties and dangers). See José Juan Berbel Rodríguez, "El *Rodrigo* de Montengón y tres tragedias sobre Don Pelayo," in *Actas del I Congreso Internacional sobre la novela del siglo XVIII*, ed. F. García Lara (Almería: Universidad de Almería, 1998), p. 111 [101–12].

22. *The Plays of Mary Pix and Catharine Trotter*, ed. Edna L. Steeves (New York and London: Garland Publications Inc., 1982), p. xvi.
23. *The Plays of Mary Pix and Catharine Trotter*, p. xli.
24. *The Plays of Mary Pix and Catharine Trotter*, p. xlviii.
25. Pilar Cuder-Domínguez, "The Islamization of Spain in William Rowley and Mary Pix," p. 329.
26. See Bridget Orr, *Empire on the English Stage 1660–1714* (Cambridge: Cambridge University Press, 2001), p. 136–37.
27. Orr, *Empire on the English Stage 1660–1714*, p. 181.
28. Operas on the Roderick legend were performed in Rome (1677 and 1694), Milan (1684), Bologna (1686), Mantua (1686), Verona (1687), Naples (1687 and 1702), Florence (1692), Parma (1695), Ferrara (1696), and Palermo (1703). The famous Reinhard Keiser's *Desiderius* (1709) was partly based on the same story. See Winton Dean and John Merrill Knapp, *Handel's Operas 1704–1726* (Oxford: Clarendon Press, 1987), p. 97.
29. Dean and Merrill Knapp, *Handel's Operas 1704–1726*, p. 85.
30. The *Argomento* of the musical drama indicates Foresti as the source: "Aquesta Istoria raccolta con orrore de nostri Secoli dalle penne tutte Spagnuole, è frà l'Italiane dal P. Foresti, s'aggiungono nel Drama i seguenti Verisimili" (This legendary story taken from Spanish writers, which has horrified the present time, is from the Italian version by P. Foresti, and the following likely details have been added to the drama), and can be viewed at http://www.concordi.it/bdigitale/Libretti/Pag%20Libretti/Silv%20Op%20371/pages/00. 8 October 2004.
31. Reinhard Strohm, *Essays on Handel and Italian Opera* (Cambridge: Cambridge University Press, 1985), pp. 4–5.
32. Strohm, *Essays on Handel and Italian Opera*, p. 36.
33. Strohm, *Essays on Handel and Italian Opera*, p. 11.
34. See Georg Friedrich Handel, *Vincer se stesso è la maggior vittoria* (*Rodrigo*, performed by Il Complesso Barocco, direction) and English libretto by Alan Curtis (London: Virgin Classics Limited, 1999), Introduction by Anthony Hicks, p. 13.
35. Dean and Merrill Knapp, *Handel's Operas 1704–1726*, p. 99.
36. Dean and Merrill Knapp, *Handel's Operas 1704–1726*, p. 101.

Chapter 7   Romanticism and Renewal

1. *Eclectic Review*, 1811, p. 673.
2. John Sutherland, *The Life of Walter Scott: A Critical Biography* (Oxford: Blackwell, 1995), p. 144.
3. Edmund Spenser, *Edmund Spenser's Poetry*, ed. Hugh MacLean and Anne Lake Prescott, 3rd edn. (New York: W.W. Norton and Company, 1993), p. 499.
4. Spenser, *Spenser's Poetry*, p. 499.
5. Spenser, *Spenser's Poetry*, p. 3.
6. R.H. Super, *Walter Savage Landor: A Biography* (London: John Calder, 1957), p. 85.
7. Menéndez Pidal, *Floresta*, III, p. 41.
8. Malcolm Elwin, *Savage Landor* (London: MacMillan and Co., 1941), p. 124.
9. Elwin, *Savage Landor*, p. 124.
10. Elwin, *Savage Landor*, p. 109.
11. Edward Waterman Evans, *Walter Savage Landor: A Critical Study* (Port Washington: Kennikat Press, 1892, repr. 1970), pp. 81–82.
12. Quoted in Elwin, *Savage Landor*, p. 125.
13. Elwin, *Savage Landor*, p. 111.
14. Elwin, *Savage* Landor, p. 113.
15. Indeed Southey told Landor that he would make a list of 'the passages which appear so difficult that ordinary readers may be supposed incapable of understanding them' (*Letters of Robert Southey: A Selection*, ed. Maurice H. Fitzgerald (London: Oxford University Press, 1912).
16. Southey, *Letters*, p. 110.
17. Walter Savage Landor, *Landor's Poetical Works Vol. 1*, ed. Stephen Wheeler, 3 vols. (Oxford: Clarendon Press, 1937), p. 161. All quotations from the play are from this edition.
18. Harry Berger Jr., *Making Trifles of Terrors: Redistributing Complicities in Shakespeare* (Stanford: Stanford University Press, 1997), p. 26.
19. Menéndez Pidal, *Floresta III*, p. 42.
20. Elwin, *Savage Landor*, p. 123.
21. Journeys from La Coruña to Madrid and to Lisbon in 1795–96 plus another journey to Portugal in 1800–1801.
22. Robert Southey, *The Poetical Works of Robert Southey* (London: Longman, Brown, Green and Longmans, 1845), p. 113.
23. Southey, *The Poetical Works*, p. 112.
24. Southey has an interesting note on the origin of the name La Caba. He quotes Bleda's "*Crónica de los moros de España*," pp. 193–94, where the historian alleges that the Hebrew name Eva is pronounced 'Cavah,' '. . .de suerte que tuvieron un mesmo nombre dos mugeres que fueron ruyna de los hombres, la una en todo el mundo, y la otra en España' ('. . .so that two women who were the ruin of men, one throughout the world and the other in Spain, both shared the same name.') (Southey, *The Poetical Works*, p. 113).

25. See Menéndez Pidal, "El Rey Rodrigo en la literatura," *Boletín de la Real Academia Española* 11, vol. 11, p. 570 [519–85].
26. Southey, *Letters*, p. 184.
27. Southey, *Letters*, p. 210.
28. Southey, *Letters*, p. 174.
29. Mark Storey, *Robert Southey: A Life* (Oxford and New York: Oxford University Press, 1997), p. 221.
30. Storey, *Robert Southey: A Life*, p. 214 and p. 232.
31. See Edward Meachen, "History and Transcendence in Robert Southey's Epic Poems," *Studies in English Literature 1500–1900* 19:4 (1979), p. 590 [589–608].
32. For a fuller view of modern critical opinion on *Roderick, Last of the Goths*, see Brian Wilkie, *Romantic Poets and Epic Tradition* (Madison and Milwaukee: University of Wisconsin Press, 1965); Kenneth Curry, *Southey* (London : Routledge and Kegan Paul, 1975); Richard Hoffpauir, "The Thematic Structure of Southey's Epic Poetry," *The Wordsworth Circle* 6:4 (1975), pp. 240–48; Meachen, "History and Transcendence," pp. 589–608 and Diego Saglia, "Nationalist Texts and Counter-Texts: Southey's *Roderick* and the Dissensions of the Annotated Romance," *Nineteenth Century Literature* 53:4 (1999), pp. 421–51.
33. Curry, *Southey*, p. 170.
34. Meachen, "History and Transcendence," p. 594.
35. Wilkie, *Romantic Poets and Epic Tradition*, p. 4 and p. 9.
36. Wilkie, *Romantic Poets and Epic Tradition*, p. 9.
37. Wilkie, *Romantic Poets and Epic Tradition*, p. 15 and p. 33.
38. Hoffpauir, "The Thematic Structure of Southey's Epic Poetry," p. 240.
39. Hoffpauir, "The Thematic Structure of Southey's Epic Poetry," p. 242.
40. For a taste of the opinion of nineteenth-century reviewers of *Roderick*, which were on the whole very favourable, see the selection on pages 175–193 of *Robert Southey:The Critical Heritage*, vol. 2, ed. Lionel Madden (London: Routledge and Kegan Paul, 1995, c. 1972).
41. Saglia, "Nationalist Texts and Counter-Texts," p. 425.
42. Saglia, "Nationalist Texts and Counter-Texts," p. 427.
43. Saglia, "Nationalist Texts and Counter-Texts," p. 428.
44. Washington Irving, *The Crayon Miscellany*, ed. Dahlia Kirby Terrell (Boston: Twayne Publishers, 1979), p. xlii.
45. Irving, *The Crayon Miscellany*, p. xlv.
46. Irving, *The Crayon Miscellany*, p. xlviii.
47. S.P. Scott, *History of the Moorish Empire in Europe*, vol. 1 (Philadelphia: J.B. Lippincott, 1904), p. vi.
48. Irving, *The Crayon Miscellany*, p. 241.
49. Irving, *The Crayon Miscellany*, p. xlvi.
50. Irving, *The Crayon Miscellany*, p. 242.
51. Irving, *The Crayon Miscellany*, p. 256.
52. Irving, *The Crayon Miscellany*, p. 349.
53. For a full account of these analogies, see Mary Weatherspoon Bowden, *Washington Irving* (Boston: Twayne Publishers, 1981), pp. 155–57.

54. Telesforo de Trueba, *The Romance of History: Spain*, 3 vols. (London: Edward Bull, 1830), p. v.
55. Trueba, *The Romance of History*, p. 16.
56. Trueba, *The Romance of History*, p. 54.
57. Marquis de Sade, *Oeuvres Complètes du Marquis de Sade*, vol. 9 (Paris: Chêne et Rousseau, 1967), p. 22.
58. Sade, *Oeuvres Complètes*, p. 20, footnote.
59. Sade, *Oeuvres Complètes*, p. 258.
60. Sade, *Oeuvres Complètes*, p. 271.
61. Menéndez Pidal shrewdly observes that Italy and Germany were much later than England and France in poeticizing the story of Roderick and La Cava because the former two countries were not involved in the peninsula war.
62. See Menéndez Pidal , *Floresta*, III, p. 57.
63. Émile Deschamps, *Oeuvres complètes, Deuxième Partie: Poésie* (Paris: Alphonse Lemerre, 1873), p. 294.
64. Deschamps, *Oeuvres complètes*, p. 294.
65. Menéndez Pidal, *Floresta*, III, p. 59.
66. Menéndez Pidal , *Floresta*, III, p. 60, notes that Victor Hugo refers to the legend on at least three occasions, in *La bataille perdue, Hernani*, and also in *Nôtre Dame de Paris*.

Chapter 8   Multiple Perspectives in Hispanic Romanticism

1. See Raymond Carr, "Spanish History from 1700," in *Spain: A Companion to Spanish Studies*, ed. P.E. Russell (London: Methuen, 1973, repr. 1987), p. 153 [145–90].
2. For a fuller account of Romanticism in Spain, see Derek Flitter, "Romanticism in Spain," in *The Cambridge History of Spanish Literature*, ed. David T. Gies (Cambridge: Cambridge University Press, 2004), pp. 345–49.
3. Geoffrey Ribbans, "Spanish Literature after 1700," in Russell, *Spain: A Companion to Spanish Studies*, p. 394 [381–428].
4. Menéndez Pidal, *Floresta*, III, p. 29.
5. Gálvez María Rosa, *Florinda*. Obras poéticas Tomo II—Biblioteca Virtual Miguel de Cervantes: http://www.cervantesvirtual.com/servlet/SirveObras/12371176449019390754624/p00.
6. Menéndez Pidal, *Floresta*, III, p. 32 and *Autoras en la Historia del Teatro Español (1500–1994), Vol 1 (Siglos XVII–XVIII–XIX)*, dir. Juan Antonio Hormigón (Madrid: Publicaciones de la Asociación de Directores de Escena de España, [1996]–2000), p. 489.
7. *Hormigón Autoras en la Historia del Teatro Español*, p. 489.
8. Daniel S. Whitaker, "Clarissa's Sisters: The Consequences of Rape in Three Neoclassic Tragedies of María Rosa Gálvez," *Letras Peninsulares* (Fall 1992), p. 249 n. 12 [239–51].

9. Gies, *The Cambridge History of Spanish Literature*, p. 356.
10. See Antonio Gil y Zárate, *Obras dramáticas de Don Antonio Gil y Zárate*, ed. Eugenio de Ochoa (Paris: Baudry, Librería Europa, 1850), p. x.
11. Menéndez Pidal, *Floresta*, III, pp. 36–37.
12. Miguel Agustín Príncipe, *El Conde Don Julián: drama original e histórico en siete cuadros y en verso*, 2nd edn. (Madrid: Repullés, 1840), p. 137.
13. Menéndez Pidal, *Floresta*, III, p. 88.
14. Pilar León Tello, *Judíos de Toledo, Tomo I* (Madrid: Consejo Superior de Investigaciones Científicas, 1979), p. 17.
15. Agustín Príncipe, *El Conde Don Julián*, p. 137.
16. Menéndez Pidal, *Floresta*, II, pp. 92–99.
17. See Gies, *The Cambridge History of Spanish Literature*, p. 392.
18. In addition to the interest of eighteenth-century writers in the character of Egilona, partly fostered by the prohibition of the depiction of Roderick by the censors, in 1804 Josef de Vargas Ponce wrote a tragedy entitled *Abdeláziz y Egilona*, described in highly negative terms by Menéndez Pidal, *Floresta*, III, p. 25–26.
19. For more details of these minor works, see Menéndez Pidal, *Floresta*, III, pp. 113–14.
20. See Menéndez Pidal, *Floresta*, III, pp. 79–81.
21. Joséde Espronceda, *El Diablo Mundo. El Pelayo. Poesías*, ed. Domingo Ynduráin (Madrid: Cátedra, 1992), p. 28.
22. E. Allison Peers, "Florinda," *Revue Hispanique* 58 (1923), p. 187, n. 4 [186–98].
23. Menéndez Pidal, *Floresta*, III, p. 69.
24. Gerald Brenan, *The Literature of the Spanish Peopl*, 2nd ed. (Cambridge: Cambridge University Press, 1976), p. 338.
25. Peers, "Florinda," p. 191.
26. Alexandre Herculano, *Eurico o presbítero* (Mem Martins: Publicaçoes Europa-América, LDA, Colecção 'Livros de Bolso Europa-América, 1844), p. 29, n. 1.
27. Herculano, *Eurico o presbítero*, p. 33.
28. Herculano, *Eurico o presbítero*, p. 43.
29. Herculano, *Eurico o presbítero*, p. 67.
30. Menéndez Pidal, *Floresta*, III, p. 110.
31. Juande Dios de Mora, *Florinda o La Caba* (Madrid: D.M. Prats, 1853), p. 492.

Chapter 9   The Once and Future King

1. Menéndez Pidal, *Floresta*, III, p. 116.
2. Menéndez Pidal, *Floresta*, III, p. 116.
3. Florentino Soria López, *Los Titanes de la Raza*, 2 vols. (Madrid: Hernando, 1925), p. xii.
4. Soria López, *Los Titanes de la Raza*, p. 118.

5. Juan Goytisolo, *Reivindicación del Conde don Julián*, ed. Linda Gould Levine (Madrid: Cátedra, 1970, 2nd edn. 1995), p. 126.
6. Goytisolo, *Reivindicación del Conde don Julián*, p. 89.
7. Juan Goytisolo, "From *Count Julian* to *Makbara*: A Possible Orientalist Reading," in *Saracen Chronicles: A Selection of Literary Essays*, trans. Helen Lane (London: Quartet Books, 1992), pp. 213–17.
8. Juan Goytisolo, "Vigencia actual del mudejarismo," in *Contracorrientes* (Barcelona: Montesinos, 1985), p. 11.
9. Goytisolo, *Reivindicación del Conde don Julián*, p. 79.
10. Goytisolo, "From *Count Julian* to *Makbara* ," pp. 217–18.
11. Goytisolo, *Saracen Chronicles*, p. 40.
12. See Jo Labanyi, *Myth and History in the Contemporary Spanish Novel* (Cambridge: Cambridge University Press, 1989), p. 205.
13. Goytisolo, "From *Count Julian* to *Makbara*," p. 220.
14. Alison Ribeiro de Menezes, *Juan Goytisolo: The Author as Dissident* (Woodbridge: Tamesis, 2005), p. 86.
15. Juan Goytisolo, *Disidencias* (Barcelona: Seix Barral, 1977), p. 292.
16. Goytisolo, *Reivindicación del Conde don Julián*, p. 143.
17. See Goytisolo's essay "Vigencia actual del mudejarismo," in *Contracorrientes*, p. 4.
18. See C. Colin Smith, "An Approach to Góngora's *Polifemo*," *Bulletin of Hispanic Studies* 42 (1965), pp. 217–38.
19. Goytisolo, *Reivindicación del Conde don Julián*, p. 158.
20. Goytisolo, *Reivindicación del Conde don Julián*, p. 204.
21. Goytisolo, *Reivindicación del Conde don Julián*, p. 206.
22. Goytisolo, *Reivindicación del Conde don Julián*, p. 208.
23. Goytisolo, *Reivindicación del Conde don Julián*, p. 267.
24. Goytisolo, *Disidencias*, p. 292.
25. See Menéndez Pidal, *Floresta*, III, p. 110–11. Only the first half of the play has been conserved.
26. Menéndez Pidal, *Floresta*, III, p. 111.
27. Frank Merkling, "New York, Don Rodrigo," in *Opera News*, 26 March 1966.
28. Juan Orrega-Salas, "*Don Rodrigo* de Ginastera," *Artes hispánicas* i/1 (1967), p. 94 [95–133].
29. Orrega-Salas, "*Don Rodrigo* de Ginastera," p. 94.
30. Dana Broccoli, *Florinda* (New York: Two Continents Publishing Group, 1977), p. 180.
31. Broccoli, *Florinda*, p. 8.
32. Broccoli, *Florinda*, p. 92.
33. Promotional leaflet for *La Cava*, 2000.
34. At http://www.theatreguidelondon.co.uk/reviews/lacava.htm on 28/08/03.
35. The Mail on Sunday, from http://www.theatreguidelondon.co.uk/reviews/lacava.htm on 28/08/03.
36. *The Daily Telegraph*, excerpt on promotional leaflet for *La Cava*.

Conclusion

1. Menéndez Pidal, *Floresta III*, pp. 125–26.
2. Quoted in White, *Tropics of Discourse*, p. 56.
3. White, *Tropics of Discourse*, p. 91.
4. White, *Tropics of Discourse*, p. 88.
5. White, *Tropics of Discourse*, pp. 69–70.
6. Mary M. Gaylord, "Spain's Renaissance Conquests and the Retroping of Identity," *Journal of Hispanic Philology* 16:2 (1992), p. 131 [125–36].
7. Gaylord, "Spain's Renaissance Conquests," p. 132.
8. Menéndez Pidal, *Floresta*, III, pp. 6–7.
9. Menéndez Pidal, *Floresta*, I, p. 7.

BIBLIOGRAPHY

Ackerlind, Sheila, R. *King Dinis of Portugal and the Alfonsine Heritage*. New York and Bern: Peter Lang, 1990.
Akhbār al-Majmū'a. Ed. and trans. E. Lafuente y Alcántara. Madrid: M. Rivadeneyra, 1867.
Alfonso X. *Crónica general de Espana: los cinco libros primeros de la Crónica de Espana*. Ed. Florián de Ocampo. Medina del Campo, 1553.
Allison Peers, E. "Florinda." *Revue Hispanique* 58 (1923): 186–98.
All's Lost by Lust and the Spanish Gypsy. Ed. Edgar C. Morris. Belles Lettres Series. Boston and London: D.C. Heath and Co., 1908.
Almagro, Martín. *Qusayr 'Amra: residencia y baños omeyas en el desierto de Jordania*. Madrid: Instituto Hispano-Árabe de Cultura, 1975.
Álvarez-Hesse, Gloria. *La Crónica sarracina: estudio de los elementos novelescos y caballerescos*. American University Studies Series II, Romance Languages and Literatures, Vol. 124. New York: Peter Lang, 1990.
Anstice, Sir R.H. *The Poetical Heroes of Sir Walter Scott*. Aberdeen: Cornwall and Sons, 1917.
Araluce Cuenca, Ramón. "Lope de Vega y la pérdida de España: El Último godo," in *Lope de Vega y los orígenes del teatro español*. Ed. Manuel Criado de Val. 6th edn. Madrid: EDI-6, 1961. 473–77.
Arolas, J. "Florinda," in *Floresta de Leyendas Heróicas Españolas: Rodrigo, el último godo, Tomo III, La Edad Moderna*, Ramón Menéndez Pidal, Clásicos Castellanos 84. Madrid: La Lectura, 1927. 214. Edición aumentada. Valencia: M. Cabrerizo, 1850.
Autoras en la Historia del Teatro Español (1500–1994), Vol 1 (Siglos XVII–XVIII–XIX). Dir. Juan Antonio Hormigón. Madrid: Publicaciones de la Asociación de Directores de Escena de España, 1996–2000.
Battesti Pelegrin, Jeanne. "Du nom de 'la Cava': ou, comment l'habit fait le moine et le surnom la diablesse." *Cahiers d'Études Romanes* 8 (1983): 7–16.
———. "La penitencia del rey Rodrigo: rituel chrétien, rite initiatique." *Cahiers d'Études Romanes* 8 (1983): 17–40.
Battista Andreini, Giovanni. *La Florinda*. Milan: Bordone, 1606.
Battista Bottalino, Giovanni. *Il Roderico*. 1684.
Berbel Rodríguez, José Juan. "El *Rodrigo* de Montengón y tres tragedias sobre Don Pelayo," in *Actas del I Congreso Internacional sobre la novela del siglo XVIII*. Ed. F. García Lara. Almería: Universidad de Almería, 1998. 101–12.

Berger Jr., Harry. *Making Trifles of Terrors: Redistributing Complicities in Shakespeare.* Stanford: Stanford University Press, 1997.

Black, Stanley. *Juan Goytisolo and the Poetics of Contagion: The Evolution of a Radical Aesthetic in the Later Novels.* Liverpool: Liverpool University Press, 2001.

Blázquez, J.M. "Las pinturas helenísticas de Qusayr 'Amra (Jordania) y sus Fuentes." *Archivo Español de Arqueología* 56 (1983): 157–90.

Brenan, Gerald. *The Literature of the Spanish People.* 2nd edn. Cambridge: Cambridge University Press, 1951.

Brito, Fray Bernardo de. *A Monarchia Lusitana.* 8 vols. Lisbon: Academia Real das Sciencias, Colleccão dos Principes Auctores da Historia Portugueza, 1809.

Broccoli, Dana. *Florinda.* New York: Two Continents Publishing Group, 1977.

Brown, David. *Walter Scott and the Historical Imagination.* London, Boston, and Henley: Routledge and Kegan Paul, 1979.

Burshatin, Israel. "Alárabes en figuras: metáfora, emblema, parodia y silencio," in *Texto y sociedad: problemas de historia literaria.* Ed. B. Aldaraca, E. Baker, and J. Beverley. Amsterdam: Rodopi, 1990.

———. "Narratives of Reconquest: Rodrigo, Pelayo and the Saints," in *Saints and Their Authors: Studies in Medieval Hispanic Hagiography in Honour of John K. Walsh.* Madison: Hispanic Seminary of Medieval Studies, 1990. 13–26.

Cacho Blecua, Juan Manuel. "Los historiadores de la Crónica sarracina," in *Historias y ficciones: coloquio sobre la literatura del siglo XV.* Ed. R. Beltrán, J.L. Canet, and J.L. Sirera. Valencia: University of Valencia, 1992. 37–55.

Cadalso, José. *Obra poética.* Ed. Rogelio Reyes Cano. Cádiz: Universidad de Cádiz, 1983.

The Cambridge History of Spanish Literature. Ed. David T. Gies. Cambridge: Cambridge University Press, 2004.

Campoamor, Ramón de. *Obras Completas de Ramón de Campoamor, Doloras y Humoradas.* Barcelona: Casa Editorial Maucci, n.d.

Carmona González, María Ángeles. *Escritoras andaluzas en la prensa de Andalucía en el siglo XIX.* Cádiz: Servicio de Publicaciones de la Universidad de Cádiz, 1999.

Castillo, Julián del. *Historia de los reyes godos que vinieron de la Scitia de Europa, contra el Imperio Romano, y a España: y la succession dellos hasta el Catholico y potentissimo don Philippe segundo Rey de España: a quien va dirigida.* Burgos: Philippe de Junta, 1582.

Cervantes Saavedra, Miguel de. *Don Quijote.* Ed. Luis Andrés Murillo. 2 vols. Madrid: Castalia, 1978.

Chalmeta, Pedro. *Invasión e Islamización: la sumisión de Hispania y la formación de al-Andalus.* Colección Al-Andalus. Madrid: Editorial Mapfre, 1994.

Chase, Gilbert and Lionel Salter. "Ginastera, 1916–1983," in *The New Grove Dictionary of Opera,* Vol. 2. Ed. Stanley Sadie. London: MacMillan, 1992. 420–21.

Cohen, Walter. "The Politics of Golden Age Spanish Tragicomedy," in *Renaissance Tragicomedy: Explorations in Genre and Politics.* Ed. Nancy Klein Maguire. New York: AMS Press, 1987. 155–76.

Collins, Roger. *The Arab Conquest of Spain 710–797.* Oxford: Basil Blackwell, 1989.

———. *Early Medieval Spain: Unity in Diversity, 400–1000.* New Studies in Medieval History. London and Basingstoke: MacMillan, 1983.

Corpus scriptorum Muzarabicorum. Ed. J. Gil. 2 vols. Madrid: Consejo Superior de Investigaciones Científicas, Instituto Antonio de Nebrija, 1973.
Corral, Pedro de. *Crónica del rey Don Rodrigo, postrimero rey de los Godos* (*Crónica sarracina*). 2 vols. Ed. James Donald Fogelquist. Madrid: Clásicos Castalia, 2001.
Correa, Pedro. *Los romances fronterizos, Vols I and II*, edición comentada. Granada: Universidad de Granada, 1999.
Cotarelo Valledor, Armando. *Alfonso III el Magno, Último rey de Oviedo y primero de Galicia*. Madrid: Colegio Universitario de Ediciones Istmo, 1991.
Creswell, K.A.C. *Early Muslim Architecture: Ummayads A.D. 622–750*. 2 vols. Oxford: Clarendon Press, 1969.
Crónica general de España de 1344: edición crítica del texto español de la Crónica de 1344 que ordenó el Conde de Barcelos donPedro Alfonso. Ed. Diego Catalán and María Soledad Andrés. Madrid: Editorial Gredos S.A., 1971.
Crónica mozárabe de 754. Ed. and trans. José Eduardo López Pereira. Zaragoza: Anubar, 1980.
Coupe, Laurence. *Myth*. London and New York: Routledge, 1997.
Cuder-Domínguez, Pilar. "The Islamization of Spain in William Rowley and Mary Pix: The Politics of Nation and Gender." *Comparative Drama* 36:3–4 (2002): 321–36.
Curry, Kenneth. *Southey*. London and Boston: Routledge and Kegan Paul, 1975.
D'Amico, Jack. *The Moor in English Renaissance Drama*. Tampa: University of South Florida Press, 1991.
Dante's Modern Afterlife: Reception and Response from Blake to Heaney. Ed. Nick Havely. Basingstoke: MacMillan, 1998.
Dean, Winton and John Merrill Knapp. *Handel's Operas 1704–1726*. Oxford: Clarendon Press, 1987.
Delgado, María M. and David Price-Uden. "Alejandro Casona (1903–1965)," in *Modern Spanish Dramatists*. Ed. Mary Parker. London: Greenwood Press, 2002.
De Sade, Marquis. *Oeuvres Complètes du Marquis de Sade*, Vol. 9. Paris: Chêne et Rousseau, 1967.
Dent, Edward J. *Opera*. Harmondsworth: Penguin Books, 1940, repr. 1949, 1951.
Deschamps, Émile. *Oeuvres complètes, Deuxième Partie: Poésie*. Paris: Alphonse Lemerre, 1873.
Deyermond, Alan. "The Death and Rebirth of Visigothic Spain in the *Estoria de España*." *Revista Canadiense de Estudios Hispánicos* 9 (1985): 345–67.
———. *A Literary History of Spain: The Middle Ages*. London and New York: Benn, Barnes and Noble Inc., 1971.
Díaz y Díaz, M.C. "La historiografía hispana desde la invasión árabe hasta el año 1000." *Settimane di Studio del Centro Italiano di Studi sull'alto medioevo* 17:1 (1975): 313–43.
Dios de Mora, Juan de. *Florinda o La Caba*. Madrid: D.M. Prats, 1853.
Domínguez Ortiz, Antonio and Bernard Vincent. *Historia de los moriscos: vida y tragedia de una minoría*. Madrid: Biblioteca de la Revista de Occidente, 1978.
Donner, Fred. *Narratives of Islamic Origins. The Beginnings of Islamic Historical Writing*. Studies in Late Antiquity and Early Islam 14. Princeton: Princeton University Press, 1998.

Duri, A.A. *The Rise of Historical Writing among the Arabs.* Ed. and trans. Lawrence I. Conrad. Princeton: Princeton University Press, 1983.

Eisenberg, Daniel. "No hubo una Edad 'Media' española," in *Propuestas teórico-metodológicas para el estudio de la literatura hispánica medieval.* Ed. Lillian von der Walde Moheno. Mexico: Universidad Autónoma Metropolitana—Iztapalapa, 2003.

Elwin, Malcolm. *Savage Landor.* London: MacMillan, 1941.

———. *Landor: A Replevin.* London: MacDonald, 1958.

English Drama Online Database at http://www.collections.chadwyck.co.uk/

Espronceda, José de. *El Diablo Mundo. El Pelayo. Poesías.* Ed. Domingo Ynduráin. Madrid: Cátedra, 1992.

Ettinghausen, Richard. *Arab Painting.* Geneva: Editions d'Art Albert Skira, 1962.

Ettinghausen, Richard, Oleg Grabar, and Marilyn Jenkins. *Islamic Art and Architecture 650–1250.* New Haven and London: Yale University Press, 2001.

Fatho-l-Andaluçi. Ed. and trans. Joaquín González. Algiers: Leon Remordet and Co., 1889.

Fernández Guerra, Aureliano. *Caída y Ruina del Imperio Visigótico Español: primer drama que las representó en nuestro teatro.* Madrid: Manuel G. Hernández, 1883.

Fletcher, Richard. *The Cross and the Crescent: Christianity and Islam from Muhammad to the Reformation.* London: Allen Lane, 2003.

Fowden, Garth. *Empire to Commonwealth: Consequences of Monotheism in Late Antiquity.* Princeton: Princeton University Press, 1993.

France: A Companion to French Studies. Ed. D.G. Charlton. London: Methuen and Co Ltd., 1972.

———. *Qusayr Amra: Art and Ummayad Élite in Late Antique Syria.* Berkeley and London: University of California Press, 2004.

Franze, Juan Pedro. "Argentina," in *The New Grove Dictionary of Opera Vol. 1.* Ed. Stanley Sadie. London: MacMillan, 1992. 166–67.

Fray Luis de León. *The Original Poems of Fray Luis de León.* Ed. Edward Sarmiento, Manchester: Manchester University Press, 1953.

Gallego, Juan Andrés (coord.), J.M. Blázquez, E. Mitre, F. Sánchez Marcos, and J.M. Cuenca Toribio. *Historia de la historiografía española.* Madrid: Ediciones Encuentro, 1999.

Gálvez, María Rosa. *Florinda.* Obras poéticas Tomo II—Biblioteca Virtual Miguel de Cervantes: http://www.cervantesvirtual.com/servlet/SirveObras/12371176449019390754624/p00

García Moreno, Luis A. *El fin del reino visigodo de Toledo, decadencia y catástrofe, una contribución a su crítica.* Madrid: Universidad Autónoma, 1975.

García Moreno, Manuel. "Las primeras crónicas de la Reconquista: el ciclo de Alfonso III." *Boletín Real de la Academia de la Historia* 100 (1932): 562–623.

Gaylord, Mary M. "Spain's Renaissance Conquests and the Retroping of Identity." *Journal of Hispanic Philology* 16:2 (1992): 125–36.

Genette, Gérard. *Narrative Discourse: An Essay in Method.* Trans. Jane E. Lewin. Oxford: Blackwell, 1980.

Gil y Zárate, Antonio. *Obras dramáticas de Don Antonio Gil y Zárate.* Ed. Eugenio de Ochoa. Paris: Baudry, Librería Europa, 1850.

Ginastera, Alberto. *Don Rodrigo, Opus 31*, opera in three acts and nine scenes. Libretto by Alejandro Casona. London: Boosey and Hawkes Inc., libretto 1967, vocal score 1969.

Glendinning, Nigel. *The Eighteenth Century. A Literary History of Spain*. London and New York: Benn, Barnes and Noble, 1972.

Godoy Alcántara, José. *Historia crítica de los falsos cronicones*. Madrid: Real Academia de la Historia, 1868.

Gómez de Avellaneda, Gertrudis. *Obras de doña Gertrudis Gómez de Avellaneda, Vol. III.* Ed. José María Castro y Calvo. Madrid: Ediciones Atlas, 1979.

Gómez Redondo, Fernando. "Historiografía medieval: constantes evolutivas de un género." *Anuario de Estudios Medievales* 19 (1989): 4–15.

Goytisolo, Juan. *Reivindicación del Conde don Julián*. Ed. Linda Gould Levine. Madrid: Cátedra, 1970, 2nd edn. 1995.

———. *Contracorrientes*. Barcelona: Montesinos, 1985.

———. *Disidencias*. Barcelona: Seix Barral, 1977.

———. *Saracen Chronicles: A Selection of Literary Essays*. Trans. Helen Lane. London: Quartet Books, 1992.

Grabar, Oleg. "The Paintings of the Six Kings at Quṣayr 'Amrah." *Ars Orientalis* 1 (1954): 185–87.

———. "La place de Qusayr 'Amra dans l'art profane du Haut Moyen Âge." *Cahiers Archeologiques* 36 (1988): 75–83.

Grosart, Alexander B. *The Life and Complete Works in Prose and Verse of Robert Greene M.A.* 15 vols. New York: Russell and Russell, 1181–86, repr. 1964, Vol. 2, *Mamillia Parts 1 and 11 and Anatomie of Flatterie*.

Gunn, Peter. *A Concise History of Italy*. London: Thames and Hudson, 1971.

Hafter, Monroe J. "The Spanish Version of Scott's *Don Roderick*." *Studies in Romanticism* 13 (Summer 1974): 225–34.

Handel, Georg Friedrich. *Vincer se stesso è la maggior vittoria (Rodrigo)*. Performed by Il Complesso Barocco, direction and English libretto by Alan Curtis. London: Virgin Classics Limited, 1999.

Harding, Anthony John. *The Reception of Myth in English Romanticism*. Colombia and London: University of Missouri Press, 1995.

Harvey, Leonard Patrick. "The Moriscos and Don Quixote." *Inaugural Lecture in the Chair of Spanish Delivered at University of London, King's College.* 1974.

Heiss, Aloïss. *Description générale des monnaies des rois wisigoths d'Espagne*. Paris: Á l'Imprimerie Nationale, 1872.

Herculano, Alexandre. *Eurico o presbítero*. Mem Martins: Publicaçoes Europa-América, LDA, Colecção 'Livros de Bolso Europa-América, 1844.

Hillgarth, J.N. *Visigothic Spain, Byzantium and the Irish*. London: Variorum Reprints, 1985.

Historia silense. Ed. Francisco Santos Coco. Madrid: Centro de Estudios Históricos, 1921.

Hoffpauir, Richard. "The Thematic Structure of Southey's Epic Poetry." *The Wordsworth Circle* 6:4 (Autumn 1975): 240–48.

Ibn al-Qutiyya. *Tārīkh Iftitāh al-Andalus*. Ed. and trans. Julián Ribera. Madrid: Real Academia de la Historia, 1926.

Irving, Washington. *The Crayon Miscellany*. Ed. Dahlia Kirby Terrell. Boston: Twayne Publishers, 1979.
Jiménez de Rada, Rodrigo. *Historia de rebus Hispaniae (Historia de los hechos de España)*. Intro. and trans. Juan Fernández Valverde. Madrid: Alianza, 1989.
Johnson, Harriet. "Brilliant Opening at State Theatre." *New York Post*, 23 February 1966 at http://www.tenorissimo.com.domingo/Articles/ny022366.htm, 28.02.05.
Kahiluoto Rudat, Eva M. "María Rosa Gálvez de Cabrera (1768–1806) y la Defensa del Teatro Neoclásico." *Dieciocho* 9 (1986): 238–48.
Kamen, Henry. *Spain 1469–1714: A Society of Conflict*. London and New York: Longman, 1983.
Kendrick, Thomas. *Saint James in Spain*. London: Methuen and Co. Ltd., 1960.
Kennedy, Hugh. *Muslim Spain and Portugal: A Political History of al-Andalus*. London and New York: Longman, 1996.
Kerner, Leighton. "Don Rodrigo." *The Village Voice*, 3 March 1966 at http://www.tenorissimo.com.domingo/Articles/ny022366.htm, 28.02.05.
Krappe, Alexander Haggerty. *The Legend of Rodrick, Last of the Visigothic Kings and the Ermanarich Cycle*. Heidelberg: Carl Winters Universitätsbuch-handlung, 1923.
Kuss, Malena. "Type, Derivation and Use of Folk Idioms in Ginastera's *Don Rodrigo*(1964)." *Latin American Music Review* 1:2 (1980): 176–95.
La Cava: The Musical, original London cast recording.
Labanyi, Jo. *Myth and History in the Contemporary Spanish Novel*. Cambridge: Cambridge University Press, 1989.
Laboa, Juan María. *Rodrigo Sánchez de Arévalo, Alcaide de Sant'Angelo*. Madrid: Fundación Universitaria Espronceda, Seminario Nebrija, 1973.
Landor, Walter Savage. *Landor's Poetical Works Vol. 1*. Ed. Stephen Wheeler. 3 vols. Oxford: Clarendon Press, 1937.
Laviano, Manuel Fermín de. *Triunfos de valor y honor en la corte de Rodrigo*. Barcelona: Pablo Nadal, 1797.
Ledford-Miller, Linda. "History as Myth, Myth as History: Juan Goytisolo's *Count Julian*." *Revista Canadiense de Estudios Hispánicos* 8 (1983): 21–30.
The Legend of the Siete Infantes de Lara (Refundición toledana de la Crónica de 1344 version). Ed. Thomas A. Lathrop. Studies in the Romance Languages and Literatures, Number 122. Chapel Hill: University of North Carolina Press, 1971.
León Tello, Pilar. *Judíos de Toledo, Tomo I*. Madrid: Consejo Superior de Investigaciones Científicas, 1979.
Lévi-Provençal, E. *Histoire de l'Espagne musulmane*. Paris: G.P. Maisonneuve, 1950, Intro. and trans. Emilio García Gómez in *Historia de España, Vol. I*, comp. Ramón Menéndez Pidal. Madrid: Espasa-Calpe, 1987.
Lockhart, J.G, trans. *The Spanish Ballads*. Trans. London and New York: Frederick Warne and Co., n.d.
Lockyer, Roger. *Tudor and Stuart Britain 1471–1714*. Harlow: Longman, 1964, 2nd edn. 1985.
López-Baralt, Luce. *Islam in Spanish Literature from the Middle Ages to the Present*. Trans. Andrew Hurley. Leiden: E.J. Brill, 1992.

López Navia, Santiago Alfonso. *La ficción autorial en el Quijote y en sus continuaciones e imitaciones.* Ediciones EUM—CEES. Madrid: Universidad Europea de Madrid, 1996.
Lowenthal, David, "Authenticity? The Dogma of Self-delusion," in *Why Fakes Matter: Essays on Problems of Authenticity.* Ed. Mark Jones. London: British Museum Press, 1992.
Lozano, Cristóbal. *David Perseguido y alivio de lastimadas: Historia sagrada parafraseada con exemplos, y varias historias humanas y divinas,* Vol. 3. Barcelona: Pablo Campius, 1745.
Luna, Miguel de. *Historia verdadera del rey Don Rodrigo, compuesta por el sabio Alcayde Abulcácim Tarif Abentarique.* Valencia: en casa de Pedro Patricio Mey junto a S. Martín, 1606.
Maalouf, Amin. *The Crusades through Arab Eyes.* Trans. Jon Rothschild. London: Al Saqi Books, 1984.
Malatesta Garuffi, Giuseppe. *Il Rodrigo.* 1677.
Maravall, José Antonio. "La 'morada vital hispánica' y los visigodos." *Clavileño 34* (1955): 28–34.
Márquez Villanueva, Francisco. "La voluntad de leyenda de Miguel de Luna." *Nueva Revista de Filología Hispánica* 30:2 (1981): 359–95.
Marshall, Tristan. *Theatre and Empire: Great Britain on the London Stages under James VI and 1.* Manchester: Manchester University Press, 2000.
Martin, Georges. "La chute du Royaume Visigothique d'Espagne dans l'historiographie chrétienne des VIIIe et IXe siècles." *Cahiers de Linguistique Hispanique Médiévale* 9 (1984): 207–33.
Mas'udi. *Les Prairies d'Or.* Trans. C. Barbier de Meynard and Pavet de Courteille. Paris: Imprimerie Impériale, 1866.
Maura, Juan F. "Leyenda y nacionalismo: alegorías de la derrota en La Malinche y Florinda 'La Cava.'" http://www.ucm.es/info/especulo/numero23/malinche.html, 25.6.2004.
McKendrick, Melveena. *Playing the King: Lope de Vega and the Limits of Conformity.* London: Tamesis, 2000.
———. *Theatre in Spain 1490–1700.* Cambridge: Cambridge University Press, 1989.
Meachen, Edward. "History and Transcendence in Robert Southey's Epic Poems." *Studies in English Literature 1500–1900* 19:4 (Autumn 1979): 589–608.
Meli, Marcello. "El Último godo: legittimazione e delegittimazione della regalità nella Spagna visigotica e altrove." *Quaderni di Lingue e Letterature* 18 (1993): 461–73.
Menéndez Pidal, Juan. "Leyendas del último rey godo" *Revista de Archivos, Bibliotecas y Museos V* (1901): 858–95.
Menéndez Pidal, Ramón. *El Rey Rodrigo en la literatura.* Madrid: La Lectura, 1924.
———. "El Rey Rodrigo en la literatura." *Boletín de la Real Academia Española* 11, Vol. 11, February 1924: 157–97, June 1924: 251–86, October 1924: 349–87, December 1924: 519–85.
———. *Floresta de Leyendas Heróicas Españolas: Rodrigo, el último godo, Tomo I, La Edad Media.* Clásicos Castellanos 25. Madrid: La Lectura, 1925.
———. *Floresta de Leyendas Heróicas Españolas: Rodrigo, el último godo, Tomo II, La Edad Media.* Clásicos Castellanos 71. Madrid: La Lectura, 1926.

Menéndez Pidal, Ramón. *Floresta de Leyendas Heróicas Españolas: Rodrigo, el último godo, Tomo III, La Edad Moderna.* Clásicos Castellanos 84. Madrid: La Lectura, 1927.

———. *Romancero tradicional de las lenguas hispánicas: Romanceros del Rey Rodrigo y de Bernardo del Carpio.* Madrid: Editorial Gredos, 1957.

Merkling, Frank. "New York, Don Rodrigo." *Opera News,* 26 March 1966 at http://www.tenorissimo.com.domingo/Articles/ny022366.htm, 28.02.05.

Merritt Cox, R. "A New 'Novel' by Cadalso." *Hispanic Review* 41 (1973): 655–68.

Miller, Julie B. "Eroticized Violence in Medieval Women's Mystical Literature: A Call for a Feminist Critique." *Journal of Feminist Studies in Religion* 15:2 (1999): 25–49.

Miquel, André. *La géographie humaine du monde musulman jusqu'au milieu du 11e siècle.* Paris: Mouton, 1975.

Moner, Michel. "Deux figures emblématiques: la femme violée et la parfaite épouse, selon le 'Romancero General' compilé par Agustín Durán." *Images de la femme en Espagne au XVIe et XVIIe siècles.* Colloque International. Ed. Augustin Redondo. Paris: Presses de la Sorbonne Nouvelle, 1994. 77–90.

Montengón, Pedro. *El Rodrigo.* Ed. Guillermo Carnero. Madrid: Cátedra, 2002.

Mora, José Joaquín de. *Don Opas (en cuatro partes)* in *Leyendas Españolas.* London: C. and H. Senior, 1840.

Morby, Edwin S. "Some observations on 'Tragedia' and 'Tragicomedia' in Lope." *Hispanic Review* 11:3 (1943): 185–209.

Moulton, Ian. *Before Pornography: Erotic Writing in Early Modern England.* Oxford: Oxford University Press, 2000.

Musil, Alois. *Kusejr 'Amra.* 2 vols. Vienna: Oesterreichische Akademie der Wissenschaften, 1907.

The New Grove Dictionary of Opera. Ed. Stanley Sadie. London: MacMillan, 1992.

Niehoff, Susan. "The Unity of Lope de Vega's *El Último godo.*" *Kentucky Romance Quarterly* 29:3 (1982): 261–72.

Noth, Albrecht. *The Early Arabic Historical Tradition: A Source-Critical Study.* 2nd edn. with Lawrence I. Conrad. Trans. Michael Bonner. Princeton: The Darwin Press Inc., 1994.

O'Callaghan, James. *A History of Medieval Spain.* Ithaca and London: Cornell University Press, 1975.

Orr, Bridget. *Empire on the English Stage 1660–1714.* Cambridge: Cambridge University Press, 2001.

Orrego-Salas, Juan. "*Don Rodrigo* de Ginastera." *Artes hispánicas* 1:1 (1967): 95–133.

Palau, Bartolomé. *Historia de la Gloriosa Santa Orosia.* Ed. Oleh Mazur. Colección Nova Scholar. Madrid: Editorial Playor, 1986.

Papadopoulo, Alexandre. *Islam and Muslim Art.* Trans. Robert Erich Wolf. Paris: Mazenod, 1976. Trans. London: Thames and Hudson, 1980.

Pattison, David G. Pattison, David G. "Legendary Material and Its Elaboration in an Idiosyncratic Alphonsine Chronicle." *Belfast Spanish and Portuguese Papers* 1979: 173–81.

The Plays of Mary Pix and Catharine Trotter. Ed. Edna L. Steeves. New York and London: Garland Publications Inc., 1982.

———. *From Legend to Chronicle: The Treatment of Epic Material in Alfonsine Historiography*. Oxford: Medium Aevum Monographs New Series 13, The Society for the Study of Medieval Languages and Literature, 1983.

Príncipe, Miguel Agustín. *El Conde Don Julián: drama original e histórico en siete cuadros y en verso*. 2nd edn. Madrid: Repullés, 1840.

Refundición toledana de la Crónica de 1344. Madrid, Biblioteca Nacional, MS 7594 (old T-282), folio 44 "vuelto."

Ribeiro de Menezes, Alison. *Juan Goytisolo: The Author as Dissident*. Woodbridge: Tamesis, 2005.

Robert Southey: The Critical Heritage. Ed. Lionel Madden. London: Routledge and Kegan Paul, 1995, c. 1972.

Rowley, William. *All's Lost by Lust*. London: Thomas Harper, 1633.

———. *All's Lost by Lust and a Shoemaker, a Gentleman*. Ed. Charles Wharton Stork. Series in Philology and Literature. Philadelphia: University of Pennsylvania, 1910.

———. *A Shoemaker, A Gentleman*. Ed. Trudi Darby. London: Nick Hern Books, 2002.

Saavedra, Ángel de, Duque de Rivas. *Obras Completas*. Ed. Enrique Ruiz de la Serna. Madrid: Aguilar, 1945.

Saavedra Fajardo, Diego de. *Obras de Don Diego de Saavedra Fajardo y del licenciado Pedro Fernández Navarrete*. Biblioteca de Autores Españoles desde la Formación del lenguaje hasta nuestros días. Madrid: M. Rivadeneyra, 1853.

Saglia, Diego. "Nationalist Texts and Counter-texts: Southey's *Roderick* and the Dissensions of the Annotated Romance." *Nineteenth Century Literature* 53:4 (March 1999): 421–51.

Scheibe, Regina. "Aspects of the Snake in the Legends of the Saints." *Bryght Lanternis, Essays on the Language and Literature of Medieval and Renaissance Scotland*. Aberdeen: Aberdeen University Press, 1989. 67–89.

Schonberg, Harold C. "City Opera Company Sparkles in Its Rich New Setting." *The New York Times*, 23 February 1966 at http://www.tenorissimo.com. domingo/Articles/ny022366.htm, 28.02.05.

Scott, S.P. *History of the Moorish Empire in Europe, Vol. 1*. Philadelphia: J.B. Lippincott, 1904.

Scott, Walter. *The Works of Sir Walter Scott*. The Wordsworth Poetry Library. Ware: Wordsworth Editions Ltd., 1995.

Shakespeare, William. *King Lear*. Ed. Kenneth Muir. The Arden Shakespeare. London and New York: Routledge, 1972, repr. 1990.

Silvani, Francisco. *Il duello d'amore e di vendetta*. Libretto at http://www.concordi.it/bdigitale/Libretti/Pag%20Libretti/Silv%20Op.%20371/, 8.10.2004.

Simmons, Jack. *Southey*. London: Collins, 1945.

Smalley, Beryl. *Historians in the Middle Ages*. London: Thames and Hudson, 1974.

Smith, C. Colin. "An Approach to Góngora's *Polifemo*." *Bulletin of Hispanic Studies* 42 (1965): 217–38.

———. *Spanish Ballads*. 2nd edn. Bristol: Bristol Classical Press, 1996.

Smith, Craig S. "Where the Moors Held Sway, Allah Is Praised Again." *New York Times*, 21 October 2003.

Soons, Alan. *Juan de Mariana*. Boston: Twayne Publishers, 1982.
Soria López, Florentino. *Los Titanes de la Raza*. 2 vols. Madrid: Hernando, 1925.
Southey, Robert. *Letters of Robert Southey: A Selection*. Ed. Maurice H. Fitzgerald. London: Oxford University Press, 1912.
———. *The Poetical Works of Robert Southey*. London: Longman, Brown, Green and Longmans: 1845.
Spain: A Companion to Spanish Studies. Ed. P.E. Russell. London and New York: Methuen and Co. Ltd., 1973, repr. 1987.
Spenser, Edmund. *Edmund Spenser's Poetry*, 3rd edn. Ed. MacLean, Hugh and Anne Lake Prescott. New York and London: W.W. Norton and Company, 1993.
Storey, Mark. *Robert Southey: A Life*. Oxford and New York: Oxford University Press, 1997.
Storni, Eduardo. *Ginastera*. Madrid: Espasa-Calpe, 1983.
Strohm, Reinhard. *Essays on Handel and Italian Opera*. Cambridge: Cambridge University Press, 1985.
Suárez Urtubey, Pola. *Alberto Ginastera*. Buenos Aires: Ediciones Culturales Argentinas, 1967.
Super, R.H. *Walter Savage Landor: A Biography*. London: John Calder, 1957.
Sutherland, John. *The Life of Walter Scott: A Critical Biography*. Oxford: Blackwell, 1995.
Sutherland, Susan. *Opera*. London: Hodder and Stoughton, 1997.
Sylva Mascarenhas, André da. *A destruiçam de Espanha e restauraçam summaria da mesma*. Lisbon: Antonio Craesbeeck de Mello, 1671.
Ṭāha, 'Abdulwāhid Dhanūn. *The Muslim Conquest and Settlement of North Africa and Spain*. London and New York: Routledge, 1989.
Talbot Rice, David. *Islamic Art*. London: Thames and Hudson, 1965, 2nd edn., 1975.
Tate, Robert B. 1954. "Mythology in Spanish Historiography of the Middle Ages and the Renaissance." *Hispanic Review* 22 (1954): 1–18.
Tolan, John V. *Saracens: Islam in the Medieval European Imagination*. New York: Colombia University Press, 2002.
Trigueros, C.M. *La Egilona, viuda del Rey don Rodrigo*. Barcelona: Juan Francisco Piferrer, 1760.
Trueba, Telesforo de. *The Romance of History: Spain*. 3 vols. London: Edward Bull, 1830.
Túy, Lucas de. *Crónica de España*. Ed. Julio Puyol. Madrid: Real Academia de la Historia, 1926.
Vega Carpio, Lope de. *El Último godo*. Ed. Marcelino Menéndez y Pelayo. *Obras de Lope de Vega XVI*. Biblioteca de Autores Españoles. Madrid: Ediciones Atlas, 1915, repr. 1966. 345–93.
———. *Jerusalén conquistada, epopeya trágica*. 3 vols. Edición y estudio crítico de Joaquín de Entreambasaguas, Vol. 3. Madrid: CSIC, 1954.
von Richthofen, Erich. *Estudios épicos medievales*. Madrid: Gredos, 1954.
Waterman Evans, Edward. *Walter Savage Landor: A Critical Study*. Port Washington, New York, and London: Kennikat Press, 1892, repr. 1970.
Weatherspoon-Bowden, Mary. *Washington Irving*. Boston: Twayne Publishers, 1981.

Weir, Anthony and James Jerman. *Images of Lust: Sexual Carvings on Medieval Churches.* London: B.T. Batsford Ltd., 1986.
Weissberger, Barbara. *Isabel Rules: Constructing Queenship, Wielding Power.* Minneapolis: University of Minnesota Press, 2003.
Wheatcroft, Andrew. *Infidels: The Conflict between Christendom and Islam 638–2002.* London: Viking, 2003.
Whitaker, Daniel S. "Clarissa's Sisters: The Consequences of Rape in Three Neoclassic Tragedies of María Rosa Gálvez." *Letras Peninsulares* (Fall 1992): 239–51.
White, Hayden. *Tropics of Discourse: Essays in Cultural Criticism.* Baltimore and London: Johns Hopkins University Press, 1978.
Wilkie, Brian. *Romantic Poets and Epic Tradition.* Madison and Milwaukee: University of Wisconsin Press, 1965.
Woolf, Stuart. *A History of Italy 1700–1860: The Social Constraints of Political Change.* London: Methuen and Co. Ltd., 1979.
Zorrilla, José de. *Obras Completas, Tomo 2. Dramas.* Madrid: Manuel P. Delgado, 1905.

Contemporary Reviews of *The Vision of Don Roderick*

The British Critic, Vol. 38 (September 1811), pp. 280–84.
The Christian Observer, Vol. 11 (January 1812), pp. 29–33.
The Critical Review, 3rd series, Vol. 23 (August 1811), pp. 337–49.
The Eclectic Review, Vol. 7, Pt. 2 (August 1811), pp. 672–88.
The Edinburgh Review, Vol. 18 (August 1811), pp. 379–92.
The Monthly Review, N.S., Vol. 65 (July 1811), pp. 293–307.
The Portfolio, N.S., Vol. 6 (October 1811), pp. 381–399.
The Quarterly Review, Vol. 6 (October 1811), pp. 221–235.

INDEX

Abbasid dynasty, 10, 16
Abdalaziz, 56, 142, 184, 185, 186
Acosta, imaginary king, 29, 31, 32
Ajbār Machmuā, 14, 22
Akhila, son of Witiza, 17–18
Alfonso III of Asturias, 16, 19, 20
Alfonso VI of Castile, 22
Alfonso X the Learned of Castile, 25–7, 28, 48, 50, 51, 62, 65, 78, 202, 215, 217, 220
All's Lost by Lust, 90–100, 116, 117, 119, 223
al-Quaeda, 7
Álvarez-Hesse, Gloria, 40
Álvaro de Luna, 37, 48
al-Walid I, 12, 14
al-Zawahiri, 7
ambiguity (ambivalence), 10, 45, 47, 62, 90, 97, 115, 130–6, 142, 155, 211, 215, 217, 221
  in portrayal of La Cava (Florinda), 38, 67, 70, 207, 208, 212, 219
  in relations between Christians and Muslims, 61, 84, 89, 153
  see also Roderick
Andalusia, 7, 19
  see also al-Andalus, 7, 15, 21, 28, 42
Andrés, María Soledad, 28
Arolas, J.
  Florinda, 192–3
Asturias, 150, 151, 182, 207, 208
  chronicles, 15, 19, 20, 110

ballads, 44, 54, 59–73, 104, 127, 162, 164, 182, 199, 206, 210, 217
  the Roderick cycle, 45, 59, 61, 64, 67, 71, 77; "Afirmada cuello y brazos", 70; "Amores trata Rodrigo", 63–4; "Cartas escribe la Cava", 68; "Cuando las pintadas aves", 70–1; "Dando suspiros al aire", 69–70; "Después que el rey don, Rodrigo", 64, 162, 199; "De una torre de palacio", 67–8; "Don Rodrigo, rey de, España", 65–6; "En Ceupta está Julián", 65; "En Toledo está Rodrigo", 66; "Gran llanto hazía la Cava", 66–7; "Las huestes de Don Rodrigo", 62–3, 208; "Los vientos eran contrarios", 62, 76; "XO canas ignominiosas!", 70; "Revuelta; en sudor y llanto", 68–9; "Triste estava don Rodrigo", 68
Basques, 3
Basque region, 14
Bathsheba, 5, 32
Baudrillard, Jean, 47, 52, 57
Bede, The Venerable, 2, 50
Boabdil, 7
Boán, Pedro Fernández de, 102, 220
  Cronicón de San Servando, 101–2

Brighten, Julie-Alanah, 211–12
Brito, Fray Bernardo de, 58, 155, 182, 220
   A Monarchia Lusitana, 58, 155, 220
Broccoli, Dana, 1, 210–12, 219
   Florinda, 210–12

Cacho Blecua, Juan Manuel, 36, 38
Cadalso, José, 110–12, 216
   Carta de Florinda a su padre el conde D. Julián después de su desgracia, 110–12, 216
Campoamor, Ramón de, 193–4
   Los dos cetros, 193–4
Casona, Alejandro, 206–10, 221
Castillo, Julián del, 47, 49, 62, 64, 102, 104
Catalán, Diego, 28
Catholicism, 3, 26, 37, 57, 95, 99, 120, 153, 156, 215
censorship, 108, 109, 110, 116, 127, 168, 169, 175, 176, 216, 218, 220
Cervantes Saavedra, Miguel de, 55, 63, 79, 203
   Don Quijote, 55, 63
Ceuta, 4, 21, 22, 30, 142, 210
Chalmeta, Pedro, 17, 21, 22, 24
Christianity, 2, 14, 15, 77, 85, 109, 151, 153, 168, 222
   see also Christians, 13, 26: Christians and Muslims, 37, 45, 61, 82, 84, 212, 219, 222, 223
Collins, Roger, 3, 4, 5, 18, 20, 21, 55, 57
comedy, 175, 192
Concha, Josef, 175
   Perder el reino y poder, por querer a una muger, 175
Corral, Pedro de, 34, 35–45, 48, 49, 50, 54, 55, 56, 58, 59, 60, 62, 66, 68, 109, 113, 139, 155, 156, 199, 202, 208, 215, 216, 220, 222
Count Julian, 44, 129, 136–43, 177–8, 205, 219
Covadonga, 19, 24, 160, 182, 194

Creswell, K.A.C., 10, 11, 12
Crónica albeldense, 19
Crónica bizantino-arábiga, 15, 17
Crónica de Alfonso III, 15, 20, 33
Crónica del moro Rasis, 22, 28, 30, 36, 42, 44, 157
Crónica general de España de 1344, 27–31, 34, 36, 38, 58, 144, 215, 220
Crónica mozárabe de 754, 15, 17, 18, 19, 54, 75
Crónica profética, 19, 20
Crónica pseudo-Isidoriana, 22
Crónica sarracina or Crónica del rey don Rodrigo, 34, 35–45, 47, 54, 55, 59, 60, 63, 64, 65, 78, 155, 156, 202, 215, 222
cultural appropriation, 13, 15

Damascus, 10, 14, 16, 20
Dean, Winton, 121, 123, 125
Deschamps, Émile, 57, 64, 73, 129, 130, 161, 162–5
   Romances sur Rodrigue, dernier roy des Goths, imités de l'espagnole, 162
Deyermond, Alan, 1
Dinis, King of Portugal (1279–1325), 28, 30, 31
divine punishment, 19, 20, 23, 54
Donner, Fred, 9, 20, 55, 57
Duque de Rivas, *see* Saavedra, Angel

Egilona, wife of King Roderick, 32, 56, 110, 116, 138, 140, 143, 149, 150, 171, 179, 184–7, 196
   see also Esilena, 123–7, 218: Exilona, 211
El Rodrigo, 112–16, 161, 190, 216
empire
   Byzantine, 10, 15
   motif of loss of, 24, 25
   Roman, 14
   Sassanian, 10
   see also Sassanian emperor, 11
Enrique IV of Castile, 48

INDEX

Espronceda, José de, 62, 182, 216
   El Pelayo, 62, 182, 187–9, 190, 216
Eusebius, 18

Fatho-l-Andaluçi, 14
Feijóo, Fray Benito, 107, 218
   Teatro crítico universal, 107
Felipe II of Castile, 49, 52, 56, 82
Felipe III of Castile, 81, 82, 83, 86
Ferdowsī, 12
Ferdinand, King and Queen Isabella (Catholic Monarchs), 7, 60, 61, 72
Fletcher, Richard, 2
Florinda, 1, 55, 56, 67, 69, 82, 91, 101, 102, 103, 107–8, 158, 159, 163, 194, 218
   in *El último godo*, 80–1, 84, 86, 89
   in *Carta de Florinda a su padre* (Cadalso), 111–12
   in *Don Rodrigo* (Ginastera), 207–10
   in *El Rodrigo*, 113–14, 116
   in *Florinda* (Arolas), 192–3
   in *Florinda* (Broccoli), 210–12
   in *Florinda* (Duque de Rivas), 189–92
   in *Florinda o La Caba* (Juan Dios de Mora), 196–8
   in *Rodrigo*, opera, 123–6
   in *Roderick, the Last of the Goths*, 144, 146, 148, 150, 151
Fogelquist, James, 36, 38, 42, 44
Fowden, Garth, 12–14
fragmentation, 167, 187, 188, 189, 194, 195, 198, 199, 216

Gálvez de Cabrera, María Rosa, 44, 168–75, 179, 184, 218, 220
   Florinda, 44, 169–75, 176, 179, 218
gender issues, 43, 45, 62, 63–4, 66–7, 68, 70, 71, 72, 105, 107, 119, 124, 127, 143, 145, 151, 159, 160, 165, 167, 175, 184, 186, 187, 194, 198, 216, 218, 221, 223
Florinda in disguise, 191, 192

General estoria, 26
genre, 35, 59, 75, 77, 79, 100, 105, 108, 115, 121, 199, 208, 216, 221
Gil Perez, priest and translator, 28, 29
Gil y Zárate, Antonio, 176, 184
   Rodrigo, 176–8
Ginastera, Alberto, 206–10, 221
   Don Rodrigo, 206–10, 221
Gómez de Avellaneda, Gertrudis, 184–7, 218, 223
   Egilona, 184–7, 218, 223
Góngora, Luis de, 203–4
Grabar, Oleg, 11, 12
Granada, 7, 43, 47, 61, 156
   Lead Books of, 51, 52, 53, 56, 57
Guadalete, river, 3, 70, 115, 173, 176
   battle of, 35, 48, 146, 150, 152, 163, 169, 175, 181, 182, 184, 188, 193, 196, 227
Goytisolo, Juan, 1, 76, 143, 200–6, 214, 216, 219, 221, 223

hagiographical literature and legends, 39, 41, 43, 77
Handel, George Friedrich, 1, 121–7, 179, 206, 208, 216, 218
Harvey, L.P., 55, 56
Herculano, Alexandre, 194–6
   Eurico o presbítero, 194–6
Hercules, 5
Historia de los reyes godos, 47, 49–50, 62, 64
Historia de Santa Orosia, 77–9, 216
Historia general de España, 47, 51–2
Historia Hispanica, 47
Historia silense, 22
historiography, 32, 47, 214, 215
   Christian, 16, 17, 20–23, 25–7, 28, 31, 37, 54, 132, 215
   Arab, 16, 17, 20–23, 54, 55, 56, 57, 111, 215
History and myth, 2, 202, 214
   see also history and legend, 5, 25, 147, 157: fact and fiction, 5,

INDEX

History and myth—*continued*
    17, 21, 44, 47, 56, 135, 155,
    159, 160, 201, 215–16; 'historia
    fingida' (false history), 49, 51,
    54, 58, 101, 215; 'historia
    verdadera' (true history), 44,
    49, 51, 53, 54, 55, 58; nature
    of history, 34, 44, 52, 57, 135,
    198, 205, 214, 221, 223
Hugo, Abel, 60, 73, 129, 130, 162
    *Romancero e historia del rey de España
    don Rodrigo, postrero de los godos,
    en lenguaje antiguo*, 162
Hugo, Victor, 66, 73, 162

incest theme, 38, 39, 113
innovation, 98, 111
    first historical drama, 77, 216
    first historical novel in Spain, 35, 216
    first historical novel of Spanish
        romanticism, 115, 216
invasion, 1, 2, 23, 131, 133, 135, 168,
    221, 222
    see also invasion of Spain in 711, 2, 4,
    5, 7, 14, 15, 16, 17, 20, 23, 25,
    30, 33, 35, 38, 50, 52, 62, 81,
    82, 89, 92, 100, 103, 123, 130,
    147, 167, 181, 186, 194, 201,
    205, 208, 214, 217, 223, 224
Irving, Washington, 57, 156–9, 210, 221
    Legends of the Conquest of Spain, 156–9
Isaac, 2, 13
Isidore of Seville, 18, 24, 54, 65, 155
Islam, 2, 6, 7, 11, 13, 15, 16, 21, 55,
    65, 88, 94, 109, 120, 157, 167,
    201, 211, 222, 223

Jerusalem, 4, 10, 15, 19, 54
Jews, 13, 26, 34, 35, 43, 61, 148, 157,
    181, 188, 198, 220, 223
    as fictional characters, 179, 180, 190,
        196, 197
    Jewish authorship, 27, 32
    Jewish tales, 21
    Judaism, 2
John of Damascus, 2

*Dialogue between a Saracen and a
    Christian*, 2
Jiménez de Rada, Rodrigo, archbishop
    of Toledo, 23, 26, 29, 36, 48, 51,
    52, 58, 79, 91
    De rebus hispaniae, 23, 29
Juan II of Castile, 37, 43, 48
Julian, Count, 4, 5, 14, 19, 20, 21, 22,
    40, 64, 109, 165, 199, 219–20
    as dishonoured father, 22, 29, 70,
        136–43
    exoneration of, 118, 200–6
    in *Reivindicación del Conde don Julián*,
        200–6
    revenge of, 30, 113, 177, 199
    as traitor, 22, 27, 38, 50, 63–4, 65,
        70, 72, 86–7, 107, 195, 200–6,
        219
    wife of, 23, 58, 91

King David, 5, 32, 37, 102
King Lear, 138–9, 140, 141
Krappe, Alexander, 24, 25, 214

Laboa, Juan María, 48
La Caba, 143–5, 218
La Cava, 1, 4, 6, 8, 19, 20, 22, 23, 25,
    35–6, 38–9, 55, 63, 89, 91, 102,
    107, 114, 115, 218–9
    as Covilla in *Count Julian*, 139
    as Jacinta in *All's Lost by Lust*, 90–100
    as Jacincta in *The Conquest of Spain*,
        117–20
    early name of Alacaba, 29, 30, 31
    love for Roderick, 69
    She-devil, 36, 38, 40, 43, 45
    sympathetic portrayal, 66–7, 68, 69,
        70, 72
La Cava, the Musical, 1, 55, 125, 179,
    211–12, 219
Landor, Walter Savage, 1, 44, 129,
    130, 136–43, 145, 171, 178–9,
    189, 205, 219, 221
Lathrop, Thomas, 32, 34
Latin America, 2, 73, 130
    Argentina, 206, 207

INDEX

La Verdadera historia del rey don Rodrigo, compuesta por el sabio alcayde Abulcacim Tarif Abentarique, 53–7, 64, 82, 143, 158, 189, 215
Laviano, Manuel Fermín de, 108–9
  Triunfos de valor y honor en la corte de Rodrigo, 108–9
Leclerq, Jules, 64, 73, 199
  Rimes Héroïques, 64, 199
legends
  Arabic, 6, 16
  enchanted tower/palace in Toledo, 4–5, 16, 21, 22, 29, 30, 49, 60, 65–6, 81, 85, 92, 99, 104, 114, 130, 156, 158, 159, 160, 174, 175, 179, 188, 189, 196, 208, 211
  Germanic, 5, 6, 214
  Gothic, 24
  Nordic, 5, 24, 214
  Siete Infantes de Lara, 34, 65
  snake or serpent, 33–4, 35, 40–2, 56, 60, 64, 162–3, 199, 202, 204
Lockhart, J.G., 60, 73, 159, 162
Lope de Vega, 1, 52, 57, 72, 79, 105, 155, 158, 203, 222
  Abindarráez y Jarifa, 45
  El mejor mozo de España, 61
  El remedio en la desdicha, 88
  El último godo (El postrer godo de España), 45, 63, 64, 66, 79, 81–90, 157, 175, 223
  Jerusalén Conquistada, 64, 79–80, 84, 157
  La desdicha por la deshonra (novel), 89
  La donzella Teodor, 66
Lozano, Cristóbal, 102–4, 218
  David perseguido, 102–4, 218
Lucas, bishop of Tuy, 23, 27, 48, 52
  Chronicon mundi, 23
Lucretia, 5, 24, 68, 108, 143, 178
Luis de León, Fray, 72, 75–6, 79, 144, 203, 216
Luna, Miguel de, 47, 49, 52–7, 58, 64, 67, 82, 85, 108, 111, 112, 130, 143, 144, 145, 155, 158, 160, 163, 189, 215, 218, 222

Maravall, José Antonio, 18
Mariana, Father Juan de, 47, 51, 53, 56, 57, 83, 100, 104, 159
Martin, Georges, 18, 19, 20
Mas'ūdī, 12
Mazur, Olem, 77, 78, 79
McKendrick, Melveena, 81, 83, 84, 88
Medrano, Francisco de, 75, 76
  Profecía del Tajo en la pérdida de España, 75
Menéndez Pidal, Don Ramón, 6, 22, 28, 30, 35, 43, 47, 49, 53–4, 55, 56, 57, 58, 60, 62, 63, 65, 67, 68, 70, 75, 79, 82, 85, 101, 102, 105, 108, 110, 137, 145, 163, 173, 176, 178, 181–2, 183, 187, 189, 196, 199, 200, 205, 206, 213
Merritt Cox, R., 111–12
Middle East, 2, 9, 44, 132
Mohammed, 2, 10, 20, 115
Montengón, Pedro, 112–16, 161, 190, 191, 216, 223
Moors, 1, 14, 24, 26, 27, 44, 69, 76, 78, 80, 89, 99, 114, 119, 120, 145, 146, 147, 148, 151, 153, 202, 220
  as fictional characters, 65, 86, 88, 94, 95, 98, 118, 140, 160, 161, 172, 173, 175, 179, 192, 196–7, 211
Mora, Juan de Dios de, 179, 196–8, 210, 223, 227
  Florinda o La Caba, 196–8, 227
Moras, José Joaquín de
  Don Opas, 192
Moratín, Nicolás Fernández de, 109–10
  Hormesinda, 109
moriscos, 47, 52, 53, 56–7, 61, 81, 82, 88, 89, 90, 222
Mudejarism, 200, 201, 202, 223
Mūsa ibn Nuṣayr, 3, 4, 14, 21
  see also Muza, 81, 86–7, 142, 186

Musil, Alois, 9, 11
Muslims, 2, 5, 7, 9, 13, 14, 18, 19, 20, 38, 61
myth, 5–6, 16, 19, 20, 23–5, 78, 114, 153, 201–2, 203, 205, 208, 214, 215

Negus of Abyssinia, 11
Noth, Albrecht, 56

Oppas, bishop of Seville, 159, 170, 172, 175, 190, 192, 196
see also Orpas, 26, 65, 81, 150, 153, 219

Palau, Bartolomé, 77–9, 216, 220
Pattison, David, 32
Pedro Afonso, Count of Barcelos, 28, 29, 30, 31, 33, 220
Pelayo, 16, 19, 20, 43, 44, 81, 88, 109–10, 147, 149, 150, 152, 159, 160, 165, 169, 170, 173, 177, 179, 180, 182, 193–4, 196, 197, 221
sister of, 24, 104, 194
Peninsular War, 129, 131, 136, 138, 143, 149, 151, 161, 167
see also War of Independence, 189
Piccadilly Theatre, London, 1, 211, 212
Pix, Mary, 116–20, 124, 127–8, 220
politics, 56, 57, 58, 71, 83, 127, 129, 137, 138, 143, 158, 165, 175, 181, 198, 204, 216, 220, 221, 223
political legitimation, 13
kingship, 71, 92, 168, 174, 198, 220, 221
Peninsular War, 130, 134, 136, 146, 152
Francoist regime, 201, 202–3, 205, 221
Primera crónica general (also known as *Estoria de España*), 26, 28, 29, 31, 33, 50, 62, 65, 202
Príncipe, Miguel Agustín, 178–81, 184, 198, 206, 221, 223

El Conde Don Julián, 178–81, 196, 221
Procopius of Caesarea, 24
Bellum Vandalicum, 24
Profecía del Tajo, 72, 75–7, 203, 216
prophecy and prediction, 16, 19, 62, 115, 190, 208

Qazwini, 12
Qusayr 'Amra, palace of, 9, 10, 11, 12, 13, 15, 16, 158, 215, 217, 220, 222, 227

Racine, 169, 174
rape, motif of, 24, 25, 27, 52
Refundición toledana de la Crónica de 1344, 27, 28, 31–5, 36, 38, 43, 202, 206, 215, 220
Reivindicación del Conde don Julián, 1, 76, 200–6, 216, 219, 221, 223
Ricoeur, Paul, 5, 215
Roderick (Rodrigo, Rudericus), King of the Visigoths, 1, 3, 5, 6, 8, 9, 16,
ambivalence, 15–16, 215, 217, 221
as hero, 147–56, 164
as Janus, 15, 158, 222
as usurper, 3, 17, 29
as tyrant, 70, 90, 92, 96, 99, 120, 123, 125, 131, 138, 198
death or disappearance of, 17, 20, 27, 37, 42, 64, 80, 115, 130, 173, 193, 211
in Six Kings painting, 11–14, 215, 217, 220
penance of, 33, 35, 36, 39, 40–2, 58, 64, 71, 163, 164, 184, 202, 217
Theudofredo, father of Roderick, 26
visual images, 11–14, 16, 227
Roderick, the Last of the Goths, 129, 130, 137, 143–56, 159, 165, 216
Rodrigo (Vincer se stesso è la maggior vittoria), opera, 121–7, 179
Rowley, William, 1, 90–100, 105, 116, 118, 119, 120, 124, 223

INDEX

Saavedra, Angel, Duque de Rivas, 189–92, 198, 218, 221
  Florinda, 62, 186, 189–92, 218, 221
Saavedra Fajardo, Diego de, 100–1, 204, 220, 227
  Corona gótica, castellana y austríaca, 100–1, 204, 227
Sade, Marquis de, 160–1, 191
  Crimes de l'amour, 160–1
Sánchez de Arévalo, Rodrigo, 47–8, 51, 61
Scott, Sir Walter, 1, 57, 66, 115, 129–36, 143, 145, 158, 161, 168, 187, 189, 190, 194, 196, 212, 221
Silvani, Francesco, 121, 122
Six Kings painting, 9, 10–15, 215, 217, 220, 222, 227
Smith, C. Colin, 60, 63, 71, 204
Soons, Alan, 51, 52
Southey, Robert, 1, 57, 109, 129, 130, 131, 136, 138, 143–56, 157, 158, 159, 165, 171, 182, 183, 187, 189, 191–2, 215, 216, 218, 221
Spenser, Edmund, 133, 135
  Spenserian stanza, 134
supernatural events, 4, 39, 114, 127, 147, 148, 154, 164, 183, 188, 211
Sutherland, John, 131

Talbot Rice, David, 10
Ta'rikh Iftitāh al-Andalus, 22
Tarik (Tariq), 3, 4, 21, 24, 51, 81, 142
Tarquin, 5, 68, 94, 178
The Conquest of Spain, 116–20
Tobias, Oliver, 211–12
Tolan, John, 7
Toledo, 4, 14, 15, 17, 19, 21, 22, 29, 32, 76, 81, 82, 156, 207, 210
Troy, 15, 18, 24, 54, 75, 76, 174
treachery, 4, 24, 31, 77, 82, 86, 168, 175, 178, 200, 219

see also betrayal, 23, 38, 62, 96, 174, 203
Trueba, Telesforo de, 156, 159–60
  The Romance of History: Spain, 159–60

Ummayad dynasty, 10, 11, 12, 13, 14, 16, 220

vengeance, 4, 24, 27, 30, 62, 67, 142, 147, 175, 180
Viseu, 27, 33, 35, 38, 50, 152, 193, 196, 206
Visigoths, 3, 36, 179
  See also references to the Visigothic era, 1, 4, 5, 9, 11, 15, 17, 18, 22, 32, 37, 56, 99, 100, 195
  Visigothic coinage, 16, 163
Vision of Don Roderick, 66, 129–36, 145, 158, 190

War of Spanish Succession (1702–13), 119, 122
Weissberger, Barbara, 61, 63, 64
Wheatcroft, Andrew, 2
White, Hayden, 28, 35, 214
Winterhalter, Franz-Xaver, 227
  Florinda, 227
Witiza, 3, 18, 19, 22, 23, 26, 27, 29, 34, 56, 100, 103, 132, 149, 157, 195
  as fictional character, 81, 85, 113, 177
  sister of, 104
  sons of, 17, 101, 104, 123, 195, 197

Yazid 111, 21

Zorrilla, José de, 104, 181–4, 198
  El puñal del godo, 104, 181–3
  La Calentura, 183–4